# THE KILLING

*of*

# UNCLE SAM

# THE KILLING

## *of*

# UNCLE SAM

### THE DEMISE OF THE UNITED STATES OF AMERICA

**RODNEY HOWARD-BROWNE** *and* **PAUL L. WILLIAMS**

**River Publishing**

# THE KILLING OF UNCLE SAM

ISBN 978-1-64007-097-4

*Printed in the United States of America*

FOR THE RIVER SCHOOL OF GOVERNMENT:
OUR HOPE FOR THE FUTURE

# CONTENTS

*Then the LORD put forth His hand and touched my mouth,*
*and the LORD said to me:*
*"Behold, I have put My words in your mouth.*
*See, I have this day set you over the nations and over the kingdoms,*
*To root out and to pull down,*
*To destroy and to throw down,*
*To build and to plant."*

—JEREMIAH 1:9-10

# A MESSAGE TO THE READER

MANY YEARS AGO, I began asking questions about how things work in the world: governments, banking, etc. The answers to my questions were not what I wanted to hear. I realized that people in leadership—and those who guide them from behind the scenes—were not altruistic, as we would hope they would be, but rather, they were greedy, ambitious, and destructive.

This book, *The Killing of Uncle Sam*, was born out of a desire to explore the journey of how we arrived at this place in history. How do we change it? Where do we go from here? To understand history, you must understand people's motivation, not just their actions.

After years of traveling the world, trying to help people, I had a hard time grasping how hard-hearted people in positions of power could be. I didn't understand how people could sell out their nations and people just for money.

Truly, the love of money is the root of all evil. Pride, greed, and power drive men to do the unthinkable. We have politicians who promise one thing and do another. It seems that many have sold their soul to the highest bidder.

How does a "legalized" system of the private central banks go unchecked? The Ponzi scheme of Bernie Madoff was called the crime of the century, but it was not. The crime of all crimes is the legalized central banking system of the globe, where, with the help of politicians, the banks fabricate money out of nothing and pillage billions of people!

The only consolation is that there is coming a day when everyone will give an account of their lives, as they stand before Almighty God on Judgment Day—with no lawyer, no lies, no facade—just them and the true record of their life.

I come from South Africa, and I always knew something was wrong. I just could not put my finger on it. I found out that the *modus operandi* of the cabal is to pit people against each other, and then, while they are fighting, dispossess them of their wealth. There are wars and genocide as men fight over the mineral wealth of nations: oil, gold, diamonds—and the list goes on.

You will find this book well documented, with over 1,000 footnotes. I believe this book will tell the tale of the past 200 years with the common thread throughout being greed and covetousness—the love of money!

In this book, you will find quotes from former presidents, prime ministers, mayors, and other leaders, trying to warn the people, even though, for the most part, the warnings were overlooked by the masses. You can't see something if you don't know what you are looking for.

From Cecil John Rhodes to the present day, nothing much has changed. Many, who endeavor to expose the problem and to do something about it, are silenced. However, it is time for people to stand up and say, "Enough is enough," and draw a line in the sand.

As far as we are concerned, we will not tolerate these things while it is our watch. We will stand, expose, speak out, and move to bring about a reformation. We feel so strongly about this, that if it means death, then so be it. Our Founding Fathers, the fifty-six signers of the Declaration of Independence, were prepared to lose everything for their nation and their freedom, and many did. Out of respect for them, in our generation, we will stand up!

It's time.

—DR. RODNEY M. HOWARD-BROWNE
TAMPA, FLORIDA, USA

# PROLOGUE

# KILLING UNCLE SAM

*To destroy a people, you must first sever their roots.*
—ALEXANDER SOLZHENITSYN

THE TITLE SEEMS ABSURD. How is it possible to kill a nation? America is not a flesh-and-blood entity but rather an ideology—a shared belief in the principles set forth in such documents as the Bill of Rights and the Constitution. This concept of America dates back to 1910, when British author G. K. Chesterton wrote: "America is the only nation in the world that is founded on a creed, one set forth with theological lucidity in the Declaration of Independence."[1]

This concept, known as Creedalism, has been advanced by sociologists, historians, and political theorists, such as Gunnar Myrdal, Allan Bloom, and Arthur M. Schlesinger Jr. Bill Bennett said: "The American national identity is based on a creed, on a set of principles and ideas."[2] Senator John McCain has sanctioned Creedalism by saying: "We have a nation of many races, many religious faiths, many points of origin, but our shared faith is the belief in liberty, and we believe this will prove stronger, more enduring and better than any nation ordered to exalt the few at the expense of the many or made from a common race or culture or to preserve traditions that have no greater attribute than longevity."[3]

Modern US presidents have endorsed this view of America. In his first inaugural address, George W. Bush proclaimed: "America has never been united by blood or birth or soil. We are bound by ideals that move us beyond our backgrounds, lift us above our interests, and teach us what it means to be citizens."[4] Similarly, Barack Obama, at a press conference in Turkey, said: "One of the great strengths of the United States [is] that we have a very large Christian population [but] we do not consider ourselves a Christian nation or a Jewish nation or a Muslim nation. We consider ourselves a nation of citizens who are bound together by ideals and a set of values."

Creedalism has been ingrained in the contemporary American psyche. It has been proclaimed by Democrats and Republicans. It has been taught

**The Declaration of Independence**
There were fifty-six signers of the Declaration of Independence representing the thirteen American colonies who severed their political connections to Great Britain declaring that they were no longer under British rule. Adopted by the Continental Congress on July 4, 1776, these states would found a new nation—the United States of America.

in schools and upheld in courts of law. It remains a truism virtually beyond dispute in the public forum and serves as the basis of political correctness. Who can argue that America is not *unique*; that, aside from the remnants of the Indian tribes, the United States has no autochthonous population; that all of the 308.7 million people who inhabit our nation are either themselves immigrants or descendants of more or less

**The Constitution of the United States of America**

Written in 1787 by James Madison, it is the supreme law of the United States of America. The Constitution's first three words are: "We the People," which affirms that the government of the United States exists to serve its citizens.

recent immigrants?[5] America remains linguistically and ethnically the most diverse country on earth. And since Americans are from different countries, they must be united by something—and that something *has* to be their basic beliefs as expressed by the Founding Fathers and upheld by US jurisprudence. What else can it be?

The belief that the American people are united by scraps of paper may be a comforting conceit for modern multiculturalists, but it has no basis in reality. Sure, the United States is the land of immigrants. But all nationalities, races, and religions have not been blended into a mythical melting pot and recast into something that is genuinely American. Americans throughout history have not been a vague commodity, an unidentifiable mass, or a nebulous conglomerate. Until the turn of the twenty-first century, they were a clearly discernible people—recognizable when traveling abroad by their speech, mannerisms, and appearance, not by their shared belief in a free marketplace or a federal union of independent states. Americans could be characterized as cartoon figures in German newspapers and lampooned as stock characters in French films. Few, even inhabitants of Outer Mongolia, had trouble spotting a Yank from a Yaqui.

There was a reason for this recognizability. The colonists who came to its shores from the founding of Jamestown in 1607 to the outbreak of the Revolutionary War were, by and large, of English and Scottish stock, augmented by a sizeable number of settlers from Holland, Sweden, Germany, and Ireland. They were predominantly Protestant and gave a Protestant direction to American life from the beginning.[6] America, for them, was the new Zion in the wilderness—where they would establish a "holy community," bound together by faith, covenant, and blood. This vision gave rise to the country's sense of a great calling, a providential plan, a Manifest Destiny.

At the time of the American Revolution, the British-Protestant element constituted at least 76 percent of the 3 million whites. In addition, the land was occupied by three quarter of a million blacks who had been imported as slaves from Africa.[7] Hailing the lack of diversity in the colonies, John Jay wrote in *The Federalist*: "Providence has been pleased to give this one connected country to one united people—a people descended from the same ancestors, speaking the same language, professing the same religion, attached to the same principles of government, very similar in their manners and customs."

The great influx came in the next century. The population of America soared in the years from 1840 to 1920 as over 35 million immigrants washed upon our shores in three great waves. By the time the great migrations came to an end, the British-Protestant element had been reduced to less than half the population, and America became linguistically and ethnically the most diverse country in the world. Racially, however, it was a different story, since the new arrivals were white Europeans.

The cause of the Great Migrations was a profound upheaval in the social and economic order of the Old World. The revolution in industry and agriculture that began in the eighteenth century had shattered the time-worn structures of towns and villages throughout Europe, giving rise to large numbers of displaced peasants, merchants, and artisans who could not eke out an existence by performing the work that had provided a measure of security for their ancestors. The sharp rise in population, coupled with the radical transformation in technology, created a buildup of economic and social pressure that could only be alleviated by emigration—and emigration, of course, meant setting sail for the New World.

By the 1840s, the annual rate of immigrants was in the hundreds of thousands. In each year in the decade between 1847 and 1857, more than 200,000 Europeans arrived in America—the high point being 1854 with the arrival of 400,000. The newcomers were predominantly from Britain, southwest Germany, and, after the great potato famine of 1846, Ireland. This inundation represented the first wave.

The second wave, bridging the years from the conclusion of the Civil War in 1865 to the start of the new century, brought millions more from Britain, Germany, and Ireland, along with Scandinavians and eastern Europeans. In fifteen of these thirty-five years, the annual influx exceeded 400,000, with some 800,000 arriving in 1882 alone.

But even these figures could not prepare the New Land for the third and final wave which swept our shores from 1900 to the outbreak of World War I, in 1915. In three of these fifteen years, the figure reached a million; in 1907 it topped 1.25 million. This wave carried immigrants from Italy, Poland, Austria, Russia, Greece, and the Balkans.

The epic story of the great migrations came to an end with the legislative restrictions of the 1920s. By this time, 35 million Europeans—not Asians, Africans, or Hispanics—had arrived to start a new life in the new republic: 4.5 million from Ireland, 4 million from Great Britain, 6 million from central Europe, 2 million from the Scandinavian countries, 5 million from Italy, 8 million from Eastern Europe, and 3 million from the Balkans. The people were diverse ethnically but not religiously, culturally, or even linguistically. They shared a common Western heritage; 95 percent were Protestants, Catholics, or Jews (63

**The Federalist**
John Jay, Alexander Hamilton, and James Madison penned The Federalist, a collection of articles and essays promoting the ratification of the US Constitution.

percent Protestant, 23 percent Catholic, and 4 percent Jews), and all, in time, became obliged for the purposes of education and employment to speak English. America is a product of the English language, European culture, and Western religion.

At the turn of the twentieth century, proponents of the "melting pot" looked forward to a genuine blending of cultures for the creation of the new American culture—a culture that was no more English than German or Italian but something transcendent and all-embracing—a culture with its own unique language, a race of people who were white chocolate with slightly slanted eyes.

To a certain degree this happened. American cuisine came to include antipasto and spaghetti, frankfurters and sauerkraut, filet mignon and French fried potatoes, borscht and pickled herring, on a perfect equality with fried chicken, ham and eggs, and pork and beans.

But, the model for assimilation was never an ambiguous entity—a bronze composite of mixed races who spoke a universal language and proclaimed a new religion of international brotherhood. The model remained as fixed as Plymouth Rock. Will Herberg points this out as follows in *Protestant, Catholic, Jew*: "It would be a mistake to infer that the American's image of himself—and that means the ethnic group's image of himself as he becomes an American—is a composite or synthesis of the ethnic elements that have gone into the making of an American. It is nothing of the kind: the American's image of himself is still the Anglo-American ideal it was at the beginning of our national existence."

To be an American meant not only to be a European but an *Anglo-Saxon*. America's self image had been defined by the *Mayflower*, John Smith, Benjamin Franklin, George Washington, Davy Crockett, *The Alamo*, and Abraham Lincoln, and this image remained etched in granite whether the American in question was a direct descendant of the Pilgrims or the grandson of an immigrant from the steppes of the Ural Mountains. Various ethnic groups tried to set forth various individuals with a kind of putative colonial past—Salem Poor, Pulaski, and Steuben—but these characters remained fringe figures in the story of America. The only exceptions were the descendants of African slaves, who developed their own uniquely American culture and, although never racially assimilated, became accepted as adopted members of the American family. The process of assimilation in the New Land took place not in a "melting pot" but a "transmuting pot" in which all the elements of the various ethnic groups became transformed to an idealized Anglo-Saxon model—a model that came to apply even to African-Americans, as evidenced by the evolution of such stereotypical characters as Uncle Remus, Amos 'n' Andy, and Sanford and Son.

**James Madison**
Author of the US Constitution.

Bonded by blood, history, and heritage, Americans were never united by a political ideology, not even by the concept of democracy.

"Democracy wastes, exhausts, and murders itself," John Adams wrote in a letter to John Taylor in 1814.[8] Even Thomas Jefferson, the most "democratic" of the Founding Fathers, possessed doubts about this system of government. "A democracy," he wrote to Isaac Tiffany in 1816, "is the only pure republic, but impracticable beyond the limits of a town."[9] James Madison, the author of the Constitution, was considerably more guarded in his opinion of this system of government. In *The Federalist* #10, he maintained: "Democracies have been spectacles of turbulence and contention; have ever been incompatible with personal security or the rights of property; and have in general been as short in their lives as they have been violent in the death."[10] Alexander Hamilton, the most undemocratic of the Founding Fathers, wrote: "The ancient democracies, in which the people themselves deliberated, never possessed one feature of good government. Their very nature was tyranny."

Recognizing that the United States was an organic entity, a unique blend of Western Europeans within an Anglo-American model, legislation was enacted to safeguard the racial and ethnic composition of the country as it existed at the turn of the twentieth century. Such laws culminated in the Immigration Act of 1924, which limited immigration by a quota system. The number of newcomers was now limited to two percent of each nationality who lived in the country not in 1924 but in 1890. The reliance of this legislation on the ethnic composition of America before the turn of the century guaranteed that the majority of new arrivals in the future would be from Northern Europe.[11]

It is hard to conceive of an act of Congress that could be more culturally biased, and yet it received nearly unchallenged bipartisan support. The *New York Times* editorialized: "The country has a right to say who shall and who shall not come in. . . . The basis of restriction must be chosen with a view not to the interest of any group or groups in this country . . . but rather with a view to the country's best interests as a whole."[12] The quota system held firm until 1965, when it was decried as "racist" and "intolerable" by Teddy Kennedy and Lyndon Johnson.

America was a nation. But what is a nation?

"Nation" comes from the Latin word *nascere*, meaning "to be born." Over one hundred years ago, the French historian Ernest Renan defined a nation as follows:

> A nation is a living soul, a spiritual principle. Two things, which in truth are but one, constitute this soul, this spiritual principle. One is in the past, the other in the present. One is the common possession of a rich heritage of memories; the other is the actual consent, the desire to live together, the will to preserve worthily the undivided inheritance which has been handed down. . . . The nation, like the individual, is the outcome of a long past of efforts, and sacrifices, and devotions. . . . To have common glories in the past, a common will in the present; to have done great things together, to will to do the like again—such are the essential conditions for the making of a people.[13]

America was a nation because of its lack of diversity. Its organic nature stemmed from its very tribalism, the fact that the people who inhabited the country shared a common heritage, a common history, and a common faith. As a nation, it was personified by Uncle Sam, a character derived from Samuel Wilson, a meatpacker from Troy, New York, who supplied rations for American soldiers during the War of 1812. Gradually, however, this figure came to resemble Andrew Jackson, the rough and tumble president who won the Battle of New Orleans, abolished the nation's central bank, and nearly clubbed to death a would-be assassin with his cane. But even fictitious characters, no less than nations, can be killed.

The demise of the United States emerged from a cabal of British aristocrats who sought to establish a global government. Their motive was not idealistic. It did not stem from a dream of universal brotherhood, but rather from their desire to lay hold of the world's riches. Riches do not come from paper currency but natural resources: gold, oil, natural gas, silver, copper, iron ore, uranium, coal, cobalt, and bauxite. The scramble for these resources causes the breakdown of borders, the uprooting of native populations, and the onset of war. Since no one possessed greater wealth than Uncle Sam, he had to be killed.

The killing was slow and painful. It began with the foundation of the Federal Reserve, which allowed the cabal to take control of the American economy. It proceeded with the creation of the Council on Foreign Relations, which allowed the plotters to gain control of the US State Department. And it ended with the establishment of international agencies (the United Nations, the World Bank, and the International Monetary Fund), the institution of free trade agreements and organizations, such as NAFTA and the WTO, the creation of the CIA and the onset of covert activities, and radical legislation such as the Hart-Cellar Act of 1965 that opened the gates of the United States to the Third World.

Uncle Sam is gone—visible only on Turner Classic Movies and reruns of "Ozzie and Harriet." In his wake, the country has transformed into a place unrecognizable—a place plagued by drugs, poverty, pornography, and violence. Schools have become war zones and racial conflict commonplace. Forty percent of the present-day inhabitants of the United States do not have a Northern European heritage. There is no blood that binds them. Fifty percent of Americans never darken the doorway of a church; one in five has no religious affiliation; and the country is now inhabited by more Muslims than Jews. There is no faith that unites them. Modern Americans remain almost completely oblivious of their history, with the vast majority (84 percent) unable to identify the author of the Constitution. There is no history that grounds them. Seventy percent believe that the strength of America lies in its diversity, and ninety percent remain unaware that a quota system ever existed. The country is not unified by language, let alone morality and religion. "One half of America," as Pat Buchanan points out, "sees the other as 'a basket of deplorables . . . racist, sexist, homophobic, xenophobic, Islamophobic bigots.'"[14] American unity and sense of patriotism has given way to a country rift with riots, in which one half of the populace views the other half as hateful and repellent. And the land of opportunity has given way to a country in which 46 percent say they are underemployed and 49 percent remain on government assistance to make ends meet.

What happened to America?

The story starts with Cecil Rhodes and South Africa.

# NOTES

1.  G. K. Chesterton, quoted in Forrest Church, "The American Creed," *Nation*, August 9, 2002, https://www.thenation.com/article/american-creed/.
2.  Bill Bennett, quoted in Patrick J. Buchanan, *State of Emergency: The Third World Invasion and Conquest of America* (New York: Thomas Dunne Books, 2006), p. 143.
3.  John McCain, "Keynote Address at the Alfred E. Smith Memorial Dinner," *John McCain website* October 21, 2005, https://www.mccain.senate.gov/public/index.cfm/speeches?ID=c1b67c86-f43c-4d9a-b4c6-a3454264c7e1.
4.  George W. Bush, "First Inaugural Address," January 20, 2001, http://www.bartleby.com/124/pres66.html.
5.  Will Herberg, *Protestant, Catholic, Jew* (Garden City, New York: Anchor Books, 1960), p. 6.
6.  Ibid.
7.  Ibid.
8.  John Adams, Letter to John Taylor, December 17, 1814, Founders Online, https://founders.archives.gov/documents/Adams/99-02-02-6371.
9.  Thomas Jefferson, quoted in Brion McClanahan, "Why the 10th Amendment?" *LewRockwell.com*, May 6, 2004, https://www.lewrockwell.com/2009/05/brion-mcclanahan/why-the-10th-amendment/.
10. James Madison, *The Federalist Papers*, No. 10, 1787, Bill of Rights Institute, http://www.billofrightsinstitute.org/founding-documents/primary-source-documents/the-federalist-papers/federalist-papers-no-10/.
11. The Immigration Act of 1924 (The Johnson-Reed Act), Office of the Historian, US Department of State, https://history.state.gov/milestones/1921-1936/immigration-act.
12. Roger Daniels and Otis L. Graham, *Debating American Immigration, 1882–Present* (New York: Rowan and Littlefield, 2001), p. 198.
13. Ernest Renan, quoted in Buchanan, pp. 140-141.
14. Patrick J. Buchanan, "Is Democracy in a Death Spiral?" *Patrick J. Buchanan Official Website*, April 11, 2017, http://buchanan.org/blog/democracy-death-spiral-126837.

# PART ONE

# OUT OF AFRICA

*"When we get piled upon one another in large cities, as in Europe, we shall become as corrupt as Europe."*
—THOMAS JEFFERSON

*"The real menace of our Republic is the invisible government which like a giant octopus sprawls its slimy legs over our cities, states and nation."*
—MAYOR (1918-1925) JOHN F. HYLAN OF NEW YORK.

*President Franklin Roosevelt said this on November 21, 1933: "The real truth of the matter is, as you and I know, that a financial element in the larger centers has owned the government since the days of Andrew Jackson."*

# 1

## THE VISION OF A FREEMASON

*Take up the White Man's burden,*
*Send forth the best ye breed!*
*Go bind your sons to exile,*
*To serve your captives' need;*
*To wait in heavy harness,*
*On fluttered folk and wild—*
*Your new-caught, sullen peoples,*
*Half-devil and half-child.*

—RUDYARD KIPLING, "WHITE MAN'S BURDEN," 1899

THE DEMISE OF UNCLE SAM began with a brainstorm that struck Cecil John Rhodes on June 2, 1877, the day he became a lifetime member of the Oxford University Apollo Chapter of the Masonic Order. Rhodes immediately put the revelation to paper in a document that he called his *Confession of Faith*: "The idea gleaming and dancing before one's eyes like a will-of-the-wisp at last frames itself into a plan. Why should we not form a Secret Society with but one object the furtherance of the British Empire and the bringing of the whole uncivilized world under British rule for the recovery of the United States for the making the Anglo-Saxon race but one Empire."[1]

Surely, he believed, if a group of wealthy Englishmen could spread the ideal of a universal brotherhood under the Gnostic religion of freemasonry to every civilized country, a similar group by breeding and blood could bring about the union of mankind under British rule.

The revelation that Rhodes received as a student at Oxford that spring day would give rise to the Anglo-American Establishment and the mad scramble for Africa. It would inaugurate global warfare, the rise of communism, Keynesian economics, and free-trade agreements. It would bring about the formation of the Pilgrim Societies, the Council on Foreign Relations, the United Nations, the Central Intelligence Agency, and the Trilateral Commission. It would produce the plague of heroin addiction, the creation of the military-industrial complex, the globalization of poverty, and the demise of nationalism. And it would result in unprecedented mass migrations, widespread coups d'état, the onset of covert operations such as Operation Gladio, Operation Mockingbird, and Operation Condor, and the emergence of radical Islam and international terrorism.

**Cecil Rhodes**
Rhodes received his vision of a New World Order on the very day that he underwent the initiation rite of freemasonry in which he was pledged to serve as a light bearer.

At six foot three and 200 pounds, Rhodes was an imposing figure on the campus of Oxford University. He had a leonine head, light blue eyes, wavy brown hair, a carefully groomed mustache, and a ruddy complexion. The forcefulness of Rhodes's appearance was offset only by his tinny voice. Still and all, he possessed so much charisma that one contemporary claimed that "belief in Rhodes was a substitute for religion."[2] At the age of twenty-four, Rhodes already had developed habits that would lead to his early demise. He was a chain smoker with a preference for nicotine-rich Turkish tobacco and a prodigious consumer of alcohol. Day in and day out, he drank huge quantities of wine, whiskey, beer, champagne, and Russian Kummel liqueur.[3]

## THE MASONIC ROOTS

Rhodes's dream of a world ruled by a small cadre of Englishmen was rooted in freemasonry, which had been created in 1716, when a group of British nobles gathered at the Goose and Gridiron Ale House to establish the Grand Lodge of London.[4] The nobles, including Anthony Sayer, John Theophilus Desaquliers, and George Payne, were imbued with the thought of Sir Isaac Newton, who had insisted the doctrine of the Trinity was a "massive fraud" that had perverted the legacy of primitive Christianity. Newton further maintained that the worship of Christ in place of God, the first cause and grand architect of the universe, was idolatrous.[5]

Like Newton, the men at the ale house shared a fascination with the geometry of Solomon's Temple, as described in the Book of First Kings, believing, like Newton, that the Temple's harmonious components—the golden sections, the conic sections, and the spirals of orthographic projection, belied an ancient history, which contained the secrets of the true God of the universe, a Being of infinite light whose existence could be uncovered by proper use of abstract mathematics and Newtonian physics.[6] The fact that this shared belief smacked of Gnosticism, an ancient heresy that had been condemned by the fathers of western Christianity, proved to be of little concern to the forgers of modern freemasonry.

## GNOSTICISM

Within the Gnostic Gospels, including the *Gospel of Truth* and the *Secret Teaching of John*, Christ was sent by the Monad, the unknown God of Acts 17:23, to inform man of his true nature as a spiritual being and to enable the soul to escape from Ialdabaoth or the Demiurge (the malevolent God of the Old Testament) by a series of secret passwords and to return to the realms of true light. Like the Gnostics, the founders of freemasonry saw themselves as emissaries of the highest God, a being of immeasurable light.[7] Knowledge of the spark of the Monad that is implanted in every human being, they came to believe, can only be obtained by members of freemasonry through a series of gradual steps or "degrees" until they are worthy of entering the *arcanum arcanorum* (the fraternity within the fraternity) and to receive "the Truth which it calls Light."[8] Upon receiving this truth, freemasons came to realize that "the Prince of Darkness . . . made Adam, whose soul was of the Divine Light. . . . so that he belonged to both Empires, that of Light and that of Darkness."[9]

Those who remain in the lesser degrees remained unaware that "he who bears the light," that is, the divine being whom they professed to seek, is, in fact, Lucifer, "the Son of Morning."[10] Manly P. Hall, the leading exponent of freemasonry, maintained that the "seething energies of Lucifer are in the hands" of every freemason who has learned the true "mystery of his Craft."[11]

On a supernatural level, it remains remarkable that Rhodes received his vision of a New World Order on the very day he underwent the initiation rite of freemasonry in which he was pledged to serve as a light-bearer. It remains equally remarkable that every member of his Secret Society (and its American counterparts) would also belong to Masonic lodges.

## THE NEW CATHOLIC FAITH

The founders of freemasonry, who gathered at the Goose and Gridiron Ale House, wanted their society to be open "to men of various professions," provided they were approved by the leaders of the lodge and submitted to a secret rite of initiation. "The religion of Freemasonry," Albert G. Mackey wrote in his Encyclopedia of Masonry, "is not sectarian. It admits men of every creed within its hospitable bosom, rejecting none and approving none for his particular faith. It is not Judaism . . . it is not Christianity. It does not meddle with sectarian creeds or doctrines, but teaches fundamental truth. At its altar, men of all religions may kneel; to its creed, disciples of every faith may subscribe."[12]

The Masonic religion quickly spread to South Africa, India, Ireland, Germany, the Netherlands, Russia, Spain, and France, where it helped to spark the French Revolution. In the United States, the list of freemasons came to include George Washington, Benjamin Franklin, John Jay, Ethan Allen, Patrick Henry, Paul Revere, John Brown, John Paul Jones, John Hancock, John Marshall, Thomas Paine, William Randolph, and Roger Sherman. The federalism that constituted the core of the US Constitution was identical to the federalism laid out in the *Freemasonry Constitution of 1723*.[13] By the time Rhodes received the brainstorm, Masonic lodges had sprouted up in China, Japan, Australia, New Zealand, and South America.

Freemasonry espoused a religion that could be embraced by Protestants, Catholics, Jews, Muslims, Hindus, Zoroastrians, and Buddhists—a religion that served to unite all of mankind in one system of belief. *The Constitution of 1723* stated: "No private piques or quarrels must be brought within the door of the lodge, far less any quarrels about religion, or nations, or state policy, we being only, as masons, of the Catholic religion above mentioned, we are also of all nations, tongues, kindreds, and languages."[14] But this one world religion, Rhodes believed, could only be established on the basis of global political and economic unification. He wrote in his *Confession*: "I see the wealth and power Masons possess, the influence they hold, and I think over their ceremonies and I wonder that a large body of men can devote themselves to what at times appear the most ridiculous and absurd rites without an object and without an end."[15]

## AN ACHIEVABLE GOAL

The religious, political, and economic unification of the world, Rhodes realized by his vision, was an achievable goal. The process, in fact, had already begun. Almost overnight, England had been industrialized by a revolution that gave birth to spinning machines and high-pressure steam engines that could be used not only in mining and manufacturing but also to power locomotives and cargo ships. Huge foundries, munitions plants, canneries, and silk mills had sprouted up in cities throughout England, thanks to the newborn concept of financial capitalism. Raw material was being shipped to English plants and factories from the four corners of the globe. Goods were being created in such quantity that the surplus could be shipped out to ports throughout the world, and the English banking system came to the fore as the leading force in international affairs and economics.[16]

The population of England soared from 8.3 million in 1801 to 30.1 million at the time of Rhodes.[17] Wealth became confined to those who controlled the means of production and finance. The industrial merchant became replaced by the industrial millionaire. Marx and Engel in their *Communist Manifesto* explained: "All old-established national industries have been destroyed or are daily being destroyed. They are dislodged by new industries, whose introduction becomes a life and death question for all civilized nations, by industries that no longer work up indigenous raw material, but raw material drawn from the remotest zones; industries whose products are consumed, not only at home, but in every quarter of the globe. In place of the old wants, satisfied by the production of the country, we find new wants, requiring for their satisfaction the products of distant lands and climes. In place of the old local and national seclusion and self-sufficiency, we have intercourse in every direction, universal inter-dependence of nations."[18] The thought of Cecil Rhodes was inexorably bound to these changes in material productivity.

## THE MASTER RACE

The superiority of the British race was evident to Rhodes by the fact

**Cecil Rhodes**
Known as the "Colossus," Rhodes planned to construct a railroad from Cairo
to Cape Town.

that the tiny island of England already ruled an Empire that consisted of over 25 percent of the world's population and land mass. The Empire included India, Australia, Canada, New Zealand, Hong Kong, Gibraltar, the West Indies, and several colonies in Africa. The inhabitants of these colonies, Rhodes believed, were beings who had not fully evolved from their apelike ancestors, and, therefore, were totally incapable of self rule. "The native is to be treated as a child and denied the franchise. We must adopt a system of despotism in our relations with the barbarians of South Africa." Casting aside any attempt at eloquence, Rhodes added:

"I prefer land to niggers."[19]

This racial awareness provided the impetus to Rhodes's *Confession*. "I contend that we are the finest race in the world and that the more of the world we inhabit the better it is for the human race," Rhodes wrote. "Just fancy those parts that are at present inhabited by the most despicable specimens of human beings; what an alteration there would be if they were brought under Anglo-Saxon influence, look again at the extra employment a new country added to our dominions gives. I contend that every acre added to our territory means in the future birth to some more of the English race who otherwise would not be brought into existence. Added to this the absorption of the greater portion of the world under our rule simply means the end of all wars. Having these ideas what scheme could we think of to forward this object?"[20]

And he, Cecil John Rhodes, the son of a country vicar in England, had been singled by divine providence and the process of natural selection to establish British rule over all creation and to bring an end, at long last, to the sad human spectacle of war and ruin.

# NOTES

1.  Cecil John Rhodes, *Confession of Faith*, June 2, 1877, http://pages.uoregon.edu/kimball/Rhodes-Confession.htm.
2.  Sidney Low, "Some Conversations in London," in *The Nineteenth Century and After*, Vol. LI (New York: Leonard Scott, 1902), p. 840.
3.  Robin Brown, *The Secret Society: Cecil John Rhodes's Plan for a New World Order* (Cape Town, South Africa: Penguin Books, 2015), pp. 163–164.
4.  Sanford Holst, "Founding of the Grand Lodge of England in 1717," *Masonic Sourcebook*, n. d., http://www.masonicsourcebook.com/grand_lodge_of_england.htm. See also Albert Gallatin Mackey, *The History of Masonry*, Volume 2, Chapters XXIA-XXXI, 1898, available online at Petre-Stones Review of Freemasonry, http://www.freemasons-freemasonry.com/mackeyhi08.html.
5.  Laurence Gardner, *The Shadow of Solomon: The Lost Secret of the Freemasons Revealed* (London: HarperCollins, 2009), pp. 63–65.
6.  Tessa Morrison, "Principia Mathematica: Issac Newton and Solomon's Temple—A Fifty Year Study," Avello Publishing Journal, University of Newcastle, Australia, Issue 1, Volume 3, September, 2013
7.  W. H. C. Frend, *The Early Church* (Philadelphia: J. P. Lippincott Company, 1966), pp. 60–68.
8.  Albert Pike, *Morals and Dogma* (Charleston, South Carolina: Supreme Council of the Thirty-Third Degree of the Scottish Rite, 1871), p. 105.
9.  Ibid., p. 567.
10. Ibid., p. 321.
11. Manly P. Hall, *The Lost Keys of Freemasonry* (Richmond, Virginia: Macoy Publishing, 1923), p. 48.
12. Albert G. Mackey, *Encyclopedia of Freemasonry*, Volume 1, (Chicago: Masonic History Company, 1924), p. 641.
13. Dean Henderson, "The Federal Reserve Cartel: Freemasons and the House of Rothschild," *Global Research*, June 8, 2011, http://www.globalresearch.ca/the-federal-reserve-cartel-freemasons-and-the-house-of-rothschild/25179.
14. John Anderson, *The Freemasonry Constitution of 1723*, http://freemasonry.bcy.ca/history/anderson/charges.html.
15. Rhodes, *Confession of Faith*.
16. Geraldine Corrodus, et alia, *Oxford Big Ideas - - Geography, History* (South Melbourne, Australia: Oxford University Press, 2013), pp. 272–275.
17. E. A. Wrigley, ed., *Nineteenth-Century Society: Essays in the Use of Quantitative Methods for the Study of Social Data* (Cambridge: Cambridge University Press, 2008), pp. 32–36.
18. Karl Marx and Frederick Engel, "The Manifesto of the Communist Party," February 1848. Creative Commons Attribution – Share Alike License, p. 16, https://www.marxists.org/archive/marx/works/download/pdf/Manifesto.pdf.
19. Rhodes quoted in Matthew Sweet, "Cecil Rhodes: A Bad Man in Africa," *IPOAA* (Indigenous People of Africa and America) Magazine, n. d., http://www.ipoaa.com/cecil_rhodes.htm.
20. Rhodes, *Confession of Faith*.

# 2

# THE AFRICAN HELL-HOLE

*Of all the targets of European empire-builders, Africa was nearest; and "black Africa" among the least advanced. Yet, save for its far south, it was the last to be grabbed. Its coast had been known to Europeans for centuries and was dotted with their trading posts. But until around 1860 the interior was protected. Fevers killed off intruding white men, roads were few and cataracts blocked access by river. Then, setting off from their enclaves along the shores, European explorers began to walk old Arab trade routes. They searched for the truth of ancient stories about the Dark Continent and the sources of its mighty rivers. By 1862 they had reached the source of the Nile. A little later, they traced the route of the Niger. They confirmed the reality of Africa's fabled riches—ivory, gold, diamonds, emeralds, copper. Entrepreneurs also saw that, instead of buying crops like cotton or palm oil from its villagers, they could set up plantations and use cheap local labor to work them. Africa was becoming too valuable to be left to the Africans.*

—"THE SCRAMBLE FOR AFRICA," *THE ECONOMIST*, MILLENNIUM ISSUE

PROVIDENCE IN 1873 had brought Rhodes at the age of sixteen to the mining settlement of Kimberley. He had arrived in Africa to work on his elder brother Herbert's cotton farm in Natal. After two years of drought and crop failure, Cecil headed off for fame and fortune at the newly discovered diamond fields five hundred miles away on the Vaal River.[1]

For months, Rhodes had eked out a meager existence by working in a pit with hundreds of other prospectors. The pit would become the largest hole ever dug on the surface of the earth—a crater measuring 42 acres across and 3,583 feet deep that had been dug by 5,000 miners with picks and shovels. When the miners unearthed chunks of crystalline carbon, they sold the rocks to the dozens of Jewish merchants, including Alfred Beit, who had descended on the settlement. These merchants, in turn, cut and polished the stones into luminescent diamonds.[2]

The mining settlement consisted of thousands of canvas tents and iron clad shacks along with forty bars and brothels. Typhus was prevalent, the temperature averaged 100 degrees Fahrenheit in the shade, and the air was perpetually thick with clouds of flies. Visiting Kimberley in 1887, Anthony Trollope wrote: "If there be a place on God's earth in which a man can thoroughly make or mar himself within that space of time, it is the town of Kimberley. I know no spot more odious in every way to a man who has learned to love the ordinary modes of English life. It is foul with dust and flies; it reeks with bad brandy; it is fed upon potted meats; it has not a tree near it. It is inhabited in part by tribes of South African Niggers, who have lost all the picturesqueness of niggerdom in working for the white man's wages. The white man himself is insolent, ill-dressed, and ugly. The weather is very hot, and from morning till night there is no occupation other than that of looking for diamonds, and the works attending it. Diamond-grubbers want food and brandy, and lawyers and policemen. They want clothes also, and a few horses; and some kind of education is necessary for their children. But diamond-searching is the occupation of the place; and if a man be sharp and clever, and able to guard what he gets, he will make a fortune there in two years more readily perhaps than elsewhere." Adding to the hellish conditions, Trollope noted, the settlement was subjected to torrential downpours that transformed the deep pit into a massive yellow quagmire.[3]

In order to augment his income, Rhodes teamed up with Charles

Rudd, another fortune seeker, to import an ice machine from England in order to manufacture ice cream for the sun-scorched miners. The ice cream business became such a success that Rhodes and Rudd were able to buy old agricultural steam engines which they converted into water pumps to drain the mines when they became flooded with rainwater.[4] By 1876, when Rhodes returned to Oxford to continue his studies and to become a freemason, he already had become a very wealthy man.

### SETTING THE STAGE

In those days, Oxford remained under the spell of John Ruskin, the celebrated don who in his inaugural lecture of February 8, 1870, had called upon the university community to take up the cause of British imperialism. "There is a destiny now possible to us—the highest ever set before a nation to be accepted or refused," Ruskin said. "We are still a race mingled with of the best northern blood. We have a firmness to govern and the grace to obey. We are rich in an inheritance of honor, bequeathed to us through a thousand years of noble history. . . . Britain must found more and more colonies as fast and as far as she is able, formed by her most energetic and worthiest men—seizing every fruitful waste ground she can set her foot on, and there teaching her colonists that their chief virtue is fidelity to their country, and that their first aim is to advance the power of England. . . ."[5]

Such colonization, Ruskin insisted, would result in the institution of global socialism. He said: "The first duty of a State is to see that every child born therein shall be well housed, clothed, fed, and educated, till it attain years of discretion. But in order to the effecting of this, the Government must have an authority over the people of which we now do not so much as dream." Such stirring words had set the stage at Oxford for the appearance of Cecil Rhodes who embraced this teaching.

The first step toward a new world order, Rhodes believed in accordance with his brainstorm, was the conquest of Africa with its vast reserves of diamonds, gold, iron ore, coal, and timber. "Africa is still lying ready for us; it is our duty to take it," he wrote in his *Confession*.

"It is our duty to seize every opportunity of acquiring more territory and we should keep this one idea steadily before our eyes: that more territory simply means more of the Anglo-Saxon race, more of the best, the most human, most honorable race the world possesses."[6]

Throughout his life, Rhodes's belief in the necessity of the British conquest of Africa remained unswerving. Fifteen years after penning his *Confession*, he confided the following to William H. Stead, one of his most ardent disciples: "If there is a God, it is clear that He would like me to do what He is doing Himself. And He is manifestly fashioning the English-speaking race as the chosen instrument by which He will bring in a state of society based upon Justice, Liberty, and Peace. He would like me to paint as much of the map of Africa British red as possible, and to do what I can elsewhere to promote the unity and extend the influence of the English-speaking race."[7]

The second step was the restoration of America to the imperial fold of Great Britain. Rhodes wrote:

> I once heard it argued by a fellow in my own college, I am sorry to own it by an Englishman, that it was good thing for us that we have lost the United States. There are some subjects on which there can be no arguments, and to an Englishman this is one of them, but even from an American's point of view just picture what they have lost, look at their government, are not the frauds that yearly come before the public view a disgrace to any country and especially theirs which is the finest in the world. Would they have occurred had they remained under English rule great as they have become how infinitely greater they would have been with the softening and elevating influences of English rule, think of those countless number of Englishmen that during the last 100 years would have crossed the Atlantic and settled and populated the United States. Would they have not made without any prejudice a finer country of it than the low class Irish and German emigrants? All this we have lost and that country loses owing to whom? Owing to two or three ignorant pig-headed statesmen of the last century, at their door lies the blame. Do you ever feel mad? do you ever feel murderous. I think I do with those men.[8]

When Rhodes penned these words, America was only beginning to acquire significant economic status and its wealth remained confined to families like the Astors, the Vanderbilts, the Morgans, and the Rockefellers, all of whom had deep roots in Britain and strong ties to the House of Rothschild, which had funded their business ventures.[9]

## SEEING A GHOST

Before returning to South Africa at the close of the summer semester, Rhodes suffered what has been described as a "heart attack" and "nervous breakdown." His friends found him in his room "blue with fright, his door barricaded by a chest of drawers, while insisting that he had seen a ghost."[10] This experience served to convince Rhodes that his life would be short and that little time remained to make his dream of a new world order a reality. And so, to his *Confession*, Rhodes added these words:

> The Society should inspire and even own portions of the press for the press rules the mind of the people. The Society should always be searching for members who might by their position in the world by their energies or character forward the object but the ballot and test for admittance should be severe).
>
> Once make it common and it fails. Take a man of great wealth who is bereft of his children perhaps having his mind soured by some bitter disappointment who shuts himself up separate from his neighbors and makes up his mind to a miserable existence. To such men as these the society should go gradually disclose the greatness of their scheme and entreat him to throw in his life and property with them for this object. I think that there are thousands now existing who would eagerly grasp at the opportunity. Such are the heads of my scheme.
>
> For fear that death might cut me off before the time for attempting its development I leave all my worldly goods in trust to S. G. Shippard and the Secretary for the Colonies at the time of my death to try to form such a Society with such an object.[11]

Sidney Godolphin Shippard, a fellow adventurer from South Africa, had joined Rhodes at Oxford. He would become the first administrator of the British Protectorate of Bechuanaland (now known as Botswana).[12]

## GATHERING GUESTS

In September, 1877, Rhodes returned to Kimberley and his "very small two-roomed corrugated iron house with a wooden floor . . . iron walls and roof." [13] To this humble dwelling, he invited his closest friends and confidants for a dinner meeting. The guests included Joseph Orpen, who would become an influential administrator for the British Crown in South Africa; Henry Caesar Hawkins, son of the resident magistrate of the Umkomaas Valley; Alfred Beit, a German Jew, who dealt in diamonds; Leander Starr Johnson, a youthful physician; Charles Rudd; Shippard; and Lewis Michell, a prominent South African banker, who recorded the words of Rhodes to the gathering as follows:

> Gentlemen: I have asked you to dine because I want to tell you what I want to do for the remainder of my life. I think that if a man when he is young determines to devote his life to one worthy object and persists in that he can do a great deal during his life even if it is to be a short one as I know my life will be. The object to which I intend to devote my life is the defense and the extension of the British Empire. The British Empire stands for the protection of all the inhabitants of a country in life, liberty, fair play, and happiness and is the greatest platform the world has ever seen for these purposes. . . It is mainly the extension of the Empire northwards that we have to watch and work for in South Africa.[14]

The men in attendance were so moved by these remarks that they agreed to join with Rhodes in devoting their lives and wealth to the extension of British rule over all creation. Their commitment was to be without personal reservation. For this reason, Rhodes urged his "band of brothers" to avoid all emotional entanglements, including marriage. "I hate people getting married," he said, "because they simply become machines and have no ideas beyond their respective spouses and off-spring."[15] The new initiates to the "Kimberley Club" took this advice to heart, thereby granting a hint of monasticism to their society, which would evolve into a hotbed of homosexuals and pederasts.

# NOTES

1.  Philip Ziegler, *Legacy: Cecil Rhodes, The Rhodes Trust, and Rhodes Scholarships* (New Haven, CT: Yale University Press, 2008, p. 4.
2.  Robin Brown, *The Secret Society: Cecil John Rhodes's Plan for a New World Order* (New York: Penguin Books, 2015), p. 25.
3.  Anthony Trollope, *South Africa* (Cape Town: A. A. Balkema, 1973), pp. 369–370.
4.  Brown, *The Secret Society*, p. 47.
5.  John Ruskin, "Inaugural Lecture at Oxford," February 8, 1870, in *Selected Writings of John Ruskin* (New York: Oxford University Press, 2009), pp. 94–95.
6.  Rhodes, *Confession of Faith*. 1877, http://pages.uoregon.edu/kimball/Rhodes-Confession.htm.
7.  William T. Stead, *The Last Will and Testament of Cecil John Rhodes* (London: Review of Review Books, 1902), pp. 97–98.
8.  Rhodes, *Confession of Faith*.
9.  Brown, *The Secret Society*, p. 107.
10. Robert I. Rotberg, *The Founder: Cecil Rhodes and the Pursuit of Power* (New York: Oxford University Press, 1988), p. 102.
11. Rhodes, *Confession of Faith*.
12. Kevin Shillington, ed., *Encyclopedia of African History*, Volume 1 (A-G) (New York: Routledge, 2004), p. 286.
13. Rotberg., *The Founder*, p. 103.
14. Sir Lewis Michell, *The Life of Rt. Hon. C. J. Rhodes, 1853 – 1902*, Volume I, (London: Edward Arnold, 1910), p. 223, https://archive.org/stream/lifeofrthoncecil01michuoft/lifeofrthoncecil01michuoft_djvu.txt.
15. Cecil John Rhodes, *Letter to Charles Rudd*, October 1876, in *Diamonds Fields Advertiser*, December 25, 1906.

# 3

# MEETING ROTHSCHILD

*I care not what puppet is placed on the throne of England to rule the Empire. The man who controls Britain's money supply controls the British Empire and I control the British money supply.*

—NATHAN MAYER ROTHSCHILD, 1815

RHODES TRAVELED BACK AND FORTH from South Africa to England until the time of his graduation from Oxford in 1881. By then, he had acquired claims to over forty diamond mines in Kimberley. Throughout the next seven years, he continued to purchase mine after mine. Unfortunately, Rhodes ignored safety rules and disaster struck in March 1888, when one of his most profitable mines collapsed and 178 African laborers and 24 white miners perished.[1] After the disaster, he returned to London to seek funding from NM Rothschild and Sons for the takeover of the remaining mines in Kimberley, including *Compagnie Française,* a company that owned a multitude of diamond-rich claims.[2]

### PAPER MONEY

By the time of Rhodes's arrival, NM Rothschild and Sons, under Lord

Nathan Rothschild, possessed complete control of the Bank of England, which regulated the country's currency. The Rothschilds performed this task simply by printing or burning the paper money. They increased the money supply to promote prosperity and decreased the supply to prevent inflation. These manipulations were based on the distinction between money and goods. Goods were the real wealth that a person possessed, while money remained only a person's claim on the wealth that was being retained by someone or something else (i.e., a bank). Goods were tangible assets, while money represented a statement of the debt that was owed to the holder.[3] The use of money rather than goods as payment for a transaction dated back to the creation of the Bank of England by William Paterson, a retired pirate, in 1694.[4] Paterson alleviated his customers of the burden of transferring heavy bags or chests of gold for business transactions by producing paper certificates, which entitled the bearers to exchange them for gold upon demand.[5]

**Nathan Rothschild**

"I care not what puppet is placed on the throne of England to rule the Empire. The man who controls Britain's money supply controls the British Empire and I control the British money supply."—Nathan Mayer Rothschild

Thanks to the convenience of paper, only a small fraction of certificate holders ever sought redemption in the precious metal. Paterson quickly realized that they only needed to keep enough gold in hand to cover the fraction of certificates presented as payment. The rest of the gold could be used to mount a myriad of public and private ventures, including the building of ships and the waging of war. The excess volume, which rose to 90 percent, of the paper claims against reserves became known as "bank notes." An economic miracle had been performed. The issuance of paper claims greater than the gold at hand meant that the Bank of England was creating most of its money out of nothing, a practice that eventually became adopted by the other central banks in existence at the time of Rhodes's meeting with Rothschild, viz., Swedish Riksbank, Banco de España, Banque de France, Bank of Finland, De Nederlandsche Bank, Norges Bank, Osterreichische Nationalbank, Danmarks Nationalbank, Banco de Portugal, National Bank of Belgium, Bank of Indonesia, German Reichsbank, Bulgarian National Bank, National Bank of Romania, Bank of Japan, and the National Bank of Serbia.[6]

## WEALTH BY STEALTH

The Rothschild family took control of the Bank of England in 1815 by an act of stealth. At the Battle of Waterloo, Nathan ("Natty") Rothschild, Lord Nathan Rothschild's grandfather, funded the British forces under the Duke of Wellington, while Jacob Rothschild funded the French army under Napoleon. Receiving preliminary news from his couriers that Wellington had won the battle, Natty Rothschild appeared at the London stock exchange in a feigned mood of depression and commenced selling his British war bonds. This started a chain reaction. Traders en masse unloaded their bonds at rock-bottom prices to buyers, who were shills from the Rothschild family. When news arrived that Wellington had actually won the battle, Natty had received a twenty-to-one return on his investment. This forced England, now the financial hub of the world, to set up a new Bank of England with the Rothschilds as principal shareholders.[7]

## ROTHSCHILD IN AMERICA

The involvement of the Rothschilds in American history dates back to 1791, when the banking family became the principal shareholders of the First National Bank of the United States, thanks to the efforts of Alexander Hamilton, their agent in the Washington cabinet. America's first central bank produced the country's currency and became the sole provider of loans—all interest bearing—to the federal government.[8]

By 1796, the American government had borrowed $8.2 million from the central bank, and prices on consumer goods rose by 72 percent. Mayer Amschel Rothschild, the head of the banking family, demanded partial payment of the loan, which the government, under Thomas Jefferson, could provide by selling all of its shares in First National. In this way, the bank became 100 percent privately owned, with 75 percent of its shares held by the Rothschilds and other foreign bankers.[9]

**Mayer Amschel Rothschild**
was the founder of the House of Rothschild and the father of internationalism.

## THE WAR OF 1812

In 1811, when the charter for First National was set to expire, "Natty" Rothschild, the new head of the family, issued this order: "Either the application for renewal of the charter is granted or the United States will find itself in a disastrous war." But the members of Congress refused to buckle under this threat and voted against renewal.[10]

The War of 1812 erupted because of Britain's attempts to restrict trade between the United States and France and the impression (the seizing and forcing into service) of US seamen into the Royal Navy.[11] The Rothschilds' role in creating such policies remains unknown. But the banking family, nevertheless, provided the British government with loans without interest for the war effort. At the end of the struggle, America may have won its second war of independence, but the country was left with a huge war debt of $105 million relative to a population of 8 million.[12] Faced with this financial burden, Congress approved the creation of the Second Bank of the United States in 1816. To no one's surprise, the Rothschilds emerged as the major shareholders.[13]

**Andrew Jackson**
In 1828, Andrew Jackson ran for president with the slogan, "Jackson and No Bank." The slogan was in keeping with his plan to seize control of the currency and to end the profiteering of the Rothschilds.

## THE SECOND NATIONAL BANK

Nicholas Biddle, the point man to James Rothschild, was appointed president of Second National, which opened a string of branches in every major city. These branches extended loans to businessmen, banks, farmers, and settlers who wished to purchase land in the American West. In 1819, the Second Bank drastically reduced the money supply. Loans were no longer available. Thousands of Americans suddenly discovered they were unable to pay off their bank debts. Farmers were forced into foreclosure. Businesses went belly up. Speculators and settlers lost their lands and savings. The widespread financial disaster and depression, which provoked popular resentment against banking and business enterprise, enabled the shareholders of Second National, namely, the Rothschilds, to purchase enormous assets at greatly depressed prices.[14]

In 1828, Andrew Jackson ran for president with the slogan, "Jackson and No Bank." The slogan was in keeping with his plan to seize control of the currency and to end the profiteering of the Rothschilds. As soon as he assumed the oath of office, Jackson began to withdraw government money from the Second Bank and to deposit it in state banks. This action prompted the Rothschilds to contract the money supply and to create another depression. Jackson, who was known for his fiery temper, responded by swearing: "You are a den of thieves and vipers and I intend to rout you out. If the people understood the rank injustices of our money and banking system there would be a revolution before morning."

## ROUTING THE ROTHSCHILDS

Rout the Rothschilds, Jackson did. On September 10, 1833, he revoked the charter for the Second Bank, five years before it was set to expire. In defense of his action, Jackson condemned the legislation that brought the bank into existence by saying:

> The Act seems to be predicated on an erroneous idea that the present shareholders have a prescriptive right to not only the favor, but the bounty of the government . . . for their benefit does this Act exclude the whole American people from competition in the purchase of this monopoly. Present stockholders and those inheriting their rights as successors be established a privileged order, clothed both with great political power and enjoying immense pecuniary advantages from their connection with government. Should its influence be concentrated under the operation of such an Act as this, in the hands of a self-elected directory whose interests are identified with those of the foreign stockholders, will there not be cause to tremble for the independence of our country in war . . . controlling our currency, receiving our public monies and holding thousands of our citizens independence, it would be more formidable and dangerous than the naval and military power of the enemy. It is to be regretted that the rich and powerful too often bend the acts of government for selfish purposes . . . to make the rich richer and more powerful. Many of our rich men have not been content with equal protection and equal benefits, but have besought us to make them richer by acts of Congress. I have done my duty to this country.[15]

On January 30, 1835, Richard Lawrence, an English immigrant, attempted to shoot President Jackson in front of the Capitol building. His pistols misfired, and the president clubbed Lawrence to the ground with his cane. The would-be assassin was deemed mentally unsound and confined to an asylum for the criminally insane. Jackson said that the Rothschilds were responsible for the attempt on his life, and Lawrence insisted that he had been commissioned to commit the murder by a group of "powerful people in Europe."[16]

## THE MONEY CARTEL

Despite their setback in America, the Rothschilds continued their global expansion by establishing financial ties to such countries as Austria, Germany, Russia, Italy, France, Egypt, China, South Africa, India, New Zealand, and Australia. In the process, they established close relations with other Jewish banking families, including the Cohens, Warburgs, Schiffs, Kuhns, Loebs, Lazards, Lehmans, and Goldmans. These families worked together, shared resources, and engaged in joint business ventures. They shared a common Jewish heritage, maintained close social ties, and often intermarried.[17] "Natty" Rothschild married the oldest daughter of Levi Barent Cohen, a prominent London financier. Jacob Schiff, who had lived with the Rothschilds, moved to America and married the daughter of Solomon Loeb, the head of the Kuhn Loeb banking dynasty. The two daughters of Marcus Goldman married the sons of Samuel Sachs to form Goldman Sachs. Paul Warburg left Hamburg for New York, where he married Nina Loeb, the daughter of Solomon Loeb.[18] United by blood, marriage, and ethnicity, they provided funding to American businessmen and industrialists, including Andrew Carnegie, John D. Rockefeller, and J. P. Morgan.[19] In this way, they created a money cartel that has become the most powerful force on planet Earth.

## A NEW ALLIANCE

Although they were freemasons and members of the same social clubs in London, Rhodes was not acquainted with Lord Nathan Rothschild, even though the banker was the major shareholder of DeBeers, one of the largest diamond mines in Kimberley.[20] Lord Rothschild was not easily approachable. He was described by his contemporaries as "aristocratic," "haughty," "fiercely conservative," and "unbearably rude."[21] Yet Rothschild was beguiled by Rhodes and provided him with the funding not only to purchase all the diamond mines in Kimberley but also to develop what Rhodes called "the simply endless" gold fields that existed beyond the Limpopo River in Matabeleland.[22] Rothschild's beguilement was coupled with his realization that Rhodes and his Society could be instrumental in achieving the following objectives of his banking family: (1) the creation of a Jewish homeland and (2) the reestablishment of a central bank in America.

By November 1888, the relationship between the two men had grown so close that Rhodes drafted a new will in which he named Rothschild the sole beneficiary of his estate. This raises the question: why would Rhodes bequeath his fortune to the world's wealthiest financier? The answer resides in the codicil to the will which instructed Rothschild to use the wealth accumulated by Rhodes to establish a British secret society as a counterpart to the Kimberley Club that Rhodes had set up in South Africa. The British secret society, which Rhodes dubbed "the Society of the Elect," was to be modeled after the Society of Jesus, which St. Ignatius Loyola had established in 1544. And Rhodes, in the codicil, requested Rothschild "to take the Constitution of the Jesuits, if obtainable, and insert the English Empire for the Roman Catholic Church."[23]

## A NEW JESUIT ORDER

The Society of Jesus began in 1540, when six men under the leadership of Ignatius Loyola met in secret to create a religious military order devoted to waging war against unbelief and apostasy.[24] The Jesuits were obliged to relinquish their individual wills so that they could be moved about "like corpses" by the provincial general.[25] By the time of Loyola's death in 1556, the order had 3,500 members living in 130 houses in eighteen countries and 100 colleges. Through herculean efforts, the Society of Jesus had turned back much of the Protestant tide, recapturing much of Germany, most of Hungary and Bohemia, and all of Poland.[26] The fact that the Jesuits accomplished so much in so little time convinced Rhodes that his Secret Society, thanks to modern advancements in transportation and communication, could produce even greater results: they could bring "the most despicable specimens of human beings" under the dominance of the English race and religion.[27]

This task was advanced by Rothschild, who attracted a host of influential aristocrats to the newly dubbed "Society of the Elect," including Lord Reginald Baliol Brett, Queen Victoria's closest advisor; Lord Archibald Primrose, the Fifth Earl of Rosebery and Rothschild's son-in-law, who would serve as Britain's prime minister from 1894 to 1895; and Arthur James Balfour, First Earl of Balfour, who would become the British prime minister from 1902 to 1905. Rhodes's ties to these three men would become tightened by their shared homosexuality and their preference for "burly, blue-eyed boys."[28] Among the other recruits were Albert Lord Grey and Robert Armstrong Yates, two prominent members of the British Parliament; William Palmer, the Second Earl of Selborne; and Alfred Milner, under-secretary of finance in Egypt.[29] Milner, who was also of questionable sexual orientation, merits special mention. Rhodes recognized in him the kind of steel that was required to pursue the dream of world domination: "I support Milner absolutely without reserve. If he says peace, I say peace; if he says war, I say war. Whatever happens, I say ditto to Milner."[30]

## RICHES BEYOND MEASURE

Returning to Kimberley with funding from Rothschild, Rhodes purchased every diamond field in South Africa, including those owned by Barney Barnato, who had been one of his fiercest competitors.[31] By 1889, he had gained control of 90 percent of the world's diamond trade and established the DeBeers Consolidated Mining Company.[32] Young men so smitten by their sweethearts that they pledged their troth by

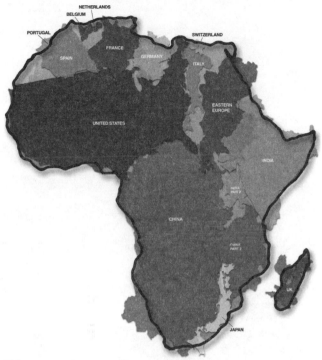

**Africa**
Map of Africa that displays its enormity.

purchasing a tiny chip of crystalline carbon now—almost inevitably—contributed to the Rhodes fortune.

Fortune continued to smile upon Rhodes. He bought up the farms of dirt-poor Boers outside Johannesburg. As luck would have it, a few hundred feet under the dirt, the world's richest and deepest seam of gold was unearthed.[33]

Thanks to Rothschild, Rhodes was granted a charter for his British South Africa Company. The charter provided him with almost limitless power over vast tracts of unconquered lands, including Mashonaland and Matabeland, a mass of land the size of Spain, France, and the Low Countries, which became known as Rhodesia, and the right to govern Bechuanaland, present-day Botswana, and Nyasaland, now known as Malawi.[34] Rhodes was now rich beyond measure and powerful enough to transform the course of human history.

# NOTES

1.  John Cooper, *The Unexpected Story of Nathaniel Rothschild* (New York: Bloomsbury Publishing, 2015), p. 74.
2.  Ibid.
3.  Ibid., p. 44.
4.  Ibid., p. 46
5.  Ibid.
6.  Stephen Mitford Goodson, *A History of Central Banking and the Enslavement of Mankind* (London: Black House, 2014), p. 92.
7.  Andrew Hitchcock, "The History of the House of Rothschild," *Rense.com,* October 31, 1999, http://rense.com/general88/hist.htm.
8.  Ibid.
9.  Stephen Mitford Goodson, *A History of Central Banking and the Enslavement of Mankind* (London: Black House Publishing, 2014), p. 61.
10. Hitchcock, "The History of the House of Rothschild."
11. Staff, "The War of 1812," *The History Channel*, A&E Network, 2009, http://www.history.com/topics/war-of-1812.
12. Hitchcock, "The History of the House of Rothschild."
13. Ibid.
14. Bray Hammond, "Jackson's Fight with the Money People," *American Heritage*, Vol. VII, No. 4, June 1956.
15. Andrew Jackson, quoted in Dean Henderson, "The Federal Reserve Cartel: Freemasons and the House of Rothschild," *Global Research*, June 8, 2011, http://www.globalresearch.ca/the-federal-reserve-cartel-freemasons-and-the-house-of-rothschild/25179.
16. Hitchcock, "The History of the House of Rothschild."
17. Dean Henderson, "The Federal Reserve Cartel: The Eight Families," *Global Research,* June 1, 2011, http://www.globalresearch.ca/the-federal-reserve-cartel-the-eight-families/25080.
18. Ibid.
19. Eustace Mullins, "Mayer Rothschild and the Five Arrows," *Modern History Project*, 1984, http://modernhistoryproject.org/mhp?Article=WorldOrder&C=1.1.
20. Robert Rotberg, *The Founder: Cecil Rhodes and the Pursuit of Power* (London: Oxford University Press, 1988), p. 203.
21. Neil Ferguson, *Empire: The Rise and Demise of the British World Order and the Lessons for Global Power* (New York: Basic Books, 2002), p. 187.
22. Rotberg, *The Founder*, p. 203.
23. Robin Brown, *The Secret Society: Cecil John Rhodes's Plan for a New World Order* (Cape Town, South Africa: Penguin Books, 2015), p. 80.
24. Ibid., p. 47.
25. Will Durant, *The Reformation*, Volume VI, *The Story of Civilization* (New York: Simon and Shuster, 1957), p. 911.

26.  Ibid., p. 915.
27.  Cecil John Rhodes, *Confession of Faith*, June 2, 1877, http://pages.uoregon.edu/kimball/Rhodes-Confession.htm.
28.  Ibid., p. 36.
29.  Ibid., pp. 83–86.
30.  William T. Stead, *The Last Will and Testament of Cecil John Rhodes* (London: Review of Review Books, 1902), p. 108.
31.  Brown, *The Secret Society*, pp. 47–48.
32.  Eric Goldschein, "The Incredible Story of How DeBeers Created and Lost the Most Powerful Monopoly Ever," *Business Insider*, December 19, 2011, http://www.businessinsider.com/history-of-de-beers-2011-12
33.  Brown, *The Secret Society*, p. 48.
34.  Philip Ziegler, *Legacy: Cecil Rhodes, The Rhodes Trust, and Rhodes Scholarships* (New Haven, CT: Yale University Press, 2008), p. 10.

# 4

# THE LURE OF THE OCCULT

*He [Cecil Rhodes] remained in the Lodge because it gave him access to the money he needed to purchase the gold and diamond mines of southern Africa. If you study the lives of those who joined him, you will discover that most of them were either Freemasons, spiritualists, Theosophists, or members of the Society of Psychical Research. Lord Milner was a 33rd Degree Mason; William Stead was a spiritualist and a Theosophist; and Arthur Balfour was a spiritualist, a Mason, and a member of the Society of Psychical Research. What most researchers have missed is the fact that most of the men who joined Cecil Rhodes' secret society were involved in the occult.*

—STANLEY MONTEITH, *BROTHERHOOD OF DARKNESS*

DURING HIS TRIP TO ENGLAND to receive the charter for the British South Africa Company from Queen Victoria in 1889, Rhodes sought out William T. Stead, the editor of the *Pall Mall Gazette,* who had written an article stating that Britain and the United States should be reunited for the sake of world peace. Stead, who would emerge as a leading character in the saga of the Society of the Elect, was neither an aristocrat nor an Oxford graduate. The son of a Congregational min-

ister, he became one of England's leading muckrakers. In
1885, Stead wrote a series of
articles on child prostitution.
To establish the truth of his revelations, he arranged to "buy"
Eliza Armstrong, the thirteen-
year-old daughter of a chimney
sweep, for five pounds. Stead's
"purchase" of the child led to his
conviction for abduction and
a well-publicized three-month
prison stay at Coldbath Fields
and Holloway prisons.[1] By the
time he emerged from his jail
cell, Stead had become the most
famous journalist in England.

**William T. Stead**
emerged as a leading character in the saga of the
Society of the Elect.

At his three-hour lunch
meeting with Stead, Rhodes
"poured out the long dammed-
up flood of his ideas" and offered
Stead $2.5 million in today's money for a stake in the *Gazette*. The jour-
nalist was overwhelmed and later recorded the following in his journal:

> The talk concentrated presently upon the Secret Society—the Society
> of the Elect (Rhodes liked that word), who were to bind themselves
> to work for the British Empire in the way in which the Jesuits worked
> for the Church of Rome. . . . I telegraphed for Brett, who came two
> hours later and we had a long talk. The net upshot of which was that
> the ideal arrangement would be, as far as we could see at present:
> Rhodes, General of the Society; Stead, Brett, Milner, to be the Junta of
> Three. After Rhodes, Stead to be General, with a third, who might be
> Rothschild in succession; behind them, Manning, Booth, little Johnson,
> Albert Grey, Arthur Balfour, to constitute a circle of Initiates.[2]

The Society of the Elect would be structured as circles within circles. The nucleus would consist of a Junta of three or four individuals of power and wealth. The Junta would chart the course of events that would culminate in a New World Order. Surrounding this nucleus would be a Circle of Initiates. These Initiates, while not privy to the decision-making process of the Society, would be willing to follow the dictates of the Junta without question. Finally, the Society would be enclosed by an Association of Helpers, who would constitute the broad mass of the organization. The Helpers would work to make the dream of Cecil Rhodes a reality without concern of the inner machinations of the organization and the covert manner in which policy was adopted. This same organization would come to characterize the various offshoots of the Society of the Elect, including the Pilgrim Societies, the Round Table, the Royal Institute of International Affairs, the Council on Foreign Relations, the Bank of International Settlements, the World Bank, and the Trilateral Commission.

## THE MOWBRAY HOUSE MEETING

The names of several men who met in Stead's office at Mowbray House remain telling. (Cardinal Henry Edward) Manning was a member of the Oxford Movement and the leading Roman Catholic prelate in England. During the London Dock Strike of 1889, where he became the principal mediator, the cardinal developed a close relationship with Stead. The appearance of his name among the "circle of Initiates" signifies the Society's belief that Manning could be highly instrumental in gaining the Vatican's approval of the formation of a global government, if not a one-world religion.[3]

(General William) Booth was a Methodist minister and the founder of The Salvation Army, which had established chapters in the United States, Canada, France, Switzerland, Sweden, India, the Cape Colony, Australia, and New Zealand. Booth had worked closely with Stead in revealing the wretched conditions of England's slums and, by 1890, had gained Rhodes's esteem. His name displays the belief by Stead and

Rhodes that Booth could serve as Manning's Protestant counterpart in forging the New World Order.[4]

"Little (Harry) Johnson, whom Rhodes had met in 1889 during his visit to London, had served for years in the British consular service for West Africa. Rhodes had sent Johnson on a mission to forge treatises with the African chiefs ruling from the Shire Highlands along the western shores of Lake Malawi to the southern tip of Lake Tanganyika. His success in this venture laid the foundation for the British colony of Nyasaland and granted Rhodes the assurance that the United States of Africa could be created.[5]

## COMMON INTERESTS

At the Mowbray House, Rhodes agreed to advance the objectives of the Society of the Elect through the establishment of schools and universities, the acquisition of newspapers, the creation of lectureships, and "the dispatch of emissaries of propaganda throughout the Empire."[6] The Society's original members shared much in common. Apart from Stead, they were personages of means who had been educated at Oxford or Cambridge. They were Masons—most members of the Apollo Chapter, even Manning, prior to receiving Holy Orders, had been a lodge member. They were imperialists, who had been influenced by the thought of John Ruskin and his belief that the world must be reshaped into an aesthetically pleasing whole. They were Social Darwinists, who believed by the British people, by the process of natural selection, had evolved into the master race. With the exception of Stead, they held positions of political power that would impact the course of British affairs. And they all had cultivated strong ties to the Rothschild family, even Manning, who had served as the governor of the Bank of England before becoming a prelate.[7]

Of equal importance was their interest in the occult. Rhodes and Rothschild shared an interest in the Jewish cabala, a mystical interpretation of Scripture based on the concealed meaning in its letters and words, and the mystery religions that flourished at the time of Christ.

This interest resulted in Rhodes's belief in preexistence and reincarnation.[8] Arthur Balfour established the Society for Psychical Research in 1882 and The Synthetic Society in 1890. Both groups espoused the doctrine that "departed spirits" can communicate "great truths." These revelations from the grave, they maintained, should be used to form the basis of a "one world religion."[9]

But, of all the founders of the Society of the Elect, Stead was the most grounded in the "dark arts." He was a well-known medium and a prominent member of the Hermetic Order of the Golden Dawn. This closed society, founded by three freemasons, specialized in esoteric philosophy, astrology, geomancy, astral travel, and alchemy.[10] Stead was also a theosophist and a devout disciple of Helena Petrovna Blavatsky.

Rhodes came to share a similar interest in theosophy. The bookshelves of Groote Schurr, the Rhodes estate in Cape Town, South Africa, remain to this day weighed down with hundreds of works by Blavatsky and other theosophists, including Anne Besant, Henry Olcott, and Judge William Q. Nilakant.[11] The sheer number of these books shows that Rhodes's interest in this subject had deepened into an obsession.

## THE WORSHIP OF SATAN

As espoused by Blavatsky, theosophy purports to reveal the ancient path to enlightenment and salvation on the basis of the teachings of freemasonry. Her teachings, as expressed in *The Secret Doctrine*, are centered on the belief that Satan is "the God of our planet and our only God."[12] In this work, she writes:

> Demon est Deus inversus: that is to say, through every point of Infinite Space thrill the magnetic and electrical currents of animate Nature, the life-giving and death-giving waves, for death on earth becomes life on another plane. Lucifer is divine and terrestrial light, the "Holy Ghost" and "Satan," at one and the same time, visible Space being truly filled with the differentiated Breath invisibly; and the Astral Light, the manifested effects of the two who are one, guided and attracted by ourselves, is the Karma of humanity, both a personal

and impersonal entity: personal, because it is the mystic name given by St. Martin to the Host of divine Creators, guides and rulers of this planet; impersonal, as the Cause and effect of universal Life and Death.

The Fall was the result of man's knowledge, for his "eyes were opened." Indeed, he was taught Wisdom and the hidden knowledge by the "Fallen Angel," for the latter had become from that day his Manas, Mind and Self-consciousness. In each of us that golden thread of continuous life—periodically broken into active and passive cycles of sensuous existence on Earth, and super-sensuous in Devachan— is from the beginning of our appearance upon this earth. It is the Sutratma, the luminous thread of immortal impersonal monadship, on which our earthly lives or evanescent Egos are strung as so many beads—according to the beautiful expression of Vedantic philosophy.

And now it stands proven that Satan, or the Red Fiery Dragon, the "Lord of Phosphorus" (brimstone was a theological improvement), and Lucifer, or "Light-Bearer," is in us: it is our Mind—our tempter and Redeemer, our intelligent liberator and Savior from pure animalism. Without this principle—the emanation of the very essence of the pure divine principle Mahat (Intelligence), which radiates direct from the Divine mind—we would be surely no better than animals.[13]

Blavatsky's disciples came to include Thomas Edison, Sir Arthur Conan Doyle (author of *The Adventures of Sherlock Holmes*), Margaret Sanger (the founder of Planned Parenthood), poet William Butler Yeats, L. Frank Baum (author of *The Wizard of Oz*), Helen Keller (the subject of *The Miracle Worker*), Aleister Crowley (the father of modern Satanism), Adolph Hitler, Alice Bailey (the founder of Lucis Trust, the publishing arm of the United Nations), India's "liberator" Mahatma Gandhi, and Henry Wallace (Franklin Delano Roosevelt's vice-president during World War II).[14] The Theosophical Society, under Madame Blavatsky, established its headquarters in Madras, India, to fulfill a three-fold purpose: (1) to promote universal brotherhood and world peace, (2) to encourage the study of comparative religion, and (3) to engage in a systematic investigation of the mystical powers of human beings who, through successive stages of reincarnation, may transform into gods.[15]

Although few members of the Society of the Elect upheld traditional Biblical beliefs, they all believed that supernatural assistance was required to create a New World Order. Small wonder, therefore, that they turned to a force that promised to provide them with "the world and all its riches."

# NOTES

1. Owen Mulpetre, "The Great Educator: A Biography of W. T. Stead," W. T. Stead Research Site, 2012, http://www.attackingthedevil.co.uk/bio.php.
2. Frederick Whyte, *Life of W. T. Stead*, Volume II (New York: Houghton Mufflin, 1925), p. 209.
3. F. L. Cross, editor, *The Oxford Dictionary of the Catholic Church* (London: Oxford University Press, 1957), pp. 849–850.
4. Roger J. Green, *The Life and Ministry of General William Booth: Founder of The Salvation Army* (Nashville: Abingdon Press, 2006), pp. 15–16.
5. Robin Hallett, *Africa Since 1875. A Modern History* (Ann Arbor: University of Michigan Press, 1974), p. 496.
6. Brown, *The Secret Society*, p. 1.
7. Ibid.
8. Ibid., p. 81
9. James Bruggeman, "The Political and Occult Connections of Wescott and Hort," *Great Conspiracy*, n. d., http://thegreatcontroversy.info/the-political--occult-conne. html.
10. Brown, *The Secret Society*, p. 156.
11. Ibid., p. 110.
12. H. P. Blavatsky, *The Secret Doctrine*, "Cosmogenesis," Volume II (Madras, India: The Theosophical Publishing House, 1938), p. 215.
13. Ibid., p. 513.
14. Stanley Monteith, *Brotherhood of Darkness* (Oklahoma City: Bible Belt Publishing, 2000), p. 128. See also David J. Stewart, "Theosophy Is of the Devil," n.d., http://www.jesus-is-savior.com/False%20Religions/New%20Age/theosophy.htm.
15. "What Is Theosophy?" Theosophy Library Online (Phoenix, Arizona: United Lodge of Theosophists, n.d.), http://theosophy.org/.

# 5

# BOERS AND BLOOD

*If you can talk with crowds and keep your virtue,*
*Or walk with Kings—nor lose the common touch,*
*If neither foes nor loving friends can hurt you,*
*If all men count with you, but none too much;*
*If you can fill the unforgiving minute*
*With sixty seconds' worth of distance run,*
*Yours is the Earth and everything that's in it,*
*And—which is more—you'll be a Man, my son!*

—RUDYARD KIPLING, "IF," A PAEAN FOR CECIL RHODES AND
LEANDER STARR JAMESON

IN 1891, Rhodes became prime minister of the Cape Colony, a position he would hold for the next five years. Addressing the Cape Parliament, Rhodes proclaimed: "If you were to sleep for five and twenty years, you might find a gentleman called your prime minister sitting in Cape Town and controlling the whole, not only to the Zambezi, but to Lake Tanganyika."[1] Now known as the "Colossus," he initiated railway systems that ran from the Cape through the Orange State of the Boers and onto Johannesburg and from southern (Matabeleland) to northern (Mashonaland) Rhodesia.

The dream that Rhodes expressed in his *Confession of Faith* was coming to fruition. Tens of thousands of British immigrants lured by reports of gold, including the location of the fabled "King Solomon's mines," and the offer of free land moved from the overpopulated cities of England to the lands owned and controlled by Rhodes in South Africa. Within the new country that Rhodes called Zambezi,[2] the new settlers came to produce more wheat, maize, and tobacco than anywhere else save America.[3] Beef cattle thrived in the lowlands north of Bulawayo, and fruit—apples, oranges, lemons, pears, peaches, apricots, pineapples, strawberries, coconuts, and melons—grew in such prodigious quantity that the highly profitable Rhodes Fruit Farms came into existence.[4]

To unify the vast continent into one enormous country, Rhodes laid plans for a Cairo-to-Cape Town railroad—a train that would traverse the Zambezi with its mighty falls, run through the meandering Congo, scale massive mountains like Kilimanjaro and Mount Kenya, stretch boundless savannahs and vast deserts, and circle lakes the size of small seas. The jungles would be cleared. The timber would be transported on railroad cars to the cities that would sprout up at the railroad stations.

The natives would be pushed from their lands in accordance with the Glen Gray Act (legislation that Rhodes initiated) and sent to work on the farms, factories, and industrial plants. This work, Rhodes believed, would assist the black natives in shedding their slovenly habits. "It must be brought home to them," Rhodes said, "that, in the future, nine-tenths of them will have to spend their lives in manual labor, and the sooner that is brought home to them the better."[5] The inexhaustible minerals (iron ore, coal, copper, nickel, lead, bauxite, and gold) of Africa would be mined by the black labor force. Riches beyond measure would be added to the British Empire. And it all seemed well within the grasp of Cecil Rhodes in 1895, when Zambesia was renamed Rhodesia in his honor.

### THE BOER PROBLEM

But before this venture got underway, matters within the Cape Colony remained to be settled. The discovery of seemingly limitless gold reserves in Witwatersrand brought thousands of "Uitlanders" ("foreigners") to the Transvaal, which remained under the rule of the "Boers" (Dutch settlers). The foreigners, for the most part, came from Great Britain, Australia, and the United States. Few spoke Dutch or German, the dominant European languages in the Transvaal and the Orange Free State, and they were subjected to restrictions, including a four-year residency in the Boer territories before receiving the right to vote in public elections. The Uitlanders were also subjected to heavy taxes, including an onerous tax on dynamite that did not apply to Boers.

Rhodes, believing that the situation in Johannesburg was on the verge of armed insurrection, organized an invasion of the Boer Republic under Sir Leander Starr Jameson. A physician by profession, Jameson was also a member of the Secret Society, a director of the British South Africa Company, a drunkard, a fool-hardy adventurer, and one of Rhodes's sexual partners.[6] If successful, the raid would have eliminated the two Boer Republics—the Transvaal and the Orange Free State— and enabled Rhodes to paint more of the "dark continent" a bright British "red."[7] It also would have represented a step toward the creation of a world federation of English-speaking dominions and allowed the Rothschilds to greatly increase their gold reserves.[8]

**Leander Starr Jameson**
was Cecil Rhodes's right-hand man. He conducted the Jameson Raid that brought about the Second Boer War.

## POWER AND PEDERASTS

The mounting of the raid showed that the Society of the Elect had become, within a few short years of its existence, a formidable force. Thanks to the machinations of Lord Rothschild, Rhodes, who maintained a stable of "angels and lambs" (young boys to furnish his sexual needs) had gained his appointment as the Cape Colony's prime minister, and Archibald Primrose, the Fifth Earl of Rosebery, a new member of the Society, had become Britain's prime minister. Lord Rosebery had married Hannah Rothschild, the daughter of Mayer Amschel Rothschild II, in 1874. A notorious pederast, Rosebery was sheltered from scandal by his father-in-law, even when he was condemned of "buggering" the son of the Marquess of Queensberry.[9] Reginald Brett, Second Viscount Esher, became permanent secretary to the Office of Works and Queen Victoria's closest advisor. Brett, too, engaged in pederasty and had a string of affairs with a host of Eton boys, including his own son, Maurice.[10] Arthur Balfour, yet another accused pederast and alleged sado-masochist, became First Lord of the Treasury.[11]

## THE JAMESON RAID

On December 29, 1895, Sir Jameson set out for Johannesburg with a meager force of 494 men, including 400 members of the Matabeleland Mounted Police. He thought that this small army was sufficient to conquer the seventeen districts of the Transvaal since it was equipped with eighteen Maxims, the first recoil-operated machine guns.[12] "I will simply blow [the Boers] away," Jameson bragged to Frederick Hamilton, editor of the *Johannesburg Star*. "I shall draw a zone of lead a mile on each side of my column, and no Boer will be able to live in it."[13]

The Boers knew that the raid was coming. Armed with German Mauser rifles, they waited until Jameson and his column marched into a valley beneath the hills of Krugersdorp before opening fire. Thirty of Jameson's men fell at once. Thirty more, including Jameson and Frank Rhodes (Cecil's brother), were captured. The remainder retreated in disarray.[14]

## UNEXPECTED BLOWBACK

The effects of the debacle were immediate. Rhodes was forced to resign as prime minister and as chairman of the Charter Company. A heavy ransom for the prisoners was paid to the Transvaal by Rhodes and Alfred Beit. And Jameson was brought to England, where he was charged with mounting a military attack on a friendly state. He was sentenced to fifteen months' imprisonment.[15]

Then came an unexpected blowback. Upon hearing the news of the raid, Kaiser Wilhelm of Germany sent a telegram to Paul Kruger, the president of the Transvaal, in which he said: "I express my sincere congratulations that, without calling on the aid of friendly Powers, you and your people, by your own energy against the armed bands which have broken into your country as disturbers of the peace, have succeeded in re-establishing peace, and defending the independence of the country against attacks from without."[16] The cable caused such an uproar that the British people clamored for war against Germany. The Kaiser had congratulated Kruger for killing English settlers without mentioning a word about the plight of the Uitlanders. Under mounting pressure, Queen Victoria sent this telegram to her grandson, Kaiser Wilhelm: "I cannot refrain from expressing my deep regret at the telegram you sent to President Kruger. It is considered very unfriendly towards this country, which I feel it is not intended to be, and has, I grieve to say, made a most unfavorable impression."[17] The English hatred of Germany, provoked by the Kaiser's condemnation of Jameson, was a contributing cause to the outbreak of World War I.[18]

## THE RAID LIONIZED

Thanks to the cable, Rhodes regained the esteem of his countrymen, and Jameson became a folk hero. Alfred Austin's first published poem as Britain's Poet Laureate was a tribute to the leader of the raiders called "Jameson's Ride." It appeared in *The Times* of London on January 11, 1896, and opened with these words:

*Wrong! Is it wrong? Well, may be;*
*But I'm going, boys, all the same.*
*Do they think me a Burgher's baby,*
*To be scared by a scolding name?*
*They may argue, and prate, and order;*
*Go, tell them to save their breath:*
*Then, over the Transvaal border,*
*And gallop for life or death!*

*Let lawyers and statesmen addle*
*Their pates over points of law:*
*If sound be our sword, and saddle,*
*And gun-gear, who cares one straw?*
*When men of our own blood pray us*
*To ride to their kinsfolk's aid,*
*Not Heaven itself shall stay us*
*From the rescue they call a raid.*[19]

In the wake of the raid, the Boers, thanks to the Germans, became armed to the teeth, and Alfred Milner, thanks to Lord Rothschild, became the new governor of the Cape Colony. The gold of Witwatersrand could be left to the Dutch. And so, a war was rigged.

The rigging was made possible not only by the Milner appointment but also by Jan Smuts, a prominent Boer, who had graduated from Cambridge. Smuts was a vigorous supporter of Rhodes and had acted for many years as his agent in Kimberley. In 1898, he settled in the Transvaal and became the state secretary and the chief political advisor to President Kruger. As soon as Smuts was in place, Milner ordered provocative troop movements on the Boer frontier. In keeping with the script, the movements persisted until Smuts drew up an ultimatum, which threatened war if the threatening troop activity persisted. Milner rejected the ultimatum and Kruger declared war on October 9, 1899.[20] The conflict was, as G. Edward Griffin writes in *The Creature from Jekyll Island*, "an act of careful engineering" by Milner, Rothschild, and the Society of the Elect on *both* sides (British and Boer)—"one making outrageous demands and the other responding to those demands in pretended indignation."[21] In the first weeks of fighting, the British suffered casualties that exceeded 3,000. In 1902, by the time the conflict came to an end, 7,582 British soldiers had been killed in action, 13,139 died of disease, 40,000 were wounded, and one had been eaten by a crocodile.[22] Six thousand Boers were killed in action, while 26,000 white civilians and 17,182 African natives died of disease and starvation in concentration camps that had been set up in the Cape and Orange River colonies.[23] The war had salubrious results for Rhodes and Milner, including the incorporation of the Transvaal and the Orange Free State into the British Empire.[24]

**Alfred Milner**

The 20,000 children who had died in the British concentration camps were of little consequence to Milner. When faced with criticism about the atrocities, Milner responded, "If we are to build up anything in South Africa, we must disregard, and absolutely disregard, the screamers."

### DISREGARD THE SCREAMERS

When Stead expressed his outrage at the war in an article that appeared in the *Review of Reviews*, Rhodes chastised his journalistic friend as follows:

That is the case which will be fatal to our ideas—insubordination. Do not you think that it is very disobedient of you? How can our Society be worked if each sets himself up as the sole judge of what ought to be done? Just look at our position here. We three are in South Africa, all of us your boys I myself, Milner, and Garrett, all of whom learned politics from you. We are on the spot, and we are unanimous in declaring this war to be necessary. You have never been in South Africa, and yet, instead of deferring to the judgment of your own boys, you fling yourself in violent opposition to the war.[25]

However, Milner had the grace to confess his role in the war. "I precipitated the crisis, which was inevitable, before it was too late," he wrote in a letter to Lord Frederick Roberts. "It is not very agreeable, and in many eyes, not very creditable piece of business to have been largely instrumental in bringing about a big war."[26] However, the 20,000 children who had died in the British concentration camps were of little consequence to Milner. When faced with criticism about the atrocities, Milner responded: "If we are to build up anything in South Africa, we must disregard, and absolutely disregard, the screamers."[27]

# NOTES

1.  Robin Brown, *The Secret Society: Cecil John Rhodes's Plan for a New World Order* (Cape Town, South Africa: Penguin Books, 2015), p. 129.
2.  Robert Blake, *A History of Rhodesia* (London: Eyre Methuen, 1977), p. 114.
3.  Brown, *The Secret Society*, p. 174.
4.  Robert I. Rotberg, *The Founder: Cecil Rhodes and the Pursuit of Power* (New York: Oxford University Press, 1988), p. 640.
5.  Martin Meredith, *Diamonds, Gold, and War: The British, the Boers, and the Making of South Africa* (New York: Public Affairs, 2008), p. 265.
6.  Russ Winter, "Cecil Rhodes and His Warmongering Buggery Hegemony," *The New Nationalist*, May 1, 2017, http://www.newnationalist.net/2017/05/01/cecil-rhodes-and-his-warmongering-buggery-hegemony/.
7.  Brown, *The Secret Society*, pp. 179–180.
8.  Ibid., p. 184.
9.  Ibid., p. 159.
10. Ibid., p. 161.
11. Winter, "Cecil Rhodes and His Warmongering Buggery Hegemony."
12. P. E. Aston, *The Raid on the Transvaal by Dr. Jameson* (London: Dean and Sons, 1897), p. 173.
13. Jameson, quoted in Meredith, *Diamonds, Gold, and War*, p. 89.
14. John Hays Hammond, *The Truth about the Jameson Raid* (Boston: Marshall Jones, 1918), p. 36.
15. Brown, *The Secret Society*, p. 201.
16. The Kruger telegram in Jean van der Poel, *The Jamestown Raid* (Cape Town: Oxford University Press, 1951), p. 135.
17. Queen Victoria's telegram, in Ibid.
18. Brown, *The Secret Society*, p. 180.
19. Alfred Austin, "Jameson's Ride" (1896), in *Books and Boots*, July 10, 2012, https://astrofella.wordpress.com/2012/07/10/jamesons-ride-1896-2/.
20. Carroll Quigley, *Tragedy and Hope: A history of the World in Our Time* (New York: Macmillan, 1966), pp. 137–138.
21. G. Edward Griffin, *The Creature from Jekyll Island: A Second Look at the Federal Reserve* (Westlake Village, CA: American Media, 2008), p. 278.
22. Megan French, "Boer War Soldiers' Records Published Online," *The Guardian*, June 24, 2010, https://www.theguardian.com/uk/2010/jun/24/boer-war-soldiers-records-online.
23. Owen Coetzer, *Fire in the Sky: The Destruction of the Orange Free State* ( Johannesburg: Covos Day, 2000), pp. 82–83.
24. Philip Ziegler, *Legacy: Cecil Rhodes, The Rhodes Trust, and Rhodes Scholarships* (New Haven, CT: Yale University Press, 2008), p. 12.
25. William T. Stead, *The Last Will and Testament of Cecil John Rhodes* (London: Review of Review Books, 1902), pp. 109–111.
26. Milner, quoted in Thomas Pakenham, *The Boer War* (New York: Random House, 1979), p. 115.
27. Ibid., p. 483.

# 6

# SO LITTLE DONE, SO MUCH TO DO

*The fact that Rhodes awarded the United States so many more scholarships than were given to all the colonies put together showed how much importance he still attached to the Anglo-American partnership. He never wholly abandoned the hope that the United States might one day rejoin the Empire. He realized that this would have to be more of a merger than a takeover and was even prepared to accept the possibility that the balance of power might one day shift so far that Washington rather than London would become the seat of government.*

—PHILIP ZIEGLER, *LEGACY: CECIL RHODES, THE RHODES TRUST, AND RHODES SCHOLARSHIPS*

DURING HIS FINAL YEARS, Rhodes's symptoms of obsessive compulsion became more and more pronounced. He drank prodigious amounts of booze—champagne, beer, and bourbon—from morning to night. He shaved so often that he removed layers of skin from his face. After each shave, he would soak in a tub—drink in hand—for several hours. Following this ritual, he would roam about his estate stark-naked in the company of his "angels and lambs." Keir Hardie, leader of Britain's Labor Party, labeled him "a confirmed drunkard and dipsomaniac."[1]

His thoughts began to focus more and more on the United States. Stead observed: "He [Rhodes] was devoted to the old flag [the Union Jack] but in his ideas he was an American, and in his latter years he expressed to me his unhesitating readiness to accept the reunion of the [English] race under the Stars and Stripes if it could not be obtained in any other way. Although he had no objection to the monarchy, he unhesitatingly preferred the American to the British Constitution, and the textbook which he laid down for his novitiates was a copy of the American Constitution."[2] Rhodes believed that the unification of Britain and the United States would secure "the peace of the world for all eternity" and the creation of a "universal language."[3]

This merger could be effected, Rhodes argued, by the strengthening of economic trade between the two nations—trade unencumbered by tariffs; by the planting of "Pilgrim Societies" in London and New York, where American and British bankers, businessmen, and industrialists could meet in private to outline their joint goals and objectives; and by the awarding of Rhodes Scholarships to Oxford University for the best and brightest American students so that they could play an integral part in the formation of the New World Order.[4] Once sufficient support for the merger was achieved, he believed, the British House of Commons would unite with the US Congress for the formation of an "Imperial Parliament," the members of which would remain seated for five-year terms, alternating their location between London and Washington, DC.[5]

## THE LAST DAYS

By the early months of 1902, Rhodes's health deteriorated rapidly. He was only forty-eight years old but looked decades older. His failing heart had left him gasping for breath and racked with pain. Compounding his misery was the oppressive heat of that summer. During the daytime, Rhodes stayed at Groote Schuur, but, when evening came, he retreated to a small cottage on the seafront at Muizenberg, where he sought relief from breezes blowing off False Bay. One of his aides, Gordon le Sueur, recalled: "Rhodes would wander about the house like a caged animal, his clothes all thrown open, his hand thrust characteristically inside his trousers, the beads of perspiration glistening on his forehead beneath his tousled hair as he panted for breath. Into the darkened drawing room he would go and fling himself upon a couch, then he would start up and huddle himself up in a chair . . . and anon painfully toil upstairs to his bedroom and pace to and fro, every now and then stopping at the window which gave him that wondrous view of Table Mountain."[6]

### "A GREAT EXAMPLE"

The end came on March 26, 1902. Jameson, who remained with Rhodes to the end, reported his last words as follows: "So little done, so much to do." Over the Easter weekend, some 30,000 people filed through Groote Schuur to view the catafalque. On Monday, the coffin was moved to the Parliament in Cape Town, where thousands more came to pay their respects. The next day, it was transported from Parliament on a gun carriage draped with a Union Jack to a funeral service at the Anglican cathedral. For his eulogy, the Archbishop of Cape Town used 2 Samuel 3:38 as his text: "Know ye not that there is a prince and a great man fallen this day in Israel."[7] He urged the congregation to follow Rhodes's "great example" and dedicate their lives "to the expansion and consolidation of the British Empire, to the provision of new markets for British merchandise, and to a new country for British colonists." No mention was made of his disdain for Christianity, his hedonistic lifestyle, or his treatment of natives. Then, in another procession, the coffin was taken to the railway station for a journey to the north.

On April 10, a memorial service was held at St. Paul's Cathedral in London. The occasion provided proof that the assassination of Uncle Sam already was in the works. Seated with Lord Rothschild was J. P. Morgan. Among the others who packed into the cathedral were General William Booth, Mr. and Mrs. William Stead, Sir Arthur Balfour, and Albert Lord Grey, who became one of the trustees of the Rhodes Scholarships.[8]

## POSTMORTEM

Lord Milner assumed leadership of the Society of the Elect, which he renamed the Round Table. Under his direction, hundreds of prominent British statesmen, writers, and bankers were recruited to the secret society, including Sir Patrick Duncan, governor general of South Africa, Philip Henry Kerr, 11th Marquess of Lothian and the British ambassador to America, 1st Baron Robert Henry Brand, managing director of the House of Lazard in England; Lionel Curtis, professor of colonial history at Oxford University; George Geoffrey Dawson, editor of *The London Times*; John Buchan, 1st Baron Tweedsmuir, author of *The 39 Steps* and future governor general of Canada; T. E. Lawrence, one of the first Rhodes scholars, who would become known as "Lawrence of Arabia"; Leo Amery, Britain's colonial secretary; Stanley Baldwin, First Earl Baldwin of Bewdley, who would serve as prime minister of England under three monarchs; Sir Edward Peacock, a partner at Barings Bank and a director of the Bank of England; and Rudyard Kipling, the first English-language writer to receive the Nobel Prize for Literature.[9] Before the group, Milner gave the following address in 1905:

> What I pray for hardest is, that those with whom I have worked in a great struggle and who may attach some weight to my words should remain faithful, faithful above all in the period of reaction, to the great idea of Imperial Unity. When we who call ourselves Imperialists talk of the British Empire, we think of a group of states, all independent in their local concerns, but all united for the defense of their own common interests and the development of a common civilization; united, not in an alliance—for alliances can be made and unmade, and are never more than nominally lasting but in a permanent organic union. Of such a union the dominions as they exist today, are, we fully admit, only the raw material. Our ideal is still distant but we deny that it is either visionary or unattainable. . . . The road is long, the obstacles are many, the goal may not be reached in my lifetime—perhaps not in that of any man in this room. You cannot hasten the slow growth of a great idea like that by any forcing process. But what

you can do is to keep it steadily in view, to lose no opportunity to work for it, to resist like grim death any policy which leads away from it. I know that the service of that idea requires the rarest combination of qualities, a combination of ceaseless effort with infinite patience. But then think on the other hand of the greatness of the reward; the immense privilege of being allowed to contribute in any way to the fulfillment of one of the noblest conceptions which has ever dawned on the political imagination of mankind.[10]

Milner's period of stewardship in South Africa proved to be of significant consequence. He administered the defeated Transvaal and Orange Free State as occupied territories, and recruited into the upper layers of his civil service a band of young men from well-to-do, upper-class, frequently titled families who became known as "Milner's Kindergarten."[11] They replaced the governors, administrators, and bureaucrats of the Boer republics and worked to rebuild the broken country.[12] The Kindergarten comprised new blood—young educated men—mostly Oxford graduates, who could serve as Rhodes's clones. After months of indoctrination, they were dispatched to the United States, Canada, Australia, New Zealand, and British colonies throughout the world. In time, the Kindergarten proved itself capable of populating the next generation of the Secret Society.[13]

## A ROTHSCHILD LACKEY

As the High Commissioner for South Africa and the first governor of the Transvaal and Orange River Colony, Milner drafted a plan at the behest of Lord Rothschild to transform the territory of Uganda into a homeland for the Jews. This was the territory that Rhodes required for his Cairo-to-Cape Town railroad. A Zion in central Africa would grant Britain control of the headwaters of the Nile and, therefore, a means of driving foreign interests from the continent.[14]

Milner retired from political office in 1905. He returned to England to assume a position of director at the Joint Stock Bank, which was owned by Lord Rothschild. He, together with Rothschild, continued to supervise the Round Table Movement which had established branches in Australia, New Zealand, and Canada. The movement now published *The Round Table*, its own quarterly magazine. The names of the editors and writers were never mentioned.[15]

## THE RHODES SCHOLARS

Along with Lord Rothschild, Milner was also co-executor of the Rhodes estate and an administrator of the Rhodes Scholarships. These post-graduate awards for study at Oxford University were granted to "young colonists" with the purpose of "instilling into their minds the advantages of the colonies as well as to England for the retention of the Unity of the Empire."[16] The lion's share of the awards were singled out for enterprising American scholars. At the completion of their two years at Oxford, these scholars were to return to the United States so that they could obtain prominent positions in academics, politics, and the media. In this way, they could serve to undermine the nation's sovereignty. As soon as the Rhodes fund was established, massive amounts of money poured into its coffers from the estate of Alfred Beit, the Carnegie United Kingdom Trust, and organizations associated with J. P. Morgan and John D. Rockefeller.[17]

By 1915, the impact of the Rhodes scholars in America was decried by William Fulton of the *Chicago Herald Tribune* as follows: "Rhodes scholars dominate the United States Department of State, which directs the doling out of billions in foreign aid, with the United Kingdom getting the major share. The savants also hold down important positions in the economic cooperation administration, mutual defense assistance programs, and other foreign handout setups."[18] Despite this warning, the infiltration of Rhodes scholars into top political positions in the US government persisted throughout the twentieth century. These scholars came to include:

- Dean Rusk (Secretary of State, 1961–69)

- Walt Whitman Rostow (special assistant for National Security Affairs, 1966–69)

- Harlan Cleveland (assistant Secretary of State for International Organization Affairs in the Kennedy Administration, ambassador to NATO under Presidents Johnson and Nixon)

- Nicholas Katzenbach (US Attorney General, 1965–66)

- Sen. James William Fulbright (Arkansas, 1945–74)

- Sen. Frank Church (Idaho, 1956–81)

- Sen. Bill Bradley (New Jersey, 1979–97)

- Sen. David Boren (Oklahoma, 1979–94)

- Sen. Richard D. Lugar (Indiana, 1976–2013)

- Sen. Larry Pressler (South Dakota, 1979–97)

- Sen. Paul Sarbanes (Maryland, 1977–2007)

- Rep. Elliot H. Levitas (Georgia, 1975–85)

- Rep. Carl Albert (Ohio, 1947–77; Speaker of the House 1971 to 77)

- Rep. John Brademas (Indiana, 1959–81; later New York University President)

- President William Jefferson Clinton (Arkansas governor, 1979–81, 1983–92; President, 1993–2001)

- Gov. Richard Celeste (Ohio, 1983–91)

- Supreme Court Justice Byron "Whizzer" White (1962–93)

- Gen. Bernard W. Rogers (Supreme Commander of the NATO forces in Europe, 1979–87)

- Gen. Wesley Clark (Supreme Commander of the NATO forces in Europe, 1997–2000)

- Stansfield Turner (CIA Director, 1977–81)

- R. James Woolsey (CIA Director, 1993–95)

- Charles Collingwood (TV commentator)

- Howard K. Smith (TV commentator)

- George Jerome Goodman (writer known as "Adam Smith")

- Hedley Donovan (former Editor-in-Chief of *Time* magazine; later a senior advisor to President Carter)

- Robert Penn Warren (Pulitzer Prize–winning poet and novelist, best known for his book *All the King's Men*).[19]

### EYEING THE CONQUEST OF AMERICA

America continued to remain the central focus of the secret society that came about because of a brainstorm. By the time the tombstone for Rhodes was set in place on a hill in the Matopos, J. P. Morgan had been persuaded by Nathan Rothschild to establish a central bank in the United States as a counterpart to the Bank of England and to serve as a founding member of the Pilgrim Society in New York. Cornelius Vanderbilt was called upon by Rothschild and Lord Rosebery to become a pilgrim and to dedicate a portion of his wealth to the grandiose endeavor of forging a one-world government. Waldorf Astoria, the New York real estate tycoon, was recruited by Milner and Lord Brett to become a key member of the British Round Table. Andrew Carnegie, arguably America's richest man, was persuaded by Lord Rosebery and William Stead to devote much of his vast fortune to further the cause of a one-world government. Behind such men of wealth and influence, the House of Rothschild loomed in the shadows. Against such forces, a backwoods character like Uncle Sam didn't have a ghost of a chance.

# NOTES

1.  H.L. Wesseling, *Divide and Rule: The Partition of Africa, 1880–1914* (Westport, Connecticut: Praeger, 1996), p. 291.
2.  William T. Stead, *The Last Will and Testament of Cecil John Rhodes* (London: Review of Review Books, 1902), p. 63.
3.  Ibid., p. 73.
4.  Ibid., pp. 23–45.
5.  Ibid., p. 73.
6.  Gordon Le Sueur, *Cecil Rhodes: The Man and His Work* (London: John Murray, 1913), p. 313.
7.  Ibid., p. 329.
8.  "Memorial Service in London," *New York Times*, April 11, 1902, http://query.nytimes.com/mem/archive-free/pdf?res-9803E4D91230E733A25752C1A9629C946397D6CF.
9.  Alexander C. Bay, *The Round Table, 1910-66* (Bodleiun Library: University of Oxford, 1995), https://archive.org/stream/ShadowGovernmentAndBankingEliteTopSecret145/Round%20Table%20Papers,%201910-1966-593_djvu.txt.
10. Alfred Milner, *The Milner Papers, 1897–1905*, Volume II (London: Cassell, 1933), p. 507.
11. Carroll Quigley, *The Anglo-American Establishment: From Rhodes to Cliveden* (New York: Books in Focus, 1981), p. 7.
12. Gerry Docherty and Jim Macgregor, "New World Order: Founding Fathers," *Global Research*. April 26, 2015, http://www.globalresearch.ca/new-world-order-the-founding-fathers/5445255.
13. Ibid.
14. Robin Brown, *The Secret Society: Cecil John Rhodes's Plan for a New World Order* (Cape Town, South Africa: Penguin Books, 2015), p. 256.
15. Brown, *The Secret Society*, p. 273.
16. Stead, *The Last Will and Testament of Cecil John Rhodes*, p. 23.
17. G. Edward Griffin, *The Creature from Jekyll Island: A Second Look at the Federal Reserve* (Westlake Village, CA: American Media, 2008), p. 272.
18. William Fulton, quoted in Brown, *The Secret Society*, p. 283.
19. "Rhodes Scholars: The Complete List, 1903-2015, The Rhodes Trust, n.d., http://www.rhodeshouse.ox.ac.uk/about/rhodes-scholars/rhodes-scholars-complete-list.

# PART TWO

# THE NEW WORLD

*"Some of the biggest men in the United States, in the field of commerce and manu-facture, are afraid of something. They know that there is a power somewhere so organized, so subtle, so watchful, so interlocked, so complete, so pervasive, that they had better not speak above their breath when they speak in condemnation of it."*
—WOODROW WILSON

*"The democracy will cease to exist when you take away from those who are willing to work and give to those who would not."*
—THOMAS JEFFERSON

*"The world is governed by very different personages from what is imagined by those who are not behind the scenes."*
—ENGLISH PRIME MINISTER BENJAMIN DISRAELI, IN 1844

# 7

# CONVERTING CARNEGIE

*Behind the visible government there is an invisible government upon the throne*
*that owes the people no loyalty and recognizes no responsibility. To destroy this*
*invisible government, to undo the ungodly union between corrupt business and*
*corrupt politics is the task of a statesman.*

—THEODORE ROOSEVELT, PRESIDENTIAL CAMPAIGN OF 1912

AT THE TURN OF THE TWENTIETH CENTURY, Andrew Carnegie was the richest man in America. He made his fortune in partnership with George Pullman, who sold railroad cars to the railroad companies. Carnegie next purchased a string of steel mills in Pittsburgh to form Carnegie Steel, which became a vertically integrated business, the prototype for the modern industrial corporation. The company owned not only the mills where the steel was made but also the mines where the iron ore was extracted and the coal mines that supplied the coal. It controlled the ships and the railroads that transported the iron ore and the coal to the factories. The company also developed its managerial pool internally from the bottom up, rather than hiring managers from other businesses.[1]

In 1883, Carnegie fell under the spell of Herbert Spencer, whom he met at a dinner in the great British philosopher's honor at Delmonico's restaurant in New York. He sought out Spencer's company whenever he visited London and showered the philosopher with lavish presents, including a grand piano. In his autobiography, Carnegie claimed that it was with Spencer's help that he finally "got rid of theology and the supernatural and found the truth of evolution."[2] Through Spencer, the American steel magnate met and befriended Matthew Arnold, the esteemed British poet, social commentator, and agnostic. Arnold maintained that the notion of a personal God is "unintelligible and unverifiable," a stance which Carnegie adopted.[3]

## ROSEBERY AND STEAD

During his visits to London, Carnegie was soon rubbing elbows with the British ruling elite, including Prime Minister William Gladstone and Lord Archibald Primrose, the Fifth Earl of Rosebery, who was Lord Nathan Rothschild's son-in-law. A member of Rhodes's Society of the Elect, Rosebery served as Britain's prime minister from 1894 to 1895.

When Rosebery visited America in the spring of 1883, Carnegie served as his tour guide and secured a private train to show the British aristocrat the anthracite deposits and collieries of eastern Pennsylvania, the natural oil fields of western Pennsylvania, and the steel rail mills of Pittsburgh, "the dirtiest place on earth."[4] The tour was such a success that Rosebery offered to put his American friend up for a seat in the House of Commons as a representative from Edinburgh, an offer which Carnegie rejected.[5]

Carnegie met Stead in the fall of 1883 at a dinner party hosted in London by Dolly Thompson, the wife of the owner of the *Pall Mall Gazette*, where Stead served as the editor.[6] Stead, who liked to bask in the company of the rich and powerful, sought Carnegie's favor. He defended Carnegie's suppression of the striking steel workers in Homestead, Pennsylvania; lavished praise on the industrialist's literary efforts; and even served as Carnegie's caddy at Skibo Castle, the American millionaire's 40,000-acre estate in Scotland.

## THE "GREAT RAPPROCHEMENT"

Through Rosebery and Stead, Carnegie became familiar with the plans of Cecil Rhodes to bring about the reunification of Great Britain and the United States.[7] In *Triumphant Democracy*, which was published in London in 1886, Carnegie wrote: "Let men say what they will, I say that as surely as the sun in the heavens once shone upon Britain and America united, so surely is it one morning to rise, to shine upon, to greet again the reunited states: the British-American Union."[8] This "great rapprochement," he believed was inevitable for racial reasons. "The American," he argued, "remains three-fourths purely British. The mixture of the German, which constitutes substantially all of the remainder, though not strictly British, is yet Germanic. The Briton of today is himself composed in large measure of the Germanic element, and German, Briton, and American are all of the Teutonic race."[9] Once the British-American Union came into being, Carnegie believed, it would dominate the world and establish universal peace. "Such a giant among pigmies as the British-American Union," he wrote, "would never need to exert its power, but only to intimate its wishes and decisions."[10]

## AMERICAN SUPREMACY

But Carnegie stood in opposition to the Society of the Elect's claim that England must rule the world. America, in his estimation, had come to supersede Great Britain in wealth, industrial and agricultural production, and inventiveness. He wrote:

> Many of the most important practical inventions which have contributed to the progress of the world have originated with Americans. No other people have devised so many labor-saving machines and appliances. The first commercially successful steamboat navigated the Hudson, and the first steamboat to cross the Atlantic sailed under the American flag from an American port. Americans gave the world the cotton gin and the first practical mowing, reaping and sewing machines. In the most spiritual, most ethereal of all departments in which man has produced great triumphs, viz.: electricity, the position of the American is specially noteworthy.[11]

What's more, America displayed a higher literacy rate, produced the greatest number of newspapers, and established political institutions that were "comparatively pure and free from corruption." For this reason, the United States must spearhead the effort to create a one world government. Britain, he insisted, possessed no other choice but to reunite with "her giant child" in order to avoid "sure decline to comparative insignificance in the future annals of the English-speaking race."[12]

While Rosebery blanched at the notion of American supremacy in the new order of things, Stead embraced it and presented Carnegie's argument to Cecil Rhodes. "Rhodes," Stead wrote, "expressed his readiness to adopt the course from which he had at first recoiled. . . . That of securing the unity of the English-speaking race by consenting to the absorption of the British Empire in the American Union if it could not be secured any other way. . . . He expressed his deliberate conviction that English-speaking re-union was so great an end in itself as to justify even the sacrifice of the distinctive features and independent existence of the British Empire."[13]

Although they never met, Carnegie and Rhodes shared much in common. Both men were freemasons.[14] Carnegie was instrumental in obtaining the most complete collection of published works by and about Scottish poet Robert Burns, an ardent freemason, for the Library of the Supreme Council of the Scottish Rite of Freemasonry in Washington, DC.[15] Both were avowed agnostics. Both espoused the doctrine of evolution and the "survival of the fittest." Both possessed an interest in the occult. Carnegie, as a young man, had been a Swedenborgian, a religious cult with ties to theosophy.[16] Both, despite their vast wealth, were socialists. In an interview with the *New York Times*, Carnegie said: "I believe socialism is the grandest theory ever presented, and I am sure some day it will rule the world. Then we will have obtained the millennium. . . . That is the state we are drifting into. Then men will be content to work for the general welfare and share their riches with their neighbor."[17] And both had ties to the House of Rothschild. Carnegie Steel had been financed by Jacob Schiff, who worked in tandem with the

European Rothschilds, and Schiff, at the instigation of Lord Rothschild, would introduce Carnegie to J. P. Morgan.[18]

## THE GOSPEL OF WEALTH

Thanks to his association with members of the Society of the Elect, Carnegie developed his "Gospel of Wealth," which he first proclaimed in an article that appeared in a 1889 edition of the *North American Review*. While the government should supervise the distribution of wealth and provide for the needs of its citizenry, he reasoned, a cadre of millionaires should preside over the government. The emergence of such a ruling elite, he insisted, was the "beneficent necessity" of human evolution.

The gap between the rich and the poor, he argued in the article, was "inevitable" and caused by "laws of nature" that were immutable. But the same laws of nature dictated that the wealthy with their "talent for organization and management" were obliged to use their surplus revenue to benefit the vast majority of mankind, who had evolved into serviceable drones. In exchange for such public benefactions, the men of means should be afforded the right to determine public policy concerning trusts, tariffs, monopoly, and regulation.[19] With this gospel, Carnegie provided the blueprint for the formation of a shadow government that was to rule over America.

## THE PRINCE OF PEACE

After Carnegie sold his steel company to J. P. Morgan for $480 million (the highest price ever paid for a business at the time), Stead persuaded the industrialist to provide the funding ($40 million in today's money) for the construction of the Peace Palace at The Hague to house a "permanent court of arbitration."[20] The task of this court would be to settle disputes between nations and to bring about the "complete banishment of war."[21] The construction of the Peace Palace represented the first attempt to dissolve national sovereignty and national law under an institution with global jurisdiction. When the building was completed,

Carnegie called it "the most holy building in the world."[22]

Carnegie now embarked on a crusade to create a "League of Peace" or "League of Nations," which would comprise a combination of the leading imperial powers, complete with an international police force.[23] He even publicized his proposal in a short article entitled "A League of Nations," which appeared in the pages of *Outlook* magazine May 25, 1907.[24]

The creation of such an organization, Carnegie realized, would require control of America's educational and political institutions—control that could only be achieved by the expenditure of vast sums of cash from a charitable foundation. These institutions would become reliant on these benefactions for their continued existence, and the trustees of the foundation thereby would gain control over their operations.

In 1910, the Carnegie Endowment for International Peace (CEIP) set up its headquarters in Washington, DC. Carnegie appointed twenty-eight trustees, including Elihu Root, senator from New York and former Secretary of War; Harvard president Charles W. Eliot; shipping and real estate magnate Robert Brookings; former ambassador to Great Britain Joseph H. Choate; former Secretary of State John W. Foster; Cleveland Hoadley Dodge, president of Phelps Dodge; James T. Shotwell, professor of history at Columbia University, and Nicholas Murray Butler, president of Columbia University.[25]

CEIP displayed Carnegie's continual close ties to J. P. Morgan to whom he had sold his steel company. Throughout the first decade of the twentieth century, the ties between the two industrialists tightened. Root, who became CEIP's first president, was Morgan's personal lawyer, while Cleveland Hoadley Dodge was a director of the Morgan-owned National City Bank in New York, and Joseph H. Choate served as one of Morgan's corporate lawyers.[26] And Morgan remained under the control of the Rothschilds.

# NOTES

1. Burtom Folsom, *The Myth of the Robber Barons: A New Look at the Rise of Big Business in America* (Herndon, Virginia: Young America's Foundation, 1991), p 65.
2. Andrew Carnegie, *The Autobiography of Andrew Carnegie and His Gospel of Wealth* (New York: Signet Classics, 2006), pp. 164 165.
3. Matthew Arnold, quoted in David L. DeLaura's *Hebrew and Hellene in Victorian England* (Austin: The University of Texas Press, 1969), p. 106.
4. Andrew Carnegie, quoted in David Nasaw's *Andrew Carnegie* (New York: Penguin Press, 2006), p. 238.
5. Ibid.
6. Nasaw, *Andrew Carnegie*, p. 229.
7. Andrew Carnegie, *Triumphant Democracy: Sixty Years' March of the Republic* (New York: Charles Scribner's Sons, 1886), p. 77.
8. Ibid., p. 549.
9. Andrew Carnegie, "A Look Ahead," *North American Review,* June, 1892, https://babel.hathitrust.org/cgi/pt?id=njp.32101013404601;view=1up;seq=21.
10. Ibid.
11. Andrew Carnegie, *Triumphant Democracy*, pp. 7–8.
12. Andrew Carnegie, "A Look Ahead," *The North American Press*, Volume 156, June 1893.
13. William T. Stead, *The Last Will and Testament of Cecil Rhodes* (London: Review of Reviews, 1902), p. 63.
14. "The Masonic Trowel," http://www.themasonictrowel.com/freemasonry/Famous/famous_masons.htm.
15. "Our Collections," The Scottish Rite of Freemasonry, Supreme Council, 33rd Degree, Southern Jurisdiction, U.S.A., n. d., https://scottishrite.org/headquarters/library/our-collections/.
16. Nasaw, *Andrew Carnegie*, pp. 48–49.
17. Andrew Carnegie, quoted in Ibid., p. 267.
18. Dean Henderson, "The Federal Reserve Cartel: The Eight Families," *Global Research,* June 1, 2011, http://www.globalresearch.ca/the-federal-reserve-cartel-the-eight-families/25080.
19. Ibid.
20. Ron Chernow, *The House of Morgan: An American Banking Dynasty and the Rise of Modern Finance* (New York: Grove Press, 2001), p. 84.
21. Nasaw, *Andrew Carnegie*, p. 650.
22. Andrew Carnegie, quoted in Samuel Bostaph, *Andrew Carnegie: An Economic Biography* (New York: Rowman and Littlefield, 2015), p. 111.
23. Andrew Carnegie, "A Look Ahead," *North American Review,* June 1893, http://www.unz.org/Pub/NorthAmericanRevie1893jun-00685.
24. Peter Koss, *Carnegie* (New York: John Wiley and Sons, 2002), p. 474.
25. "Endowment History," Carnegie Endowment for International Peace, n.d., https://web.archive.org/web/20091013002726/http://www.carnegieendowment.org/about/index.cfm?fa=history.
26. Charles Burns, "The Men Who Built America," Lew Rockwell.com, November 13, 2012, https://www.lewrockwell.com/lrc-blog/126276/.

# 8

## THE RISE OF FOUNDATIONS

*The foundation's direct power is the power of money. Privately financed educational institutions have had a bad time during the period of rapidly increasing costs. Foundation grants have become so important a source of support that college and university presidents cannot often afford to ignore the opinions and wishes of the executives who distribute foundation largess. Such administrators will freely admit that they do not like to receive restricted or earmarked grants and would far prefer to be unfettered in their disposition of money given to their institutions. But they will also admit that they usually dare not turn down a grant, however inconsistent with their policy, priority of goals, or urgent needs it may be, for fear they might earn the displeasure of the granting foundation.*

—RENE WORMSER, *FOUNDATIONS: THEIR POWER AND INFLUENCE*

KNOWING THE RISE of global government required social engineering, the Carnegie Foundation for the Advancement of Teaching (CFAT), which was established in 1905, gained control of America's educational system. The original purpose of the foundation was "to provide retiring pensions for teachers of universities, colleges, and technical schools . . . without regard to race, sex, creed, or color."[1] The foundation also provided general endowments to institutions that complied with its prescribed scholastic standards and entrance requirements. By 1909, the CFAT had become the national unofficial accrediting agency for colleges and universities.[2] It possessed the power to create the curricula,

**Andrew Carnegie**
Since Carnegie was an avowed socialist, an agnostic, a globalist, and an associate of the Rhodes Society, universities throughout America began to reflect his ideology and beliefs. Carnegie was seeking control of the American political and education systems to further a New World Order.

to oversee the faculty, and to supervise the actions of the administration.

Since Carnegie was an avowed socialist, an agnostic, a globalist, and an associate of the Rhodes Society, universities throughout America began to reflect his ideology and beliefs. In *Foundations: Their Power and Influence,* Rene Wormser, special counsel to the Reece Committee, wrote: "The growing radicalism which was beginning rapidly to permeate academic circles was no grass-roots movement. Mr. [Aaron] Sargent cited a statement by Professor Ludwig Von Mises that socialism does not spring from the masses but is instigated by intellectuals that form themselves into a clique and bore from within and operate that way. It is not a people's movement at all. It is a capitalization on the people's emotions and sympathies toward a point these people wish to reach."[3]

## THE SWORD OF DAMOCLES

Funding from the CFAT came to hang over the country's institutions of higher learning like the sword of Damocles. Those who complied with the dictates of the Foundation's trustees received massive benefactions; those who failed to comply did not. New subjects became mandatory college courses, including anthropology, comparative religions, and social science—all of which served to stress the relativity of cultural practices and ideals. The need to introduce such subjects had been brought on by the advent of the global conflict. Students had to be conditioned to abandon the isolationist stance of their fathers and forefathers before they could be expected to engage in a war on European soil.

The effects of the Carnegie Foundation on America's religious colleges were decried as follows in a speech delivered by Thomas W. Churchill, president of the New York Board of Education, on June 14, 1914: "Mr. Carnegie's efforts are crushing individuality out of American colleges and lessening their contributions to public service. The Carnegie Foundation has deliberately and conspicuously made a mark of religious colleges—particularly of the small institutions which in their own field carried on a great Samaritan work with limited equipment but a splendid spirit. One after another many religious colleges have been seduced by great wealth to give up the independence that should have been found in a college if nowhere else, and to forsake the faith of their founders. It makes me boil with shame to think that in this generation and in this Republic any body of men would so blazingly employ the tremendous power of great wealth as to permit it to buy the abandonment of religion."[4]

At the same time, Ernest Victor Hollis, the chief of college administration in the US Department of Education, also voiced his objection to the "sinister" influence of CFAT. The method used by the endowment, he said, was one of indirection—"indirectly through general and non-controversial purposes." "For instance," Hollis elaborated, "there is little connection between giving a pension to a college professor or giving a sum to the general endowment of his college, and reforming entrance requirements, the financial practices, and the scholastic standards of his institution." Yet, he insisted, the one was bound to the other. It was a case of conform, or no grant! When to conform meant bathing in a stream of millions, Hollis concluded that college and university administrators and their faculties were inclined to conform.[5]

## THE GENERAL EDUCATION BOARD

Carnegie was not alone in seeking control of the American political and educational systems to further a New World Order. John D. Rockefeller was greatly impressed by Carnegie's philanthropy, and when the Carnegie Library opened in Pittsburgh, he sent this congratulatory note: "I would that more men of wealth were doing as you are doing with your money; but, be assured, your example will bear fruits, and the time will come when men of wealth will more generally be willing to use it for the good of others."[6]

In 1905, Rockefeller with Frederick Gates, his investment manager, created the General Education Board (GEB) that came with an ultimate price tag of $129 million. The task of this organization was spelled out by Gates as follows:

> In our dreams, we have limitless resources and the people yield themselves with perfect docility to our molding hands. The present education conventions fade from their minds, and unhampered by tradition, we work our own good will upon a grateful and responsive rural folk. We shall not try to make these people or any of their children into philosophers or men of learning, or men of science.

We have not to raise up from among them authors, editors, poets or men of letters. We shall not search for embryo great artists, painters, musicians nor lawyers, doctors, preachers, politicians, statesmen, of whom we have an ample supply.

The task we set before ourselves is very simple as well as a very beautiful one, to train these people as we find them to a perfectly ideal life just where they are. So we will organize our children and teach them to do in a perfect way the things their fathers and mothers are doing in an imperfect way, in the homes, in the shops and on the farm.[7]

In compliance with GEB guidelines, blacks would receive vocational training since they were intellectually inferior to whites and, therefore, ill-equipped to meet academic challenges. Gates wrote: "Latin, Greek, and metaphysics form a kind of knowledge that I fear with our colored brethren tend to puff up rather than build up."[8] The American educational system was to serve not only as a branch of industry but also as a tool for governance.

## STANDARDIZED EDUCATION

In no time at all, the GEB was working in tandem with the CFAT to develop standardized curricula with standardized textbooks for all American children. This development was to be expected since Daniel Gilman, one of GEB's four incorporators, was also the president of the Carnegie Institution of Washington. Nevertheless, it provoked considerable public outcry. In 1914, the newly formed National Education Association passed this resolution: "We view with alarm the activity of the Carnegie and Rockefeller Foundations—agencies not in any way responsible to the people—in their efforts to control the policies of our State educational institutions, to fashion after their conception and to standardize our courses of study, and to surround the institutions with conditions which menace true academic freedom and defeat the primary purpose of democracy as heretofore preserved inviolate in our common schools, normal schools, and universities."[9]

The Rockefeller Foundation was set up in 1913 with an initial $100

"MY INTERESTS IN THE UNITED STATES STEEL CORPORATION ARE WELL REPRESENTED BY MY SON."—JOHN D. ROCKEFELLER, SR.

**John D. Rockefeller Sr.**
In 1905, Rockefeller with Frederick Gates, his investment manager, created the General Education Board (GEB), which came with an ultimate price tag of $129 million.

million endowment "to promote the well being of mankind throughout the world."[10] The nebulous nature of this charter gave the Rockefeller family carte blanche to manipulate the foundation to feather its own nest. As soon as the charter was approved, Rockefeller dumped an additional $82.8 million into the foundation's coffers, thereby insulating a large portion of his vast wealth from federal and state taxation.[11]

Since the family business was oil production and refinement, millions of dollars were contributed by the Rockefeller Foundation to the American Petroleum Institute, a trade association whose chief function was lobbying for tariffs on imported oil and arranging marketing agreements between the various oil companies.[12]

### JUNIOR'S INDOCTRINATION

John D. Rockefeller Junior, who served as the first president of the Rockefeller Foundation, retained a very close relationship with Carnegie, whom he held in avuncular affection. Junior spent several weeks every summer at Skibo and agreed with Carnegie that their foundations should direct their resources toward common global goals.[13] Carnegie's last public appearance was at a gathering of Junior's Bible Class at the Fifth Avenue Baptist Church in New York. The appearance was telling since Carnegie was instrumental in persuading Junior to shed his religious fundamentalism. Shortly after Carnegie addressed the Bible Class, Junior announced to the group his belief that anyone who manifested "the moral spirit" of Jesus merited entrance into the Kingdom of Heaven, even if he or she refused to practice Christian rituals.[14]

Junior's internationalism was further enhanced by his friendship with Raymond B. Fosdick, who became his lawyer and closest adviser. Fosdick had been appointed to serve as undersecretary of the League of Nations by President Wilson.[15] In his fawning biography, *John D. Rockefeller, Jr.: A Portrait* (1956), Fosdick wrote: "More and more Mr. Rockefeller began to think in international terms. It is true that he had not favored the League of Nations when it was first proposed. Just as he had taken his church affiliations from his father, so his political loyalties were similarly inherited, and he had followed the Republican Party in its opposition to President Wilson. But his opinions were invariably marked by tolerance, and inflexibility was not part of his character."[16]

### REWRITING HISTORY

Before the outbreak of World War I, Carnegie and Junior came to an understanding. The Carnegie Endowment would center on international education, while the Rockefeller Foundation would focus on national education.[17] Both men agreed that the key to conditioning the American people for war required a drastic rewriting of American history. In textbooks throughout the country, England became "the mother country," who watched over her American sons and daughters with loving affection. No longer were the British portrayed as the oppressors of the American colonists. Nor were they presented as tyrants who engaged in the brutal practice of impressment that sparked the War of 1812. The contributions of Germans to the building of America were greatly downplayed. German was banned from school curricula, and the music of German composers was eliminated from school repertories. University professors and high school teachers who objected to these changes or opposed the war were fired or cowed into silence.[18]

Ground zero for the educational reforms was the Rockefeller-funded Columbia Teachers College, where Harold Rugg, a distinguished professor, said: "Through schools of the world we shall disseminate a new conception of government—one that will embrace all the collective activities of men; one that will postulate the need for scientific control and operation of economic activities."[19]

## GLIMPSING EVIL

One of the first glimpses into the inherent nefarious nature of the Carnegie and Rockefeller Foundations influence came in 1912, when the Commission on Industrial Relations studied labor conditions and the treatment of workers by the major US industrial firms. Starting with a study of labor exploitation, the Commission on Industrial Relations went on to investigate concentrations of economic power, interlocking directorates, and the role of the then relatively new large charitable foundations.[20] Questions arose from the fact that Junior appointed William Lyon King to serve as the head of the Rockefeller Foundation's Department of Industrial Relations. King's main task was not to further the goal of compromise between labor and industry but rather to defend Junior's role in the Ludlow Massacre, a labor dispute which resulted in the deaths of two men and eleven children.[21]

During the commission hearings, future Supreme Court Justice Louis D. Brandeis testified that he was seriously concerned about the emerging danger of such a concentration of power. He said: "When a great financial power has developed which can successfully summon forces from all parts of the country to carry out what they deem to be their business principle, [there] develops within the State a state so powerful that the ordinary social and industrial forces existing are insufficient to cope with it."[22] The commission's report concluded that, "As regards the 'foundations' created for unlimited general purposes and endowed with enormous resources, their ultimate possibilities are so grave a menace [that] it would be desirable to recommend their abolition."[23]

## DENYING CHRIST

But no efforts were undertaken by government officials to curtail their activities, let alone to abolish the foundations. This permitted Junior to use his tax-exempt organization to further the development of a one-world religion. Under the influence of the Reverend Harry Emerson Fosdick, Raymond's elder brother, he funded and spearheaded the Interchurch Movement (ICM), which sought to consolidate the Protestant churches into a corporate-like structure that would exercise control over their activities.[24] The ideology of the ICM sprang from the sermons of the Rev. Fosdick, who had become indoctrinated in the employment of "higher criticism" to the New Testament by Charles Briggs, his professor at Union Theological Seminary. Fosdick believed that Christianity should be "demythologized" and stripped of all "theological accretions, including the Virgin Birth, the miracles, and the Resurrection, so that the "kergyma" or "original message" of the historic Jesus could recaptured for modern man.[25]

As a young pastor in lower Manhattan, Fosdick came upon the "social gospel" of Walter Rauschenbusch, who taught that Christianity is in its nature revolutionary, that Jesus did not perform an act of atonement on the cross, and that the Kingdom of Heaven "is not a matter of getting into heaven but of transforming life on earth into the harmony of heaven."[26] This was the message, Fosdick believed, that could unite all of mankind. The message struck a chord with Junior, who, in a 1917 speech at the Baptist Social Union, had said that a new, unified church "would pronounce ordinance, ritual, creed, as non-essential for admission into the Kingdom of God or His Church."[27]

Harry Emerson Fosdick and Junior became bound together after Fosdick delivered a sermon called "Shall the Fundamentalists Win?" at the First Presbyterian Church in New York. In the sermon, the Rev. Fosdick denounced interpretations of the Bible which upheld the supernatural aspects of the life of Jesus as "intolerant."[28] When the congregation reacted to the sermon by demanding Fosdick's ouster as their pastor, Junior rallied to Fosdick's support and distributed copies of the sermons to ministers and seminarians throughout the country.[29] In addition, he arranged for Fosdick to be selected as the senior pastor of the Riverside Church in upper Manhattan, which had been constructed by the Rockefeller Foundation at a cost of $4 million.[30]

With the Fosdick brothers at his side, Junior initiated a policy of funding seminaries that complied with the dictates of higher criticism and the debunking of the New Testament. A new breed of minister, who believed neither the account of the resurrection nor the divinity of Jesus, was unleashed on the American people. The seeds of doubt and skepticism would be spread from sea to shining sea so that deeply held convictions would be surrendered for the sake of ecumenism.

# NOTES

1. Ibid., p. 671.
2. Joseph Frazier Wall, *Andrew Carnegie* (Pittsburgh: The University of Pittsburgh Press, 1989), p. 877.
3. Rene Wormser, *Foundations: Their Power and Influence* (New York: Covenant House Books, 1993), p. 31.
4. Thomas W. Churchill, "The Carnegie Attitude to the Religious College," *The Evening Post* (New York), June 17, 1914.
5. Ernest Victor Hollis, quoted in Rene Wormster, *Foundations*, p. 140.
6. John D. Rockefeller's note to Carnegie in Ron Chernow, *Titan: The Life of John D. Rockefeller, Sr.* (New York: Vintage Books, 2004), p. 313.
7. General Education Board, Occasional Papers (New York: General Education Board, 1913), p. 6.
8. Frederick Tyler Gates, *Chapters in My Life* (New York: the Free Press, 1977), p. 134.
9. "Industrial Relations: Final Report and Testimony," U.S. Commission on Industrial Relations, 1914, p. 7883, https://books.google.com/books?id=0-keAQAAMAAJ&pg=PA7883&lpg=PA7883&dq=1914+national+education+association+st+paul+ resolution+carnegie+rockefeller&source=bl&ots=S phDo-cpw4&sig=HIkguQsB9 W7K2vuUeI6IRh1v6pc&hl=en&sa=X&ved=0ahUKEwiTqcXgxp 3SAhVM3IM KH QEmC9wQ6AEIMTAE#v=onepage&q=1914%20national%20education%20 association%20st%20paul %20resolution%20carnegie%20rockefeller&f=false.
10. Chernow, *Titan*, p. 564.
11. Ibid.
12. Ferdinand Lundberg, *America's 60 Families* (New York: Vanguard Press, 1937), p.330.
13. Nasaw, *Andrew Carnegie*, p. 615.
14. Chernow, *Titan*, pp. 639–640.
15. Ibid, p. 638.
16. Raymond E. Fosdick, *John D. Rockefeller, Jr.: A Portrait* (New York: Harper and Brothers, 1958), p. 216.
17. Jamie Lee, "The Untold History of Modern U.S. History," *Waking Times*, January 28, 2014, http://www.wakingtimes.com/2014/01/28/untold-history-modern-u-s-education-founding-fathers/.
18. Stone and Kuznick, *The Concise Untold history of the United States*, p. 15.
19. Harold Rugg, quoted in James F. Troy, "New World Order Education: Useful Engines in the 'One World Schoolhouse,'" *Global Research*, October 19, 2012, http://www.globalresearch.ca/new-world-order-education-useful-engines-in-the-one-world-schoolhouse/5308822.
20. Mark M. Rich, "The Hidden Evil: The Financial Elite's Covert War against the Civilian Population," 2009, http://www.bibliotecapleyades.net/sociopolitica/hiddenevil/hiddenevil07.htm.
21. Chernow, *Titan*, pp. 578–583.
22. Louis D. Brandeis, quoted in Rich, "The Hidden Evil."
23. Ibid.
24. Chernow, *Titan*, p. 639.
25. Robert Moats Miller, *Harry Emerson Fosdick: Preacher, Pastor, Prophet* (New York: Oxford University Press, 1985), pp. 408–409.

26. Walter Rauschenbusch, *A Theology of the Social Gospel* (New York: Abington Press, 1918), pp. 131–137.

27. John D. Rockefeller, Jr., quoted in Fosdick, *John D. Rockefeller: A Portrait*, p. 206.

28. Harry Emerson Fosdick, "Shall the Fundamentalists Win," a sermon delivered in 1922 at the First Presbyterian Church in New York City, http://historymatters.gmu. edu/d/5070/.

29. James Perloff, "The War on Christianity, Part 1," jamesperloff.com, 2013, https://jamesperloff.com/tag/national-council-of-churches/.

30. Ibid.

# 9

# NEW AMERICAN PILGRIMS

*What an extraordinary episode in the economic progress of man that age was, which came to an end in August 1914. The projects and politics of militarism and imperialism, of racial and cultural rivalries, of monopolies, restrictions, and exclusion, which were to play the serpent to this garden of paradise, were little more than the amusements of the daily newspaper, and appeared to exercise almost no influence at all on the ordinary course of social and economic life, the internationalization of which was nearly complete in practice.*

—JOHN MAYNARD KEYNES, *THE ECONOMIC CONSEQUENCES OF PEACE*

THE TASK OF CREATING A SECRET SOCIETY in America to advance the goals of Cecil Rhodes was left to J. P. Morgan. In 1854, the Morgan Bank had been established in London by two American financiers: George Peabody and Junius Morgan. The Rothschilds developed a close relationship with Peabody and Morgan, and following a financial crash in 1857, they saved the Morgan Bank by organizing a bailout from the Bank of England.

The Morgan Bank, with unlimited funding from the Rothschilds, became the driving force behind Western expansion in the United States.

It financed and controlled West-bound railroads through voting trusts. In 1879, Cornelius Vanderbilt's New York Central Railroad, which was financed by J. P. Morgan ( Junius's son), gave preferential shipping rates to John D. Rockefeller's budding Standard Oil monopoly, thereby cementing the Rockefeller/Morgan relationship and the formation of a new cartel. In 1904, economic analyst John Moody, founder of Moody's Investor Services, said it was impossible to talk of Rockefeller, Carnegie, and Morgan interests as separate.[1]

## ENTER J. P. MORGAN

Like Carnegie, Rhodes, and members of the Society of the Elect, J.P. Morgan was an Anglophile, a freemason, and a practitioner of the occult. Raised in England, the young Morgan regularly consulted famed fortune-teller Evangeline Adams and, later in his life, planned an expedition to Egypt to explore the supernatural origins of the ancient mystery religions.[2] Through his business connection with Lord Nathan Rothschild, Morgan became acquainted with members of the Society of the Elect, including Lord Alfred Milner. In 1901, Morgan offered Milner a then-massive income of $100,000 per annum to become a partner in the London branch. But Milner, who was then serving as the administrator of the Transvaal, would not be distracted from the vital business of the Boer War.[3]

## THE PILGRIM SOCIETY

In 1903, at the bidding of Rothschild and Milner, Morgan established the American chapter of the Pilgrim Society at the Waldorf Astoria in New York. The purpose of this clandestine club, whose motto was *Hic et Ubique* ("Here and Everywhere") was to further the Anglo-American union. The London headquarters of the Society had been set up as a spin-off of the Society of the Elect and catered to the rich and influential, including Alfred Milner, Lord Rosebery, Robert Brand of the Lazard Bank, Waldorf Astor, Alfred Beit, and Charles Dawes.

The New York chapter included such notables as Elihu Root,

J. P. MORGAN (WHO IS TO GIVE WAY TO HIS SON AND TAKE A LONG REST): "WELL, BOY, THERE'S THE PUMP AND THE HOSE, AND I BELIEVE THAT FELLOW OVER THERE HAS MONEY LEFT. REMEMBER, THERE IS NOTHING LIKE WATER—FOR STOCK."

**J. P. Morgan**
created a secret society in America to advance the goals of Cecil Rhodes.

Thomas W. Lamont, Percy Rockefeller, Ogden Mills Reid, Otto Kahn, Andrew Mellon, W.B. Whitney, Cornelius Vanderbilt, Vincent Astor, Mortimer I. Schiff, Frank Vanderlip, Henry Davison, Charles D. Norton, Nelson Aldrich, and Paul Warburg. Joseph Choate, the

Morgan lawyer who became a CEIP trustee, was one of the Society's Founding Fathers, and Nicholas Murray Butler, another founder, would emerge several years later as a CEIP trustee. The interlocking interest of the group was best exemplified by Root, who became instrumental not only in the work of the Carnegie and Rockefeller Foundations but also in the creation of the League of Nations and the Council on Foreign Relations. Similarly, the fact that the pilgrims were controlled by the Rothschild money cartel was verified by the presence of Paul Warburg. Warburg, a prominent member of the Warburg banking consortium in Germany, which was allied to the House of Rothschild, had married Nina Loeb, the daughter of one of the founders of Kuhn, Loeb and Company, a financial firm tightly connected to Rothschild.[4] The incredible importance of this "dining club" to the future of America became clear in 1910, when prominent pilgrims, including Warburg, Vanderlip, Davison, Norton, and Aldrich, set off for Jekyll Island off the coast of Georgia to plan the formation of the Federal Reserve System.[5]

## A CLANDESTINE SOCIETY

The pilgrims from the London and New York societies were welcomed guests at each other's clubs and shared in each other's efforts to advance a concept that they called "the New World Order." The meaning of this phrase was clarified by William Lyon Mackenzie King, the premier of Canada, in his dinner address to New York pilgrims in 1912. King envisioned a future in which the world would be united in peace and harmony under an Anglo-American alliance. "When victory and peace came," he prophesized, "the peoples of the British Commonwealth and of the United States would be united more closely than ever—as all the nations who have united in the defense of freedom would remain united in the defense of mankind."[6] These remarks prompted Andrew Carnegie, one of the leading members of the Society, to stand up and cheer.

The meetings of the Pilgrim Society were held in secret. No guests were allowed to attend. No minutes were kept. No financial records were disclosed. Proof of the commitment of members to the cause of their society came in 1919, when US pilgrim Irving T. Bush plunked down the funding for the Bush House in downtown London. Cut from Portland stone at a cost of $20 million, it was at the time the most expensive building in the world. To dispel any doubts about the purpose of the building, Bush commissioned the erection of a large statue at its entrance of two semi-naked men holding aloft the torch of liberty while brandishing two swords. One sword was emblazoned with lions; the other with eagles. The inscription read: "To the friendship of English-speaking peoples."[7]

Thirty-seven years after its founding, an obscure American journalist took notice of the clandestine club. In 1940, *Sir Uncle Sam: Knight of the British Empire*, a book that sold less than 500 copies, John Whiteford wrote:

> There are several curious things about these Pilgrim functions. In the first place, there is present at these dinners an array of notables such as it would be impossible to bring together under one roof for any other purpose and by any other society. . . Among the guests were John D. Rockefeller and J. P. Morgan, Thomas W. Lamont and other members of the House of Morgan. . . . We are entitled to know what the Pilgrim Society is, what it stands for, and who these powerful Pilgrims are that can call out the great to hear a British Ambassador expound to Americans the virtues of a united democratic front.[8]

The lack of public interest in the workings of the Pilgrim Society through the years remained mind-boggling, since its members would come to include John Foster Dulles, Allen Dulles, General George Marshall (of the Marshall Plan), W. Averill Harriman, Joseph P. Kennedy, Henry Luce (founder of *Time* magazine), Henry Kissinger, General Alexander Haig, William Paley (CBS president), Walter Cronkite, Sandra Day O'Connor, Elliot Richardson, Jacob Schiff, Paul Volker, and David Rockefeller.[9]

## THE AMERICAN ROUND TABLE

In 1912, the Pilgrim Society spawned the American Round Table. Stead's mission resulted in ultimate success. Its Founding Fathers were George Louis Beer, an associate of J. P. Morgan, who served as a professor of British history at Columbia University; Walter Lippmann, editor of *The New Republic* and the author of Woodrow Wilson's "Fourteen Points" speech; Jerome D. Greene, chief executive officer of the London branch of Lee, Higginson, and Company and a trustee of the Rockefeller Foundation; Frank Aydelotte, a Rhodes scholar and president of Swarthmore College; Whitney Shepardson, a Rhodes scholar and director of the Carnegie Corporation's British and Colonies Fund; Thomas Lamont, a partner of J. P. Morgan Company; and Erwin D. Canham, a Rhodes scholar and editor of *The Christian Science Monitor*.[10] Their names displayed the coalescence of wealth and power between the Houses of Morgan, Rockefeller, and Carnegie with the Rhodes Trust and the Rothschild cartel. Planning to attend the opening ceremony of this new extension of the society, which had been created by Rhodes, William T. Stead boarded the Titanic and passed into history.

# NOTES

1. Ibid.
2. Nick Levine, "The Dignity of Exact Science: Evangeline Adams, Astrology, and the Profession of the Probable, 1890–1910," Senior Thesis, Yale University, April 2014, http://hshm.yale.edu/sites/default/files/files/2014-levine.pdf.
3. Carroll Quigley, *Tragedy and Hope: A History of the World in Our Time* (San Pedro, CA: GSG and Associates, 2004), p. 451.
4. G. Edward Griffin, *The Creature from Jekyll Island* (Westlake Village, CA: 2017), p. 5.
5. Joel van der Reijden, "The Pilgrim Society," *The Journal of History,* September 21, 2005, http://www.truedemocracy.net/hj31/37.html.
6. William Lyon Mackenzie King, quoted in Robin Brown, *The Secret Society: Cecil John Rhodes's Plan for a New World Order* (Cape Town, South Africa: Penguin Books, 2015), p. 279.
7. Robin Brown, *The Secret Society: Cecil John Rhodes's Plan for a New World Order* (Cape Town, South Africa: Penguin Books, 2015, p. 282.
8. John T. Whiteford, *Sir Uncle Sam: Knight of the British Empire*, 1940, https://archive. org/details/SirUncleSamKnightOf TheBritishEmpire.
9. Van der Reijden, "The Pilgrim Society."
10. Quigley, *Tragedy and Hope,* pp. 950–955.

# 10

# THE DUCK HUNTERS

*The composition of the Jekyll Island meeting was a classic example of cartel structure. A cartel is a group of independent businesses which join together to coordinate the production, pricing, or marketing of their members. The purpose of a cartel is to reduce competition and thereby increase profitability. This is accomplished through a shared monopoly over their industry. . . . Here [at Jekyll Island] were representatives of the world's leading banking consortia: Morgan, Rockefeller, Rothschild, Warburg, and Kuhn-Loeb. They were often competitors, and there is little doubt that there was considerable distrust among them. . . . But they were driven together by one overriding desire to fight their common enemy. The enemy was competition.*

—G. EDWARD GRIFFIN, *THE CREATURE FROM JEKYLL ISLAND*

## PLANNING THE FED

The House of Morgan, which remained bound to the House of Rothschild, emerged as the dominant force in the creation of a deep state which would rule the United States from the shadows. It gave rise to the Pilgrim Society and the American Round Table. And it would strip the country of liberty by fashioning the Federal Reserve System.

From the time of its creation on December 23, 1913, the Fed represented the ultimate political and economic power in the country. It alone possessed the ability to manufacture currency, to establish interest rates, and to precipitate prosperity or depression. By its sole decision, money became available for industrial expansion and business growth or

**Federal Reserve**

From the time of its creation on December 23, 1913, the Federal Reserve represented the ultimate political and economic power in the country. It is a private, profit-making company. It is not federal; the government owns no shares of it.

it became withdrawn from circulation, making it impossible for entrepreneurs to launch new ventures, for couples to purchase houses, or people to gain employment. No other agency is more formidable or important to the everyday lives of American citizens, although few are unaware of its function.

Almost everything about the Federal Reserve System is shrouded in mystery. The chairman is appointed by the president of the United States, thereby eluding the impression that the twelve branches of the central bank are under the control of the federal government. But the person really in charge is the director of the Federal Reserve in New York. The very name of America's central bank is deceptive. It is not federal. The government owns no shares. It is a private, profit making company. The shareholders are the private banks that united to it.[1] The Reserve System has no reserves. The money deposited is used by the directors of the twelve banks at their discretion. Finally, the System is not a system. It is a syndicate of bankers whose interests are often at odds with the welfare of the American people.

## THE WORKINGS OF THE SYNDICATE

When the government needs money, the Treasury Department issues bonds, which are sold by bond dealers. When the Fed wants to expand the money supply, it purchases the Treasury bonds from the bond dealers by the transfer of newly issued dollars. The dollars are created *ex nihilo*—out of nothing—they're not even printed. The dollars are made to materialize by the simple click of a mouse on the Fed computer. This practice is called "open market operations," because the Fed buys the bonds on an open market from the bond dealers.[2] The bonds, which

**David Rockefeller**
would serve as the chief executive officer of the Chase Manhattan Corporation and the founder of the Trilateral Commission.

the Fed now owns, become the "reserves" to back up the banking establishment's loans, and, through "fractional reserve lending," the same reserves are lent over and over again, thereby expanding the money supply and generating interest through each loan.[3] Every act within this process represents an illusion. No material wealth is exchanged. And the value of the dollar is determined by fiat, that is, by a mere declaration of its worth by the Fed's Board of Governors.

Louis McFadden, who chaired the House Committee on Banking and Currency from 1920 to 1931, said at the time of his retirement: "When the Federal Reserve Act was passed, the people of the United States did not perceive that a world banking system was being set up here, a super-state controlled by international bankers and international industrialists acting together to enslave the world for their own pleasure. Every effort has been made by the Fed to conceal its power, but the truth is—the Fed has usurped the government."[4]

## THE PANIC OF 1907

The origin of the Federal Reserve System dates back to the Panic of 1907, when snowballing bank runs, prompted by Morgan-generated stories about the insolvency of the Knickerbocker Trust Company, caused the

**Nelson Aldrich Rockefeller**
would become the vice-president under Gerald Ford in 1974.

collapse of banks throughout the country. Depositors were left with no means of recovering their savings, Wall Street brokers could not obtain the loans required for their daily transactions, and no central agency existed to clean up the mess.[5]

After creating the crisis, Morgan came to the rescue. He dispatched an army of clerks to troubled banks in order to look into their vaults and verify their assets. If the banks were solvent, he sent more clerks with satchels of gold coins, which he imported from Europe, to the banks in order to place them on display, so that depositors would be assured of the safety of their money. On Wall Street, Morgan convinced several of his fellow bankers to offer $25 million in loans to brokers in order to keep the stock market afloat.[6] He also met with US Treasury Secretary George Cortelyou, who placed $25 million of Treasury funds in national banks and provided $36 million in small bills to meet the bank runs. By the middle of November, the working capital of the US Treasury had dwindled down to $5 million.[7]

## MAESTRO MORGAN

Morgan's "rescue" measures resulted not only in averting a financial meltdown but also in producing sizeable interest payments on all the loans the House of Morgan provided to the nation's banks and to Wall Street. The measures also served to solidify Morgan's position as the leader of the American money trust and the driving force behind the emergence of the shadow government. As Morgan biographer Frederick Lewis Allen pointed out: "Where there had been many principalities, there was now one kingdom and it was Morgan's."[8]

The panic caused Congress to approve the Aldrich-Vreeland Act of 1908, which brought into being the National Monetary Commission. This, too, was a result of orchestration. Senator Nelson Aldrich, who received the appointment to head the Commission, was "J. P. Morgan's floor broker in the Senate."[9] Aldrich's daughter, Abby, was married to John D. Rockefeller Jr. His grandson

**John D. Rockefeller Jr.**
Senator Nelson Aldrich's daughter, Abby, was married to John D. Rockefeller Jr.

Nelson Aldrich Rockefeller would become the vice-president under Gerald Ford in 1974, while his grandson David Rockefeller would serve as the chief executive officer of the Chase Manhattan Corporation and the founder of the Trilateral Commission. Aldrich's chief advisor on the Commission was Harry Davison, a senior partner at J. P. Morgan and Company.[10] For two years, Aldrich and his entourage visited Europe's central banks, including the Bank of England, at the cost of $300,000 to US taxpayers. It was all a ruse to lead Congress to believe that the commission was engaged in a massive study to prevent a future financial crisis.[11]

## THE DUCK SHOOTING PARTY

On November 22, 1910, shortly after the return of the commission members to America, Davison, at the behest of Morgan, invited Aldrich and a small group of Wall Street bankers to a "duck shooting party" on Jekyll Island, off the coast of Georgia. The group included Frank A. Vanderlip, president of the National City Bank of New York (a Rockefeller firm in which Morgan was a principal shareholder); Abraham Platt Andrew, Assistant Secretary of the Treasury; Charles D. Norton, president of J. P. Morgan's First National Bank of New York; Benjamin Strong, president of J. P. Morgan's Bankers Trust Company; and Paul Warburg. Vanderlip described how the participants came together as follows:

> Despite my views about the value to society of greater publicity for the affairs of corporations, there was an occasion, near the close of 1910, when I was as secretive—indeed, as furtive—as any conspirator. . . . I do not feel it is any exaggeration to speak of our secret expedition to Jekyll Island as the occasion of the actual conception of what eventually became the Federal Reserve System. . . . . We were told to leave our last names behind us. We were told, further, that we should avoid dining together on the night of our departure. We were instructed to come one at a time and as unobtrusively as possible to the railroad terminal on the New Jersey littoral of the Hudson, where Senator Aldrich's private car would be in readiness, attached to the rear end of a train for the South. . . . Once aboard the private car we began to observe the taboo that had

been fixed on last names. We addressed one another as "Ben," "Paul," "Nelson," and "Abe." Davison and I adopted even deeper disguises, abandoning our own first names. On the theory that we were always right, he became Wilbur and I became Orville, after those two aviation pioneers, the Wright brothers. . . . Discovery, we knew, simply must not happen, or else all our time and effort would be wasted.[12]

The gathering was to serve the following purposes: (1) to ensure that the money trust would gain complete control over the nation's financial resources, (2) to make the money supply elastic in order to reverse the trend of private capital formation and to recapture the industrial loan market, (3) to pool the resources of the nation's banks into one reserve that would serve to protect a few of them from currency drains and bank runs, and (4) to shift inevitable financial losses from the money trust to the US taxpayers.[13] It had been instigated by the problem of competition. In 1910, the number of banks in America had doubled to over twenty thousand within a decade. Most of these banks were in the South and West, causing the New York banks to suffer a steady decline of market share. Forty percent of the institutions were national banks that had been chartered by the federal government. These banks, which were located in every major American city, were allowed to issue their own currency in the form of bank notes.[14] This ability served as a safeguard to financial independence, since it prevented a single, centralized agency from gaining control of the nation's economy.

## FASHIONING THE FED

At the Jekyll Island Hunt Club, a property owned by Morgan, Warburg told the group that the bill that they would compose for Congress must avoid any reference to a "central bank," since several American presidents, including Thomas Jefferson and Andrew Jackson, had railed against the establishment of such an entity.[15] It was sound advice. In 1910, America was the only major economic power without a central bank. Throughout its history, the country had deep suspicion against the very idea of central banking. East Coast bankers with ties to the

House of Rothschild pressed the case for centralizing control over the nation's monetary system in a single overarching bank. Their efforts met with resistance from average citizens, who maintained, in the spirit of Jackson, that granting such power to one institution was blatantly un-American. The commoners had prevailed for seventy-seven years.[16]

### AN ECONOMIC COUP D'ETAT

Warburg further advised the group that legislation for a central bank must create an illusion that control of the system would reside with the government, since the chairman of the Federal Reserve in Washington, DC, would be appointed by the president and would remain answerable to Congress. For further camouflage, Warburg insisted that the legislation must be presented as a regional system, with the fifteen branches responsible for overseeing the financial conditions within their jurisdiction.[17] Such measures were necessary since the cabal of millionaires at Jekyll Island were plotting the greatest financial and political coup d'état in American history—the usurpation of Congress's authority, as provided in the Constitution, to create and control the country's money supply.

After spending ten days on the island, the final draft for the new banking system was written by Vanderlip from Warburg's notes. Aldrich, upon returning to Washington, inserted the draft within the pages of the report, a work of twenty-three volumes replete with copious analytical data, which was being prepared for Congress by the National Monetary Commission.[18] In 1911, when asked by his fellow Republicans to prepare a bill for financial and monetary reform, Aldrich merely plucked the draft from the voluminous report and presented it to Congress as though the legislation that sprang from three years of travel, study, and work by diligent members of the Commission and not the product of a clandestine meeting of duck hunters.[19] It was a sleight of hand that escaped detection, even of Aldrich's many biographers. But, as Robert Burns realized, "the best laid plan o' mice an' men gang aft-a-gley." The plot was to experience a surprising setback.

# NOTES

1. Ellen Brown, "Who Owns the Federal Reserve?" *Global Research*, October 8, 2008, http://www.globalresearch.ca/who-owns-the-federal-reserve/10489.

2. Ibid.

3. Ibid.

4. Louis McFadden, quoted in A. Ralph Epperson, *The Unseen Hand: An Introduction to the Conspiratorial View of History* (Tucson, Arizona: Publius Press, 1985), p. 182.

5. Alice Gomstyn, "Born of Panic: The Federal Reserve and the Panic of 1907," Part 2, *The Alert Investor*, April 8, 2016, https://www.thealertinvestor.com/born-of-panic-the-federal-reserve-and-the-panic-of-1907-part-2/.

6. Ibid.

7. Jon Moen, "The Panic of 1907," *Economic History Association*, August 4, 2001, https://eh.net/encyclopedia/the-panic-of-1907/.

8. Frederick Allen Lewis, *The Lords of Creation* (New York: Harper and Brothers, 1935), p. 142.

9. Ferdinand Lundberg, *America's Sixty Families* (New York: Vanguard Press, 1938), p. 69.

10. Ron Chernow, *The House of Morgan: An American Banking Dynasty and the Rise of Modern Finance* (New York: Grove Press, 1990), p. 129.

11. Murray N. Rothbard, "Origins of the Federal Reserve," Mises Institute (Australia), November 13, 2009, https://mises.org/library/origins-federal-reserve.

12. Frank Vanderlip, "U. S. Farm Boy to Financier," *Saturday Evening Post*, February 9, 1936.

13. G. Edward Griffin, *The Creature from Jekyll Island* (New York: American Media, 2008), p. 437.

14. Ibid., p. 12.

15. G. Vance Smith and Tom Gow, *Masters of Deception: The Rise of the Council on Foreign Relations* (Colorado Springs, Colorado: Freedom First Society, 2012), p. 20.

16. Liaquat Ahamed, *Lords of Finance: The Bankers Who Broke the World* (New York: Penguin Books, 2009), p. 52.

17. Ibid.

18. N. A. Weston, "Studies of the National Monetary Commission," The Annals of the American Academy of Political and Social Science, Vol. 99, January 1922, https://www.jstor.org/stable/1014505?seq=1#page_scan_tab_contents.

19. Nathaniel Wright Stephenson, *Nelson W. Aldrich: A Leader in American Politics* (Port Washington, New York: Kennikat Press, 1971), pp. 129-130.

# 11

## "CONTROL OF THE WORLD"

*Money, being naturally barren, to make it breed money is preposterous and a perversion for the end of its institution, which was only to serve the purpose of exchange and not of increase. . . . Men called bankers we shall hate, for they enrich themselves while doing nothing.*

—ARISTOTLE, *POLITICS*

THE SO-CALLED "ALDRICH PLAN," which had been devised at Jekyll Island, called for the creation of a massive banking octopus: the National Reserve Association (NRA). The central bank of the association would be capitalized with a minimum of $100 million and fifteen branches would be set up throughout the country. The branches were to be controlled by member banks on the basis of their financial holdings, that is, banks that were owned or controlled by the money trust. The NRA would issue currency that would be the property of the bank and would hold the deposits of the federal government. For this reason, the power of the association would increase in proportion to the size of the government. Bankers and businessmen from each of the fifteen financial districts would elect thirty out of the thirty-nine members of the NRA board.[1] This process would ensure that the system would be self-perpetuating.[2]

Aldrich's name on the plan was problematic, as Liaquat Ahamed explains in *Lords of Finance:*

**Woodrow Wilson**
For the Democratic candidate, the trust opted for Woodrow Wilson, an austere, scholarly figure, who lived his life in the shadow of Wall Street.

> Nelson Aldrich may have been the most knowledgeable member of the Senate about finance, but the cause of central banking in the United States could not have found a worse champion. In a Senate full of very rich men—it was becoming known as the "millionaires' club"—he was one of the richest, having sold his stake in the United Traction and Electric Company of Rhode Island for $10 million; he boasted a grand estate in Newport, Rhode Island, and his daughter Abby had married John D. Rockefeller, Jr. He was a fervent supporter of big business, a bitter enemy of regulation, an advocate of high tariffs; rumors abounded, furthermore, that he traded political favors for financial contributions. In short, he was the living embodiment of everything that opponents of a central bank most feared.[3]

The surprise came when the plan met with fierce opposition. Charles A. Lindbergh (R–Minnesota), father of the famous aviator, decried the proposed legislation as an attempt by a handful of unscrupulous bankers to gain unlimited power. In a speech before Congress on June 13, 1911, he said: "Wall Street, backed by Morgan, Rockefeller, and others, would control the Reserve Association, and those again, backed by all the deposits and disbursements of the United States, and also backed by the deposits of the national banks holding the private funds of the people, which is provided in the Aldrich plan, would be the most wonderful financial machinery that finite beings could invent to take control of the world."[4]

### THE CURTAIN LIFTED

In response to Lindbergh's comments, Congress authorized the formation of a committee, under the leadership of Arsene Pujo (D–Louisiana), to determine if a money trust had been created to gain control of the US economy. The committee verified that a financial cartel had been established under J. P. Morgan, which controlled over $22 billion in revenue and 112 corporations. It further maintained that the Morgan cartel manipulated the daily transactions on the New York Stock Exchange.[5]

Republican President William Howard Taft also hastened the Congress's instantaneous rejection of the Aldrich Plan by vowing to veto the bill as soon as it arrived at his desk.[6] The plan went down in flames even before it was brought to the floor for a vote. And Taft, by making the vow, had unwittingly secured his own political demise.

### THE RIGGED ELECTION

But the money trust remained undeterred by the setback. To ensure the defeat of Taft in the 1912 election, Morgan provided the funding for former president Theodore Roosevelt to run as a candidate for the newly created Progressive ("Bull Moose") Party. Morgan also dispatched two of his most trusted agents—banker George Perkins and publisher Frank Munsey—to accompany Roosevelt throughout the campaign. The two men helped with the speeches, drummed up large crowds, and provided the feisty candidate with a steady supply of cash.[7] For the Democratic candidate, the trust opted for Woodrow Wilson, an austere, scholarly figure, who lived his life in the shadow of Wall Street. He was close to Andrew Carnegie, shared Carnegie's ideology, and became a trustee of the Carnegie Foundation. As president of Princeton University, his salary was augmented by a yearly stipend from Cleveland Dodge and Cyrus McCormick, directors of Rockefeller's National City Bank. In the midst of the Panic of 1907, Wilson said that the country should be guided by a panel of financial experts with J. P. Morgan as chairman.[8] The Wall Street cabal could not have found a more submissive candidate.

In 1912, Wilson was brought by prominent banker Bernard Baruch "like a poodle on a string" to Democratic headquarters in New York, where Wilson agreed, if elected president, to support a revision of the Aldrich Plan, to advocate a graduated income tax, and to seek the approval of Wall Street for appointees to his cabinet.[9] Following the meeting, Wilson received financial backing for his presidential campaign from Baruch, Cleveland Dodge, and Jacob Schiff of Kuhn, Loeb.[10] The selection of the bespectacled academician was a masterful subterfuge. It seemed inconceivable that any Wall Street banker would support a Democrat, especially when the Party platform contained this plank: "We oppose the so-called Aldrich Bill or the establishment of a central bank, and what is known as the money trust."[11]

The election went precisely as planned. Wilson won with only 42 percent of the popular vote. Had Roosevelt not entered the race, most of his votes undoubtedly would have gone to Taft, and Wilson's place in American history would consist of a footnote.[12]

## THE BELL TOLLS

With Wilson in the White House, the Aldrich Bill was repackaged and reintroduced as the Glass Act (named for Senator Carter Glass, who had been an opponent of the Aldrich Bill). In order to convince the public and Congress that the "new" legislation was really "a people's bill," central bankers, including Frank Vanderlip, denounced it, and Senator Aldrich refused to support it. Years later, Vanderlip wrote in his memoirs: "Now, although the Aldrich Federal Reserve Plan was defeated, when it bore the name Aldrich; nevertheless its essential points were all contained in the plan that was finally adopted."[13]

On December 23, 1913, the Federal Reserve Act became law.

**Nelson Wilmarth Aldrich**
Senator who advanced the plan for the Federal Reserve. He was also appointed head of the National Monetary Commission and was J.P. Morgan's floor broker in the Senate.

The House vote was 298 to 60; the Senate, 43 to 25. Upon its approval, Congressman Lindbergh, one of the few who realized the bell was now tolling for Uncle Sam, said:

This Act establishes the most gigantic trust on earth. . . . When the President signs this Act, the invisible government by the Money Power, proven to exist by the Money Trust Investigation, will be legalized. . . . The money power overawes the legislative and executive forces of the Nation and of the States. I have seen these forces exerted during the different stages of this bill. The new law will create inflation whenever the trusts want inflation. It may not do so immediately, but the trusts want a period of inflation, because all the stocks they hold have gone down.

. . . Now, if the trusts can get another period of inflation, they figure they can unload the stocks on the people at high prices during the excitement and then bring on a panic and but them back at low prices. . . . The people may not know it immediately, but the day of reckoning is only a few years removed.[14]

The Federal Reserve began operations on November 16, 1914, with a capital base of $143 million. The money came from the sale of shares in the twelve district banks. The payments to the Fed's Board of Governors in Washington, DC, arrived in the form of gold bullion. Each district bank of the Fed was a separate tax-exempt corporation with nine directors from its region's banking and business community. The shares, in accordance with Section 7 of the Federal Reserve Act, were all owned by private banks and individuals, who received yearly dividends in the amount of 6 percent of the net revenue.[15] The remaining revenue was transferred to the Board of Governors as a franchise fee. This money was used by the governors to supplement the gold reserves since gold remained the sole standard of the nation's currency.[16]

## THE SHAREHOLDERS

A partial listing of the 1914 principal shareholders in the Fed's district banks contains the names of N. M. Rothschild, London; Lord Montagu Norman, London; Brown, Shipley, and Company, London; Alex Brown and Sons, Baltimore; Brown Brothers Harriman, New York; Morgan et Cie, Paris; Morgan, Grenfell and Company, London; J. P. Morgan Company, New York; Morgan Guaranty Company, New York; Morgan Stanley Company, New York; Lazard Brothers, London; Lazard Freres, Paris; Lazard Brothers, New York; J. Henry Schroder Banking Corporation, New York; Schroder Bank, Hamburg, New York, and Montgomery, Alabama; Lehman-Stern, New Orleans; Drexel and Company, Philadelphia; National City Bank, New York; William Rockefeller; J. P. Morgan; Percy Rockefeller; New York Trust; New York Edison; Sherman and Sterling; National Bank of Commerce (later identified as Morgan Guaranty Trust Company); New York Equitable Life ( J. P. Morgan); H. P. Davison ( J. P. Morgan; North British Mercantile Insurance, London; Levi P. Morgan, New York; First National Bank of New York; Goldman Sachs Bank of New York; Israel Moses Seif Bank of Italy; Royal Bank of Scotland; Bank of Nova Scotia; First National Bank of Boston; First National Bank of Cincinnati; Philadelphia National Bank; First National Bank of Minneapolis; First National Bank of Kansas City; and the American Foreign Banking Corporation, New York.[17] The largest shareholder was the Rockefeller-controlled National City Bank with 30,000 shares; the second largest was the Morgan-controlled First National Bank with 15,000 shares.[18]

The fact that foreign banks purchased substantial shares in the Federal Reserve system ensured that the economic course of the United States no longer would be controlled and directed solely by representatives of the American people or duly appointed officials of the Treasury Department, but also by a clique of very wealthy bankers from London, Paris, Hamburg, Berlin, and Rome.

### THE REAL POWER

The Federal Reserve Bank of New York quickly emerged as the fountainhead of the system, since Manhattan remained the financial capital of the nation. The other eleven banks, in the words of Frederick Lundberg, became "so many expensive mausoleums erected to salve the local pride and quell the Jacksonian fears of the hinterland."[19] These banks were set up in Boston, Philadelphia, Cleveland, Richmond, Atlanta, Chicago, St. Louis, Minneapolis, Kansas City, Dallas, and San Francisco.

The May 19, 1914, organization chart of the New York Fed showed that of the 203,053 shares issued, Rockefeller's National City Bank purchased 30,000 shares, while the Morgan-Baker First National Bank took 15,000 shares. The National Bank of Commerce, of which Paul Warburg was a principal shareholder, acquired 21,000 shares; Hanover Bank with Lord Rothschild as a director gained 10,200 shares; the Rockefeller-owned Chase National Bank took 6,000 shares as did the Morgan-affiliated Chemical Bank. These six banks owned 40 percent of the stock in the New York Fed.[20] Other shareholders, according to European trade specialist Gary Kah, were the Rothschild Bank of London and Berlin, the Lazard Brothers Bank of Paris, the Warburg Bank of Hamburg and Amsterdam, the Israel Seif Bank of Italy, Lehman Brothers of New York, and Goldman Sachs of New York.[21]

Benjamin Strong, president of the (Morgan) Bankers Trust Company, served as the first Governor of the New York Fed. Under Strong's leadership, the Federal Reserve of New York, unsuspected by the nations, became interlinked with the Bank of England and the Banque de France.[22] It alone became authorized to receive massive deposits of gold from other central banks. By 1924, a massive vault, half the size of a football field, was built eighty-six feet beneath the Federal Reserve Bank on the corner of William and Nassau Street in lower Manhattan. Three years later, the vault contained 10 percent of the world's entire supply of monetary gold.[23]

## A PROGRESSIVE INCOME TAX

By authorizing a central bank to control the country's money supply and the value of a dollar, Congress enabled government spending to skyrocket beyond all expectation. Politicians now could commit to projects that cost millions of dollars more than the existing revenue. The Fed, in turn, could purchase the "excess" debt by printing more paper money, thereby inflating the economy. States, seduced by the federal deep pockets but lacking any mechanism to manufacture debt, would become dependent on Washington, DC, for revenue, thereby reversing the traditional relationship that existed between state and federal governments. And the taxpayers would bear the brunt of bloated governments, thanks to the enactment of a graduated income tax.[24]

Prior to 1913, there was no income tax in America, except for a period during the Civil War and the early years of Reconstruction. The federal government existed on other sources of revenue, including tariffs and excise taxes. Not being able to spend or borrow heavily, the federal government remained limited in its scope of operations. Moreover, in 1895, the US Supreme Court in the case of *Pollock v. Farmers Loan Trust* ruled that the 2 percent income tax that President Grover Cleveland attempted to impose on the American people to be unconstitutional.[25] Due to this ruling, a federal income tax could only be imposed by Constitutional amendment. The man who proposed this amendment to Congress was the same senator who advanced the plan for the Federal Reserve: Nelson Aldrich.[26]

The average John Doe who voted for the approval of the Amendment fancied that the progressive tax would "soak the rich." He was unaware that the rich could channel their wealth into their tax-exempt foundations or that they would manufacture losses and expenses to lessen their reported earnings. Twenty years after the passage of the Revenue Act of 1933, a congressional committee discovered that J. P. Morgan Jr., one of the richest men in the country, was not paying any income tax at all.[27] The people had been duped.

# NOTES

1. Arthur Link, *Wilson and the Progressive Era* (New York: Harper and Brothers, 1954), pp. 44–45.
2. Verle B. Johnston, "The Aldrich Plan," Research Department, The Federal Reserve of San Francisco, January 6, 1984, https://fraser.stlouisfed.org/files/docs/historical/frbsf/frbsf_let/frbsf_let_19840106.pdf.
3. Liaquat Ahamed, *Lords of Finance*, p. 56.
4. Charles A. Lindbergh, Sr., Congressional Record, June 13, 1911, p. 1992.
5. Arsene Pujo, "Report of the Committee Appointed Pursuant to House Resolutions 429 and 504 to Investigate the Concentration of Control of Money and Credit," Washington, D. C.: Government Printing Office, February 28, 1913.
6. Smith and Gow, *Masters of Deception*, p. 20.
7. Lundberg, *America's Sixty Families*, pp. 110–112.
8. Chernow, *The House of Morgan*, p. 128.
9. Charles B. Dall, *FDR: My Exploited Father-in-Law* (Washington, D. C.: Action Associates, 1970), p. 137.
10. James Perloff, *The Shadows of Power: The Council on Foreign Relations and the American Decline* (Appleton, Wisconsin: Western Islands, 2005), p. 27.
11. G. Edward Griffin, *The Creature from Jekyll Island*, p. 454.
12. Ibid., p. 455.
13. Vanderlip, "U.S. Farm Boy to Financier."
14. Charles A. Lindbergh, Sr., Congressional Record, Volume 52, December 22, 1913, p. 1446.
15. Federal Reserve Act of 1913, Section 7, https://www.federalreserve.gov/aboutthefed/fract.htm.
16. V. Gilmore Iden, *The Federal Reserve Act of 1913: History and Digest* (Philadelphia: The National Bank News, 1914), p. 47.
17. Eustace Mullins, *Secrets of the Federal Reserve* (New York: Kasper and Horton, 1982), http://arcticbeacon.com/books/Eustace_Mullins-SECRETS_of_the_Federal_ Reserve_Bank.pdf.
18. Ibid.
19. Lundberg, *America's 60 Families*, p. 122.
20. Eustace Mullins, *The World Order: A Study in the Hegemony of Parasitism* (Staunton, VA: Ezra Pound Institute of Civilization, 1985), http://vho.org/aaargh/fran/livres10/MULLworldor.pdf.
21. Gary Kah, *En Route to Global Occupation: A High Ranking Government Liaison Exposes the Secret Agenda for World Unification* (Lafayette, Louisiana: Huntington House, 1991), p. 13.
22. Ibid.
23. "The Founding the Fed," Federal Reserve of New York, n. d., https://www.newyorkfed.org/aboutthefed/history_article.html.
24. Smith and Gow, *Masters of Deception*, p. 27.
25. Joseph Henchman, "Today in History: Income Tax Ruled Unconstitutional in Pollock v. Farmers Loan Trust," Tax Foundation, April 8, 2013, https://taxfoundation.org/today-history-income-tax-ruled-unconstitutional-pollock-v-farmers-loan-trust-co/.
26. James Perloff, *The Shadows of Power*, p. 25.
27. Ibid.

# PART THREE

## WAR TO END ALL WARS

*"I am concerned for the security of our great nation; not so much because of any threat from without, but because of the insidious forces working from within."*
—GENERAL DOUGLAS MACARTHUR

*"It is incumbent on every generation to pay its own debts as it goes. A principle which if acted on would save one-half the wars of the world."*
—THOMAS JEFFERSON

*"The invisible Money Power is working to control and enslave mankind. It financed Communism, Fascism, Marxism, Zionism, Socialism. All of these are directed to making the United States a member of a World Government."*
—*AMERICAN MERCURY MAGAZINE*, DECEMBER 1957, PG. 92.

# 12

# THE SERPENT'S EGG

*Men of wealth [should] form a synthetic free enterprise system based on cradle-to-grave schooling. The people who advance through schooling will be given licenses to lead profitable lives. All licenses will be tied to forms of schooling. This way, the entire economy can be controlled and people will have a motivation. . . . to learn what you want them to learn. It also places the minds of all children in the hands of a few social engineers.*

—ANDREW CARNEGIE, "WEALTH," 1889

WITHIN THE CARNEGIE ENDOWMENT for International Peace's plan to create a world without war, a serpent's egg had been planted. This came to light in 1964, when the research staff of the Reece Commission, a congressional committee set up to probe tax-exempt foundations, came upon the minutes of a meeting of the CEIP trustees in 1911, which was held to discuss the question: "Is there any means known to man more effective than war to alter the life of an entire people?" The trustees concluded that only war could serve to set the stage for world government. At the end of the meeting, they resolved to influence the diplomatic machinery toward launching a world conflagration by gaining control of the US State Department.[1]

Their resolution produced profound results. Root gained the position as the American delegate to The Hague Tribunal. Shotwell came to write the social security clauses of the Versailles Treaty. Brookings received the appointment to chair the War Industries Board and the Price Fixing Committee. Foster became a fixture in the office of Robert Lansing, Wilson's secretary of state, who by a happy stroke of coincidence, happened to be Foster's son-in-law. Eliot, an avowed pacifist, wrote articles about the necessity of supporting the Allied forces for major US newspapers. Choate embarked on a speaking tour to promote American involvement in the European conflict. And Dodge, who commenced to sell millions in munitions to the Allies, emerged as Wilson's financier.[2]

### THE RISE OF THE ROUND TABLE

The power brokers were on the move in Great Britain as well. As soon as the Great War broke out, members of the Round Table began to dine every Monday night at the residence of Leopold Amery, who had been recruited to join the group while serving as a correspondent for *The London Times* during the Boer War. The Monday night diners included Lord Milner, Philip Kerr (Lord Lothian), Lord Robert Brand, Reginald Brett (Lord Esher), Geoffrey Dawson, Lord Waldorf Astor, Baron John Buchan, and Sir Leander Jameson (of the infamous Jameson Raid). By producing a flow of "leaks" to the British press, they managed to obtain Herbert Henry Asquith's ouster as Britain's prime minister. In his place, they arranged the appointment of David Lloyd George, an adjunct member of the Secret Society that Cecil Rhodes had created.[3]

As soon as Lloyd George assumed occupancy of 10 Downing Street, Milner became Secretary of War; Philip Kerr became Lloyd George's personal secretary; Leopold Amery became assistant secretary to the war cabinet; Waldorf Astor became Lloyd George's parliamentary secretary; Robert Brand became deputy chairman of the British mission in Washington, DC; John Buchan became Lloyd George's director of intelligence; and Reginald Brett became the *de facto* head of the British Intelligence Service.[4] The British Empire was now firmly in the hands of a cabal intent upon making the dream of Cecil Rhodes a political reality.

## AMERICAN ISOLATIONISM

Prior to 1917, the United States remained an isolationist nation that stayed clear from all foreign entanglements. This was in keeping with the advice of George Washington, who said in his Farewell Address: "The great rule of conduct for us in regard to foreign nations is in extending our commercial relations, to have with them as little political connection as possible. So far as we have already formed engagements, let them be fulfilled with perfect good faith. Here let us stop. Europe has a set of primary interests which to us have none; or a very remote relation. Hence she must be engaged in frequent controversies, the causes of which are essentially foreign to our concerns. Hence, therefore, it must be unwise in us to implicate ourselves by artificial ties in the ordinary vicissitudes of her politics, or the ordinary combinations and collisions of her friendships or enmities."[5]

Similarly, Thomas Jefferson in his inaugural address pledged "peace, commerce, and honest friendship with all nations, entangling alliances with none."[6] This tradition of isolationism was fortified by the millions of immigrants who came to America to escape from oppression. During the 1800s, the United States spanned North America without departing from its stance of isolationism. It fought the War of 1812, the Mexican War, and the Spanish American War without forming foreign alliances or fighting on European soil.[7]

## THE MONEY MEN'S MOLE

But with Wilson in the White House, America's money trust gained control of the Oval Office, thanks to Edward Mandell House, the president's closest friend and advisor. House, an ardent Anglophile who had been educated in England, was credited with swinging the 1912 Democratic Convention in Baltimore behind Wilson's nomination.[8]

He became Woodrow Wilson's constant companion from that point onwards, with his own suite of rooms in the White House. He was also in direct, sometimes daily, contact with J. P. Morgan Jr., Jacob Schiff, Paul Warburg, and Democrat senators who sponsored the Federal Reserve Bill.[9] House guided Wilson in every aspect of foreign and domestic policy, chose his cabinet, and established the first policies of his new administration.[10]

### STAGED TERRORISM

The interests between Carnegie and the House of Morgan became intertwined when Carnegie became one of the cosigners of a $500 million loan from J. P. Morgan and Company to the Anglo-French Financial Commission in 1914. The $500 million to fund the Allied war against Germany represented the largest foreign loan in Wall Street history. It was five times greater than the previous record holder, the $100 million loan to Great Britain for the Boer War.[11] With such a tremendous amount at stake, it was essential to tip the scales in favor of the Allies by securing the participation of the United States in the conflict.

An incident had to be manufactured that would provoke the American people to abandon their stance of isolationism and to enter the fracas. It came with the sinking of the *Lusitania* by a German submarine on May 7, 1915. One thousand, one hundred, and ninety-eight civilians, including 128 Americans, died when the ship went down and the seemingly unprovoked act of aggression against a passenger ocean liner served to arouse anti-German sentiment throughout the country. Many of the 767 survivors popped up and down in the waves for three hours while seagulls swooped from the sky to peck out the eyes of the floating corpses.[12] Few Americans realized that the sinking and delayed rescue had been planned by Winston Churchill and members of the British Admiralty who were acting in tandem with Britain's Board of Trade, Colonel Edward M. House of the Wilson Administration and American industrialists, including J. P. Morgan, who had provided massive loans to Great Britain and the Allied forces.

The American public was not informed that the *Lusitania* was transporting six million rounds of ammunition and other military munitions to Britain. Upon the order of President Wilson, the ship's original manifest was hidden away in the archives of the treasury department.[13] Nor were they made aware that Churchill and other members of the Admiralty had directed the *Lusitania* to proceed at considerably reduced speed and without escort to the precise location within the Irish sea where the German U-boat was lying in wait.[14] And the public, for the most part, remained oblivious that the Germans had placed large ads in the New York newspapers to dissuade Americans from boarding the ocean liner.[15]

## FAKE NEWS

After the sinking of the *Lusitania*, stories about German atrocities began to capture headlines in US newspapers, including the *New York Times*. One story reported that German soldiers were deliberately mutilating Belgian babies by cutting off their hands, in some cases even eating them. Another atrocity story involved a Canadian soldier, who had supposedly been crucified with bayonets by the Germans. Many Canadians claimed to have witnessed the event, yet they all provided different versions of how it had happened. The Canadian high command investigated the matter, concluding that it was untrue. Other reports circulated of Belgian women, often nuns, who had their breasts cut off by the Germans. A story appeared in *The Times* about German corpse factories where bodies of German soldiers were supposedly turned into glycerin for weapons, or food for hogs. The stories produced moral outrage throughout America and a hatred for the bloodthirsty "Hun."

Few realized that the news came from Milner's Round Table and was circulated by J. P. ("Jack") Morgan Jr., who had gained control of America's newspapers. On February 9, 1917, Congressman Oscar Callaway inserted this statement within the *Congressional Record* about Morgan's ability to control and manipulate the national news:

In March, 1915, the J.P. Morgan interests, the steel, ship building and powder interests and their subsidiary organizations, got together 12 men high up in the newspaper world and employed them to select the most influential newspapers in the United States and sufficient number of them to control generally the policy of the daily press in the United States.

These 12 men worked the problems out by selecting 179 newspapers, and then began, by an elimination process, to retain only those necessary for the purpose of controlling the general policy of the daily press throughout the country. They found it was only necessary to purchase the control of 25 of the greatest papers.

The 25 papers were agreed upon; emissaries were sent to purchase the policy, national and international, of these papers; an agreement was reached; the policy of the papers was bought, to be paid for by the month; an editor was furnished for each paper to properly supervise and edit information regarding the questions of preparedness, militarism, financial policies and other things of national and international nature considered vital to the interests of the purchasers.

This contract is in existence at the present time, and it accounts for the news columns of the daily press of the country being filled with all sorts of preparedness arguments and misrepresentations as to the present condition of the United States Army and Navy, and the possibility and probability of the United States being attacked by foreign foes.

This policy also included the suppression of everything in opposition to the wishes of the interests served. The effectiveness of this scheme has been conclusively demonstrated by the character of the stuff carried in the daily press throughout the country since March, 1915. They have resorted to anything necessary to commercialize public sentiment and sandbag the National Congress into making extravagant and wasteful appropriations for the Army and Navy under false pretense that it was necessary. Their stock argument is that it is 'patriotism.' They are playing on every prejudice and passion of the American people.[16]

In the postwar years, investigations in Britain and France revealed that these stories were false and had been generated to increase popular support for America's entry into World War I.[17]

## THE REAL WAR

With the media in the control of Morgan, and, in turn, Rothschild, the American people never really knew the reason the doughboys were being dispatched to the trenches of France. They had been informed by leading journalists, including Roundtable member Walter Lippmann, that the cause of the war was the assassination of Archduke Franz Ferdinand, the heir to the Austro Hungarian Empire, by a Serbian nationalist on June 28, 1914. The murder, most Americans were led to believe, prompted conflict between Russia, Serbia's ally, and Germany, the Austro-Hungarian protector. They were shielded from the fact that the war—like all wars—had been sparked by economic interests and that the conflict had been in the works for decades. The creation of the German empire under Bismarck upset the balance of powers that had existed in Europe for more than two centuries. England ruled supreme over the continent until 1871. This supremacy had been repeatedly challenged by Spain and by France, but England always remained victorious. The fact that Germany now grew stronger by acquiring colonies in Africa and by building up its military force was a severe threat to the economic hegemony of England.

To counteract the rise of Germany, the international bankers, who at that time were excluded from the economic development in Germany, sought for ways to limit and control Germany. Between 1894 and 1907 a number of international treaties were signed to have Russia, France, England, and other nations unite against Germany in the case of war. It was the task of the so-called "Committee of 300" at the Round Table (which later became known as Chatham House) to set the stage for World War. Members of the committee included Lord Albert Grey, Lord Arnold Toynbee, Lord Alfred Milner, and H. J. Mackinder, who became known as the father of geopolitics.[18] Edward

Bernays, the so-called "father of public relations," and Walter Lippmann, the founding editor of *The New Republic*, were the American "specialists" of the Committee. Lord Rothermere, aka Harold Harmsworth, used his newspaper (*The Daily Mail*) as a tool to try out their "social conditioning" techniques on his readers. After a test period of six months they had found that 87 percent of the public had formed opinions without rational or critical thought processes. Thereupon the English working class became subjected to a constant onslaught of propaganda, designed to convince them that they were obliged to send their sons by the millions to their deaths.[19] The experiment verified that human beings can be conditioned as easily as rats.

# NOTES

1. William H. McIlhany, *The Tax-Exempt Foundations* (Westport, Connecticut: Arlington House, 1980), pp. 60–61.

2. James Perloff, *The Shadows of Power: The Council on Foreign Relations and the American Decline* (Appleton, Wisconsin: Western Islands, 2005), p. 29.

3. Robin Brown, *The Secret Society: Cecil John Rhodes's Plan for a New World Order* (Cape Town, South Africa: Penguin Books, 2015), p. 310.

4. Ibid.

5. George Washington, "Farewell Address," 1796, http.//avalon.law.yale.edu/18th_ century/washing. asp.

6. James Simon, "Isolationism," *U.S. History,* n. d., http://www.u-s-history.com/pages/h1601.html.

7. Ibid.

8. Gerry Dockerty and Jim Macgregor, "New World Order: The Founding Fathers," *Global Research,* April 26, 2015, http://www.globalresearch.ca/new-world-order-the-founding-fathers/5445255.

9. Ibid.

10. George Sylvester Vierick, *The Strangest Friendship in History: Woodrow Wilson and Colonel House* (New York: Praeger, 1976), p. 4.

11. Chernow, *The House of Morgan,* p. 197.

12. Erik Larson, *Dead Wake: The Last Crossing of the Lusitania* (New York: Crown, 2015), p. 296.

13. Sam Greenhill, "Secret of the Lusitania: Arms Find Challenges Allied Claim It Was Solely a Passenger Ship," *Daily Mail,* December 19, 2008, http://www.dailymail.co.uk/news/article 1098904/Secret-Lusitania-Arms-challenges-Allied-claims-solely-passenger-ship.html.

14. Gary Allen with Larry Abraham, *None Dare Call It Conspiracy* (San Diego, CA: Dauphin Publications, 2013), p. 38.

15. Ibid.

16. U.S. Congressional Record, February 9, 1917, p. 2947.

17. Thomas Fleming, "The Historian Who Sold Out," History News Network, August 8, 2005, http://historynewsnetwork.org/article/1489.

18. Jan Van Helsing, "Geheimgesellschaften und Ihre Macht in 20 Jahrhundert," n. d., http://www.bibliotecapleyades.net/sociopolitica/secretsoc_20century/secretsoc_20century.htm#Contents.

19. Jan van Helsing, "Secret Societies and Their Power in the 20th Century, 1998, https://www.bibliotecapleyades.net/sociopolitica/secretsoc_20century/secretsoc_20century.htm.

# 13

## MAKING HAY

*My God! This is living History! Everything we are doing and saying is thrilling—*
*it will be read by a thousand generations, think of that! Why I would not be out*
*of this glorious delicious war for anything the world could give me.*
—WINSTON CHURCHILL, JANUARY 1915

JOINED AT THE RIGHT HIP to the Bank of England and the left
hip to J. P. Morgan, the House of Rothschild was deeply involved in
manipulating events to ensure that the massive loans it had provided to
the Allied forces would be repaid. After the Battle of Jutland in 1916,
when Germany appeared on the verge of winning the war, Lord Rothschild worked to secure America's intervention in the struggle with the
aid of Morgan and Louis Brandeis, one of Wilson's trusted advisors.[1]
In exchange for this effort, Rothschild received assurance from Lord
Arthur Balfour—England's former prime minister, present foreign
secretary, and leading member of the Round Table—that his group of
Zionists would be granted a homeland in Palestine at the end of the
struggle. This assurance came in the form of a letter, dated November
2, 1917, which read as follows:

Dear Lord Rothschild,

I have much pleasure in conveying to you, on behalf of His Majesty's Government, the following declaration of sympathy with Jewish Zionist aspirations which has been submitted to, and approved by, the Cabinet: 'His Majesty's Government view with favor the establishment in Palestine of a national home for the Jewish people, and will use their best endeavors to facilitate the achievement of this object, it being clearly understood that nothing shall be done which may prejudice the civil and religious rights of existing Jewish colonies in Palestine, or the rights and political status enjoyed by Jews in other countries.

I should be grateful if you would bring this declaration to the knowledge of the Zionist Federation.

Yours,

Arthur Balfour[2]

This declaration was of inestimable value to the House of Rothschild since it possessed vast economic holdings in the Middle and Far East and wanted its own state, replete with its own military, to ward off any aggressor that threatened these interests.[3]

## PROLONGING THE WAR

Once America entered World War I, the Carnegie trustees under Elihu Root sent a telegram to President Woodrow Wilson in which they urged him not to end the war too soon.[4] Jennings C. Wise, Wilson's biographer, acknowledged that the war had been escalated and prolonged to lay the foundation for world government. He wrote: "Whether or not [British Ambassador Sir Cecil] Spring-Rice was correct in his belief that [Theodore] Marburg [the force behind the Carnegie-funded League to Enforce Peace] and the Internationalists had brought on the war, certain it is they proposed to 'make hay' out of it."[5]

The prolongation of the war was in keeping with Carnegie's wishes. In an article for *The Washington Post* that appeared on January 24, 1915, two years before Wilson deployed troops to Europe, Carnegie wrote: "In these times when half of our fair world is being blackened by the fire and smoke of shot and shell, when men are at each other's throats and civilization's progress has suffered its most serious setback of centuries, I am asked if I can find any possible prospect for lasting peace. To this I answer an emphatic 'yes.' It is my firm belief and opinion that never at any time in the history of the world did the future hold out such definite promise for permanent peace as it does now. The present war is so appalling and shocking that it in itself is probably doing more to put an end to war than any peace propaganda could have accomplished in half a century. The longer that this war continues and the more terrible its results, the stronger the argument for permanent world peace."[6] He should have added that war was also incredibly profitable.

### BLOOD MONEY

By 1917, the British War Office had borrowed $2.5 billion from the House of Morgan and other Wall Street banks. Only $27 million had been loaned to the Germans.[7] As soon as war was declared, Congress voted $1 billion in credit for England and France. Two hundred million dollars was sent to England immediately and was applied to the Morgan account. The vast quantity of money needed to finance the war was created by the Federal Reserve system, which means it was collected from Americans through that hidden tax called inflation.[8]

As soon as the American troops were deployed, the House of Morgan took every possible step to assure itself that the private debts that the British government owed the bankers and bondholders would be transferred to the US Government in exchange for US bonds or treasury notes. "In other words," historian Roberta Dayer writes, "the Morgans ensured that it was repaid before the war was over, while the American Treasury, that is, the American people, assumed the British debts, which, because of postwar debt renunciation, were never fully paid."[9]

## PROFITS OF WAR

The exigencies of the massive conflict forced England and France to go heavily into debt. When their respective central banks and local merchant banks no longer could meet the ever-increasing demand for cash, the beleaguered governments, under the guidance of the Rothschilds, turned to the House of Morgan to serve as sales agent for their bonds. Most of the money raised in this fashion was recycled to the United States through the purchase of weapons and materiel from Morgan holding companies or firms within the orbit of the Morgan bank. Price gouging remained unchecked since The House of Morgan had been singled out by the Wilson Administration to serve as the US purchase agent for the Allies. A commission was paid on all transactions: when the money was borrowed and again when the money was spent.[10] Under such a lucrative arrangement, Morgan and his associates were hardly anxious to see hostilities come to a close.

In 1915, Thomas W. Lamont, a partner of Morgan and Company, delivered the following speech to the American Academy of Political and Social Science in Philadelphia:

> We are turning from a debtor into a creditor. . . We are piling up prodigious export trade balance. . . . Many of our manufacturers and merchants have been doing a wonderful business in articles relating to the war [WWI]. So heavy have been the war orders running into the hundreds of millions of dollars, that now their effect is beginning to spread to general business. . .
>
> The question of trade and financial supremacy must be determined by several factors, a chief one of which is the duration of the war. If the war should come to an end in the near future . . . we should probably find Germany, whose export trade is now almost wholly cut off, swinging back into keen competition very promptly.
>
> [Another factor that] is dependent on the duration of the war, is as to whether we shall become lenders to foreign nations upon a really large scale. . . Shall we become lenders upon a really stupendous scale to these foreign governments? If the war continues long enough

to encourage us to take such a position, then inevitably we would become a creditor instead of a debtor nation, and such a development, sooner or later, would tend to bring about the dollar, instead of the pound sterling, as the international basis of exchange.[11]

The money began to flow in January of 1915 when the House of Morgan signed a contract with the British Army Council and the Admiralty. At the advent of modern warfare, the first purchase, curiously, was for horses, and the amount tendered was $12 million. But that was but the first drop in the banker's bucket. Total purchases from the Allies eventually climbed to an astronomical $3 billion. Morgan's office at 23 Wall Street became mobbed by brokers and manufacturers seeking to cut a deal. Each month, Jack Morgan presided over purchases that equaled the gross national product of the entire world just one generation before.[12]

## THE PROMISE OF COMMUNISM

In 1917, America's money trust, who created the Pilgrim Societies and the Round Table, funded the Russian Revolution with the conviction not only that it would spark a universal movement for global government, but also that the revolution would permit them to give control of Russia's vast natural resources. Jacob Schiff, head of the New York investment firm Kuhn, Loeb and Company, shelled out $20 million to the Bolsheviks. Millions more came from the House of Morgan and members of the British and American Round Table.[13]

The appeal of Communism to the money trust resided in the fact that it represented a monopolist system of government, a government over which enterprising industrialists and bankers could gain control through loans to the government, the manipulation of the country's centralized banking system, and, of course, bribes.[14] Communism further represented government regulation of all facets of business and industry—a notion that met with the resounding approval of the leading American bankers and industrialists. Regulation, they realized, could be used to establish exclusive monopolies and to feed on tax revenue.

The first American regulatory agency—the Interstate Commerce Commission—was created at the behest of the railroad owners, not the railroad users. When the Federal Reserve came under consideration for congressional approval in 1912, Henry Davison, J. P. Morgan's partner, said: "I would rather have regulation and control than free enterprise."[15]

## THE PASSING OF THE OLD ORDER

Small wonder, therefore, that the American ruling elite saw in the rise of Communism their hope for the future. In the January 13 issue of *The New York World*, William Boyce Thompson (Federal Reserve bank director and founding member of the Council on Foreign Relations) wrote: "Russia is pointing the way to great and sweeping world changes. It is not in Russia alone that the old order is passing. There is a lot of the old order in America, and that is going too. . . . I'm glad it is so. When I sat and watched those democratic conclaves in Russia, I felt that I would welcome a similar scene in the United States."[16]

After the Bolsheviks seized power, Standard Oil, under the direction of the House of Rockefeller, purchased the Russian oil fields, set up a refinery for the Soviets, and made arrangements to market the refined oil in Europe. During the 1920s, the Rockefellers' Chase Bank set up the American-Russian Chamber of Commerce, financed the raw material exports of the Soviets, and sold Russian bonds to American investors.[17]

## CONDITIONING THE MASSES

The war had been orchestrated from start to end not by politicians and military officials but rather by British bankers and businessmen who sought to preserve, at all costs, British economic hegemony. It was fueled by American financiers and industrialists, who made immense profits from the bloody conflict. And it was prolonged by the efforts of the trustees of leading American foundations, including the Carnegie Endowment for International Peace, which believed that the phoenix of a new world order would emerge from the ashes of the conflagration.

Few American scholars questioned the necessity for the conflict and the fact that the incredible bloodshed was not produced (what St. Augustine would call) a "just cause." In schools and colleges throughout America, students were conditioned to accept the carefully prepared script that explained the causes of the conflict in terms of conflicting alliances. Almost no one took the effort to look behind the curtain.

## WAR AND INSCRIPTION

On April 6, 1917, the joint sessions of Congress approved President Wilson's request for a declaration of war against the German Empire. US intervention in the conflict was justified by Wilson's belief that the war would make the world "safe for democracy." Six senators voted against the declaration, including Robert La Follette of Wisconsin, and fifty members of the House of Representatives opposed it, including Jeannette Rankin of Montana, America's first congresswoman.[18]

Despite government appeals for a million volunteers, only sixty-three thousand enlisted in the first six weeks, forcing Congress to institute compulsory military inscription. Under the 1917 Espionage Act, hundreds of Americans who opposed the draft were tossed into prison, including political activist Eugene Debs who said: "Let the capitalists do their own fighting and furnish their own corpses and there will never be another war on the face of the earth."[19]

## THE BIRTH OF THE MILITARY-INDUSTRIAL COMPLEX

The war gave rise to modern warfare. Huge plants sprouted up throughout the United States to produce military aircraft, submarines, battleships, aircraft carriers, tanks, portable machine guns, flamethrowers, and automatic rifles. Military spending rose until it constituted 22 percent of the GNP in 1918. The principal beneficiaries were US Steel, Bethlehem Steel, Du Pont Chemical, Kennecott, and General Electric—all of which were related to the House of Morgan.[20] Enterprising defense companies set up shop, including General Dynamics, which produced submarines, and Boeing, which produced aircraft. The military-industrial complex had come into existence.

By the end of the war, oil had become the most valuable commodity on earth. Prior to the war, industry was fueled by coal, and places like Scranton and Wilkes Barre became boomtowns, attracting thousands of immigrants to eke out a living in the anthracite mines of Northeast Pennsylvania. But oil was cheaper, cleaner, and more labor efficient since it produced no residue that required removal.

No naval issue would affect Britain's foreign policy more than the crucial debate over whether or not the Royal Navy should be converted from coal propulsion to oil. Oil was not only superior to coal, but the Rothschilds were, together with the Rockefellers, supreme rulers of the oil business, having entered into a world cartel with Standard Oil. On June 17, 1914, Winston Churchill introduced a bill proposing that the British government invest in an oil company, after which it acquired 51 percent of Anglo-Persian, which in actuality was already partially owned by the British government and was financed by the Rothschilds' bank. Britain had acquired its first oil concession and kept its involvement secret. By the summer of 1914, the British Navy was fully committed to oil, and the British government had assumed the role of majority stockholder in the Anglo Persian Oil Company, now known as British Petroleum (BP).[21] But 80 percent of the oil that was used to fuel the British Navy and Army came from America, and 90 percent of the oil in America was owned by the Rockefellers.[22]

## THE WAR'S AFTERMATH

On November 11, 1918, the long war came to an end. Of the two million Americans who took part in the struggle, 116,000 were killed and 204,000 wounded. The European losses were staggering. Eight million soldiers and six to ten million civilians were dead. The civilian casualties were caused by disease and starvation. No country suffered more than Russia with 1.7 million dead and 5 million wounded.[23]

The survivors found themselves in a strange new world. Britain and France had been severely weakened and no longer represented a threat to rising American political and economic hegemony. The German

Empire had collapsed into financial shambles. The Austro-Hungarian Empire vanished, necessitating the restructuring of Eastern Europe. The Ottoman Empire, which had stood for six hundred years, no longer ruled over the Middle East and Central Asia. And the reign of the czars in Russia had been overthrown by Bolshevik revolutionaries, who pledged to inaugurate a world revolution.[24]

# NOTES

1. Stephen Mitford Goodson, *A History of Central Banking and the Enslavement of Mankind* (London: Black House, 2014), p. 89.

2. "Balfour Declaration: Test of the Declaration (November 2, 1917)," *Jewish Virtual Library,* http://www.jewishvirtuallibrary.org/text-of-the-balfour-declaration.

3. Andrew Hitchcock, "The History of the House of Rothschild," *Rense.com,* October 31, 1999, http://rense.com/general88/hist.htm.

4. William H McIlhany, *The Tax-Exempt Foundations* (New York: Arlington House, 1980), p. 61.

5. Jennings Wise, *Woodrow Wilson: Disciple of Revolution* (New York: Paisley Press, 1938), p. 220.

6. Andrew Carnegie, quoted in David Nasaw, *Andrew Carnegie* (New York: Penguin Press, 2008), pp. 786–787.

7. Oliver Stone and Peter Kuznick, *The Concise Untold History of the United States* (New York: Gallery Books, 2014), p. 14.

8. G. Edward Griffin, *The Creature from Jekyll Island* (New York: American Media, 2008), p. 260.

9. Roberta Dayer, quoted in T. Hunt Tooley, "*Merchants of Death* Revisited: Armamets, Bankers, and the First World War," *Journal of Libertarian Studies,* Winter 2005, file:///C:/Users/Spike/Downloads/19_1_4%20(1).pdf.

10. Ron Chernow, *The House of Morgan: An American Banking Dynasty and the Rise of Modern Finance* (New York: Grove Press, 2001), pp. 185–187.

11. Thomas W. Lamont, quoted in F. William Engdahl, *Gods of Money: Wall Street and the Death of the American Century* (San Diego, CA; Progressive Press, 2011), p. 67.

12. Ibid.

13. G. Edward Griffin, *The Creature from Jekyll Island: A Second Look at the Federal Reserve* (Westlake Village, CA: American Media, 2010), pp. 274–277.

14. James Perloff, *The Shadows of Power: The Council on Foreign Relations and the American Decline* (Appleton, Wisconsin: Western Islands, 1988), p. 44.

15. Henry Davison, quoted in Ibid., p. 45.

16. William Boyce Thompson, quoted in Charlotte Thomson Iseliyt, *The Dumbing Down of America* (Ravenna, Ohio: Conscience Press, 1999), p. 10.

17. Perloff, *The Shadows of Power*, p. 43.

18. Stone and Kuznick, *The Concise Untold History of the United States*, p. 15.

19. Eugene Debs, quoted in Ibid., p. 17.

20. Dean Henderson, "The Federal Reserve Cartel: The Eight Families," *Global Research,* June 1, 2011, http://www.globalresearch.ca/the-federal-reserve-cartel-the-eight-families/25080.

21. David Yergin, *The Prize: The Epic Quest for Oil, Money and Power* (New York: The Free Press, 2008), pp. 138–140.

22. David Yergin, "The Blood of Victory: World War I," *Modern History,* n. d., http://erenow.com/modern/theepicquestforoilmoneyandpower/10.html.

23. Stone and Kuznick, *The Concise Untold History of the United States*, p. 18.

24. Ibid.

# 14

## PEACE AND PUNISHMENT

*We can feel all the power of hate we must encounter in this assembly. . . . It is demanded of us that we admit ourselves to be the only ones guilty of this war. Such a confession from my mouth would be a lie. We are far from declining any responsibility for this great world war. . . but we deny that Germany and its people were alone guilty. The hundreds of thousands of non-combatants who have perished since November 11 by reason of the blockade were killed with cold blood after our adversaries had conquered and victory had been assured to them. Think of that when you speak of guilt and punishment.*

—ULRICH VON BROCKDORFF-RANTZAU, GERMAN FOREIGN MINISTER,
PARIS PEACE CONFERENCE, MAY 7, 1919

AT THE END of the war, the British government, under Prime Minister David Lloyd George, demanded the "utmost severity" for Germany. Heading off to the peace conference in Paris, Lloyd George pledged to the cheers of his countrymen that the Germans would pay "the full cost of war."[1] Similarly, Georges Clemenceau, France's prime minister, said that he would impose a treaty on "le Boche" so severe that Germany could never again threaten France. "There are twenty million Germans too many," he said.[2]

Both men attempted to live up to their word. By the Treaty of Versailles, which was signed on July 28, 1919, exactly five years after the assassination of Archduke Franz Ferdinand, Germany lost one tenth of her population and one eighth of her territory. Germany's overseas empire, the third largest in the world, was torn apart and handed over to the victors. German citizens who lived in these German colonies were obliged to forfeit all of their personal property. Japan was given the German concession in Shantung and the German islands north of the equator. The German islands south of the equator were handed over to Australia and New Zealand. Germany's African colonies were shelled out to Britain, South Africa, and France. German waterways were now internationalized and she was compelled to open her markets to Allied imports but denied access to Allied markets.[3] Germany was also required to cede to the Allies the city of Danzig and its hinterlands, including the delta of the Vistula River on the Baltic Sea.[4] This last stipulation would spark World War II, since the Germans, residing in Danzig, would call upon Adolf Hitler to liberate them from the clutches of the League of Nations.

## REPARATIONS AND REVENGE

But the loss of empire was only a part of the punishment—Germany was forbidden to build armored cars and tanks, to produce heavy artillery, and to maintain an air force. Her High Seas Fleet and merchant ships were confiscated as booty. And the German army was restricted to a force of 100,000 men.[5] And then there was the matter of finances. Germany was required not only to pay the pensions of the Allied soldiers but also to cough up thirty-two billion gold marks—an amount equivalent to the entire wealth of the country—in reparations.[6] This indemnity would be used to repay the international bankers for the loans with interest that they had provided to Great Britain and France.[7]

Germany was also required to confess that she alone had caused the war and was responsible for all the damages caused by the conflict. Under Article 227, Kaiser Wilhelm II was to be arrested and prosecuted at an international trial that was to be held in Leipzig.[8] King George V of England called his cousin, the Kaiser, "the greatest criminal in history," and Prime Minister Lloyd George issued demands that the German emperor be hanged. The Kaiser escaped this ordeal by fleeing to the Netherlands, which granted him political asylum.[9]

This portion of the treaty was particularly galling to the German people since it forced them to confess to a crime that they believed they had not committed. Commenting on this stipulation, historian Erik von Kuehnelt-Leddihn wrote: "There is no better way to generate hatred than by forcing a person to sign a confession of guilt which he is sacredly convinced is untrue. The wanton humiliation, unprecedented up to that time in the annals of Christendom, created the thirst for revenge which the National Socialists so cleverly exploited."[10]

## THE STARVATION BLOCKADE

Why would the German diplomats agree to such terms? The answer resides in the fact that the Allied forces, including US warships, had imposed a blockade on Germany, sealing entry to all points of entry so that food, medical supplies, and other vital necessities could not flow into the country. The blockade was so tight that even Baltic fishing boats were sequestered. When Berlin pleaded for permission to buy 2.5 million tons of food to save the German people from starvation, the request was denied.[11] The "starvation" blockade, which persisted from November 11, 1918, through the peace conference, was responsible for the deaths of 900,000 men, women, and children, after the Germans had laid down their arms.[12] The Germans had no choice but to sign. Decades later, Herbert Hoover, who headed the US Food Administration during World War I, continued to decry the "food blockade" of Germany as "a black chapter in human history."[13]

## THE PEACE CONFERENCE

The trustees of the Carnegie Endowment for International Peace took an active role in the Paris Peace Conference and the creation of the League of Nations. James T. Shotwell, CEIP's director of research, accompanied Wilson to the conference, along with Colonel House, Charles Haskins, a trustee of the Carnegie Corporation, and CEIP trustee John W. Foster's grandsons John Foster and Allen Dulles. Equally prominent among the entourage was Thomas W. Lamont, Morgan's leading partner, whose mission was to ensure that Britain and France would repay the enormous loans they had received from the House of Morgan, and Paul Warburg, the Chairman of the Federal Reserve, who represented America's banking interests.[14]

At the conference, the Wilson delegation teamed up with British delegates, including such prominent Round Table figures as Alfred Milner, Arthur Balfour, Philip Kerr, Robert Henry Brand, and Lionel Curtis, to draft the plans for a "world without war."[15] One of the planks of the Treaty, which was ratified at the conference, called for severe reparations to be paid to the victorious nations by the German government, including the pensions of the Allied soldiers. This stipulation precipitated the hyperinflation of the German mark between 1920 and 1923, the destruction of the German middle class, and the rise of the Third Reich. It had been written and inserted into the peace settlement by John Foster Dulles, one of the founders of the Council on Foreign Relations, and Thomas Lamont.[16] As an addendum to the Treaty of Versailles, the victorious nations drafted the Charter of the League of Nations, which was signed by President Wilson for the American government.

The League, as conceived by the trustees and espoused by President Wilson, was to establish a global forum to settle territorial disputes through arbitration and the power to enforce those settlements; to create a free-trade regime to remove "all economic barriers" between nations; to promote regional integration on both political and economic levels (including the welding together of North and South America); and to allow the United States to lead the way in the formation of a new world order.[17]

## DREAMS COME TRUE

By the time Wilson set sail for his return trip to America, the dream of Cecil Rhodes was on the threshold of becoming a reality. His secret society of aristocratic and mostly effete Masons had gained control of the empire and reshaped the world. German islands in the South Pacific had been handed over to Australia and New Zealand. Mesopotamia and Palestine, taken from the Ottoman Empire, had been granted to Britain. German South West Africa became incorporated into South Africa, which remained under British rule. The Cameroons and Togoland were divided between Britain and France. Thanks to "the war to end all wars," the British Empire had gained 950,000 square miles and millions of new subjects.[18]

Due to the war and the treaties imposed upon the Germans, one could walk from Cairo to Cape Town without ever leaving a British dominion, colony, or protectorate. The trans-African railroad, envisioned by Rhodes, could now be built without requesting transit rights from anyone except a member of the British Imperial Conference.[19] Jan Smuts, who now served as the prime minister of South Africa, bragged that the British Empire had "emerged from the War quite the greatest power in the world, and it is only un-wisdom or unsound policy that could rob her of that great position."[20]

Only one part of the grand scheme remained to be set in place: the reunification of Britain and the United States. This task could be easily accomplished through the League of Nations, since Britain would wield political and economic control over almost every member nation.

Therefore, a reunification, Lionel Curtis wrote in *The Commonwealth of Nations*, would allow America to advance beyond the concept of nationalism and to accept its obligation to join with Great Britain in an effort to impose peace, order, and good government over the "backward nations." Americans, he believed, were ready for this undertaking since "the presence of the Negro in their midst has taught them that a mixture in one country of an advanced with a backward civilization is in itself the greatest menace to liberty."[21]

## A SETBACK

When Wilson submitted the treaty for ratification in June of 1919, the Senate balked. The establishment of the League, Senator Henry Cabot Lodge maintained, would make Wilson "the President of the world."[22] The setback was so personally devastating for Wilson that he suffered a severe stroke in October of 1919 that prevented him from seeking a third term in office.[23] The only hope for the League's success resided with a Democratic sweep of the legislative and executive branches in the upcoming election. The Republicans, galvanizing support around Senator Warren G. Harding from Ohio, drafted a platform that held: "The Republican Party stands for agreement among the nations to preserve the peace of the world. We believe that this can be done without depriving the people of the United States of the right to determine what is just and fair, and without involving them as participants and not peacemakers in a multitude of quarrels, the merits of which they are unable to judge." It condemned the concept of the League as "not only intolerable for an independent people, but certain to produce the injustice, hostility and controversy which it proposes to prevent."[24]

The Democrats, uniting under James M. Cox, the governor of Ohio, endorsed a platform which favored the League as "the surest, if not the only, practical means of maintaining the permanent peace of the world and terminating the insufferable burden of great military and naval establishments." It further held: "We reject as utterly vain, if not vicious, the Republican assumption that ratification of the treaty and membership in the League of Nations would in any wise impair integrity or independence of our country."[25]

But in 1920 there was still a spirit of independence in the land. The majority of Americans had not been subjected to the social engineering of the Carnegie and Rockefeller Foundations and the national press was not under the complete control of the money trust. Harding won by a landslide, capturing 34 of the 48 states and gaining the first Republican victories in Arizona, New Mexico, and Oklahoma.[26] In retrospect, it was a Pyrrhic victory. The globalists, who already controlled the country's monetary system, now had their minds set on taking over the US State Department.

# NOTES

1. William Manchester, *The Last Lion: Winston Spencer Churchill: Visions of Glory, 1874-1932* (New York: Random House, 1991), p. 472.

2. Georges Clemenceau, quoted in Patrick J. Buchanan, *Churchill, Hitler, and the Unnecessary War* (New York: Crown Publishing, 2008), p. 72.

3. Ibid., p. 74.

4. *Treaty of Versailles*, Article 110, Section XI of Part III, June 28, 1919, Library of Congress, https://www.loc.gov/law/help/us-treaties/bevans/m-ust000002-0043.pdf.

5. Buchanan, *Churchill, Hitler and the Unnecessary War*, p. 72.

6. Stephen Mitford Goodson, *A History of Central Banking and the Enslavement of Mankind* (London: Black House, 2014), p. 91.

7. Ibid.

8. *Treaty of Versailles*.

9. Lamar Cecil, *Wilhelm II: Emperor and Exile, 1900-1941* (Chapel Hill: The University of North Carolina Press, 1996), p. 294.

10. Erik von Kuehnelt-Leddihn, quoted in Buchanan, *Churchill, Hitler, and the Unnecessary War*, p. 76.

11. Ibid., p. 77.

12. Fred Blahut, "The Allied Attempt to Starve Germany in 1919," *The Burns Review* (Washington, DC), April 1996, https://www.wintersonnenwende.com/scriptorium/english/archives/articles/starvation1919.html.

13. Herbert Hoover and Hugh Gibson, "The Problem of Lasting Peace" in *Prefaces to Peace: A Symposium* (New York: Simon and Schuster, et alia, 1948), p. 228.

14. Buchanan, *Churchill, Hitler, and the Unnecessary War*, p. 24.

15. Brown, *The Secret Society*, p. 320.

16. Ibid.

17. Will Banyon, "The Invisible Man of the New World Order: Raymond B. Fosdick (1888-1972)" *Conspiracy Archives*, February 2015, http://www.conspiracyarchive.com/2015/03/08/the-invisible-man-of-the-new-world-order-raymond-b-fosdick-1883-1972/.

18. Buchanan, *Churchill, Hitler, and the Unnecessary War*, p. 100.

19. Ibid.

20. Jan Smuts, quoted in Ibid.

21. Lionel Curtis, *The Commonwealth of Nations: An Inquiry into the Nature of Citizenship in the British Empire and into the Mutual Relations of the Several Communities Thereof, Part I* (London: Macmillan and Company, 1916), p. 697.

22. Banyon, "The Invisible Man of the New World Order."

23. G. Vance Smith and Tom Gow, *Masters of Deception: The Rise of the Council on Foreign Relations* (Colorado Springs, Colorado: Freedom First Society, 2012), p. 36.

24. 1920 Republican Platform in Warren P. Mass, "The People's Choice," *The New American*, October 26, 1987.

25. 1920 Democratic Platform in Ibid.

26. Smith and Gow, *Masters of Deception*, p. 45.

# PART FOUR

# THE AMERICAN ESTABLISHMENT

*"I predict future happiness for Americans if they can prevent the government from wasting the labors of the people under the pretense of taking care of them."*
—THOMAS JEFFERSON

*"We are grateful to the Washington Post, the New York Times, Time magazine and other great publications whose directors have attended our meetings and respected the promises of discretion for almost forty years. It would have been impossible for us to develop our plan for the world if we had been subject to the bright lights of publicity during those years. But, the world is now more sophisticated and prepared to march towards a world-government. The supranational sovereignty of an intellectual elite and world bankers is surely preferable to the National auto determination practiced in past centuries."*
—DAVID ROCKEFELLER IN AN ADDRESS TO A TRILATERAL COMMISSION
MEETING IN JUNE OF 1991

# 15

# THE SHADOW GOVERNMENT

*The CFR (Council on Foreign Relations), established six years after the Federal Reserve was created, worked to promote an internationalist agenda on behalf of the international banking elite. Where the Fed took control of money and debt, the CFR took control of the ideological foundations of such an empire—encompassing the corporate, banking, political, foreign policy, military, media, and academic elite of the nation into a generally cohesive overall world view.*

—CARROLL QUIGLEY, *TRAGEDY AND HOPE*

ON MAY 30, 1919, members of the American and British delegations, all of whom were members of the Round Table movement, met at the Majestic Hotel in Paris to create the Institute for International Affairs, which was to have two chapters: the Royal Institute of International Affairs (RIIA), also known as the Chatham House Study Group, as an advisory group to the British Government; and the Council on Foreign Relations as a think tank for the US State Department. A subsidiary organization, the Institute of Pacific Relations, was formed to deal exclusively with Far Eastern affairs. Other organizations were set up in Paris and Hamburg.

The Royal Institute, which opened in London in 1920, was simply the Round Table writ large. Its Founding Fathers included Lionel Curtis, Philip Kerr, Lord Robert Cecil, Arnold Toynbee, Arthur Balfour, Robert Brand, and Geoffrey Dawson. Initial funding came from the Carnegie Corporation, the Rockefeller Foundation, and the Rhodes Trust. RIIA became known as the Chatham House on the basis of its address at No. 4, St. James in London. The property was purchased for the group by Colonel Reuben Wells Leonard, a Canadian businessman, who named it in honor of William Pitt, the 1st Earl of Chatham, "to whom Canadians owed their status as British subjects."[1]

RIIA functioned and continues to function under this policy: "When a meeting, or part thereof, is held under the Chatham House Rule, participants are free to use the information received, but neither the identity nor the affiliation of the speaker(s), nor that of any other participant, may be revealed."[2] This rule mirrored the manner in which Rhodes believed information should be shared and disseminated—clandestinely through an elite group of decision makers, and it intimated that the inner workings of the group operates on the Society of the Elect's original rings-within-rings model. RIIA members have included a host of British prime ministers, including Winston Churchill, Harold Macmillan, Harold Wilson, and John Major. The list of foreign dignitaries who have addressed the gatherings at No. 4, St. James contains the names of Mahatma Gandhi, Ronald Reagan, Mikhail Gorbachev, Nelson Mandela, Yasser Arafat, Vladimir Putin, Alan Greenspan, Kofi Annan, and Hillary Clinton.[3]

## ANOTHER HOUSE OF MORGAN

As the House of Morgan, thanks to its ongoing ties to the House of Rothschild, took the lead in the creation of the Federal Reserve, the Pilgrim Society and the American Round Table, it also spearheaded the formation of the Council on Foreign Relations (CFR) on July 29, 1921.[4] John W. Davis, the first president of the organization, was one of Morgan's private attorneys; Paul Cravath, the vice-president, headed the

**Council on Foreign Relations**
The Council on Foreign Relations (CFR) became a place where enterprising bankers and businessmen gathered to gain access to America's power elite.

law firm that protected Morgan's business interests; Russell Leffingwell, who became the first chairman, was one of Morgan's banking business partners; Edwin Gay was president of the *New York Post*, a newspaper owned by the Morgan Company; Hamilton Fish Armstrong, another employee of the *Post*, became the first editor of *Foreign Affairs*, the CFR's monthly publication; and Elihu Root, another of Morgan's private attorneys, was named "honorary president." Many of the founders also possessed strong ties to the Carnegie and Rockefeller Foundations which provided the funding for the organization's headquarters at 58 East 68th Street in New York City, a property known as the Pratt House. John Foster Dulles, another Morgan lawyer, was the board chairman of the Carnegie Foundation for International Peace. His wife, Janet Pomeroy Avery, was the first cousin of John D. Rockefeller, and Standard Oil was one of Dulles's most important clients. In later life, he would become Secretary of State under President Dwight D. Eisenhower, while his younger brother Allen, also a CFR founding member and Morgan lawyer, would become director of the CIA.[5] Another founder was Paul Warburg, the Founding Father of the Federal Reserve system.[6] Warburg now served as the Chairman of the International Acceptance Bank, which he had organized to promote the post-war reconstruction of Europe with the Rothschilds.[7]

In post–World War I America, Morgan and Company wielded almost unlimited power. Its financial resources defied statistical measurement, since the full extent of its control over American banks and businesses remained concealed from public scrutiny. Ten years after the formation of the CFR, Ferdinand Lindberg was able to list eighty financial institutions and eighty-six nonfinancial corporations under the Morgan influence. These firms possessed combined assets of $77.6 billion, a total that represented more than one fourth of America's corporate wealth.[8] And this amount did not include the holdings of the House of Rockefeller, which had become intertwined with Morgan interests through their financial and industrial alliance. By the turn of the twentieth century, this alliance had become so close that it was difficult for financial analysts to discern what holdings belonged to Morgan and what belonged to Rockefeller. In 1904, John Moody, one of the country's leading financial experts, argued that this bond between the two houses was a salubrious development that had occurred as a "law of nature." He wrote: "No amount of blind public opposition or restrictive legislation can prevent the constant change from small scale to large scale. . . The modern trust is the natural outcome of society conditions and ethical standards which are recognized and established among men today as necessary elements in the development of civilization."[9] This interconnectedness served as the nucleus of the Council on Foreign Relations and remained the source of its power throughout the decades.

Through the years, the CFR remained under the domain of the Houses of Morgan, Rothschild, and, eventually, Rockefeller. These banking families controlled it. They financed it. They selected its staff. They set its agenda. They arranged the placement of its members in key government positions. Its purpose was to align America's foreign policy with the aim of the international money cartel, in the same manner that the Federal Reserve aligned America's economic policy. Its activities were never benign and never removed from the ultimate goal of its founders: the accumulation of the world's wealth.

## THE ESTABLISHMENT'S PRESIDIUM

The Council on Foreign Relations (CFR) became a place where enterprising bankers and businessmen gathered to gain access to America's power elite. For the most part, these individuals came from wealthy, old-line families who pursued the same path to worldly success, beginning at elite private schools, such as Groton, and then proceeding to Ivy League institutions, where they joined exclusive fraternities, such as Yale's Skull and Bones. From academia, they progressed to careers as Wall Street lawyers, corporate executives, bank officials, or high-ranking government directors. Upon their arrival in their chosen professions, they received an invitation to join the CFR. Naturally, they accepted since entry to the organization placed them among the movers and shakers of politics, business, and industry. At the CFR, they formed alliances with other members to shape public policy through lobbyists, political action committees (PACs), and political contributions.

The CFR became the first organization to unite private interests under the Houses of Morgan and Rockefeller with the purpose of influencing governmental decisions and directives. Historian Arthur Schlesinger Jr. described the CFR as a "front organization for the heart of the American Establishment."[10] David Halberstam in *The Best and the Brightest* called it "the Establishment's unofficial club."[11] Richard Rovere, in an *Esquire* article, spoke of it as "a sort of Presidium for that part of the Establishment that guides our destiny as a nation. . . . Policy and strategy are worked out by the Council and reach the President by way of the State Department, which, of course, is largely staffed and always directed by Council members."[12] Richard Harwood, managing editor of *The Washington Post*, wrote: "[CFR] members are the nearest thing we have to a ruling establishment in the United States." Harwood went on to identify CFR members in top positions as the *New York Times*, the *Wall Street Journal, Time* magazine, the *Post*, and network national news. These media officials, he concluded, "do not merely analyze and interpret foreign policy for the United States, they help to make it."[13]

## THE MEMBERSHIP ROSTER

In its brochure, the CFR presents itself as "an independent, nonpartisan membership organization, think tank, and publisher dedicated to being a resource for its members, government officials, business executives, journalists, educators and students, civic and religious leaders, and other interested citizens in order to help them better understand the world and the foreign policy choices facing the United States and other countries." Its corporate membership list contains the names of almost every major business and bank in the country, including Bank of America, Merrill Lynch, Chevron, ExxonMobil, JPMorgan Chase, Morgan Stanley, Goldman Sachs, Shell Oil, American Express, Barclays, Lockheed Martin, Lazard, Soros Fund Management, Prudential Financial, IBM, General Electric, Facebook, FedEx, Rothschild North America, Northrop Grumman, Microsoft, Raytheon, Merck and Company, Standard and Poor's, Sony Corporation of America, Time Warner, and Walmart.[14] A small sampling of the prominent names on the 2015 membership roster is as follows: Elliot Abrams, Madeleine Albright, Bruce Babbit, James Baker, Warren Beatty, Michael Bloomberg, Sidney Blumenthal, John Bolton, Zbigniew Brzezinski, Warren Buffet, Paul Bremer, Jimmy Carter, Dick Cheney, Warren Christopher, Henry Cisneros, Wesley Clark, Bill Clinton, Chelsea Clinton, George Clooney, Katie Couric, Scott Cuomo, Christopher Dodd, Alfonse D'Amato, Diane Feinstein, Timothy Geithner, Ruth Bader Ginsburg, Alan Greenspan, Chuck Hagel, Teresa Kerry Heinz, Vernon Jordan, Joseph Kennedy III, Edward Kennedy Jr., Henry Kissinger, Charles Krauthammer, John Kerry, Bernard Lewis, Joe Lieberman, John McCain, George Mitchell, Janet Negroponte, Alice Rivlin, Grover Norquist, Sam Nunn, Janet

Napolitano, Colin Powell, Condoleezza Rice, John Roberts, John D. Rockefeller IV, David Rockefeller, David Rockefeller Jr., Nicholas Rockefeller, Steven Rockefeller, Donna Shalala, Susan Rice, Douglas Schoen, Joe Scarborough, William Roper, George Soros, Jonathan Soros, Lesley Stahl, Diane Sawyer, Laura Tyson, Cyrus Vance, Barbara Walters, Paul Wolfowitz, and Janet Yellen.[15]

## A SUBVERSIVE PURPOSE

In 1957, a congressional investigative committee revealed the following finding: "In the international field, foundations, and an interlock among some of them and certain intermediary organizations, have exercised a strong effect upon our foreign policy and upon public education in things international. This has been accomplished by vast propaganda, by supplying executives and advisers to government and by controlling much research in this area through the power of the purse. The net result of these combined efforts has been to promote 'internationalism' in a particular sense—a form directed toward 'world government' and a derogation of American 'nationalism.' The CFR has become in essence an agency of the United States Government [and its] productions are not objective but are directed overwhelmingly at promoting the globalist concept."[16]

This subversive purpose has been verified by *Foreign Affairs,* the Council's own publication, which has been called "the most influential periodical in print" by *Time* magazine.[17] In its inaugural issue (September 1922), the journal condemned "the dubious doctrines expressed by such phrases of 'safety first' and 'America first.'"[18] In its second issue, Philip Kerr, a member of the British Round Table, declared: "Obviously there is going to be no peace or prosperity for mankind so long as it remains divided into fifty or sixty independent states. Equally obviously there is going to be no steady progress in civilization or self-government among the more backward peoples until some kind of international system is created which will put an end to the diplomatic struggles of every nation to make itself secure. The real problem today is that of world government."[19] This same insistence has been resounded ad nauseam in nearly every issue of *Foreign Affairs*. In "Reflections on Our National Purpose," an article published in the April 1972 issue, Kingman Brewster Jr., the US ambassador to Great Britain and president of Yale University, said: "Our national purpose should be to abolish American nationality and to take some risks in order to invite others to pool their sovereignty with ours."[20] Two years later, former deputy assistant Secretary of State Richard N. Gardner penned a piece called "The Hard Road to World Order" in which he wrote: "We are witnessing an outbreak of shortsighted nationalism that seems oblivious to the economic, political and moral implications of interdependence. . . The 'house of world order' will have to be built from the bottom up rather than from the top down." He went on to say: "An end run around national sovereignty, eroding it piece by piece, will accomplish much more than the old-fashioned frontal assault."[21]

In keeping with the founding spirit of the CFR, John Dewey, noted educator and philosopher, coauthored *The Humanist Manifesto*, which called for a "synthesis of all religions" and a "socialized and cooperative economic order."[22] Similarly, social engineer Lewis Mumford and theologian Reinhold Niebuhr, two *Foreign Affairs* correspondents, wrote in their work *The City of Man: A Declaration of World Democracy*: "Universal peace can be founded only by the unity of man under one law and one government. . . . . All states, deflated and disciplined, must align themselves under the law of the world-state . . . the new order . . . when the heresy of nationalism is conquered and the absurd architecture of the present world is finally dismantled. . . . . And there must be a common creed . . . or ethico-religious purpose."[23]

## NON-ATTRIBUTION

Within the hallowed halls of the Pratt House, including its 55,000 volume library, a carefully selected group of candidates are groomed for prominent positions of power in the federal government. "They walk in one door as acquisitive businessmen," David Halberstam said, "and come out the other as statesmen-figures."[24] Proof of this resides in the fact that by 2017, twenty secretaries of state, nineteen secretaries of the treasury, fifteen secretaries of defense, and hundreds of other federal department heads have been CFR members, along with twenty-one of the twenty-four CIA directors, and every chairman of the Federal Reserve since 1951.

The CFR holds 120 meetings a year at the Pratt House. The gatherings feature an address by a guest speaker, followed by group discussion. These meetings are held in secrecy under the rule of "non-attribution," which means that everything that transpires at the meetings is off the record. Anyone who violates this rule, which prohibits statements from members reaching the press, is subject to immediate expulsion from the organization. The CFR claims that this rule is essential to ensure candor.[25] But economist John Kenneth Galbraith, a former council member, decried it as scandalous. "Why," he asked, "should businessmen be briefed on information not available to the general public, especially since it can be financially advantageous?"[26]

## THE STUDY GROUPS

The council also sponsors a yearly average of twenty study groups that concentrate on specific foreign policy topics. These groups produce reports that are circulated among an inner core of members. The preparation of these reports do not represent idle academic exercises but rather the means to advance the agenda of the CFR inner core. Admiral Chester Ward, another former council member, wrote: "Once the ruling members of the CFR have decided that the US Government should adopt a particular policy, the very substantial research facilities of CFR are put to work to develop arguments, intellectual and emotional, to support the new policy, and to confound and discredit, intellectually and politically, any opposition."[27] Indeed, the studies generated by the council have resulted in the establishment of such international institutions as the United Nations, the World Bank, and the International Monetary Fund.

Financing for the study groups comes from the Rockefeller, Carnegie, and Ford Foundations, which are governed by boards of directors that are interconnected. The board members of the Rockefeller Foundation often pop up as trustees of the Rockefeller, Carnegie, and Ford Foundations and vice versa. For example, CFR president John W. Davis served as a trustee for the Rockefeller and Carnegie Foundations, while running for president in a campaign heavily funded by Kuhn, Loeb and Company, the bank in which Paul Warburg, the founder of the Federal Reserve, was a partner. By 1960, many of the trustees of America's three leading foundations were executives from Bechtel Construction, Chase Manhattan, Kimberly Clark, Monsanto Chemical and other leading international business and banking firms.[28] Twelve of the fifteen Rockefeller Foundation trustees, ten of the fifteen Ford Foundation trustees, and ten of the fourteen Carnegie Foundation trustees were members of the CFR.[29]

Thanks to Dwight David Eisenhower and the Dulles brothers, the US State Department, by this time, was firmly under the council's control. A pattern developed that would continue into the second decade of the twenty-first century. Corporate plans for expansion into new regions of the world were established by American's leading CEOs, many of whom served on the boards of the major foundations. The foundations would fund CFR study groups that inevitably would uphold the soundness of the expansion plans in reports that were passed on to the State Department for implementation. The result of this process would be wars without borders, ceaseless political upheavals, and mass migrations of uprooted populations, along with the concentration of wealth within a favored few and the globalization of poverty.

# NOTES

1. Robin Brown, *The Secret Society: Cecil John Rhodes's Plan for a New World Order* (Cape Town, South Africa: Penguin Books, 2015, p. 327.

2. James Corbett, "Chatham House Rule: Inside the Royal Institute of International Affairs, *The Corbett Report,* January 15, 2013, https://www.corbettreport.com/chatham-house-rule-inside-the-royal-institute-of-international-affairs/.

3. Brown, *The Secret Society*, p. 322.

4. James Perloff, *The Shadows of Power: The Council on Foreign Relations and the American Decline* (Appleton, Wisconsin: Western Islands, 2005), p 5.

5. Ibid., p. 38.

6. "History of the Council on Foreign Relations," CFR website, n. d., http://www.cfr.org/about/history/cfr/appendix.html.

7. Mira Williams, *The History of Foreign Investments in the United States, 1914 to 1945* (Cambridge, Mass: Harvard University Press, 204), p. 719.

8. Ferdinand Lundberg, *America's 60 Families* (New York: Vanguard Press, 1937), p. 37.

9. John Moody, quoted in John H. Bodley, *Cultural Anthropology: Tribes, states and the Global System* (New York: Rowman and Littlefield, 2016), p. 309.

10. Arthur Schlesinger, Jr., *A Thousand Days: John F. Kennedy in the White House* (Boston: Houghton Mifflin, 1965), p. 128.

11. David Halberstam, *The Best and the Brightest* (New York: Random House 1972), p. 6.

12. Richard Rovere, "The American Establishment," *Esquire,* May 1962, https://archive.org/stream/americanestablis001909mbp/americanestablis001909mbp_djvu.txt.

13. Richard Harwood, "Ruling Class Journalists," *The Washington Post*, October 30, 1993.

14. Council on Foreign Relations, brochure, 2017, http://i.cfr.org/content/about/About_CFR_2016.pdf.

15. Council on Foreign Relations, membership roster, http://www.cfr.org/about/membership/roster.html.

16. *Hearings Before the Special Committee to Investigate Tax-Exempt Foundations and Comparable Organizations*, House of Representatives, Eighty-Third Congress, Second Session on H. Res. 217, Part 1, Pages 1–943. (Washington, D.C.: Government Printing Office, 1954).

17. Advertisement in *Foreign Affairs,* Summer 1986.

18. Perloff, *The Shadows of Power*, p. 10.

19. Ibid., p. 11.

20. Kingman Brewster, Jr., "Reflections on Our National Purpose," *Foreign Affairs,* April 1972, https://www.foreignaffairs.com/articles/united-states/1972-04-01/reflections-our-national-purpose.

21. Richard N. Gardner, "The Hard Road to World Order," *Foreign Affairs*, April 1974, https://www.foreignaffairs.com/articles/1974-04-01/hard-road-world-order.

22. John Dewey, "A Humanist Manifesto," 1934, *Secular Web*, https://infidels.org/library/modern/edwin_wilson/manifesto/ch13.html.

23. Reinhold Niebuhr, Lewis Mumford, *et al.*, *The City of Man; A Declaration on World Democracy*, 1941, http://zeitwort.at/files/the-city-of-man.pdf.

24. John Franklin Campbell, "The Death Rattle of the Eastern Establishment," New York, September 29, 1971, https://books.google.com/books?id=xGbNXzogsxoC&pg=PA48&lpg=PA48&dq=halb erstam+%22they+walk+in+one+door+as+acquisitive+businessmen%22&source=bl&ots=8V4suF Yzkm&sig=Yl6hovEaASJehmWW9nWZW mYkZo&hl=en&sa=X&ved=0ahUKEwjYgIky9vSA hWKiFQKHbyzBicQ6AEILDAD#v=onepage&q=halberstam%20%22they%20walk%20in%20 one%20door%20as%20acquisitive%20businessmen%22&f=false.

25. Perloff, *The Shadows of Power*, p. 6.

26. John Kenneth Galbraith, quoted in Ibid.

27. Phyllis Schlafly and Chester Ward, *Kissinger on the Couch* (New Rochelle, New York: Arlington House, 1975), p. 151.

28. Daniel Estulin, *The True Story of the Bilderberg Group* (Waterville, Oregon: Trineday, 2009), p. 87.

29. Ibid.

# 16

## A DESIGNED DEPRESSION

*We ourselves are in the midst of the greatest depression we have ever known. From the Atlantic to the Pacific, our Country has been ravaged and laid waste by the evil practices of the Fed and the interests which control them. At no time in our history, has the general welfare of the people been at a lower level or the minds of the people so full of despair. Recently in one of our States, 60,000 dwelling houses and farms were brought under the hammer in a single day. 71,000 houses and farms in Oakland County, Michigan, were sold and their erstwhile owners dispossessed. The people who have thus been driven out are the wastage of the Fed. They are the victims of the Fed. Their children are the new slaves of the auction blocks in the revival of the institution of human slavery.*

—REPRESENTATIVE LOUIS MCFADDEN, REMARKS IN CONGRESS, 1934

THANKS TO THE WAR, America had become the world's largest creditor nation. The money that flowed into America from the $8 billion in war loans granted to France, Great Britain, and Italy was used to fund US business and industry and to provide loans to American workers. While Europe remained in a state of stagnancy, perpetuated by the devastation of property and loss of population caused by the war, cars, highways, bridges, manufacturing plants, hotels, theaters, and department stores were being built throughout America at an unprecedented rate. Unemployment dropped to less than 5 percent. Almost every home in the country had electricity. By 1920, the national income of the United States was greater than the combined incomes of Britain, France, Germany, Japan, Canada, and seventeen smaller countries.[1]

The House of Morgan, which remained united with the House of Rockefeller, emerged from the war as powerful as its parent, the House of Rothschild. The Morgans and the Rockefellers controlled not only America's leading national banks but also the Federal Reserve system. By the snap of their fingers, these banking families, since they had provided the funding that produced the country's prosperity and controlled the cash flow, could alter the course of the American economy, plunging the American people into the depths of poverty. Montagu Norman, the governor of the Bank of England, reminded them of their omnipotence by these remarks which he made to the United States Bankers' Association in 1924:

> Capital must protect itself in every possible way, both by combination and legislation. Debts must be collected, mortgages foreclosed as rapidly as possible. When, through the process of law, the common people lose their homes, they will become more docile and more easily governed through the strong arm of government applied by a central power of wealth under leading financiers. These truths are well known among our principal men, who are now engaged in forming an imperialism to govern the world. By dividing the voters through the political party system, we can get them to expend their energies in fighting for questions of no importance. It is, thus, by discrete action, we can ensure for ourselves that which has been so well planned and so successfully accomplished.[2]

When Norman made these remarks, which were met by a standing ovation, the House of Morgan was actively informed in establishing "the imperialism to govern the world" by the Dawes Plan.

## THE DAWES PLAN

By 1923, the reparation payments imposed upon Germany by the Treaty of Versailles had caused the Weimar Republic to print such an outrageous quantity of paper money that 100 million marks was not sufficient to buy a box of matches.[3] The hyperinflation was accompanied by an unemployment rate that soared to 33 percent. When Germany was no longer able to come up with the mandated annual payments of 132 billion gold marks to the Allies, French and Belgium forces took possession of the Ruhr Valley. As a result of the occupation, German miners in this area reduced coal production. This situation intensified the financial crisis and poised the possibility of a renewed outbreak of armed conflict.[4]

Within these dire developments, the House of Morgan spotted an opportunity to increase its wealth and came up with the Dawes Plan. As implemented in 1924, this plan called for the provision of $1.5 billion in loans from Morgan and Rockefeller to spark the German economy and stabilize the German currency. It was developed by members of the Council on Foreign Relations.[5] Germany at that time represented carrion for the money vultures. The opportunities seemed limitless. Major German businesses could be bought for pennies on the dollar. The Daimler-Benz motor company, for example, could be had for the price of 227 of its cars.[6] Some of the money was used to build theaters, sports stadiums, and even opera houses. But the lion's share went for industrialization.[7]

## THE GERMAN CHEMICAL COMPANY

The Dawes Plan was foolproof. It stipulated that the American bankers would be repaid with interest ahead of the reparation payments to France and Great Britain. And it met with immediate success. Businesses began to flourish, imports ballooned, and the austerity measures that had been imposed upon the German people were lifted. By 1926, the German government was back to running modest deficits of $200 million and inflation had been controlled.[8]

A major beneficiary of the Plan was I. G. Farben, which received a

$30 million loan from Rockefellers' National City Bank. Thanks to this funding, Farben grew into the largest chemical company in the world. It produced 100 percent of Germany's synthetic oil, 100 percent of its lubricating oil, and 84 percent of its explosives. German bankers on the Farben *Aufsichtsrat* (the supervisory board of directors) included Hamburg banker Max Warburg, whose brother Paul Warburg was a founder of the Federal Reserve system in the United States. Not coincidentally, in 1928, Paul Warburg became a director of American I. G., Farben's wholly owned US subsidiary, whose holdings came to include the Bayer Company, General Aniline Works, Agfa Ansco, and Winthrop Chemical Company.[9] By 1933, Farben had become so wealthy that it could fund the Nazi Party's rise to power. The ties to Hitler greatly increased the chemical company's worth. By 1943, it was the leading producer of Zyklon B gas, which was used in the concentration camps.[10]

### "THE TWENTY-FOUR-HOUR CALL"

Along with creating prosperity in Germany, the money cartel decided to manufacture a depression in America, which, as Norman Montagu predicted, would result in the American people losing their homes and holdings and thereby becoming "more docile and more easily governed through the strong arm of government applied by a central power of wealth under leading financiers." They produced this financial catastrophe through a process known as the "twenty-four-hour call." This process enabled investors to purchase securities on extended credit. This meant if a person wanted to purchase $1,000 in stock, he only had to shell out $100. The loan was immediate, and it was provided by every national bank in the country. If the stock increased ten percent in value, an investor could double his money.[11] Moreover, Andrew Mellon, the secretary of the treasury, proceeded to make more and more cuts to the tax rate so that Americans had more and more expendable income. For those who earned $5,000 or less, the rate fell from 15.9 percent in 1920 to 1.1 percent in 1928. Those who earned $10,000 or less saw their rate dwindle from 9.1 percent in 1920 to 2 percent in 1928. And those who earned $25,000 or less witnessed a drop in their taxable income from 16.6 percent in 1920 to 7.1 percent in 1928.[12] Between 1923 and 1929, the Federal Reserve added helium to the financial balloon by expanding the money supply by 62 percent. Much of this new money was used to build up the stock market to dizzying heights.[13]

With credit money readily available, the mass media began to ballyhoo tales of the instant riches to be made in the stock market. According to Ferdinand Lundberg: "For profits to be made on these funds the public had to be induced to speculate, and it was so induced by misleading newspaper accounts, many of them bought and paid for by the brokers that operated the pools."[14]

## WALL STREET MASSACRE

But, unbeknown to the average American investors, a time bomb had been planted within their stock portfolios. The loans, which had been given so freely with a mere 10 percent down and a glad hand from the bankers, could be recalled at a moment's notice, forcing the borrowers to come up a full repayment within twenty-four hours. For most Americans, the only way to make repayments was by selling all of their securities. The stage was set for the crisis. On February 6, 1929, Montagu Norman arrived in Washington to confer with Treasury Secretary Mellon. Immediately after the mysterious meeting, the Federal Reserve Board began to cut the money supply and to raise the interest rate.[15]

On Black Friday, October 24, 1929, the excrement hit the fan. Throughout the country, the loans were called, and the stampede to sell stocks began. The stock market crashed, banks throughout the country ran out of cash and closed up shop, and the Fed refused to come to the rescue with a printing of fresh currency.[16] On Tuesday, October 29, the exchanges were crushed by a new avalanche of selling. For many securities, there were no buyers at all. By the end of the day, over sixteen million shares had been dumped, in most cases at any price that was offered. Millions of investors were wiped out. Within several months of continual decline, $40 billion of wealth had vanished. Americans who believed they were very rich suddenly discovered they were very poor.[17]

The crash may have devastated the average American investor but not "Junior" Rockefeller, "Jack" Morgan, Bernard Baruch, Joseph P. Kennedy, Paul Warburg, and other financial insiders. They were either out of the market or had sold "short" so that they earned enormous profits as the Dow Jones plummeted. Following the crash, they swooped down on Wall Street like vultures to feast on ravaged companies. Shares that once sold for a dollar now could be bought for a few pennies.[18] John P. Kennedy's worth increased from $4 million to $100 million. Similarly, while businesses went belly up throughout the country, the Rockefeller-Morgan concerns, including US Steel, Standard Oil, General Electric, and International Harvester, experienced enormous expansion.[19]

# NOTES

1. David Jarmal, "American History: Foreign Policy during the 1920s," *Masking of a Nation*, February 2, 2011, http://learningenglish.voanews.com/a/american-history-foreign-policy-during-the-1920s-115124654/116037.html.

2. Montagu Norman, quoted in Stephen Mitford Goodson, *A History of Central Banking and the Enslavement of Mankind* (London: Black House, 2014), p. 92.

3. James Perloff, *The Shadows of Power: The Council on Foreign Relations and the American Decline* (Appleton, Wisconsin: Western Islands, 2005), p. 46.

4. Jennifer Llewellyn, Jim Southey, and Steve Thompson, "The Ruhr Occupation," *Alpha History*, 2014, http://alphahistory.com/weimarrepublic/ruhr-occupation/.

5. Perloff, *The Shadows of Power*, p. 46.

6. Liaquat Ahamed, *Lords of Finance: The Bankers Who Broke the World* (New York: Penguin, 2009), p. 283.

7. Ibid.

8. Ibid.

9. Anthony Sutton, "The Empire of I. G. Farben," *Reformed Theology*, 2004, http://www.reformation.org/wall-st-ch2.html.

10. Perloff, *The Shadows of Power*, p. 47.

11. James Perloff, *The Shadows of Power: The Council on Foreign Relations and the American Decline* (Appleton, Wisconsin: Western Islands, 2005), p. 56.

12. Veronique de Rugy, "1920s Income Tax Cuts Sparked Economic Growth and Raised Federal Revenues," CATO Institute, March 4, 2003, https://www.cato.org/publications/commentary/1920s-income-tax-cuts-sparked-economic-growth-raised-federal-revenues.

13. Gary Allen, *None Dare Call It Conspiracy* (San Diego, CA: Dauphin Publications, 1971), p. 53.

14. Ferdinand Lundberg, quoted in Gary Allen, "How a Group of International Bankers Engineered the 1929 Crash and the Great Depression," *Friends of the American Revolution*, February 11, 2008, https://21stcenturycicero.wordpress.com/2008/02/11/how-a-group-of-international-bankers-engineered-the-1929-crash-and-the-great-depression/.

15. Eustace Mullens, *The Secrets of the Federal Reserve* (Staunton, VA: Bankers Research Institute, 1983), p. 143.

16. Allen, *None Dare Call It Conspiracy*, pp. 54–55.

17. G. Edward Griffin, *The Creature from Jekyll Island: A Second Look at the Federal Reserve* (New York: American Media, 2008), p. 499.

18. Perloff, *The Shadows of Power*, p. 57.

19. William P. Hoar, *Architects of Conspiracy: An Intriguing History* (Appleton, Wisconsin: Western Islands, 1985), p. 190.

# 17

# THE POLICE STATE

*After 1933, Federal Reserve Notes and deposits were no longer redeemable in gold coins to Americans; and after 1971, the dollar was no longer redeemable in gold bullion to foreign governments and central banks. The gold of Americans was confiscated and exchanged for Federal Reserve Notes, which became legal tender; and Americans were stuck in a regime of fiat paper issued by the government and the Federal Reserve. Over the years, all early restraints on Fed activities or its issuing of credit have been lifted; indeed, since 1980, the Federal Reserve has enjoyed the absolute power to do literally anything it wants: to buy not only U.S. government securities but any asset whatever, and to buy as many assets and to inflate credit as much as it pleases. There are no restraints left on the Federal Reserve.*

—MURRAY ROTHBARD, *THE CASE AGAINST THE FED*

BY 1932, UNEMPLOYMENT STOOD AT 25 PERCENT. The gross national product slipped to 50 percent. Farmers lost 60 percent of their income. A staggering 20 percent of the country's banks went belly-up. Breadlines formed in every town and city throughout the country. The homeless walked the streets, begged for pennies and nickels, and slept in vast shantytowns called Hoovervilles.[1]

As president-elect, FDR appointed prominent CFR members to key White House positions. Edward Stettinius, former board chairman of US Steel, was named Secretary of State, and Sumner Welles, a member of the Roosevelt family, became the deputy secretary of state. Norman Davis, president of the CFR, was selected as chairman of the Advisory Committee on Problems of Foreign Relations; and James Warburg, son of Paul Warburg, rose to prominence as a leading member of the President's brain trust.[2]

## KILLING PIGS

As soon as he was ensconced in the Oval Office, Roosevelt pressured Congress to pass the Agricultural Adjustment Act (AAA), which wielded absolute control over the nation's farms. While millions of Americans faced starvation, the AAA decreed the destruction of crops to prevent overproduction and to stabilize falling prices. It also ordered the slaughter of six million pigs to prevent the cost of pork, lard, and soap from plummeting. In an effort to justify these actions, FDR took to the airwaves and said: "The ungoverned push for rugged individualism perhaps had an economic justification in the days when we had all the West to surge upon and conquer; but this country has filled up now, and grown up. There are no more Indians to fight . . . . We must blaze new trails in the direction of a controlled economy, common sense, and social decency."[3]

## THE NATIONAL INDUSTRIAL RECOVERY ACT

On June 6, 1933, Congress ratified the National Industrial Recovery Act (NIRA), which represented the heart of the New Deal. The legislation had been written by Gerard Swope, president of Morgan-owned General Electric and a prominent member of the CFR.[4] The legislation mandated the regulation of every aspect of American business in a manner that paralleled the formation of the fascist government in Italy. Every industry was to operate in collaboration with the federal government in setting prices, wages, quantity of product, and working conditions.

Under this system, the companies with the most employees had the most clout in determining policy. In the iron and steel industry, for example, Morgan's US Steel possessed 511 votes; Allegheny Steel, 17 votes; and Bethlehem Steel, 16 votes. Giant corporations now possessed the ability to impose production, salary, and price standards that would drive their competition out of business. In the iron and steel industry alone, there were more than sixty complaints against the oppressive new standards in the first months of 1934.[5]

Monopolies were now supported and sustained by federal mandate. Regulations ran amok. The agency approved 557 basic and 189 supplemental industry codes in two years. Between 4,000 and 5,000 business practices were prohibited, some 3,000 administrative orders were promulgated in documents of over 10,000 pages, and tens of thousands of legal opinions were upheld and enforced by NIRA officials.[6]

In his memoirs, Herbert Hoover maintained that Wall Street had attempted to pressure him into implementing the NIRA while he was still behind the desk in the Oval Office. He wrote:

> Among the early Roosevelt fascist measures was the National Industry Recovery Act (NIRA) of June 16, 1933. . . . These ideas were first suggested by Gerald Swope (of the General Electric Company). . . [and] the United States Chamber of Commerce. During the campaign of 1932, Henry I. Harriman, president of that body, urged that I agree to support these proposals, informing me that Mr. Roosevelt had agreed to do so. I tried to show him that this stuff was pure fascism; that it was a remaking of Mussolini's "corporate state" and refused to agree to any of it. He informed me that in view of my attitude, the business world would support Roosevelt with money and influence. That for the most part proved true.[7]

## CODE ENFORCEMENT

To enforce the regulations, the NIRA employed its own police force. In the garment district of New York, the code enforcers roamed through the area like storm troopers. They entered factories, lined up workers, and subjected them to interrogation. They expelled the factory owners from their own establishments to examine their books and records. Since night work was forbidden, the code enforcers battered down the doors of several factories with axes, looking for workers who were committing the crime of sewing a pair of pants after the mandated closing hour.[8]

The fascistic policy of the NIRA was crystallized in the case of Jack Magid, a New Jersey tailor. Magid pressed a suit for thirty-five cents, five cents less than the Tailor Code rate. For this offense, the tailor was arrested, convicted, fined $500, and sent to prison. The case created a public uproar. A judge hastily summoned Magid from his jail cell, remitted his sentence and fine, and offered to give the offender his own pants to press.[9]

## ROOSEVELT'S REVENGE

On May 27, 1935, the Supreme Court ruled that the NIRA violated the borders of the US Constitution. "Extraordinary conditions may call for extraordinary remedies," the court decreed, "but the argument necessarily stops short of an attempt to justify action which lies outside the sphere of constitutional authority. Extraordinary conditions do not create or enlarge constitutional power." The ruling may have stayed the transformation of America into a fascist state, but it failed to prevent Roosevelt and his Wall Street backers from creating an occult economy.

Roosevelt retaliated by sending a bill to Congress that would enable him to appoint as many as six additional Supreme Court justices. But eventually this assault on the checks and balances of power proved to be too much for the president's friends on Capitol Hill to swallow and the "court-packing plan" met with rejection. Former Chief Justice William Rehnquist later observed: "President Roosevelt lost the Court-packing battle, but he won the war for control of the Supreme Court—not by any novel legislation, but by serving in office for more than twelve years, and appointing eight of the nine Justices of the Court."[10]

## CHANGING TIMES

The New Deal represented more than an attempt to impose a fascist system of government upon the American people. It also constituted a concerted attempt by the House of Rockefeller to gain control of the Federal Reserve and the financial domination of the United States. The success of this coup, which toppled the House of Morgan, was due to an alliance which the Rockefeller family formed with such burgeoning American financial establishments as Harriman Brown and Company (which included George Herbert Walker and Prescott Bush as partners), Lehman Brothers, and Goldman Sachs, which had managed to push Kuhn, Loeb and Company into the background.[11]

The harbinger of this revolution was the Rockefellers' successful takeover of Morgan's flagship commercial bank, Chase National Bank of New York. After the 1929 crash, Winthrop W. Aldrich, son of Senator Nelson Aldrich and brother-in-law of John D. Rockefeller Jr., engineered a merger of his Rockefeller-controlled Equitable Trust Company into Chase Bank. From that point on, Aldrich engaged in a titanic struggle within Chase, by 1932 managing to oust Morgan's Chase CEO Albert Wiggin from office and to take his place as the head of the gigantic financial firm. Thanks to this ouster, Chase has remained the financial headquarters of the House of Rockefeller.[12]

# NOTES

1. Oliver Stone and Peter Kuznick, *The Concise Untold History of the United States* (New York: Gallery Books, 2014), p. 35.

2. James Perloff, *The Shadows of Power: The Council on Foreign Relations and the American Decline* (Appleton, Wisconsin: Western Islands, 2005), p. 60.

3. FDR's "Declaration of Interdependence," quoted in Stone and Kuznick, *The Concise Untold History of the United States*, p. 38.

4. G. Vance Smith and Tom Gow, *Masters of Deception: The Rise of the Council on Foreign Relations* (Colorado Springs, CO: Freedom First Society, 2012), p. 49.

5. Perloff, *The Shadows of Power*, p. 59.

6. Gary Dean Best, *Pride, Prejudice, and Politics: Roosevelt Versus Recovery, 1933–1938* (New York: Praeger, 1991), p. 114.

7. Herbert Hoover, *Memoirs of Herbert Hoover, 1929-1941: The Great Depression* (New York: Macmillan, 1952), p. 420.

8. John Thomas Flynn, *The Roosevelt Myth* (Auburn, Alabama: Ludwig von Mises Institute, 2008), p. 46.

9. Ibid., p. 45.

10. David Savage, "Rehnquist Sees Threat to Judiciary," *Los Angeles Times*, January 1, 2005, http://articles.latimes.com/2005/jan/01/nation/na-scotus1.

11. Murray N. Rothbard, *The Case against the Fed* (Auburn, Alabama: Ludwig von Mises Institute, 2007, p. 130.

12. Ibid.

# PART FIVE

# THE OCCULT ECONOMY

*"No free man shall ever be debarred the use of arms."*
—THOMAS JEFFERSON

*"[The New World Order] cannot happen without US participation, as we are the most significant single component. Yes, there will be a New World Order, and it will force the United States to change its perceptions."*
—HENRY KISSINGER, WORLD AFFAIRS COUNCIL PRESS CONFERENCE,
REGENT BEVERLY WILSHIRE HOTEL, APRIL 19, 1994.

*"To compel a man to subsidize with his taxes the propagation of ideas which he disbelieves and abhors is sinful and tyrannical."*
—THOMAS JEFFERSON

# 18

## CONFISCATED GOLD

*All persons are hereby required to deliver on or before May 1, 1933, to a Federal
Reserve Bank or a branch or agency thereof or to any member bank of the Federal
Reserve System all gold coin, gold bullion and gold certificates now owned by them
or coming into their ownership on or before April 28, 1933.*
—FRANKLIN DELANO ROOSEVELT, EXECUTIVE ORDER 6102

FOR CENTURIES, the banking system was based on a gold standard,
and the price of gold was established by law. In the United States, this
price, prior to the arrival of FDR in the White House, was fixed at
$20.07 per ounce. This set price served not only to prevent inflation
and deflation but also to establish the limits of the money supply, since
honest paper currency could not be issued without adequate principal,
that is, gold.

Gold represented real wealth that could protect any country from
financial collapse. For this reason, the gold reserves of the United States
were stored under armed guard in a vault eighty-six feet beneath the
first floor of the New York Federal Reserve Bank on Nassau Street. By
1927, the vault, which was half the size of a football field, contained 10

percent of all the gold reserves in the world.[1]

In 1933, when Roosevelt became president, the United States had the largest gold reserves of any nation in the world. On March 8, 1933, a few days after taking the oath of office, he announced to the American public that the gold standard was safe. Three days later,

however, he issued an executive order forbidding gold payments by banks. Treasury Secretary Henry Morgenthau Jr., the son of a CFR founding member, said that the measure was aimed at those who hoarded quantities of gold and thereby hindered the Government's plans for a restoration of public confidence."[2]

### THE GOLD BAN

The order backfired. Thousands of Americans, fearful that their paper money was becoming worthless, withdrew their savings from banks to purchase gold from foreign and domestic markets. On April 5, 1933, Roosevelt responded to the mounting banking crisis by ordering all American citizens

**Franklin D. Roosevelt**
In 1933, when Roosevelt became president, the United States had the largest gold reserves of any nation in the world. On April 5, 1933, Roosevelt responded to the mounting banking crisis by ordering all American citizens to surrender their gold to the government.

to surrender their gold to the government. No one in America was now allowed to own more than $100 in gold coins.[3] Roosevelt assured the country: "The order is limited to the period of the emergency." But the ban of owning gold remained on the books until 1974.

Nine months later, Executive Order 6102 became law: The Gold

Reserve Act of 1934. The gold began to pour into the coffers of the Federal Reserve Bank in Washington, DC. Guards, armed with machine guns, oversaw the transportation of gold bullion and coins from national and state banks throughout the country. "I am keeping my finger on the gold," Roosevelt announced to the press, and he did.[4] The gold that was confiscated and locked within the vaults of the Fed was never returned to the American people.

## CITIZENS BECOME CRIMINALS

The federal mandate implied that government was the rightful owner of all the gold in the nation, and that no American had a right to possess the precious metal. Roosevelt branded all those who did not turn over their gold as "hoarders." He defined "hoarding" as "the withdrawal and withholding of gold coin, gold bullion or gold certificates from the recognized and customary channels of trade."[5] Citizens had accepted a paper currency based on the government's pledge to redeem it in gold at $20.07 per ounce; then, when Roosevelt decided to default on that pledge, he also felt obliged to turn all citizens holding gold into criminals. Scores of Americans were now rounded up, fined, and sent to the slammer for having a fistful of gold dollars.[6]

Foreigners also had gold confiscated and were forced to accept paper money as payment. The Uebersee Finanz-Korporation, a Swiss banking company, had $1.25 million in gold coins for business use, which it entrusted to an American firm for safekeeping. In 1934, the Uebersee Finanz officials were shocked to find that their gold was confiscated by the US government. They made appeals, but the appeals were denied. The officials were told that they were only entitled to paper money but not their gold coins. The Swiss company would have lost 40 percent of their gold's value if they tried to buy the same amount of gold with the paper money they received in exchange for their confiscated coins.[7]

Roosevelt stated that the ban on private ownership of the precious metal "was the first step also to that complete control of all monetary gold in the United States, which was essential in order to give the

Government that element of freedom of action which was necessary as the very basis of its monetary goal and objective."[8] The Fed now began to churn out cash at an unprecedented level. The dollar lost 93 percent of its purchasing power, while the value of an ounce of gold rose to $35.[9]

## A CONGRESSMAN'S OUTCRY

In 1933, Representative Louis T. McFadden of Pennsylvania took to the floor of Congress to denounce FDR's action as follows:

> Roosevelt seized the gold value of forty billions or more of bank deposits in the United States banks. Those deposits were deposits of gold values. By his action he has rendered them payable to the depositors in paper only, if payable at all, and the paper money he proposes to pay out to bank depositors and to the people generally in lieu of their hard earned gold values in itself, and being based on nothing into which the people can convert it the said paper money is of negligible value altogether. . .
>
> The people of the U.S. are now using unredeemable paper slips for money. The Treasury cannot redeem that paper in gold or silver. The gold and silver of the Treasury has unlawfully been given to the corrupt and dishonest Fed. And the Administration has since had the effrontery to raid the country for more gold for the private interests by telling our patriotic citizens that their gold is needed to protect the currency.
>
> It is not being used to protect the currency! It is being used to protect the corrupt and dishonest Fed. "The directors of these institutions have committed criminal offense against the United States Government, including the offense of making false entries on their books, and the still more serious offense of unlawfully abstracting funds from the United States Treasury!" Roosevelt's gold raid is intended to help them out of the pit they dug for themselves when they gambled away the wealth and savings of the American people.[10]

In the wake of making these remarks, McFadden experienced two attempts on his life. The first came in the form of two gunmen who fired at the congressman after he alighted from a cab in front of a leading hotel in the nation's capital. The shots missed him. The second occurred when McFadden ingested food that had been poisoned at a Washington political gathering. His life was saved by a physician friend, who procured a stomach pump and administered emergency treatment.[11] The rescue, however, failed to save the country from its inevitable fate. In 1936, McFadden was voted out of office.

## A PRESIDENTIAL PUPPET

After confiscating the gold from American citizens and purchasing it from foreign sources, the Roosevelt Administration appeared to set the price of the precious metal at random. Every morning at nine o'clock, Henry Morgenthau, the secretary of the treasury, Jesse Jones, the head of the Financial Reconstruction Corporation,[12] and George Warren, the country's leading economic advisor, would meet with FDR over his breakfast of soft-boiled eggs to determine the gold price for that day.

They began at $31.36 an ounce. The next morning this rate was hiked to $31.54, then $31.76 and $31.82. It seemed as though they were acting at random. The morning exercise only served to push the price a little higher than the day before. On November 3, 1933, Roosevelt suggested that the cost of an ounce of gold should be raised twenty-one cents. When the others asked why, the president explained that it was a lucky number, three times seven.[13]

But the pricing was neither arbitrary nor capricious. Roosevelt, throughout his years in the Oval Office, remained manipulated by the money trust. In *FDR: My Exploited Father-in-Law*, Curtis Dall, a syndicate manager for Lehman Brothers who married Anna Eleanor Roosevelt, wrote:

> For a long time I felt that FDR had developed many thoughts and ideas that were his own to benefit this country, the United States. But, he didn't. Most of his thoughts, his political ammunition, as it were,

were carefully manufactured for him in advance by the Council on Foreign Relations-One World Money group. Brilliantly, with great gusto, like a fine piece of artillery, he exploded that prepared "ammunition" in the middle of an unsuspecting target, the American people, and thus paid off and returned his internationalist political support.[14]

"Roosevelt," as Liaquat Ahamed confirmed in *Lords of Finance,* "did not even pretend to grasp the subtleties of international finance."[15] He received direction, in part, from James Warburg, who served as FDR's chief financial advisor. The son of the founder of the Fed, Warburg *fils* would later tell a US Senate subcommittee: "We shall have a one world government, whether we like it or not. The question is only whether world government will be achieved by consent or conquest."[16]

## "THE END OF WESTERN CIVILIZATION"

Under the direction of Warburg, Acheson, and other prominent members of the Council on Foreign Relations, Roosevelt secretly removed America from the gold standard. Informed of this decision, Lewis Douglas, the director of the Bureau of the Budget, proclaimed "the end of Western Civilization."[17] The value of the dollar plummeted, the prices for everyday goods skyrocketed, and unemployed Americans wandered the streets and asked: "Brother, can you spare a dime?" And yet, as the Depression deepened, the Federal Reserve began to purchase the foreign debts of Germany, France, and Great Britain to provide steamer trunks filled with bonds and notes to prop up failing foreign economies, while so much gold continued to pour into the vaults of the Federal Reserve in New York that Roosevelt ordered the creation of Fort Knox, another federal gold depository, in Louisville, Kentucky.[18]

# NOTES

1. "The Founding the Fed," Federal Reserve of New York, n. d., https://www.newyorkfed.org/aboutthefed/history_article.html.

2. Gustav Cassell, *The Downfall of the Gold Standard* (New York: Augustus Kelly, 1966), pp. 118–119.

3. Barry J. Eichengreen, *Gold Fetters: The Gold Standard and the Great Depression* (New York: Oxford University Press, 1992), p. 321.

4. Eric Rauchway, "How Franklin Roosevelt Secretly Ended the Gold Standard," *Bloomberg*, March 21, 2003, https://www.bloomberg.com/view/articles/2013-03-21/how-franklin-roosevelt-secretly-ended-the-gold-standard.

5. *The Public Papers and Addresses of Franklin Roosevelt* (New York: Random House, 1938), p. 112.

6. "Bootleg Gold Ring Smashed in California," *The Evening Independent,* April 13, 1939, https://news.google.com/newspapers?id=gupPAAAAIBAJ&sjid=klQDAAAAIBAJ &pg=5059,3562795&dq=1 3+men+fall+into+trap+of+secret+service+agents+in+ four+cities&hl=en.

7. "Uebersee Finanz Korporation, etc. v. Rosen," Circuit Court of Appeals, Second Circuit, April 6, 1936.

8. Franklin Roosevelt, quoted in Benjamin Anderson, *Economics and Public Welfare* (Indianapolis: Liberty Fund Press, 1949), p. 314.

9. James Bovard, "Money: The Great Gold Robbery," Foundation for Economic Education, June 1, 1999, https://fee.org/articles/money-the-great-gold-robbery/.

10. "Congressman McFadden on the Federal Reserve Corporation," Remarks in Congress, 1934, http://home.hiwaay.net/~becraft/mcfadden.html.

11. Robert Edward Edmondson's account of the two assassination attempts in "Impeachment of the Federal Reserve," *Forbidden History*, October 27, 2015, http://home.hiwaay.net/~becraft/mcfadden.html.

12. The RFC was a federal agency established in 1932 to provide financial support to state and local governments, and loans to banks, railroads, mortgage companies, anted other businesses.

13. Liaquat Ahamed, *Lords of Finance: The Bankers Who Broke the World* (New York: Penguin Books, 2009), p. 472.

14. Curtis B. Dall, *FDR: My Exploited Father-in-Law* (Washington, D.C.: Action Associates, 1970, p. 67.

15. Ahamed, *Lords of Finance*, p. 458.

16. James Warburg, Testimony, *Revision of the United Nations Charter: Hearings before a Senate Subcommittee on Foreign Relations* (Washington, DC: U.S. Government Printing Office, 1950), p. 494.

17. Eric Rauchway, "How Franklin Roosevelt Secretly Ended the Gold Standard," *Bloomberg*, March 21, 2013, https://www.bloomberg.com/view/articles/2013-03-21/how-franklin-roosevelt-secretly-ended-the-gold-standard.

18. "Steel and Stone Fortress to Guard Our Hold," *Popular Mechanics,* December 1935, https://books.google.com/books?id=x98DAAAAMBAJ&pg=PA837&dq=Popular+ Science+1933+plane+%22P opular+Mechanics%22&hl=en&ei=T4wiTpSVB4bns QLQ5ujWAw&sa=X&oi=book_result&ct=result&resnum=9&ved=0CE kQ6AEw CDgK#v=onepage&q&f=true.

# 19

# THE MOTHER BANK

*It must not be felt that these heads of the world's chief central banks were themselves substantive powers in world finance. They were not. Rather, they were the technicians and agents of the dominant investment bankers of their own countries, who had raised them up and were perfectly capable of throwing them down. The substantive financial powers of the world were in the hands of these investment bankers (also called "international" or "merchant" bankers) who remained largely behind the scenes in their own unincorporated private banks. These formed a system of international cooperation and national dominance which was more private, more powerful, and more secret than that of their agents in the central banks. This dominance of investment bankers was based on their control over the flows of credit and investment funds in their own countries and throughout the world. They could dominate the financial and industrial systems of their own countries by their influence over the flow of current funds through bank loans, the discount rate, and the re-discounting of commercial debts; they could dominate governments by their control over current government loans and the play of the international exchanges. Almost all of this power was exercised by the personal influence and prestige of men who had demonstrated their ability in the past to bring off successful financial coups, to keep their word, to remain cool in a crisis, and to share their winning opportunities with their associates. In this system the Rothschilds had been preeminent during much of the nineteenth century, but, at the end of that century, they were being replaced by J. P. Morgan whose central office was in New York, although it was always operated as if it were in London (where it had, indeed, originated as George Peabody and Company in 1838).*

—CARROLL QUIGLEY, *TRAGEDY AND HOPE*

ON MAY 17, 1930, the start of the Great Depression, the Bank of International Settlements (BIS), a private financial institution, opened its headquarters in Basel, Switzerland. The major shareholders were the Bank of England, the Bank of France, the National Bank of Belgium, Reichsbank, the J. P. Morgan Company, the Morgan-owned First National Bank of New York, the Morgan-owned First National Bank of Chicago, and the Bank of Japan, which was controlled by the Iwasaki and Dan families, two of Japan's wealthiest clans. These families, which had formed a partnership with Jack Morgan, owned Mitsubishi and Mitsui, two companies that emerged from the seventeenth-century Shogunates.[1] Eventually, the Federal Reserve would purchase shares in the Basel bank and become the leading player in directing its activities.[2]

**BIS**

On May 17, 1930, the start of the Great Depression, the Bank of International Settlements (BIS), a private financial institution, opened its headquarters in Basel, Switzerland.

The original purpose of the BIS was to facilitate the recurring problem of the war reparations that had been imposed upon Germany. Although buoyed through the roaring twenties by the Dawes Plan, Germany was faced with a new disaster. When Wall Street crashed in 1929, American investors frantically pulled out of their German investments. Foreign capital was no longer flowing into the Rhineland. The country was, once again, broke and unable to come up with the mandated annual payment of $625 million to France and England.

To settle this new crisis, the Young Conference, named in honor of Owen Young, its chairman, was held in Paris in 1929. Young, like Dawes, was closely tied to the Houses of Morgan and Rockefeller and served as the president and chairman of the General Electric Company and RCA. A compromise had been reached at the Young Conference. The Germans would pay $500 million a year for the next thirty-six years to England and France, and $375 million for the next twenty-two years after that to cover the Allies debt to the United States.[3]

The plan was approved at the First Hague Conference. Control of the German economy was returned to Berlin, and a new bank—the Bank of International Settlements—was established to administer the payments.[4] The BIS would serve to "commercialize" the payments, that is, to issue bonds against them; and would act as a lender to the Reichsbank, Germany's central bank, if the German currency weakened and the government found itself unable to make payments.[5]

## ANOTHER MORGAN MONSTER

Among its founders of BIS were J. P. ("Jack") Morgan, Owen D. Young, Thomas Lamont, Seymour Parker Gilbert, Jackson Reynolds, and Gates W. McGarrah. Young had served as chairman of both the Radio Corporation of America (RCA), which was owned by the House of Rockefeller, and General Electric, which was owned by the House of Morgan.[6] Lamont was Morgan's banking partner, an ambassador to the Paris Peace Conference of 1919, and a member of the Jekyll Island Club.[7] Gilbert, another Morgan partner, had served as the undersecretary of treasury for the Harding Administration.[8] Reynolds was a director of the Federal Reserve of New York and a Morgan economic advisor.[9] McGarrah, who became the first President of BIS, was an official at Chase Manhattan, owned by the House of Rockefeller, and the chairman of the Federal Reserve Bank of New York.[10]

## THE CENTRAL BANKER'S CENTRAL BANK

Despite the fact that it was established as a result of the Young Conference, the BIS, in its statement of purpose, made no mention of the mandated reparations. It rather maintained that its objective was "to promote the cooperation of central banks and to provide additional facilities for international operations; and to act as trustees or agents in regard to international financial settlements entrusted to it under agreements with the parties concerned." Throughout its history, the BIS referred to itself not as an institution of settlements, but rather as "the central banker's central bank," a place where bankers could meet in secret away from the prying eyes of the press and the nagging demands of the politicians.[11] The constitution of the BIS was written by Sir Walter Layton, editor of *The Economist*. Layton, in tandem with the Rothschild family, had created a consortium of British businessmen to promote a United Europe.[12]

The concept of a central bank had been advanced during the 1920s by British economist John Maynard Keynes, who called for the creation of a "supranational bank" that would take command of all national economies, set the exchange rate of all currencies, and manage the value of gold according to a standard commodity index.[13] Since the wealth of the world was being confined more and more to eight banking families, the formation of a bank to rule all banks appeared to be inevitable. In 1925, Montagu Norman, governor of the Bank of England, sent the following note to Benjamin Strong, governor of the Federal Reserve Bank of New York: "I rather hope that next summer we may be able to inaugurate a private and eclectic Central Banks 'Club,' small, at first, large in the future."[14]

## A FORTRESS IMPREGNABLE

The headquarters of the BIS was a renovated hotel near the Basel central railroad station, where meetings were held under tight security and complete secrecy. No minutes, agenda, or attendance list was published in any form, and the building became "inviolate," meaning that the Swiss authorities possessed no authority over its premises. Correspondence to the bank was received by diplomatic couriers.[15] Such measures were necessary to safeguard the true purpose of the bank, which Carroll Quigley, one of America's leading economists, described as follows:

The powers of financial capitalism had [a] far-reaching aim, nothing less than to create a world system of financial control in private hands able to dominate the political system of each country and the economy of the world as a whole. This system was to be controlled in a feudalist fashion by the central banks of the world acting in concert, by secret agreements arrived at in frequent private meetings and conferences. The apex of the system was to be the Bank for International Settlements in Basel, Switzerland, a private bank owned and controlled by the world's central banks which were themselves private corporations.[16]

## GAINING GOLD

As soon as it was established, the BIS abandoned its effort to settle the matter of Germany's delinquent payments for reparations and took up the task of stabilizing the world's economies. To accomplish this task, it was allocated control of the gold reserves that were held by its member banks. Gold now flowed out of Japan, Europe, and the United States into Basel.[17]

But the lion's share of the precious metal came from China. During the 1930s, Chiang Kai-shek, chairman of the Nationalist Government, was facing war on two fronts—from Mao Tse-tung's Communist insurgency and imperial Japan. As his government became increasingly unstable, Chiang began to transfer massive amounts of Chinese gold to the BIS and the Federal Reserve. A story concerning the transfer of 203.43 metric tons to Basel and New York was reported by the *New York Times* on February 19, 1937. In 1938, Chiang transported an additional 125,000 metric tons of gold for safekeeping.[18]

## CONTROLLING COUNTRIES

Thanks to the power of this combined wealth, the BIS could save a country from economic disaster or drive it into a tailspin. And its transnational actions could take place without political or governmental interference. In the first six months of 1931, the BIS advanced $10 million to the Bank of Spain to stabilize the peseta; gave a credit of 100 million Austrian schillings to the Bank of Austria, when the Credit Anstaldt bank went belly-up; and advanced $5 million to the Hungarian National Bank, which was experiencing a revenue shortfall.[19]

The activities of the BIS superseded all political, moral, and religious ideologies. The sole concern was the control of capital by the flow of money. Capital represented the resources required to produce goods: coal, oil, iron ore, factories, machine tools, trucks, and roads. Money was the means of purchasing capital.[20] By manipulating the money supply and determining the value of all currencies, the directors of the BIS could hold absolute control over state and society. Personal principles were superfluous. Thus it came to pass that a group of international bankers, including members of the Reichsbank, met each month to manage international economies and to plan a one-world order, while war raged around them. And no one objected when Paul Hechler, a German deputy manager at the BIS, signed his correspondence, "Heil Hitler."[21]

# NOTES

1.  Dean Henderson, "The Federal Reserve Cartel: The Eight Families," *Global Research,* June 1, 2011, http://www.globalresearch.ca/the-federal-reserve-cartel-the-eight-families/25080.

2.  Adam Lebor, *Tower of Basel: The Shadowy History of the Secret Bank That Runs the World* (New York: Public Affairs, 2013), p. 229.

3.  Liaquat Ahamed, *Lords of Finance: The Bankers Who Broke the World* (New York: Penguin Books, 2009), p. 336.

4.  Adam Lebor, *Tower of Basel: The Shadowy History of the Secret Bank that Runs the World* (New York: Public Affairs, 2013), p. 13.

5.  Ahamed, *Lords of Finance*, p. 336.

6.  Devon Douglas-Bowers, "History of the Bank of International Settlements," *Truthout*, October 17, 2015, http://www.truth-out.org/news/item/33234-history-of-the-bank-for-international-settlements.

7.  Nick Carbone and Ishaan Tharoor, "1929: Black Thursday and Thomas William Lamont," *Time*, November 11, 1929, http://newsfeed.time.com/2013/02/27/time-turns-90-all-you-need-to-know-about-modern-history-in-90-cover-stories/slide/1929-black-thursday-and-thomas-william-lamont/.

8.  Seymour Parker Gilbert, Register of Papers, Committee on the History of the Federal reserve System, March 14, 1956, https://fraser.stlouisfed.org/files/docs/historical/brookings/16807_01_0030.pdf.

9.  Kevin Dowd and Richard Henry Timberlake, *Money and the Nation State: The Financial Revolution and the World Monetary Systems* (Oakland, CA: Independent Institute, 1998), p. 152.

10. Douglas-Bowers, "History of the Bank of International Settlements," *Truthout*, October 17, 2015, http://www.truth-out.org/news/item/33234-history-of-the-bank-for-international-settlements.

11. Roger Auboin, "The Bank for International Settlements, 1930-1955," *Essays in International Finance*, Princeton University, May 1955, https://www.princeton. edu/~ies/IES_Essays/E22.pdf.

12. Felix Klos, *Churchill on Europe: The Untold Story of Churchill's European Project* (London: I. B. Tauris, 2016), p. 82.

13. David Felix, *Biography of an Idea: John Maynard Keynes and the General Theory of Employment, Interest, and Money* (Piscataway, New Jersey: Transaction Publishers, 1955), p. 77.

14. Montagu Norman, quoted in Lebor, *Tower of Basel*, p. 3.

15. Tyler Hedge, "Meet the Secretive Group That Rules the World," *Zerohedge*, April 12, 2015, http://www.zerohedge.com/news/2015-04-11/meet-secretive-group-runs-world.

16. Quigley, *Tragedy and Hope*, p. 324.

17. Lebor, *Tower of Basel*, p. 13.

18. Brandon Tubervile, "Secret 'Occult' Economy Coming out of the Shadows," *Blacklisted News*, March 15, 2012, http://blacklistednews.com/?news_id=18463&print=1.

19. Ibid., p. 44.

20. Jason Trennert, "Big Difference between Money and Capital," *Forbes,* August 26, 2011, https://www.forbes.com/sites/greatspeculations/2011/08/26/big-difference-between-money-and-capital/#28a9b4933dc0.

21. Lebor, *Tower of Basel.*, p. 49.

# 20

## THE MOTHER BOXES

*If these bonds were indeed forgeries, it implies that the box itself might be fake as well, which raises the question: why would counterfeiters go through the effort of not only faking $6 trillion in $1 billion bonds but also go through the effort of creating a fake Treaty of Versailles Mother Box?*

*When I try to imagine the mindset of a thief, I cannot bring myself to understand why I would counterfeit two things instead of just one, thus doubling my chances of forgeries being detected.*

*Furthermore, why hide the bonds in makeshift compartments within the Mother Box? It all just makes so little sense I'm not sure what to think at this point.*

—MADISON RUPPERT, *END THE LIE*, 2012

THE SECRET SHIPMENTS OF GOLD would permit the Federal Reserve and the Bank for International Settlements to create an "occult economy." In exchange for the precious metal received for "safekeeping," bonds and notes of astronomical value were issued by the Fed and dispatched to the BIS, which deployed them to central and commercial banks throughout the world to bolster flailing economies. The worth of the bonds and notes was based on the value of the gold that had been blacklisted, that is, removed from the market and stored away from

"This box is officially declared sealed and registered by the Department of Treasury on April 22, 1934, Washington D.C. U.S.A., complete with contents of important bank documents; a lawful instrument for redemption engagement and other commercial purposes."

Turn to page 444 for additional pictures and details regarding the Mother Boxes.

circulation and scrutiny in vaults. This undertaking was conducted with utmost secrecy. If the public discovered how much precious metal actually existed in storage, economic shock waves would reverberate throughout the world, and gold would lose much of its value overnight.[1]

On the eve of the outbreak of the Sino-Japanese War, wealthy Chinese families, including members of the Dragon dynasty, delivered their gold reserves to Chaing Kai Shek, the leader of Nationalist China, for safekeeping in the Federal Reserve. Regular shipments of gold were

$500 million gold certificate.

During the onset of the Sino-Japanese War of 1937, the "Mother Control Boxes" arrived in New York containing gold bullion and global immunity certificates along with microfilm reels and coins; which validated the boxes as official financial instruments. The United States Federal Reserve then collaborated with the Bank for International Settlements (BIS) headquartered In Basel, Switzerland and placed the boxes in the Swiss central banks. The war was funded by both countries and the United States Federal Reserve gave the BIS permission to print their money backed by the US dollar which sparked the secrecy of the Swiss central banking system and the neutrality of Switzerland during the war.

loaded on US Naval ships and transported to the Federal Reserve. When the war broke out, seven tankers fully loaded with gold bars purportedly made their way to New York from China. In exchange for these massive deposits, they received guarantees from the Fed in the form of billion dollar bonds.[2]

## THE MYSTERIOUS MOTHER BOXES
The bonds arrived in sealed bronze and copper containers the size of steamer trunks and became known as "mother boxes." With each mother box were twelve 8.5 × 11-sized "baby" boxes carved out of a single piece of durable wood. They were two and a half inches deep,

making them big enough to store a ream of paper. The baby boxes were faced and sealed with bronze-colored sheet metal for protection.[3] The gold certificates that they contained were in the amount of $100,000, $1 million, $100 million, and even $1 billion.

Since the bonds were sent to Basel, presumably to resolve the issue of war reparations, the "Treaty of Versailles" was engraved in gold letters on each "mother" box, along with the insignia of the United States. The face value of every trunk was $3 trillion. The Federal Reserve notes were placed in silver-colored metal containers the size of attaché cases, with a face value of $50 billion.[4]

## FOR DEPOSIT ONLY

If the gold certificates were cashed, the payout could have crashed the US economy, which had nowhere near enough money to honor them. The plan was to keep the bonds and notes on deposit, along with the gold that was issued against them. Their total value was not derived from a vacuum. It was based on the total amount that had been squirreled away by countries and central banks in the BIS system.[5]

This extraordinary deployment of gold certificates from the Federal Reserve served to establish the dollar as the currency for international exchange and to fortify the United States as the economic bedrock of a world ravaged by war and depression. Careful measures were undertaken to protect the certificates. The bonds, boxes, and chests contained deliberate, glaring errors in spelling and grammar so that they would be dismissed as fake by almost any public official or banking authority who examined them.[6]

## HARD EVIDENCE

The truth about the boxes began to come out of the shadows at the dawn of the twenty-first century. In January 2000, Chris Estrella, a Filipino social worker, led a troop of five porters out of a Mindanao jungle with a weather-beaten iron-and-leather box crammed with $25 billion of US government bearer bonds. The elders of the Umayamnon tribe had informed him that an American plane crashed in a river near their village in the 1930s. The river dried up in the 1990s, and the natives went into the plane and found twelve boxes that contained $300 billion in bonds. Each box was emblazoned with the Great Seal of the United States and the words "Federal Reserved Bond." They rested on top of a stack of certificates purporting to have been issued by the Federal Reserve Bank of Atlanta in 1934 and to be redeemable in gold bullion.[7] The notes bore the signature of then–treasury secretary, Henry Morgenthau. The story received coverage from the mainstream press, including Bloomberg News.

On June 16, 2009, Mitsuyoshi Watanabe and Akihiko Yamaguchi, two Japanese couriers for the Chinese Dragon Family, were arrested in Italy with a stack of 1934 US Treasury bearer bonds with a face value of $134 billion. They had recently arrived in Ponte Chiasso, a small town near the Swiss border, from the same area of the Philippines where Chris Estrella had found the iron-and-leather box. Watanabe and Yamaguchi were about to board a train headed for the Bank of International Settlements in Basel. The bonds were located in the false bottom of one of their suitcases. The Guardia di Finanza (Italy's financial police) called upon Robert Gombar, head of the US Secret Service in Italy, to authenticate the certificates, which bore the signature of Henry Morganthau Jr. and a metal plate stating "Dallas Federal Reserve Bank." Gombar deemed them to be fraudulent and said: "There's no such thing as a $500 million Treasury bond. It's like counterfeiting a $3 bill, something that doesn't exist." Since the Italian authorities lacked evidence that the couriers were intent on selling the bonds, the case was closed, and the suspects were released.[8] But news later surfaced about their employer. The Dragon Family had decided to cash in their bonds.

## A TWISTED TALE

The authorities purportedly refused to release the bonds to the couriers. Instead, they turned them over to Italian Prime Minister Silvio Berlusconi, who redeemed them for cash. Half of the cash, according to this account, was turned over to the Federal Reserve in New York, and the redeemed bonds were placed in storage in a program operated by the United Nations.[9]

At this point, the curious tale becomes even more twisted. Yamaguchi, one of the couriers, now contacted Irish-American businessman Neil Keenan on behalf of the Dragons and commissioned him to liquidate another box of 1934 Federal Reserve bonds with a face value of $124.5 billion for cash. This task purportedly brought Keenan in contact with Daniele Dal Bosco, a Vatican banker, who said that he could provide adequate financial redemption. The deal seemed good to Keenan since Dal Bosco and the Vatican Bank appeared to possess the means to effect a settlement. But after Keenan turned over the securities to Dal Bosco, the Vatican banker engaged in an attempt to sell them in the global marketplace "through stealth, conversion and bribery."[10]

At his wit's end, Keenan on November 23, 2011, filed a lawsuit with the US District Court in the Southern District of New York. The lawsuit targets the Federal Reserve for refusing to honor its financial commitment and names as defendants Daniele Dal Bosco, the Office of International Treasury Control, the United Nations, the Italian Republic, the Guardia di Finanza, Silvio Berlusconi, and the World Economic Forum.[11]

## MORE MATERIAL EVIDENCE

At the same time the Japanese couriers were taken into custody, a story crossed the news wires from Barcelona that $1.64 trillion of Federal Reserve notes and bonds, dated 1934, had been seized by Spanish officials. The securities, which were owned by two unidentified businessmen, were lodged within a bronze strong box, which had been engraved with the name of the Dallas Federal Reserve Bank. They had been shipped to Barcelona from the Philippines. The US gold certificates came in bundles bearing J. P. Morgan Chase metal bands.[12]

On February 15, 2012, the Guardia di Finanza collared eight men with ties to organized crime who were involved in an alleged scheme to purchase a large quantity of plutonium from the black market in Nigeria with 1934 US Treasury bearer bonds. While arrests were made in the southern Italian region of Basilicata, the bonds were seized in Zurich. The suspects testified that the bonds, with a face value of $6 trillion, came from Hong Kong and had been issued to Chiang Kai-shek as security for the large shipments of gold he had delivered to the Federal Reserve in New York for safekeeping.[13] In addition to the bonds, which were packed within special metal compartments of a large copper-colored case, bearing a plate with the inscription "Chicago: Federal Reserve System," the Italian police also discovered a copy of the Treaty of Versailles. In an interview with the *New York Times*, Giovanni Colangelo, the chief prosecutor in the case, said: "We had heard that they weighed a lot but, frankly, we didn't expect that kind of material."[14]

## THE GOLD AND 9/11

According to Benjamin Fulford, former Asia-Pacific bureau chief for *Forbes* magazine, and David Wilcox of the website *Divine Cosmos*, the Dragon family filed a lawsuit at the International World Court in The Hague in 1998. The trial took place behind closed doors. The decision of the court was ruled in favor of the Dragons, and the Federal Reserve Bank became obligated to return 200,000 tons of gold by September 12, 2001, the day after 9/11. The gold was purportedly stored in the vaults in the basement of the World Trade Centre and disappeared after the attack of 9/11. Cantor Fitzgerald Securities, the shipping company in the possession of the insurance and transportation documents, were located in WTC 1. All 600 employees of Cantor Fitzgerald were killed, and all documents vanished with the rubble. The Treasury Police was located in WTC 7. When this building collapsed, their documents were reduced to ashes. The message to the Dragon family was loud and clear: the Fed would neither honor its notes and bonds nor return the gold that had been delivered to it during the Second Sino-Japanese War.[15]

## ANOTHER LAWSUIT

Another lawsuit involving the 1934 certificates was filed by Joseph Riad on December 22, 2011, in the Eastern District of the US Federal Court in Philadelphia. In the suit, Riad claimed that the Department of Homeland Security had seized fifteen $1 billion Federal Reserve bonds from 1934 that he had stashed away in several banks. He said that he had obtained the bonds as collateral for loans he had provided to the South African government. The case merited widespread media attention since Riad possessed written proof that the bonds were authentic from Kermit Harmon, a Security Director for the Federal Reserve System. This proof was attached to the lawsuit as an exhibit.[16] Riad produced additional statements of authenticity from A. J. Obara, a bronze metal expert who verified the date of the boxes in which the bonds were contained; Franklin Noll, a consultant with the Bureau of Public Debt with an expertise in the history of government-issued, high denomination bonds; and Stuart Eizenstat, a former deputy security director of the US Treasury Department.[17]

Riad said that he met with agents from the Department of Homeland Security, who claimed to possess the authority to redeem the fifteen bonds. The plaintiff, believing he had struck pay dirt, gave them the bonds and sat back thinking that the check would be in the mail. A week later, he was contacted by the officials who said that the bonds were fake and that they were duty-bound to destroy them. After making several attempts to secure the return of the securities, Riad filed the suit, demanding payment of $15 billion. The case was dismissed with prejudice by US District Judge Mary A. McLaughlin, not on its merits but rather because it was time-barred under the Federal Tort Claims Act. Riad hadn't filed the suit within six months of the date he had received notice that the bonds were being destroyed.[18]

With the creation of an occult economy, a cabal of international bankers and businessmen gained control of the world's wealth, not in the form of paper but of gold—vast gold reserves almost beyond imagination. With such wealth, they could cause vast armies to form, governments to topple, and economies to crash. They could control elections, manipulate the media, and manufacture the news. They could form public opinion, create consensus, and reshape beliefs. In 1938, as the world stood on the brink of war, few Americans had heard of a New World Order, and fewer still had realized that it already had come into existence.

# NOTES

1. David Wilcox, "Financial Tyranny: Defeating the Greatest Cover-Up of All Time," *Divine Cosmos*, January 13, 2013, http://www.divinecosmos.com/start-here/davids-blog/1023-financial-tyranny?start=3.

2. Ella Ster, "The Trillion Dollar Lawsuit," *Ellastar*, April 15, 2016, http://www.ellaster.nl/2016/04/15/the-trillion-dollar-lawsuit/.

3. Wilcox, "Financial Tyranny."

4. Ibid.

5. Ibid.

6. Ibid.

7. A Craig Copetas, "No One Knows the Truth about $300b Bonds from Alleged Plane Crash," *Bloomberg News*, January 19, 2012.

8. Ibid.

9. David Wilcox, "Confirmed: The Trillion Dollar Lawsuit That Could End Financial Tyranny," *Divine Cosmos,* December 12, 2011, http://divinecosmos.com/start-here/davids-blog/995-lawsuit-end-tyranny.

10. Keenan lawsuit, quoted in Brandon Turbeville, "Unprecedented Lawsuit Reveals Bizarre Worldwide Banking Connections," *Activist Post*, December 9, 2011, http://www.activistpost.com/2011/12/unprecedented-lawsuit-reveals-bizarre.html.

11. Michael Henry Dunn, "A Brief History of the Global Collateral Accounts and Keenan's Efforts to Free Them," *Group K*, June 8, 2013, http://neilkeenan.com/sample-page/.

12. Wilcox, "Financial Tyranny."

13. Rachel Donadio, "Brother, Can You Spare $6 Trillion?" *New York Times*, February 17, 2012, http://www.nytimes.com/2012/02/18/world/europe/italy-arrests-8-in-fake-us-treasury-bonds-scam.html

14. Giovanni Colangelo, quoted in Ibid.

15. Wilcox, "Confirmed."

16. Brandon Tubeville, "Massive New Lawsuit Filed against U.S. Federal Government in Bond Theft Scheme," *Activist Post*, January 2, 2012, http://www.activistpost.com/2012/01/massive-new-lawsuit-filed-against-us.html.

17. Ibid.

18. "Pennsylvania Man Who Sued U.S. Government for $15 Billion for Failure to Return Federal Reserve Bonds Has Complaint Dismissed," *Penn Record*, n.d., http://pennrecord.com/stories/510552024-pa-man-who-sued-u-s-govt-for-15-billion-for-failure-to-return-federal-reserve-bonds-has-complaint-dismissed.

# PART SIX

# THE BREAKING OF NATIONS

*"I believe that if the people of this nation fully understood what Congress has done to them over the last forty-nine years, they would move on Washington; they would not wait for an election. . . . It adds up to a preconceived plan to destroy the economic and social independence of the United States!"*

—GEORGE W. MALONE, US SENATOR (NEVADA),

SPEAKING BEFORE CONGRESS IN 1957.

*"The strongest reason for the people to retain the right to keep and bear arms is, as a last resort, to protect themselves against tyranny in government."*

—THOMAS JEFFERSON

*Winston Churchill said this back in 1920: "From the days of Spartacus-Weishaupt to those of Karl Marx, to those of Trotsky, Bela Kun, Rosa Luxembourg, and Emma Goldman, this worldwide conspiracy for the overthrow of civilization and for the reconstitution of society on the basis of arrested development, of envious malevolence and impossible equality, has been steadily growing. It played a definitely recognizable role in the tragedy of the French Revolution. It has been the mainspring of every subversive movement during the nineteenth century, and now at last this band of extraordinary personalities from the underworld of the great cities of Europe and America have gripped the Russian people by the hair of their heads, and have become practically the undisputed masters of that enormous empire."*

# 21

# THE PROBLEM WITH HITLER

*Break down the thralldom of interest is our war cry! What do we mean by the thralldom of interest? The landowner is under this thralldom, who has to raise loans to finance his farming operations, loans at such a high rate as almost to eat up the results of his labor, or who is forced to make debts and to drag the mortgages after him like so much lead. So is the worker, producing in shops and factories for a pittance, whilst the shareholder draws dividends and bonuses that he has not worked for. So is the earning middle class, whose work goes almost entirely to pay the interest on bank overdrafts.*

*Thralldom of interest is the real expression for the antagonisms, capital versus labor, blood versus money, creative work versus exploitation. The necessity of breaking this thralldom is of such vast importance that on it depends the hope of recovering happiness, prosperity, and civilization throughout the world.*

—GOTTFRIED FEDER (ADOLF HITLER'S MENTOR),
THE PROGRAM OF THE SOCIALIST GERMAN WORKERS PARTY

ON SEPTEMBER 1, 1939, Hitler invaded Poland and initiated World War II. This act of alleged "unprovoked aggression" violated a "war guarantee" that British Prime Minister Neville Chamberlain had given to a junta of Polish colonels.[1] The guarantee, which was issued several months before the invasion, proclaimed that Britain would deploy all

**Adolf Hitler**
Within his death camps, Hitler stands accused of exterminating over 6 million Jews, Gypsies, and people with physical disabilities.

of its military power to protect Polish independence. Why Chamberlain offered such a guarantee remains quizzical. Britain possessed no vital interest in Poland or Eastern Europe and had drafted no plan to ward off the *Wehrmacht* (the unified armed forces of Nazi Germany). Six months after Warsaw received its guarantee, not one British bomb or bullet had been delivered to Poland, no financial credit had been extended to Warsaw by the Bank of England, and no effort was made to dispatch a British military unit to Eastern Europe.[2]

What's more, Poland was far from a freedom-loving democracy that merited Britain's protection. Its ruling junta already had crawled into bed with Hitler by collaborating in the carving up of Czechoslovakia and annexing, with the Fuhrer's consent, the territory of Teschen, where thousands of Poles lived.[3] And verification that the guarantee did not stem from any altruistic concern came on September 17 when Britain neglected to declare war on Stalin for invading and occupying eastern Poland.

## POLISH PROVOCATION

The Nazi invasion had not been unprovoked. It had been caused by the Treaty of Versailles, which stripped Germany of its territorial holdings, including the port city of Danzig, which was handed over to Poland. The population of Danzig at the time of the invasion was 97 percent German. They turned in desperation to the Fuhrer for reunion with their countrymen. They had been subjected to ongoing attacks of wanton savagery in which 58,000 ethnic Germans were murdered by the ruling Polish junta.[4] Hitler reached out to Warsaw with the Marienwerder proposals, which offered these terms:

1. Retention of the existing 1919 borders between Poland and Germany as determined by the Treaty of Versailles.

2. The return of Danzig to Germany.

3. Construction by the Third Reich of a sixty-mile autobahn and railway that would link West and East Prussia, from Schonlanke to Marienwerder.

4. An exchange of German and Polish populations.

Regarding the proposals, Nevile Henderson, the British ambassador to Berlin, wrote: "I must admit that I regard Hitler's proposals as a fair basis of negotiation and in my innermost heart I regard the Poles as extremely unwise to make enemies of Germany and as dangerous allies for us. . . . I may be wrong but I am personally convinced that there can be no permanent peace in Europe until Danzig has reverted to Germany. The Poles cannot be masters of 400,000 Germans in Danzig—ergo Germany must be."[5] The Poles, however, turn down every effort from Hitler to negotiate a settlement.[6]

## CHURCHILL'S WAR CRY

But British officials insisted that the guarantee be honored, even though, as Winston Churchill pointed out, it "must surely lead to the slaughter of tens of millions of people." Despite the fact that the people of Danzig had cried out for deliverance, Churchill insisted that war must be waged. He wrote:

> If you will not fight for the right when you can easily win without bloodshed; if you will not fight when your victory will be sure and not too costly; you may come to the moment when you have to fight with all the odds against you and only a precarious chance of survival. There may even be a worse case. You may have to fight when there is no hope of victory, because it is better to perish than to live as slaves.[7]

Churchill's words remain problematic. Hitler had issued no threats against England, and the British people were not faced with Nazi enslavement. And his statement, as stirring as it may be, neglected to explain why it suddenly had become Britain's duty to fight and die for Poland.[8]

## PRECIOUS BRITISH BLOOD

What's more, it remains highly doubtful that Hitler wanted to wage war with Britain. The day before he ordered his storm troopers to invade the Polish Corridor, he issued this directive:

> The responsibility for the opening of hostilities in the West should rest unequivocally with England and France. . . . The German land frontier in the West is not to be crossed at any point without my express consent. The same applies to war-like actions at sea or any which may be interpreted as such. . . . Defensive measures on the part of the Air Force should at first be exclusively confined to the warding-off of enemy air attacks on the frontier of the Reich.[9]

German historian Andreas Hillgruber writes: "The European war that came on September 3 was as incomprehensible as it was contrary to his [Hitler's] aims."[10]

Proof of Hitler's desire not to create "an irreparable breach" between England and Germany came when he gave a "stop order" to his armored units that were closing in on the British forces stranded on the beach of Dunkirk. "The blood of every single Englishman is too valuable to be shed," he told his friend Frau Gerhardine Troost. "Our two people belong together racially and traditionally—this is and always has been my aim even if our generals can't grasp it."[11] Throughout the war, Hitler made at least twenty-eight attempts to establish unconditional peace with Britain. They were all refused.[12]

## HITLER'S RUSSIAN OBSESSION

Nor was Hitler intent upon world conquest. His dreams of conquest remained fixed not on the West but the East, and most particularly, Russia. In *Mein Kampf,* published in 1926, Hitler wrote:

> We, National Socialists, consciously draw a line beneath the foreign policy tendency of the pre-War period. We take up where we broke off six hundred years ago. We stop the endless German movement to the south and west of Europe, and turn our gaze on the land in the east. At long last we break off the colonial and commercial policy of the pre-War period, and shift to the soil policy of the future.
>
> If we speak of soil in Europe today, we can primarily have in mind only Russia and her vassal border states.[13]

Hitler's overriding aim was the conquest of Soviet Russia, since he viewed Jews and Bolsheviks as one and the same enemy. Hillgruber writes: "The conquest of European Russia . . . was for Hitler inextricably linked with the extermination of the 'bacilli,' the Jews. In his conception they had gained dominance over Russia with the Bolshevik Revolution. Russia thereby became the center from which a global danger radiated, particularly threatening to the Aryan race and its Germanic core."[14]

Hitler was a maniacal despot who sent millions of innocent civilians to death camps. Within his death camps, the Fuhrer of the Third Reich stands accused of exterminating over 6 million Jews, Gypsies, and people with physical disabilities.[15] But these crimes came to light when Nazi Germany was reduced to rubble and were not the reason why the Allied nations opted to go to war against him.

## THE REASON FOR WAR

Through the haze of history, one can discern that a key reason for the outbreak of World War II was financial. On January 7, 1939, Hjalmar Schacht, the president of the Reichsbank (Germany's central bank), which remained bound to the House of Rothschild and the money cartel, refused to provide a loan of three billion *Reichsmarks* to the German government unless Hitler complied with the following demands:

1. The Reich must spend only the amount covered by taxes.

2. Full financial control of the government must be placed with the Ministry of Finance, which was headed by Schacht.

3. Price and wage control must be set in place.

The use of money and investment markets must remain at the sole discretion of the Reichsbank.[16]

Schacht concluded his memo, which contained his list of demands, with this statement: "We shall be happy to do our best to collaborate with all future goals, but for now the time has come to call a halt."[17]

By making these demands, Schacht sought to collapse the German economy, which had experienced astronomical growth under Hitler's rule. From 1933 to 1939, Germany's Gross National Product increased by 100 percent. Imports rose by 31 percent and exports by 20.4 percent. Unemployment, which stood at 30.1 percent in 1933, fell to almost zero in 1939.

National income climbed by 43.8 percent. Education at Germany's technical schools and colleges was free, and every German received free medical care. Strange to say, this economic renaissance was not caused by armament production. Germany's military expenditure in 1935–1936 was less than 11 percent of the national income. The rate of military spending under Hitler, according to British historian A. J. P. Taylor, offers "decisive proof" that Hitler was "not contemplating general war, and probably not intending war at all."[18]

Hitler responded to Schacht's demands by ousting him from office and by making the Reichsbank totally subordinate to the sovereignty of the state. By transforming the central bank into a national bank, Hitler could produce paper money that he could loan without interest to the Nazi government and its citizens. The worth of the money was based entirely upon its designated worth by the state rather than a gold standard.

Article 3 of the new Reichsbank law decreed that the bank should be renamed *Deutsche Reichsbank* and that it would be directed and managed by the Fuhrer and the Reichschancellor.[19] In *A History of Central Banking,* economist Stephen Mitford Goodson writes: "It was this event which triggered World War II—the realization by the Rothschilds that universal replication of Germany's usury-free state banking system would permanently destroy their evil financial empire."[20]

## PLOTTING AMERICA'S INVOLVEMENT

Within two weeks of the outbreak of war in Europe, Walter Mallory, the executive director of the CFR, and Hamilton Fish, the editor of the CFR's periodical *Foreign Affairs,* met in Washington with Assistant Secretary of State George Messersmith, another CFR member, to set up a study group that could develop a wartime strategy for the United States. The group, which met in secret, became known as the War and Peace Studies Project.[21]

One of the tasks of the War and Peace Studies Project was to develop propaganda that would cause the American people to shed their isolationism and to support participation in the European War "to make the world safe for democracy." Another task was to lay the groundwork for a new system of global government to replace the ill-fated League of Nations. This system would become the United Nations.

The group held 362 meetings and prepared 682 papers for the State Department.[22] These papers were received by the Roosevelt Administration as Holy Writ. Ironically, while this work was taking place behind closed doors, FDR in his campaign for reelection, was making this campaign pledge to the American public: "I have said this before, but I shall say it again and again and again: Your boys are not going to be sent into any foreign wars."[23]

Why were war plans developed two years before the attack on Pearl Harbor when America was not threatened by any foreign enemy? Why would the Council on Foreign Relations be driven to usurp complete control of the US State Department? Who was manipulating these actions? Why would the United States be willing to sacrifice the lives of its sons for a struggle in which it possessed no vested interest?

The answer is lodged in the fact that the War and Studies Project was funded entirely by the House of Rockefeller, which had emerged as a principal power not only in the CFR but also the international money cartel. After creating the Bank of International Settlements and touching its goal of global economy hegemony, the cartel was not willing to sacrifice the Reichsbank and its control of the German economy to an upstart like Adolf Hitler without raising one hell of a ruckus. The fact that this cartel was able in 1940 to manipulate US foreign policy, the White House, and the national media provides demonstrable proof that Uncle Sam already was on his deathbed.

# NOTES

1. Ron Bontekoe, *The Nature of Dignity* (New York: Rowman and Littlefield, 2008), p. 175.
2. Pat Buchanan, *Churchill, Hitler, and the Unnecessary War: How Britain Lost Its Empire and the West Lost the World* (New York: Three Rivers Press, 2008), p. 297.
3. Vanessa Cortez, "Before Hitler Invaded Poland—Poland Invaded Czechoslovakia," *Weekly Universe*, June 8, 2003, http://www.weeklyuniverse.com/2003/poland.htm.
4. Stephen Mitford Goodson, *A History of Central Banking and the Enslavement of Mankind* (London: Black House, 2014), p. 128.
5. Nevile Henderson, quoted in Simon Newman, *March, 1939: The British Government to Poland* (Oxford: Clarendon Press, 1976), p. 214.
6. Goodson, *A History of Central Banking*, p. 129.
7. Winston Churchill, *The Gathering Storm* (New York: Houghton Mifflin, 1948), p. 347.
8. Buchanan, *Churchill, Hitler and the Unnecessary War*, p. 259.
9. Hitler, quoted in Ibid., p. 295.
10. Andreas Hillgruber, *Germany and the Two World Wars* (Cambridge, Mass.: Harvard University Press, 1981), p. 203.
11. Hitler, quoted in John Toland, *Adolf Hitler* (New York: Doubleday, 1976), p. 611.
12. Goodson, *A History of Central Banking*, p. 129.
13. Hitler, quoted in Buchanan, *Churchill, Hitler, and the Unnecessary War*, p. 323.
14. Hillgruber, *Germany and the Two World Wars*, pp. 51–52.
15. Polash Ghosh, "How Many People Did Joseph Stalin Kill?" *International Business Times*, March 5, 2013, http://www.ibtimes.com/how-many-people-did-joseph-stalin-kill-1111789
16. E. N. Peterson, *Hjalmar Schacht: For and against Hitler: A Political Economic Study of Germany, 1923-1945* (Boston: Christopher Publishing House, 1954), p. 179.
17. Schacht, quoted in Goodson, *A History of Central Banking*, p. 125.
18. A. J. P. Taylor, *The Origins of the Second World War* (London: Hamish Hamilton, 1961), p. 218.
19. David Marsh, *The Bundesbank: The Bank That Rules Europe* (London: William Heinemann, Ltd., 1992), p. 300.
20. Goodson, *A History of Central Banking*, p. 128.
21. James Perloff, *The Shadows of Power: The Council on Foreign Relations and the American Decline* (Appleton, Wisconsin: Western Islands, 2005), p. 64.
22. Ibid.
23. FDR, quoted in G. Vance Smith and Tom Gow, *Masters of Deception: The Rise of the Council on Foreign Relations* (Colorado Springs, CO: Freedom First Society, 2012), p. 52.

# 22

## BAITING NAZIS AND "NIPS"

*By Pearl Harbor, Hitler was overextended and blocked at the Channel and Atlantic by the Royal Air Force and Navy, and at Moscow and Leningrad by the Red Army. By 1942, he was finished in Africa. The idea that Hitler, with no surface navy or fleet of transport ships, no landing craft or seamen who had even served on a carrier, could construct in Africa or the Canary Islands ships to threaten the U.S., on the other side of an ocean the U.S. and British navies had ruled since Trafalgar is a proposition too absurd to require rebuttal.*
—PAT BUCHANAN, "AN UNNECESSARY WAR?" 1999

THERE WAS MUCH FOR THE MONEY CARTEL TO GAIN from the second global war. War broke down borders; caused mass migrations, and gave rise to new countries. It promulgated diversity and undermined the racial structures of existing nations. This benefit of war was essential for the creation of a global government. Race constituted the major component of nationalism. John Jay, coauthor of the *Federalist Papers*, recognized this fact by claiming in 1787, two years before the drafting of the Constitution, that America was a "band of brethren," who shared a common language, faith, culture, and ancestry. He wrote:

I have often taken notice that Providence has been pleased to give this one connected country to one united people—a people descended from the same ancestors, speaking the same language, professing the same religion, attached to the same principles of government, very similar in manners and customs, and, who, by their joint counsels, arms, and efforts, fighting side by side throughout a long and bloody war, have nobly established their general liberty and independence.[1]

For the money cartel, any nation that sought to safeguard the purity of its race must be obliterated. Otherwise, the New World Order could not come into being.

Economically, war produced other benefits for the cartel, including the floating of massive loans for armaments, the availability of the natural resources of vanquished countries, and the establishment of new central banks under the Bank of International Settlements.

## THE CASE OF TYLER KENT

Since economic hegemony was at stake, it was essential to bring the United States into the European conflict. This task was formidable since America possessed no vital interest in the European war, and the American people remained isolationists, who opted to remain free from all foreign entanglements. In 1940, a Gallup poll showed that 83 percent of Americans opposed any intervention in the war against Hitler.[2]

While offering public assurance that America would not become involved in the "foreign war," Roosevelt was privately corresponding with Churchill to concoct a means to drag America into the war. The secret dispatches between the two leaders were discovered by Tyler Kent, a code clerk at the American embassy in London. Kent tried to smuggle these dispatches out of the embassy in order to warn the American people, but he was caught and confined to a British prison for the remainder of the war. After the war, he was deported to the United States, where he became the subject of ongoing FBI investigations.[3]

## THE HOPKINS VISIT

Harry Hopkins, Roosevelt's closest advisor, met with Churchill at 10 Downing Street in January 1941 to offer this assurance: "I came here to see how we can defeat that fellow Hitler. The President is determined that we shall win the war together. Make no mistake about it. He has sent me here to tell you that at all costs and by all means he will carry you through, no matter what happens."[4] Following the Hopkins visit, American and British military began to hold secret meetings to concoct ways to bring the United States into the war.[5] Robert Sherwood, FDR's biographer and admirer, said: "If the isolationists had known the full extent of the secret alliance between the United States and Britain, their demands for the President's impeachment would have rumbled like thunder through the land."[6]

## FAILURE TO RESPOND

An incident had to be staged that was even more horrific than the sinking of the *Lusitania*. Thus the provocation began. At the instigation of the Century Group and the War and Peace Studies Project, both CFR organizations, the Roosevelt Administration shipped fifty destroyers to Great Britain to beef up the British fleet. He also sent millions of rounds of ammunition to England on freighters that sailed directly into the war zone. To add to the antagonism, FDR ordered the closing of all German consulates so that German officials would have no means of protesting the ongoing aid to Britain. In a final attempt to instigate a German attack, Roosevelt ordered the occupation of Iceland and used this strategic location to deploy depth-charges against German U-boats.[7] But Hitler refused to retaliate, knowing that America's entry in the war would tip the scales against him.

## ROOSEVELT'S "SECRET MAP"

On October 27, 1941, FDR announced the following to the nation in his Navy Day Address: "Hitler has often protested that his plans for conquest do not extend across the Atlantic Ocean. . . I have in my possession a secret map, made in Germany by Hitler's government. . .

It is a map of South America as Hitler proposes to reorganize it. The geographical experts of Berlin, however, have ruthlessly obliterated all the existing boundary lines . . . bringing the whole continent under their domination. This map makes clear the Nazi design not only against South America but against the United States as well."[8]

The president claimed he had another secret terrifying document from Hitler's government in his possession. "It is," he said, "a plan to abolish all existing religions—Protestant, Catholic, Mohammedan, Hindu, Buddhist and Jewish alike. . . . In the place of the churches of our civilization, there is to be set up an international Nazi Church. In the place of the Bible, the words of 'Mein Kampf' will be imposed and enforced as Holy Writ. And in place of the cross of Christ will be put two symbols: the swastika and the naked sword. . . . A god of blood and iron will take the place of the God of love and mercy."[9]

## "THE SHOOTING HAS STARTED"

All those who tuned into this address were horrified. Few knew that the documents were forgeries by William Stephenson and other British agents in New York who were operating under orders from Prime Minister Winston Churchill.[10] FDR concluded his address by describing two German submarine attacks on US destroyers Greer and Kearny, the latter of which had been torpedoed with a loss of eleven American lives. "We have wished to avoid shooting," the president said. "But the shooting has started. And history has recorded who fired the first shot." The truth was the two destroyers had been tracking German subs for British planes by dropping depth charges.[11]

The German government categorically rejected FDR's accusations. The purported secret documents, it declared in an official statement, were "forgeries of the crudest and most brazen kind." Furthermore, the statement maintained: "The allegations of a conquest of South America by Germany and an elimination of the religions of the churches in the world and their replacement by a National Socialist church are so non-sensical and absurd that it is superfluous for the Reich government to discuss them." In a separate statement, German propaganda minister Josef Goebbels said that Roosevelt's "absurd accusations" were part of a "grand swindle" designed to "whip up American public opinion."[12]

The day after the address, a reporter at a press conference asked the president for a copy of the "secret map" document. Roosevelt declined to release it but insisted that the map had come from "a source which is undoubtedly reliable."[13]

## PRODDING THE TIGER

Since Hitler refused to respond to the provocation, the Century Group and the War and Peace Studies Project, under the guidance of the House of Rockefeller, looked to Japan to mount an attack against the United States. The choice was prudent since Japan, on September 27, 1940, had signed the Tripartite Pact with Germany and Italy, which bound the three nations to the following terms:

ARTICLE 1. Japan recognizes and respects the leadership of Germany and Italy in the establishment of a new order in Europe.

ARTICLE 2. Germany and Italy recognize and respect the leadership of Japan in the establishment of a new order in Greater East Asia.

ARTICLE 3. Japan, Germany, and Italy agree to cooperate in their efforts on aforesaid lines. They further undertake to assist one another with all political, economic and military means if one of the Contracting Powers is attacked by a Power at present not involved in the European War or in the Japanese-Chinese conflict.

ARTICLE 4. With a view to implementing the present pact, joint technical commissions, to be appointed by the respective Governments of Japan, Germany and Italy, will meet without delay.

ARTICLE 5. Japan, Germany and Italy affirm that the above agreement affects in no way the political status existing at present between each of the three Contracting Powers and Soviet Russia.

ARTICLE 6. The present pact shall become valid immediately upon signature and shall remain in force ten years from the date on which it becomes effective. In due time, before the expiration of said term, the High Contracting Parties shall, at the request of any one of them, enter into negotiations for its renewal.[14]

Thanks to this pact, America could gain entry into the European war by baiting the Japanese into launching an attack against a US territory, such as Hawaii. Several weeks after the signing of the Tripartite Pact, Henry L. Stimson, FDR's Secretary of War and a CFR patriarch, met with the president and wrote the following words in his diary: "We face the delicate question of the diplomatic fencing to be done as to be sure Japan is put in the wrong and makes the first bad move. . . .The question was how we should maneuver them [the Japanese] into the position of firing the first shot."[15]

## ECONOMIC WARFARE

The matter of positioning the Japanese to take the first shot was taken up by the War and Peace Studies Commission, which recommended the imposition of a crippling trade embargo on Japan. In July 1941, FDR imposed a trade embargo of oil, rubber, scrap metal, and steel to Japan. The reason for this action, Roosevelt explained, was Japan's occupation of French Indo-China. No one questioned this action even though the French had permitted the occupation.[16] The British government and the Dutch government in exile followed suit by placing their own oil embargos on Japan. As a result, Japan lost access to three-fourths of its overseas trade and 88 percent of its imported oil.[17]

More sanctions followed. FDR froze all of Japan's financial assets in the United States and closed the Panama Canal to Japanese shipping. On July 31, 1941, Japan's Foreign Minister Teijiro Toyoda communicated to Kichisaburo Nomura, Japan's ambassador to the United States the following message: "Commercial and economic relations between Japan and third countries, led by England and the United States, are gradually becoming so horribly strained that we cannot endure it much

longer. Consequently, our Empire, to save its very life, must take measures to secure the raw materials of the South Seas."[18]

## THE DAY OF INFAMY

By the fall of 1941, US military intelligence had broken the radio code
that Tokyo used to communicate with its embassies. The decoded
intercepts made the US War Department aware that Japanese spies in
Hawaii were informing Tokyo of the locations of American warships
docked in Pearl Harbor and the suggested date of Sunday, December
7th for an attack. This information was passed on to the president,
Secretary Stimson, and General George Marshall, the army chief of
staff. By December 6th, the War Department was aware that Japanese
aircraft carriers had moved within 400 miles of Honolulu.[19]

Despite their awareness that an attack was imminent, neither FDR
nor his War Department issued an alert to Admiral Husband Kimmel
and General Walter C. Short, the leading US military commanders in
Hawaii. Rather than making an attempt to save lives, Roosevelt and
Marshall stripped Hawaii of most of its defenses immediately before the
raid, and allotted the island only one-third of the surveillance planes
necessary to detect incoming enemy movement. The attack left two
thousand Americans dead and eighteen naval vessels sunk or heavily
damaged.[20] The true perpetrators of the day of infamy were not in Japan
but in Washington, DC.

Few presidents have contributed more to the demise of Uncle Sam
than Franklin Delano Roosevelt. Thanks to his efforts, the self-reliant
land of Washington, Jefferson, Jackson, Lincoln, and Teddy Roosevelt
(FDR's distant cousin) would become a welfare state, integral matters
of national government would be placed in the hands of a global agency,
and economic control of the country would be relinquished to the Bank
of International Settlements, the International Monetary Fund, and the
World Bank. The good war was not so good. It resulted in the annihila-
tion of tens of millions of innocent civilians by Allied and Axis forces,
the rise of communism as a far greater threat than National Socialism,

the end of American isolationism, the expenditure of billions of US taxpayer dollars to rebuild Europe, the onset of covert operations, and the onset of a time when American soldiers would go to war under a foreign flag.

# NOTES

1. John Jay, "Concerning Dangers from Foreign Force and Influence," *The Federalist*, No. 2, *Independent Journal,* October 31, 1787, http://www.constitution.org/fed/federa02.htm.
2. James Perloff, *The Shadows of Power: The Council on Foreign Relations and the American Decline* (Appleton, Wisconsin: Western Islands, 2005), p. 66.
3. Mark Weber, "The Roosevelt Legacy and the Kent Case," *The Journal for Historical Review,* Summer 1983, http://www.ihr.org/jhr/v04/v04p173_kent.html.
4. Christopher D. O'Sullivan, *Harry Hopkins: FDR's Envoy to Churchill and Stalin* (New York: Roman and Littlefield, 2014), pp. 52–53.
5. Perloff, *The Shadows of Power*, p. 65.
6. Robert Sherwood, quoted in Ibid.
7. Clay Blair, *Hitler's U Boat War: The Hunters, 1939-1942* (New York: Random House, 1998), p. 360.
8. Franklin Delano Roosevelt, "Navy Day Address," October 27, 1941, https://www.ibiblio.org/pha/timeline/411027awp.html.
9. Ibid.
10. Mark Weber, "Roosevelt's 'Secret Map' Speech," *Journal of Historical Review,* Spring 1985, http://www.ihr.org/jhr/v06/v06p125_weber.html.
11. Perloff, *The Shadows of Power,* p. 65.
12. Josef Goebbels, quoted in Weber, "Roosevelt's 'Secret Map' Speech."
13. Ibid.
14. "Three Power Pact between Germany, Italy, and Japan," signed in Berlin, September 27, 1940, http://avalon.law.yale.edu/wwii/triparti.asp.
15. Henry Stimson's diary, quoted in Perloff, *The Shadows of Power*, pp. 66–67.
16. "United States Freezes Japanese Assets," *History.com,* A&E Network, 2009, http://www.history.com/this-day-in-history/united-states-freezes-japanese-assets.
17. James K. Bowen, "Increasing Tensions between the United States and Japan," *Pacific War Historical Society*, February 20, 2007, http://www.pacificwar.org.au/pearlharbor/pearloverview4.html.
18. Tejito Toyoda in Robert Higgs, "How U.S. Economic Warfare Provoked Japan's Attack on Pearl Harbor," *Independent Institute,* May 1, 2006, http://www.independent.org/newsroom/article.asp?id=1930.
19. John Toland, *Infamy, Pearl Harbor and Its Aftermath* (New York: Doubleday, 1982), p. 316.
20. Perloff, *The Shadows of Power*, p. 68.

# 23

# THE SECRET ARMY

*For more than a century ideological extremists at either end of the political spectrum have seized upon well-publicized incidents . . . to attack the Rockefeller family for the inordinate influence they claim we wield over American political and economic institutions. Some even believe we are part of a secret cabal working against the best interests of the United States, characterizing my family and me as 'internationalists' and of conspiring with others around the world to build a more integrated global political and economic structure—one world, if you will. If that's the charge, I stand guilty, and I am proud of it.*

—DAVID ROCKEFELLER, *MEMOIRS*, 2002

ON JUNE 13, 1941, the Office of Strategic Services (OSS), America's first intelligence agency, was set up in Rockefeller Center to "collect and analyze all information and data which may bear upon national security."[1] FDR placed General William "Will Bill" Donovan in charge of the agency. A scion of high society, Donovan was an Ivy League lawyer who had married Ruth Ramsey, the heiress of one of the richest families in America, and served as a director of the Rockefeller Foundation.[2] The headquarters for the new agency was Rockefeller Center in New York since it was funded and served as an appendage of the House of Rockefeller.

Six months after the attack on Pearl Harbor, the OSS set up secret training camps for agents in Maryland and Virginia. The agents were not ordinary men with ordinary means. Almost to a man, they were bankers, lawyers, businessmen and accountants deeply embedded with the Council on Foreign Relations and the international money cartel. They included Henry Sturgis Morgan (son of J. P. Morgan Jr.), Junius Morgan III (another son of J. P. Morgan Jr.), Nicholas Roosevelt (chief correspondent of the *New York Times*), Paul Mellon (son of Andrew Mellon), Thomas Childs (a Rhodes scholar and the Paris representative of Sullivan and Cromwell), David Bruce (Andrew Mellon's son-in-law), Shepherd Morgan (director of the Federal Reserve Bank of New York), John Haskell, (executive director of Rockefeller's National City Corporation), John Gardner (a director of the Carnegie Corporation), and members of the Vanderbilt, Carnegie, DuPont, and Ryan families. Donovan justified the practice of recruiting the social elite for the OSS by saying: "You can hire a second-story man and make him a better second-story man. But if you hire a lawyer or an investment banker or a professor, you have something else besides."[3]

## A PRIME EXAMPLE

Allen Dulles was a prime example of an OSS agent. A scion of the Eastern Establishment, he came from a distinguished family of political dignitaries. John W. Foster, his maternal grandfather, had served as secretary of state under Benjamin Harrison, and Robert Lansing, his uncle by marriage, had been Woodrow Wilson's secretary of state. Dulles had attended the Paris Peace Conference with Wilson, where he had been instrumental in the creation of the Royal Institute on International Affairs and the Council on Foreign Relations.[4] A tweedy, pipe-smoking corporate lawyer, Dulles, with his snake-like charm and Machiavellian ambition, had been credited with seducing over one hundred women, including Claire Booth Luce, the wife of Henry Luce, the founder of *Time* and *Life*, and Queen Frederika of Greece.[5]

Dulles entered the diplomatic service in 1916 and was stationed in Vienna and later Bern. From 1922 to 1926, he served as the chief of the Near East Division of the US State Department. He left this post to join the Wall Street law firm of Sullivan and Cromwell, where his brother John Foster Dulles was a partner. Sullivan and Cromwell floated bonds for Krupp A. G., the German arms manufacturer, and managed the finances of I. G. Farben.[6] The most important clients of the firm were Rockefeller's Standard Oil Company of New Jersey and J. P. Morgan and Company.[7]

In addition to his law practice, Allen Dulles became the first president of the CFR in 1927. Thanks to this position, he deepened his ties with the Houses of Morgan and Rockefeller, while becoming intricately involved with the Chatham House, the Round Table, and the House of Rothschild.[8]

## A SEPARATE PEACE

Dulles was placed in charge of the OSS office in Bern, Switzerland, where he decided that America was waging a war against the wrong enemy. He came to this conclusion at the close of 1942, when the German infantry remained mired in the mud and snow of the Russian steppes. He had received word via the Vatican from *Schutzstaffel* (SS) chief Heinrich Himmler and Walter Schellenberg, head of the *Sicherheitsdienst* (the SS foreign intelligence service) that the Nazi government wished to establish a separate peace with the United States. Such reconciliation would enable the Third Reich to turn its undivided attention to pulverizing the Soviets. When Dulles expressed his openness to discuss the proposal, the German High Command sent Prince Max von Hohenlobe, a Prussian aristocrat and businessman, to meet with him in Bern.[9] At the meeting, Hohenlobe was surprised to learn that Dulles not only endorsed the Nazi proposal but also maintained that a strong Germany was necessary as a bulwark against Bolshevism, the Leninist faction of the Communist Party that had seized control of Russia in 1917.[10]

In a series of communiqués with Donovan, who remained the OSS chief in Washington, Dulles expressed his eagerness to pursue the peace negotiations, believing that the Soviets posed a far greater threat to the United States and Western World stability than the Nazis.[11]

## NAZI WEREWOLVES

Having established contact with Hitler's high command, Dulles conducted meetings in Bern with Nazi General Reinhold Gehlen, the head of German military intelligence. Gehlen was a stiff, unassuming man with sparse blond hair, a toothbrush mustache, and ears that stuck out of his head like radar antennas. Knowing that the defeat of the Third Reich was inevitable, he had concocted the idea of forming clandestine guerilla squads—composed of Hitler youth and die-hard fascist fanatics, as "stay-behind units." These units, Gehlen informed Dulles, would serve as a police force to ward off a post-war Soviet invasion.[12] The Nazi general referred to the members of his secret army as "werewolves"—individuals who function as ordinary citizens by day and Communist-killers by night. Each werewolf unit, Gehlen said, had access to buried depots of food, radio equipment, weapons, and explosives.[13]

Believing the Soviets planned a takeover of Germany and Western Europe at the conclusion of the war, Dulles became convinced that the OSS must reach out to these stay-behind armies in order to supply them with tactical and strategic assistance. This task, he informed Donovan and the OSS top brass in Washington, could be accomplished through Gehlen and SS General Karl Wolff, another new Nazi friend of Dulles, who served as the SS adjutant to Mussolini and the Italian government.[14]

## OPERATION SUNSHINE

Along with securing and fortifying the "werewolves," Dulles busied himself with arranging the separate peace with the Nazis that would exclude the Soviet Union. This undertaking became known as "Operation Sunrise." The separate peace should be signed without delay, Dulles informed Donovan, since it would allow the *Wehrmacht* to deploy three divisions from northern Italy to the Eastern front, where they could combat the Red Army.[15] When Stalin became aware that such negotiations were underway, he went ballistic, accusing his US allies of bad faith and betrayal. President Franklin D. Roosevelt responded that such accusations were "vile misrepresentations" of actuality.[16]

## THE FORT HUNT CONFERENCE

The worst fears of Allen Dulles for the postwar period began to materialize in February 1945, when the leaders of the "Big Three"—the United States, Great Britain, and the Soviet Union—met at Yalta on the Black Sea to redraw the map of Europe. The eastern border of Germany was moved westward to the Oder and Neisse Rivers, and parts of eastern Poland were handed over to the Soviets. What remained of Germany was to be divided into four zones of occupation, which would be administered by a council of military generals, including the French.[17]

As soon as the ink dried on the Yalta agreement, Dulles transported Gehlen and his top representatives to Fort Hunt, Virginia, where they were wined and dined by Donovan and other US officials. An agreement was reached. Gehlen would return to Germany under US protection to establish the "Gehlen Organization," which would receive full funding from US Army G-2 resources. The primary purpose of this organization would be the maintenance of the existing stay-behind armies and the recruitment of new guerilla soldiers from the ranks of Third Reich veterans with staunch anti-Communist credentials.[18] These soldiers no longer would be known as werewolves. They were to be known as "gladiators," who were commissioned to ward off Communist invaders in the great theater of postwar Europe. And the operation in which they were engaged was to be known as "Gladio," after the short swords that the Roman gladiators used to kill their opponents.

## THE ITALIAN GLADIATORS

Gladio expanded to Italy, where OSS officials, including James Jesus Angleton, secured the participation of Prince Junio Valerio Borghese, the leader of Decima Flottiglia MAS (10th Light Flotilla), better known as X MAS, an Italian naval commando unit. After Italy signed an armistice with the Allies on September 8, 1943, Borghese and his 10,267 commandos opted to fight for the so-called "Solo Republic" that had been set up by the Nazis in northern Italy. The unit was given the task of attacking the Italian partisan bands that had sprouted up throughout Italy. The partisans were sponsored by the Italian Communist Party (*Partito Comunista Italiano* or PCI). And, thanks to X MAS, thousands were found hanging from street lights and flag posts by the end of the war.[19]

On April 13, 1945, Borghese met with General Wolff and Angleton at a villa on Garda Lake where they discussed the possibility of extending their war efforts beyond any peace treaty with the Soviets by the redeployment of X MAS under the covert direction of the OSS. Borghese was amenable to the terms, especially since his cooperation would save him from an Italian firing squad.[20]

Under Borghese, the Gladio forces in Italy were divided into forty main groups: ten specialized in sabotage; six in espionage, propaganda, and escape tactics; and twelve in guerilla activities. A special training camp for members for the stay-behind units was set up in Sardinia, off Italy's western coast. The camp, thanks to the efforts of Gehlen and Wolff, was soon swarming with new gladiators from Germany, France, and Austria. By 1946, when the OSS morphed into the Central Intelligence Group (the precursor of the CIA), hundreds of Gladio units were in place throughout Western Europe.[21]

## THE MONEY SUPPLY

But there was a problem that seemed insurmountable. Gladio was a covert operation that had been initiated not by an act of Congress or a mandate from the Pentagon. Few federal officials knew of its existence. The $200 million in original funding came primarily from the House of Rockefeller, since Gladio was to pave the way for a new world government under the control of the money cartel.[22] But a new and steady stream of revenue had to be created almost overnight, since the operation would come to cost billions of dollars. But where could the cartel secure such a source of funding? The answer would soon come from Paul E. Helliwell, who was serving as the OSS chief of special intelligence in China.

# NOTES

1.  Stephen Kinzer, *The Brothers: John Foster Dulles, Allen Dulles, and Their Secret War* (New York: Times Books, 2013), p. 64.

2.  "William J. Donovan and the National Security," CIA's Historical Review Program, March 2011, https://www.cia.gov/library/center-for-the-study-of-intelligence/kent-csi/vol3no3/html/v03i3a07p_0001.htm.

3.  Evan Thomas, *The Very Best Men: Four Men Who Dared* (New York: Touchstone, 1985), p. 9.

4.  James Corbett, "Meet Allen Dulles: Fascist Spymaster," *The Corbett Report*, August 30, 2015, https://www.corbettreport.com/episode-307-meet-allen-dulles-fascist-spymaster/comment-page-1/.

5.  Stephen Kinzer, "When a CIA Director Had Scores of Affairs," *New York Times*, November 10, 2012, http://www.nytimes.com/2012/11/10/opinion/when-a-cia-director-had-scores-of-affairs.html?_r=0.

6.  Adam LeBor, "Overt and Covert," *New York Times*, November 8, 2013, http://www.nytimes.com/2013/11/10/books/review/the-brothers-by-stephen-kinzer.html.

7.  Murray N. Rothbard, "Rockefeller, Morgan, and War," *Mises Institute*, March 20, 2017, https://mises.org/library/rockefeller-morgan-and-war.

8.  Peter Grose, *Continuing the Inquiry: The Council on Foreign Relations from 1921 to 1996* (Washington, D.C.: Council on Foreign Relations Press, 2006), p. 7.

9.  Martin A. Lee, The Beast Reawakens: Fascism's Resurgence from Hitler's Spymasters to Today's Neo Nazi Groups and Right Wing Extremists (New York: Routledge, 2011), pp. 18–19.

10. Stephen Dorril, *Inside the Secret World of Her Majesty's Secret Intelligence Service* (New York: Touchstone, 2000), p. 168.

11. Lee, *The Beast Reawakens*, p. 19.

12. Charles Higham, *American Swastika* (New York: Doubleday, 1985), p. 198.

13. Lee, *The Beast Reawakens*, p. 24.

14. John Simkin, "Karl Wolff," Spartacus Educational, September 30, 1997, http://www.spartacus.schoolnet.co.uk/Karl_Wolff.htm.

15. Heinz Hohne and Herman Zolling, *The General Was a Spy: The Truth about General Gehlen and His Spy Ring* (New York: Coward, McCann, and Geoghegan, 1972), pp. xxix–xxxv. See also Stephen P. Halbrook, "Operation Sunrise: America's OSS, Swiss Intelligence, and the German Surrender 1954," a paper delivered at *Atti del Convegno Internazionale*, Locarno, Switzerland, March 2, 2005.

16. Lee, *The Beast Reawakens*, p. 21.

17. Ibid., p. 28.

18. Hohne and Zolling, *The General Was a Spy*, p. 107.

19. "Operation Gladio," British Broadcasting Corporation (BBC), *Timeline* series, June 10, 1992, http://www.youtube.com/watch?v=AUvrPvV-KQo.

20. Jack Green and Alessandro Massignani, *The Black Prince and the Sea Devils: The Story of Valerio Borghese and the Elite Units of Decoma MAS* (Cambridge, MASS: De Capo Press, 2004), p. 181.

21. "Operation Gladio," *BBC*.

22. John Judge, "Good Americans" in *Selected Writings of John Judge*, Citizens Watch, 1983, http://www.ratical.org/ratville/JFK/JohnJudge/GoodAmericans.html.

# 24

# PRODUCING THE PLAGUE

*What cannot now be denied is that US intelligence agencies arranged for the release from prison of the world's preeminent drug lord, allowed him to rebuild his narcotics empire, watched the flow of drugs into the largely black ghettoes of New York and Washington, D.C. escalate and then lied about what they had done. This founding saga of the relationship between American spies and gangsters set patterns that would be replicated from Laos and Burma to Marseilles and Panama.*

—ALEXANDER COCKBURN AND JEFFREY ST. CLAIR,
*WHITEOUT: THE CIA, DRUGS, AND THE PRESS*

COL. PAUL E. HELLIWELL, the OSS chief in China, had one hell of an idea, which would result in a union between the US intelligence community and organized crime that in turn would produce conflicts, wars, rebellions, financial upheavals, and an epidemic that would forever alter the tide of world history.

Mainstream books about the CIA, like Tim Weiner's *Legacy of Ashes*, make no mention of Helliwell, his relationship with Lucky Luciano and Meyer Lansky, his creation of the Castle Bank in the Bahamas, or his grand experiment on the black community of Harlem. In the flood of CIA documents released since 1992, one does not find the name of Helliwell in the indices of the National Archive, the National Security Archive, or the Federation of American Scientists. In the million declassified pages stored and indexed on the website of the Mary Ferrell Foundation, Helliwell's name appears only once—on a list of documents that were withheld from inspection during the CIA's search in 1974 for records concerning Watergate. This silence about the principal architect of the postwar CIA drug connection speaks volumes about the state of contemporary journalism. The only writer who has recognized Helliwell's central importance is Peter Dale Scott, a former Canadian diplomat and an English professor at the University of California, Berkeley.[1]

## THE HELLIWELL PLAN

Within Kunming, a town within the South China province of Yunnan, Helliwell observed that General Chiang Kai-shek, leader of the Kuomintang (KMT), sold opium to Chinese addicts in order to raise funds for his army's planned war against the Communist forces of Mao Zedong.[2] Since his task was to provide covert assistance to the KMT, what better help could Helliwell provide than steady shipments of opiates for the good general?

Delighted with the concept, General Wild Bill Donovan, the OSS director, arranged to funnel money to Helliwell, who now "became the man who controlled the pipe line of covert funds for secret operations throughout Asia."[3] This expenditure, from funds provided by Rockefeller, was approved by J. P. Morgan Jr., who was in charge of the OSS finances, and James Warburg, son of Paul (the founder of the Federal Reserve), who served as Donovan's special assistant. Therefore, the involvement of the international banking establishment in the heroin venture was evident from the time of its inception.[4]

## OSS ENTERS THE DRUG TRADE

By the close of World War II, Helliwell and fellow army intelligence officers E. Howard Hunt of Watergate fame; Lucien Conein, a former member of the French Foreign Legion with strong ties to the Corsican mafia; Tommy "the Cork" Corcoran, a lawyer serving the Strategic Service Unit; and Lt. General Claire L. Chennault, the military advisor to Chiang Kai-shek and the founder of the Flying Tigers, created the Civil Air Transport (CAT) from surplus aircraft—including C-47 Dakotas and C-46 Commandos.[5]

The CAT fleet transported weapons to a contingency force of the KMT in Burma. The "empty" planes were then loaded with drugs for their return trip to China.[6] The pilots who flew these bush-type aircraft were a motley group of men, who often served as agents or go-betweens with the Chinese National guerillas and the opium buyers. Some were ex-Nazis and others, part of the band of expatriates who emerge in countries following any war.[7] Helliwell and his compatriots had created a model for the trafficking in drugs that would result in the formation of Air America. Thanks to his efforts, Burma's Stan Plateau would emerge from a relatively minor poppy-cultivating area into the largest opium-producing region of the world.[8]

### GHETTO GOLD

Knowing that Wild Bill had drafted plans to create a postwar central intelligence agency, Helliwell came up with another brainstorm—a sure-fire means of gaining covert funding for Gladio and other security operations.[9] The new agency, he realized, could obtain cold cash by adopting the same measures of General Chiang. It could supply smack to blacks in America's ghettos.

World War II had disrupted international shipping and imposed tight waterfront security that made smuggling of heroin into the United States almost impossible. Heroin supplies were small, and international crime syndicates fell into disarray. But opiates were becoming the rage of the Jazz scene in Harlem, and the demand for China White was increasing day-by-day among black musicians in New York, where a hit could cost as much as $100. Helliwell, in dealing with Du Yuesheng and other drug lords in Burma, was keenly aware of this fact.

The notion wasn't out of line with OSS protocol. Helliwell and his army intelligence buddies in China already were involved in providing shipments of opium to General Chiang, and "three sticky brown bars" to Burmese addicts who could provide information concerning the military plans of Chairman Mao.[10] If similar bars could be made available to inner city black dealers at rock bottom rates, then the market could be cornered, and the demand could be caused to increase in an exponential manner. Helliwell knew that a drug epidemic might arise. But, he reasoned, the problem would remain confined to the lowest strata of society with little impact on white middle-class America.

## ANSWERED PRAYER

Donovan and his OSS colleagues viewed Helliwell's proposal as answered prayer. Selling smack to the black jazz subculture would provide US intelligence with a steady supply of revenue for Gladio throughout the postwar era. The Truman Administration had set aside no funds for covert, postwar operations in the federal budget. And cold cash, Donovan knew, would become the key weapon of the new agency, which he remained hell-bent on establishing as soon as he got back to Washington. It alone could provide the means to purchase the services of foreign agents, foreign politicians, and foreign assassins without the approval of any elected official.[11]

Donovan's reasoning, bizarre as it might seem to modern readers, was shared by most American political leaders—Republican and Democratic alike—at the close of World War II. Alfred W. McCoy explains:

> Henry Luce, founder of the Time-Life empire, argued that America was the rightful heir to Great Britain's international primacy and heralded the postwar era as "The American Century." To justify their "entanglement in foreign adventures," American cold warriors embraced a militantly anti-Communist ideology. In their minds, the entire world was locked in a Manichaean struggle between "godless

communism" and "the free world." The Soviet Union was determined to conquer the world, and its leader, Joseph Stalin, was the new Hitler. European labor movements and Asian nationalist struggles were pawns of "international Communism," and as such had to be subverted or destroyed. There could be no compromise with this monolithic evil: negotiations were "appeasement" and neutralism was "immoral." In this desperate struggle to save "Western civilization," any ally was welcome and any means was justified.[12]

Since any ally was welcome and any means justifiable, Wild Bill decided that the implementation of Helliwell's drug scheme would enable him to make use of Charles "Lucky" Luciano and the Sicilian mafia.

### LUCKY'S HOMECOMING

In 1944, Luciano was cooling his heels in the Clinton Correctional Facility in upstate New York, where he had been sentenced to spend thirty to fifty years for "compulsory prostitution."[13] But pressure was mounting for Lucky's release. He had been so instrumental in planning the US invasion of Sicily that Walter Winchell, America's popular news broadcaster, recommended the mobster for a Congressional Medal of Honor.[14]

Instead of a medal, Lucky was granted a one-way ticket to his native Sicily in the summer of 1946. When he arrived in his hometown of Lercara Friddi in Sicily, the mobster received a hero's welcome. Hundreds of people lined the streets waving small American flags. A four-piece band played "The Stars and Stripes Forever" as the mayor, draped in a red sash, ushered the American mobster out of a police car.[15] "Half the people I met in Sicily was in the Mafia," Lucky later reflected, "and by half the people, I mean half the cops, too. Because in Sicily, it goes like this: the Mafia is first, then your own family, then your business, and then the Mafia again."[16]

In October, at the request of US intelligence agents, Lucky traveled to Cuba where he met with Frank Costello, Vito Genovese, Albert Anastasia, and Meyer Lansky to discuss Helliwell's plan. Also in attendance were Mike Miranda, Joseph Magliocco, Joe Adonis, Tommy Lucchese, Joe Profaci, Willie Moretti, the Fischetti brothers (heirs to Al Capone), and Santo Trafficante. The conference was held at the Hotel Nacional, where Frank Sinatra made his Havana singing debut in honor of Luciano.[17] Several of the mafiosi voiced their opposition to Lucky's plan by maintaining that dealing in junk was beneath them. But, at the end of the conference, all became convinced that providing heroin to blacks was simply giving them what they wanted, and who cared what happened to "niggers."[18]

Two hundred kilos of heroin for the test run would come from Schiaparelli, one of Italy's most respected pharmaceutical companies.[19] The product would be shipped by the Sicilian mob in crates of oranges. Half of the oranges in the crates would be made of wax and stuffed with 100 grams of pure heroin.[20] Additional heroin would be packed in cans of sardines, wheels of *caciocavalla* cheese, and barrels of olive oil.[21] Within Cuba, the heroin would be "cut" in laboratories under the control of the Trafficante clan. The drugs would be shipped to New York for distribution by Vito Genovese and his clan in the jazz clubs of Harlem.

The Helliwell plan got underway at the close of the year and met with incredible success. The future of Gladio and other covert ventures was no longer in jeopardy. Helliwell's analysis had been correct. The jazz clubs were the perfect spots to peddle the product. Soon some of the country's leading black musicians—Carl Drinkard (Count Basie's piano player), Theodore "Fats" Navarro, and Charlie Parker—became hopeless junkies, who would die by overdose.

Regarding this development, Harry Anslinger, then head of the Bureau of Narcotics, said: "Jazz entertainers are neither fish nor fowl. They do not get the million-dollar protection Hollywood and Broadway can afford for their stars who have become addicted—and there are many more than will ever be revealed. Perhaps this is because jazz, once considered a decadent kind of music, has only token respectability. Jazz grew up next door to crime, so to speak. Clubs of dubious reputation were, for a long time, the only places where it could be heard."[22]

## POLICE PROTECTION

Col. Albert Carone, a New York City policeman, served the new drug network as "a bagman for the CIA" by paying law enforcement officials to look the other way when drugs were being distributed in Harlem and other black communities.[23] A made-man within the Genovese crime family, Carone also collected money for drug payments and money to be laundered by the Vatican from mafia families in New York, New Jersey, and Pennsylvania. In recognition of his service, the cop/bagman became a Grand Knight of the Sovereign Military of Malta, which has been described as "the military arm of the Holy See."[24] Protection of the drug trade would become reflected in the fact that not one major drug bust was conducted by US officials from 1947 to 1967, despite the rise in heroin addicts from 20,000 to 150,000.[25]

The shadow government now possessed sufficient funds not only to sustain secret armies throughout Europe but also to establish the Central Intelligence Agency (CIA), a covert organization to do its bidding.

# NOTES

1.  Peter Dale Scott, "Deep Events and the CIA's Global Drug Connection," *Global Research*, September 8, 2008, http://www.globalresearch.ca/deep-events-and-the-cia-s-global-drug-connection/10095.
2.  Ibid.
3.  Sterling Seagrove, *The Marcos Dynasty* (New York: Harper and Row, 1988), p. 361.
4.  Eustace Mullens, "The World Order: A Study in the Hegemony of Parasitism," *Modern History Project*, 1984, http://modernhistoryproject.org/mhp?Article=WorldOrder&C=5.0.
5.  Henrik Kruger, *The Great Heroin Coup: Drugs, Intelligence and International Finance* (Boston: South End Press, 1980), p. 68.
6.  Joseph Trento, *Prelude to Terror: The Rogue CIA, the Legacy of America's Private Intelligence Network* (New York: Carroll and Graf, 2005), p. 48.
7.  Peter Dale Scott, *American War Machine: Deep Politics, the CIA Global Drug Connection, and the Road to Afghanistan* (Washington, D.C.: Rowman and Littlefield, 2010), p. 58.
8.  Alfred McCoy, Testimony before the Special Seminar focusing on allegations linking CIA secret operations and drug trafficking, convened February 13, 1997 by Rep. John Conyers, Dean of the Congressional Black Caucus.
9.  Declassified OSS documents show that Donovan's plans for the creation of a Special Intelligence Service to gather intelligence from countries throughout the world dates back to September 25, 1941. See "Memo Col. Donovan from Wallace B. Stevens," WIN #24299.
10. Penny Lernoux, *In Banks We Trust* (New York: Penguin Books, 1986), p. 79.
11. Tim Weiner, *Legacy of Ashes: The History of the CIA* (New York: Doubleday, 2007), p. 116.
12. Alfred W. McCoy, *The Politics of Heroin in Southeast Asia* (New York: Harper and Row, 1972), p. 7.
13. Staff report, "Luciania (sic) Sentenced to 30 to 50 Years, Court Warns Ring," *New York Times*, June 19, 1936.
14. Selwyn Raab, *Five Families: The Rise, Decline and Resurgence of America's Most Powerful Mafia Empires* (New York: Thomas Dunne Books, 2005), pp. 78–79.
15. Douglas Valentine, *The Strength of the Wolf*, p. 76.
16. Martin A. Gosch and Richard Hammer, *The Last Testament of Lucky Luciano,* (Boston: Little Brown, 1974), pp. 292–293.
17. Jerry Serra, "Lucky Luciano Not So Lucky in Cuba," *Cuba on My Mind: A Personal Look at Cuban History,* July 24, 2005.
18. Gosch and Hammer, *The Last Testament of Lucky Luciano*, p. 314.
19. McCoy, *The Politics of Heroin in Southeast Asia*, p. 24. See also Cockburn and St. Clair, *Whiteout*, p. 130.
20. Claire Sterling, *Octopus: Octopus: How the Long Reach of the Sicilian Mafia Controls the Global Narcotics Trade* (New York: Simon and Schuster, 1990), p. 100–101.
21. Ibid.
22. John Bevilaqua, "Harry Anslinger: Head of the Bureau of Narcotics since 1930," *Education Forum*, December 4, 2009,http://educationforum.ipbhost.com/index.php?showtopic=15084.

23. James Cameron Graham, "The Secret History of the CIA's Involvement in the Narcotics Trade," doctoral dissertation, School of Politics and International Relations, The University of Nottingham, 2009.
24. Ibid.
25. Cockburn and St. Clair, *Whiteout*, p. 141.

# PART SEVEN

## ENDLESS ENTANGLEMENTS

*John F. Kennedy held a dinner in the White House for a group of the brightest minds in the nation at that time. He made this statement: "This is perhaps the assembly of the most intelligence ever to gather at one time in the White House with the exception of when Thomas Jefferson dined alone."*

*"Fundamental Bible-believing people do not have the right to indoctrinate their children in their religious beliefs because we, the state, are preparing them for the year 2000, when America will be part of a one-world global society and their children will not fit in."*
—NEBRASKA STATE SENATOR PETER HOAGLAND, SPEAKING ON RADIO IN 1983.

*"My reading of history convinces me that most bad government results from too much government."*
—THOMAS JEFFERSON

# 25

# A CANCEROUS GROWTH

*The United Nations, for three and a half decades, has been indulging in a gigantic, unfettered conspiracy, mostly at the U.S. taxpayers' expense, to enslave our republic in a world government dominated by the Soviet Union and the Third World. Having had enough of this freewheeling conspiracy, more and more responsible officials and thinking citizens are ready to pull out.*
—US REPRESENTATIVE LARRY MCDONALD, JANUARY 27, 1982

THE UNITED NATIONS, as conceived by the Council on Foreign Relations and funded by the House of Rockefeller, was never meant to be an academic debating society. It was conceived to become an international regime that would control the world's weapons, its wars, its courts, its tax collectors, and its economy. The plans for this behemoth were drawn up in 1943 by a "secret steering committee" under Secretary of State Cordell Hull. The members of this committee—Leo Pasvolsky, Isaiah Bowman, Sumner Welles, Norman Davis, and Myron Taylor—were all prominent CFR members. The draft for the massive international agency was presented on June 15, 1944, to President Roosevelt, who promptly gave it his approval.[1]

Delegates were now chosen by the US State Department to meet with their foreign counterparts in San Francisco to devise a final plan. The list of the American delegates, which contained the following names, resembled a CFR roll call:

| | | | |
|---|---|---|---|
| 1. | Theodore C. Achilles | 23. | Foy D. Kohler |
| 2. | James W. Angell | 24. | John E. Lockwood |
| 3. | Hamilton Fish Armstrong | 25. | Archibald MacLeish |
| 4. | Charles E. Bohlen | 26. | John J. McCloy |
| 5. | Isaiah Bowman | 27. | Cord Meyer Jr |
| 6. | Ralph Bunche | 28. | Edward G. Miller Jr. |
| 7. | John M. Cabot | 29. | Hugh Moore |
| 8. | Mitchell B. Carroll | 30. | Leo Pasvolsky |
| 9. | Andrew W. Cordier | 31. | Dewitt C. Poole |
| 10. | John S. Dickey | 32. | William L. Ransom |
| 11. | John Foster Dulles | 33. | Nelson A. Rockefeller |
| 12. | James Clement Dunn | 34. | James T. Shotwell |
| 13. | Clyde Eagleton | 35. | Harold E. Stassen |
| 14. | Clark M. Eichelberger | 36. | Edward R. Stettinius Jr. |
| 15. | Muir S. Fairchild | 37. | Adlai E. Stevenson |
| 16. | Thomas K. Finletter | 38. | Robert Sweetser |
| 17. | Artemus Gates | 39. | James Swihart |
| 18. | Arthur J. Hepburn | 40. | Llewellyn E. Thompson |
| 19. | Julius C. Holmes | 41. | Herman B. Wells |
| 20. | Philip C. Jessup | 42. | Francis Wilcox |
| 21. | Joseph E. Johnson | 43. | Charles W. Yost |
| 22. | R. Keith Kane | | |

The secretary-general of the conference was US State Department official Alger Hiss, a member of the CFR and a secret Soviet agent.[2]

## THE LEAGUE REVIVED

The final draft was introduced to Congress on October 24, 1944, by Senator Glen Taylor (D–Idaho) who called upon his fellow senators to go on record favoring a world republic with an international police force.[3] When it was presented for resolution, Senator Harold A. Burton (R–Ohio) said: "We again have the chance to retrieve and establish, not a League of Nations, but the present United Nations Charter, although 80 percent of its provisions are, in substance, the same as those of the League in Nations in 1919."[4]

This statement should have alerted the Senate that the charter represented no less than the League of Nations, an abandonment of US sovereignty. It should have caused them to recall the rallying cry of Republicans in 1920 against such an organization: "The Republican Party stands for agreement among the nations to preserve the peace of the world. . . . We believe that this can be done without depriving the people of the United States in advance of the right to determine for themselves what is just and fair, and without involving them as participants and not as peacemakers in a multitude of quarrels, the merits of which they are unable to judge."[5]

## RHODES RESURGENT

The most glaring problem with the resolution, which was signed into law by President Harry S. Truman on July 28, 1945, was that it represented a treaty between the United States and a world-governing organization. By law, a treaty can only be established between two sovereign nations, and the new organization was neither sovereign nor a state. Another problem was that the treaty called upon the United States to engage in military action at the discretion of foreign governments. This violated the Constitution, which mandated that Congress alone possessed the power to declare war. A third problem came with the stipulation that the president of the United States remain the supreme commander-in-chief of the military in times of peace with the ability to engage at any time America's armed forces in military conflict.[6]

By its charter, the United Nations is governed by three principal units: the Security Council, the General Assembly, and the Economic and Social Council. Under these units, hundreds of agencies and programs have been formed to influence every aspect of human activity, from administering welfare programs to regulating the environment.

Violators of these mandates are subjected to force, arrest, and trial in an international court of law.[7] Thus the brainstorm of Cecil Rhodes has crystallized into a political and economic reality.

The center source of power within the United Nations resides with the Security Council. This council consists of five permanent member-nations—the United States, the United Kingdom, France, Russia, and China. Anyone of these member-nations possesses veto power over the final determinations. This relegation of power gives the organization a semblance of check and balance. But semblance is not reality, and the real control resides with the money cartel, which can force member-nations, even Russia, to comply with its interest since it possesses control over their economies. This control became evident on June 27, 1950, when the Security Council adopted Resolution 83, which determined that the attack on the Republic of Korea by Communist forces from North Korea constituted a "breach of peace" that warranted an immediate show of force.[8]

## POLICE ACTION

In accordance with the Potsdam Conference, Korea, a protectorate of Japan, was divided in half along the 38th parallel. The northern half was occupied by the Soviet Union, and the southern half by the United States. Stalin named Kim Il-Sung, one of his protégés, to serve as the premier of North Korea; he provided his military officials to train a North Korean army of 150,000 recruits; and he supplied the Communist army with tanks and fighter planes. On June 25, 1950, a force of 75,000 North Koreans poured over the 38th parallel in an invasion that was designed to reunite the country.[9]

Truman responded to the invasion by turning to the United Nations for a deployment of its peace-keeping force. It was a bit of a ruse since American soldiers comprised 85 percent of this force. The ruse was compounded when the Security Council voted to approve the deployment, even though the war could have been prevented if the Soviets had exercised their veto. But the Soviets were not present at the critical meeting. Instead, they had staged a walk-out in protest of the UN's refusal to provide a seat in its general assembly for Red China.[10]

## THE SOVIET MYSTERY

Why would the Soviets opt to pass up an opportunity to protect their surrogate operation in North Korea? Was a blunder of this magnitude really intentional? These questions have dogged historians for decades. The answers may be discovered by following the money. By 1927, Rockefeller-owned Standard Oil of New York and its subsidiary, the Vacuum Oil Company, had purchased the Russian oil fields and constructed a massive refinery in Batumi on the coast of the Black Sea.[11] In accordance with the deal, the Rockefellers gained the right to market Soviet oil in Europe, while the Bolsheviks received a loan of $75 million.[12] During this same time, Rockefeller-owned Chase National Bank had established the American-Russian Chamber of Commerce, which financed Soviet raw material exports and sold Soviet bonds in the United States.[13]

In 1935, Stalin expropriated many foreign investments in Russia, but the holdings of the House of Rockefeller were not touched.[14] Other Rockefeller investments were made in the Soviet Union, including the construction of a truck factory that created tanks and rocket launchers.[15] The total holdings of Chase National, Standard Oil, the Guaranty Trust Company, and other firms controlled or owned by the Rockefellers remained concealed from public scrutiny. The profits from these enterprises flowed into numbered accounts at Swiss banks so that they could never be audited by American legislators or US Treasury officials.[16] It was all a matter of high finance. The creation of another superpower by the House of Rockefeller proved to be an incredibly profitable venture. The Soviet Union began producing T 34/85 tanks and MIG 15 fighter jets for the North Korean army with financing from the House of Rockefeller.

## THE WAR BOOM

The Korean War also produced a windfall for the American holdings of the money cartel, including the Rockefeller family. It necessitated, as John Whiteclay Chambers writes in *The Oxford Companion to American Military History*, "a permanent military-industrial establishment in peacetime as well as wartime or, at least, in cold as well as hot war."[17] Since the war mandated a quadrupling in military spending, the fortunes of the Rockefellers and the other global banking families increased exponentially. The Rockefellers had heavily invested in Boeing, McDonnell Aircraft, and other leading firms that received lucrative contracts with the Department of Defense. In addition to its oil companies (Exxon, Mobil, Texaco, Atlantic-Richfield, Standard Oil of California, Standard Oil of Indiana, and Marathon), the family had acquired majority control in steel companies (Inland Steel, Wheeling-Pittsburgh Steel, and National Steel) and chemical companies (Merck, Pfizer, and Wyeth), all of which reaped enormous profits from the so-called "police action."[18] International Harvester, the Rockefeller-owned agricultural equipment company, emerged as one of the country's leading defense contractors by producing aerial torpedoes, military bulldozers, M7 tanks, 37 mm cannon shells, 57 mm antitank guns, aircraft cannons, and other munitions. An extra bonus to these earnings was the remilitarization of Japan, which not only forced the Rockefeller-owned firms to go into overdrive but also gave rise to the Rockefeller-dominated Nippon Oil and Energy.[19]

The war was particularly ugly. The UN strategy involved the mass killing of civilians through extensive bombings. On August 12, the US Air Force dropped 626 tons of bombs on North Korea; two weeks later the daily tonnage increased to 800 tons. The carpet bombings resulted in the destruction of seventy-eight cities and thousands of villages. By the time an armistice was signed on July 27, 1953, a third of the population of North Korea—over 3 million people—had been wiped out.[20] The official US casualty list showed that 36,914 American soldiers had died in the conflict, and 7,800 remained unaccounted for.[21] The struggle resulted neither in territorial gain or loss. The objective of the war had been "containment," not liberation or victory. The terms of the armistice called for the creation of a demilitarized zone (DMZ) between North and South Korea. Each side was to be 2,200 yards from the center.

The DMZ was to be patrolled by both sides at all times.[22] And so it had come to this: America's wars were to be waged with limited rules of engagement and indefinite outcomes to advance the purpose of the global bankers, who had brought the United Nations into being.

Despite the military failure of the Korean War, the CFR continued its campaign for more and more power to be granted to the United Nations, including the institution of a permanent force to police the planet. In *Freedom from War: The United States Program for General and Complete Disarmament in a Peaceful World,* a publication from the US State Department, Dean Rusk and other CFR members called for the transference of all tactical and strategic military weapons to the United States. Draftees of this document argued universal peace could only be achieved by this means.[23] They overlooked the fact that the majority of the UN member nations were dictatorships with a deep-seated repugnance for constitutional republics and that the gatherings of the General Assembly were characterized by rabid anti-American rants.

## LUCIFER'S RE-EMERGENCE

The planners of the New World Order, including Rhodes and Nathan Rothschild, were intensely interested in the occult, an interest that gave rise to the Society of Psychic Research and the Theosophist Movement. Their obsession was shared by their disciples, including the founders of the United Nations. Lucis Trust became an official consultative agency of the UN and its publishing arm. Founded in 1922 as the Lucifer Publishing Company by Alice Bailey, a disciple of Helena Petrova Blavatsky, the chartered purpose of the Trust was as follows: "To encourage the study of comparative religion, philosophy, science and art; to encourage every line of thought tending to the broadening of human sympathies and interests, and the expansion of ethical religious and educational literature; to assist or to engage in activities for the relief of suffering and for human betterment; and, in general, to further worthy efforts for humanitarian and educational ends."[24] The leading sponsors of Lucis Trust included Henry Clausen, Supreme Grand Commander of the Supreme Council, 33rd Degree, Southern District Scottish Rite; John D. Rockefeller IV; The Rockefeller Foundation; The Marshall Field family; World Bank president Robert McNamara; US ambassador to Moscow and IBM president Thomas Watson; Undersecretary of State Alexis Johnson; and The United Theosophists of New York City.[25]

Bailey's ultimate objective in establishing Lucis Trust was to bring about a one-world religion under the guiding light of Lucifer. She wrote: "The day is dawning when all religions will be regarded as emanating from one spiritual source; all will be seen as unitedly providing the one root out of which the universal religion will inevitably emerge."[26] In keeping with this objective, the Trust established World Goodwill, an agency within the UN that seeks to harness the "spiritual qualities of human beings" in order to issue forth a new era of enlightenment.

Signatories to the World Goodwill document included: Helmut Schmidt, former chancellor of West Germany; Malcolm Fraser, former Australian prime minister; Oscar Arias Sanchez, former prime minister of Costa Rica; Israeli president Shimon Peres; Robert McNamara; Federal Reserve Chairman Paul Volcker; and Jimmy Carter.[27]

Aside from Lucis Trust and World Goodwill, the scent of sulfur could also be discerned in the creation of the UN's two evil sisters: the International Monetary Fund and the World Bank.

# NOTES

1. James Perloff, *The Shadows of Power: The Council on Foreign Relations and the American Decline* (Appleton, Wisconsin: Western Islands, 2005), p. 71.

2. William F. Jaspers, *Global Tyranny. . .Step-by-Step: The United Nations and the Emerging New World Order,* Chapter Three, "The U.N. Founders," 1992, http://www.bibliotecapleyades.net/sociopolitica/global_tyranny/global_tyranny03.htm.

3. Joseph Preston Baratta, *The Politics of World Federation: United Nations, UN Reform, Atomic Control* (New York: Praeger, 2004), p. 155.

4. Harold Burton, quoted in Andrew Marshall, "Global Power and Global Government," *Global Research,* August 18, 2009, http://forum.prisonplanet.com/index.php?topic=129174.80;wap.

5. Republican platform of 1920, quoted in G. Vance Smith and Tom Gow, *Masters of Deception: The Rise of the Council on Foreign Nations* (Colorado Springs, CO: Freedom First Society, 2012), pp. 36–37.

6. Andrew Marshall, "Global Power and Global Government."

7. Marten Zwanenburg, "United Nations and International Humanitarian Law," Oxford Public International Law, October 2015, http://opil.ouplaw.com/view/10.1093/law:epil/9780199231690/law-9780199231690-e1675.

8. Yong-jin Kim, *Major Powers and Korea* (Silver Spring, MD: Research Institute on Korean Affairs, 1973), p. 46.

9. Ibid.

10. Perloff, *The Shadows of Power,* p. 91.

11. Alexander Igolkin, "Early Lessons of Mutually Beneficial Cooperation," *Lukoil International Magazine,* No. 3, 2004. http://www.oilru.com/or/17/230/.

12. Gary Allen, *The Rockefeller File* (Seal Beach, CA: '76 Press, 1976), p. 107.

13. Mark M. Rich, *The Hidden Evil: The Financial Elite's Covert War against the Civilian Population* (Raleigh, NC: Lulu Press, 2009), p. 58.

14. Ibid.

15. Mark Rich, *The Hidden Evil: The Financial Elite's Covert War against the Civilian Population* (Raleigh, NC: Lulu Press, 2009), p. 58.

16. Allen, *The Rockefeller File,* p. 107.

17. John Whiteclay Chambers, *The Oxford Companion to American Military History* (New York: Oxford University Press, 2000), p. 439.

18. Allen, *The Rockefeller File,* pp. 31–33.

19. Staff Report, "Japan: The Politics of Oil," *Executive Intelligence Review,* March 29, 1977, http://www.larouchepub.com/eiw/public/1977/eirv04n13-19770329/eirv04n13-19770329_066-japan_the_politics_of_oil.pdf.

20. Michel Chossudovsky, *The Globalization of War: America's 'Long War' against Humanity"* (Montreal, Quebec: Global Research Publishers, 2015), pp. 26–30.

21. CNN Library, "Korean War Fast Facts," *CNN News,* June 21, 2016, http://www.cnn.com/2013/06/28/world/asia/korean-war-fast-facts/.

22. Ibid.

23. Smith and Gow, *Masters of Deception*, pp. 68–71.

24. Lucis Trust Charter cited in Curtis A. Chamberlain, *The Judas Epidemic: Exposing the Betrayal of the Christian Faith in Church and Government* (Bloomington, Indiana, West Bow Press, 2011), p. 111.

25. Lyndon La Rouche, "Real History of Satanism," La Rouche Publications, January 17, 2015, http://www.rense.com/general61/satanism.htm.

26. Alice A. Bailey, *Ponder on This: A Compilation* (Washington, DC: Lucis Publishing, 2003), p. 294.

27. Terry Melanson, "Lucis Trust, Alice Bailey, World Goodwill, and the False Light of the World,"*Conspiracy Archive*, May 8, 2005, http://www.conspiracyarchive.com/NewAge/Lucis_Trust.htm.

# 26

# THE EVIL SISTERS

*Just between you and me, shouldn't the World Bank be encouraging more migration of the dirty industries to the LDCs [less-developed countries]? . . . I think the economic logic behind dumping a load of toxic waste in the lowest wage country is impeccable and we should face up to that . . . I've always thought that under-populated countries in Africa are vastly under-polluted, their air quality is probably vastly inefficiently low compared to Los Angeles or Mexico City . . . The concern over an agent that causes a one in a million change in the odds of prostate cancer is obviously going to be much higher in a country where people survive to get prostate cancer than in a country where under 5 mortality is 200 per thousand . . . The problem with the arguments against all of these proposals for more pollution in LDCs (intrinsic rights to certain goods, moral reasons, social concerns, lack of adequate markets, etc.) could be turned around and used more or less effectively against every Bank proposal for liberalization.*

—LAWRENCE H. SUMMERS, CHIEF ECONOMIST OF THE WORLD BANK, IN AN
INTERNAL MEMO DATED DECEMBER 12, 1991. SUMMERS WENT ON TO BECOME
THE US TREASURY SECRETARY IN THE CLINTON ADMINISTRATION AND PRESI-
DENT OF HARVARD UNIVERSITY

IN ADDITION TO THE UNITED NATIONS, the Council on Foreign
Relations, through its War and Peace Studies Project, also spawned the
International Monetary Fund (IMF) and the World Bank. The Articles

of Agreement for these organizations were drawn up at an international conference of 44 allied countries at the Mount Washington Hotel and Resort in Bretton Woods, New Hampshire. The agreement which brought the two sisters to life was ratified on December 27, 1945.[1]

According to A. K. Chesterton, "The World Bank and the IMF were not incubated by hard pressed governments engaged in waging war, but by a supra-national Money Power, which could afford to look ahead to the shaping of a post-war world that would serve its interests."[2]

**The United Nations**
was one the first global political institutions that impacts the lives of all Americans.

The IMF, with headquarters in Washington, DC, was set up to "control international exchange rates" and to "stabilize currencies." The funding for the organization was based on a quota system with the most industrialized countries providing the greatest share of revenue. But the lion's share (over 20 percent) came from the United States since the currencies of other countries were not transferable into gold. FDR had confiscated the gold of the American citizenry and removed the nation from the gold standard.

But everybody else in the world could still exchange their paper dollars for gold at the fixed price of $35 per ounce.[3] The result of this arrangement was the ongoing transference of America's wealth to overseas banks and the recognition of the dollar as the basis of the global economy.

## A GOAL BEYOND GOLD

As long as the dollar remained redeemable in gold, the amount of currency that could be created by the money cartel in charge of the IMF remained limited. John Maynard Keynes, the leading British economist at the Bretton Woods Conference, recognized this problem as soon as the IMF was established. He wrote: "I felt that the leading central bank would never voluntarily relinquish the then existing forms of the gold standard, and I did not desire a catastrophe sufficiently violent to shake them off involuntarily. The only practical hope lay in a gradual evolution in the forms of a managed world currency, taking the existing gold standard as a starting point."[4]

The ultimate goal of the group who gathered at Bretton Woods was the creation of a world currency called the *bancor*. At the conference, Mariner Eccles, a governor of the Federal Reserve Board, noted: "An international currency is synonymous with international government."[5] But this act, which would have driven the final nail in Uncle Sam's coffin proved to be even too radical for acceptance by the American dignitaries in attendance, including Harry Morgenthau, Jr.[6]

## THE SPECIAL DRAWING RIGHTS

The plan to wean the world from gold came to fruition on August 15, 1971, when President Richard Nixon signed an executive order declaring that the United States no longer would redeem its paper dollars for gold.[7] Nixon was acting on the advice of Secretary of State Henry Kissinger, a lifelong appendage of the Rockefeller interests, and budget adviser George Shultz, later secretary of state and chairman of the vast Bechtel construction giant.[8]

Thanks to Nixon's executive order, the IMF now could function as the world's central bank by providing an unlimited issue of its own fiat currency to member nations. This new money, based solely on the money cartel's statement of its worth, was called a Special Drawing Right (SDR). It operated, as economist Dennis Turner explains, in the following way: "SDRs are turned into loans to Third World nations by the creation of checking accounts in the commercial or central banks of the members in the name of debtor governments. These bank accounts

**President Richard Nixon**
The plan to wean the world from gold came to fruition on August 15, 1971, when President Richard Nixon signed an executive order declaring that the United States no longer would redeem its paper for gold.

are created out of thin air. The IMF creates dollars, francs, pounds or other hard currencies and gives them to a Third World dictator, with inflation resulting in the country where the currency originated. . . . Inflation is caused in the industrialized nations while wealth is transferred from the general public to the debtor nation. And the debtor nation doesn't repay."[9]

But the sword is two-edged. Nations borrow SDRs primarily to pay interest on their mounting debts. This would be fine and dandy, save for the fact that the IMF charges interest on every SDR that it produces from its computer system. And so, the loans, for the most part, do not serve to bolster failing economies. They simply create a steady flow of wealth from borrowing nations to the money changers who control the IMF and are not subjected to any international supervision.

## THE DOLLAR'S DEMISE

The dollar, severed from the gold standard, ceased to serve as the official IMF currency and was compelled to compete with other currencies—primarily the mark and the yen—on its relative value to the countries. Over the decades, the dollar became increasingly discounted. Still and all, it remained a favored medium of exchange since America as a country remained wide open to foreign investors, who could buy American real estate, American factories and industrial plants, American mining companies, and shopping centers without the restrictions placed on such purchases by other nations. For this reason, the Federal Reserve continued to churn out massive amounts of fiat paper money, since the demand for such dollars seemed to be endless.[10]

**International Monetary Fund (IMF)**
The IMF now could function as the world's central bank by providing an unlimited issue of its own fiat currency to member nations thanks to Nixon's executive order.

This situation permitted Americans to finance its enormous trade deficits with more and more money made out of nothing and allowed them to purchase cars, cell phones, computers, clothing, generic drugs, and seventy-inch high-definition television sets at cut-rate prices, while the foreign manufacturers got the greenbacks. By the twenty-first century, this flood of dollars, which continued to be discounted, caused inflation to raise its hoary head until America was rapidly approaching the time when foreign manufacturers no longer will accept dollars for their goods and the Federal Reserve no longer will be able to finance its enormous trade deficit by churning out paper money.[11]

## "THE GOOD OLD DAYS ARE GONE"

At the end of 2016, the US trade deficit stood at $502 billion.[12] This prompted the following response from Chinese officials: "The US government has to come to terms with the painful fact that the good old days when it could just borrow its way out of messes of its own making are finally gone. . . . China, the sole superpower's largest creditor, now has every right to demand that America address its structural debt problem and ensure the security of China's dollar denominated assets." The officials went on to demand that the Federal Reserve be placed under restraints and subjected to international monitoring. "International supervision over the issue of US dollars should be introduced and a new, stable and secured global currency may also be an option to avert a catastrophe caused by any single country."[13]

## THE SECOND SISTER

While the IMF purportedly provides loans to stabilize economies, the World Bank, which was set up with funds from Morgan Stanley and First Boston (another J. P. Morgan facility), shelled out loans to war-ravaged and underdeveloped nations.[14] Through the years, the majority of the presidents of the World Bank have come from the stables of the Council on Foreign Relations. Eugene Meyer, the first president of the World Bank (1945), was a CFR official and the former chairman of the Federal Reserve. He was succeeded by John J. McCloy (1947–1949), who also served at the CFR chairman.[15] All of these men had strong ties to Wall Street. McCloy was a partner of the Wall Street corporate law firm of Milbank, Tweed, Hope, Hadley & McCloy, which had long served the Rockefeller family and the Chase Bank as legal counsel.

**World Bank**
The World Bank was set up with funds from Morgan Stanley and First Boston, another J.P. Morgan facility.

From there he moved to become chairman of the board of the Chase Manhattan Bank, a director of the Rockefeller Foundation, and of Rockefeller Center.[16] Eugene Black, who replaced McCloy, was a senior vice-president at Chase Manhattan, and his son, Bill, was a Morgan Stanley executive.[17] The House of Morgan looked on the World Bank as its greatest creation. It represented the crystallization of the family's efforts, beginning with the Pilgrim Society and the Federal Reserve, to acquire, along with the Rothschilds and the Rockefellers, ultimate control over the world's financial systems.

The World Bank established its headquarters in Washington, DC. Its membership consisted of the same forty-four nations that belonged to the IMF. Like its sister agency, it was controlled by one-dollar one-vote rather than the one-country one-vote UN system. Since the United States provided nearly 20 percent of the money required to fund the World Bank, the New York bankers (Morgan, Rockefeller, and Kuhn-Loeb) gained a permanent place among the Bank's executive directors and the exclusive right to appoint the Bank president.[18]

Ostensibly, this Morgan creation was supposed to serve as the savior of mankind by enabling foreign governments to provide care for those most in need. The loans were provided on generous terms, usually at rates below market, and for durations as long as fifty years.[19] The lion's share of the cash, which amounted to $30 billion, came from the US taxpayers.[20]

## TERMS AND CONDITIONS

But there is a snare to the World Bank's every transaction. The money, like IMF loans, is provided with very exacting conditions, known as structural-adjustment programs (SAPs).[21] One SAP is the immediate reimbursement to the country's creditors, such as Morgan Stanley, Chase Manhattan, and Citibank. Another is the country's agreement to sell off its key assets, including their water supply, their pipelines, and their power systems to buyers provided by the World Bank/IMF. A third condition is the country's commitment to take remedial steps, including a restructuring of its government and the resettlement of populations, dictated by World Bank/IMF officials.[22]

The SAPs have caused devastating results for countries who accepted the loans. The World Bank/IMF forced Argentina and Ecuador to liquidate its public holdings in order to comply with the repayment demands. In this way, Rockefeller-affiliated Citibank seized control of 50 percent of Argentina's banks; Rockefeller-owned British Petroleum assumed ownership of Ecuador's pipelines; and Enron, a shell company tied to the House of Rothschild, obtained control of the great lakes that provide water to Buenos Aires.[23]

## CRY THE BELOVED COUNTRY

Other SAPs mandates include the lowering of existing wages, the raising of the interest rate, the downsizing of all state facilities, the phasing out of statutory minimal wages, and the termination of "surplus" teachers and health care workers.[24] In extreme circumstances, even the resettlement of existing populations is required.[25] Such a program got underway in Tanzania, which has received more aid per capita from the World Bank than any other country. Thousands of Tanzanians were driven from their villages, which were set ablaze, and loaded like cattle into trucks for relocation in government villages.[26]

On average, Third World countries face as many as sixty-seven conditions for every World Bank loan. Some countries are hit with a far higher number of demands. Uganda, for example, where 23 percent of all children under five are malnourished, faced a staggering 197 conditions attached to its World Bank development finance grant in 2005. Anxious to uphold the conditions, Ugandan security forces engaged in mass detentions, torture, and the killing of hundreds of prisoners.[27]

## THE FRUITS OF CECIL RHODES

Zimbabwe (formerly known as Rhodesia in honor of Cecil Rhodes) serves as a prime example of the effects of SAPs on a Third World economy. In accordance with stipulations from the IMF/World Bank, the leftist government confiscated and nationalized many of the farms that were owned by white settlers. The most desirable properties became occupied by leading government officials, while the least desirable farms were transformed into state-run collectives. The collectives were such miserable failures that the natives who worked the farms were forced to beg for food.[28]

By 1992, one year after Zimbabwe became subjected to the IMF/World Bank, the economy went into a deep recession; the GDP fell by nearly 8 percent, 25 percent of the public workers were laid off, and unemployment began to soar, reaching 50 percent in 1997. By 1999, 68 percent of the population was living on less than $2 a day.[29] The per-capita budget for health care fell from $22 in 1990 to $11 in 1996, causing a 30 percent decline in the quality of medical services. Twice as many women were dying of childbirth in Harare hospitals in 1993 than in 1990. By 1995, the number of cases of tuberculosis had quadrupled. At the dawn of the twenty-first century, one fourth of Zimbabwe's population was infected with HIV/AIDS.[30]

According to a three-year study released in 2002 by the Structural Adjustment Participatory Review International Network (SAPRIN) in collaboration with the World Bank, SAPs have been "expanding poverty, inequality, and insecurity around the world. They have torn at the heart of economies and the social fabric . . . increasing tensions among different social strata, fueling extremist movements and delegitimizing democratic political systems. Their effects, particularly on the poor, are so profound and pervasive that no amount of targeted social investments can begin to address the social crises that they have engendered."[31]

## ANTI-AMERICAN ANIMUS

Since the World Bank and the IMF are located in Washington, DC, and controlled by the Houses of Morgan and Rockefeller, the people who have been subjected to SAPs manifest a strong anti-American animus.

They assume that the twin banks are part of a corrupt capitalistic government that seeks to deprive them of life's basic necessities. Within forty years of the creation of these sister organizations, violent riots directed against Americans and caused by the austerity programs erupted in Argentina, Bolivia, Brazil, Ecuador, Egypt, Haiti, Liberia, Peru, and the Sudan.[32]

Concerning these occurrences, Luis Ignacio Silva, a prominent Brazilian politician, said: "Without being radical or overly bold, I will tell you that the Third World War has already started—a silent war, not for that reason any the less sinister. This war is tearing down Brazil, Latin America and practically all the Third World. Instead of soldiers dying there are children, instead of millions of wounded there are millions of unemployed; instead of destruction of bridges there is the tearing down of factories, schools, hospitals, and entire economies . . . It is a war by the United States against the Latin American continent and the Third World. It is a war over the foreign debt, one which has as its main weapon interest, a weapon more deadly than the atom bomb, more shattering than a laser beam."[33]

# NOTES

1. "History of the International Monetary Fund," *The Tree Center,* August 14, 2014, http://www.50years.org/history-of-imf.
2. A. K. Chesterton, quoted in Jack Kenney, "The Federal Reserve Bankers for the New World Order," *New American,* January 2014, https://www.thenewamerican. com/economy/item/17312-the-federal-reserve-bankers-for-the-new-world-order.
3. G. Edward Griffin, *The Creature from Jekyll Island,* 5th Edition (Westlake Village, CA: The Reality Zone, 2017), p. 90.
4. John Maynard Keynes, *The Collected Writings of John Maynard Keyes,* Vol. V (New York: Macmillan, 1971), p. xx.
5. Mariner Eccles, quoted in G. Vance Smith and Tom Gow, *Masters of Deception: The Rise f the Council on Foreign Relations* (Colorado Springs, Colorado: Freedom First Society, 2012), p. 60.
6. Douglas French, "Bretton Woods Final Conceit," Freedom for Economic Education, August 22, 2013, https://fee.org/articles/bretton-woods-fatal-conceit/.
7. Griffin, *The Creature from Jekyll Island,* p. 91.
8. F. William Engdahl, *Gods of Money: Wall Street and the Death of the American Century* (Wiesbaden, Germany: Edition Engdahl, 2010), p. 163.
9. Dennis Turner, quoted in Griffin, *The Creature from Jekyll Island,* p. 90.
10. Ibid., pp. 93–94.
11. Ibid.
12. Kimberly Amado, "U.S. Trade Deficit: Causes, Effects, and Trade Partners," *The Balance,* April 12, 2017, https://www.thebalance.com/u-s-trade-deficit-causes-effects-trade-partners-3306276.
13. Gus Luhin, "China: 'America Needs to Accept the Painful Fact that the Good Old Days Are Over," *Business Insider,* August 6, 2011, http://www.businessinsider.com/china-debt-addiction-short-sighted-2011-8.
14. Ron Chernow, *The House of Morgan: An American Banking Dynasty and the Rise of Modern Finance* (New York: Grove Press, 1990), p. 518.
15. Smith and Gow, *Masters of Deception,* p. 60.
16. Murray N. Rothbard, "Rockefeller, Morgan, and War," Mises Institute, April 30, 2017, https://mises.org/library/rockefeller-morgan-and-war.
17. Ron Chernow, *The House of Morgan,* p. 518.
18. Asad Ismi, "Impoverishing a Continent: The World Bank and the IMF in Africa," *Halifax Initiative Coalition,* July 2004, http://www.halifaxinitiative.org/updir/ImpoverishingAContinent.pdf.
19. Ibid., p. 95.
20. Ibid.
21. Ismi, "Impoverishing a Continent."
22. Peter Palms, "Building the New World Order with the IMF and the World Bank and Taypayers Pay the Bill," *Thomas Hartman Program,* October 9, 2015, https://www.thomhartmann.com/users/dr-peterpalms/blog/2015/10/building-new-world-order-imf-and-world-bank-and-taxpayers-pay-bill.
23. Greg Palast, "World Bank Secret Documents Consume Argentina," Greg Palast. com, March 4,

2002, http://www.gregpalast.com/world-bank-secret-documents-consumes-argentinaalex-jones-interviews-reporter-greg-palast/.

24. Michel Chossudovsky, *The Globalization of War: America's "Long War" against Humanity* (Montreal, Quebec: Global Research 2015), pp. 125–131.

25. Ibid.

26. G. Edward Griffin, *The Creature from Jekyll Island*, p. 98.

27. Ibid.

28. Ibid, pp. 98–99.

29. Ismi, "Impoverishing a Continent."

30. Ibid.

31. SAPRIN, "The Policy Roots of Economic Crisis and Poverty: A Multi-Country Participatory Assessment of Structural Adjustment, April 2002.

32. "IMF Hands Out Prescriptions for Sour Economic Medicine," *Insight*, February 9, 1987.

33. Luis Ignacio Silva, quoted in Susan George, *A Fate Worse Than Debt: The World Financial Crisis and the Poor* (New York: Grove Press, 1990), p. 238.

# 27

# THE BASTARD SON

*Now, as nearly as I can make out, those fellows in the CIA don't just report on wars and the like, they go out and make their own, and there's nobody to keep track of what they're up to. They spend billions of dollars on stirring up trouble so they'll have something to report on. . . . It's become a government all of its own and all secret. They don't have to account to anybody.*

—HARRY TRUMAN, INTERVIEW WITH MERLE MILLER, 1962.

ON SEPTEMBER 20, 1945, President Harry S. Truman abolished the OSS and placed its secret intelligence and counter-espionage branches under the war department as the Strategic Services Unit (SSU). Within months, the SSU morphed into the National Intelligence Authority and the Central Intelligence Group (CIG), the precursor of the CIA. According to Richard Helms in his memoirs, General Vandenberg, the director of CIG, recruited Allen Dulles, who had returned to his law practice in New York, "to draft a proposal for the shape and organization of what would become the Central Intelligence Agency" from the outline of Wild Bill Donovan, who remained a close confidant to the Houses of Rockefeller and Rothschild.[1] The proposal met with Truman's approval.

The Central Intelligence Agency (CIA) was created in 1947, under the National Security Act, to carry out covert operations "against hostile foreign states or groups or in support of friendly foreign states or groups but which are so planned and conducted that any US government responsibility for them is not evident to unauthorized persons." True to the vision of General "Wild Bill" Donovan, the new agency was exempt from disclosure of its "organization, functions, officials, titles, salaries, or numbers of personnel employed."[2] Even its solicitation and distribution of funds was to be concealed from Congressional and Judicial scrutiny. As Tom Braden, a senior CIA operational official in the early 1950s, explained: "The Agency never had to account for the money it spent except to the President if . . . [he] wanted to know how much money it was spending . . . otherwise the funds were not only unaccountable, they were unvouchered, so there was really no means of checking them . . . . Since it [the CIA] was unaccountable, it could hire as many people as it wanted. . . . It could hire armies; it could buy banks."[3]

The ties between the new agency and the House of Rockefeller were apparent from the start. Top secret planning meetings were held at the Pratt House, the CFR headquarters in New York.[4] These meetings were chaired by Allen Dulles, who in 1947 remained a partner in Sullivan and Cromwell, the New York law firm that represented the Rockefeller business interests, and served as the CFR president.[5] The Agency would serve the interest of the Rockefellers and the money cartel by toppling foreign governments, seizing natural resources, promoting free trade, and opening channels of communication between the world's central banks. In time, several of the CIA's covert operations, including MK-Ultra, would be funded by the Rockefeller family and the Rockefeller Foundation.[6]

The CIA represented another chapter in the linear story of the development of a shadow government that sought to rule the world. It's a story that began with the teachings of freemasonry and the creation of Rhodes's Secret Society and continued with the formation of the Round Table Movement, the Federal Reserve, the CFR, and the UN.

It was authored by the House of Rothschild and the banking families that became affiliated with it. Thanks to the Bank of International Settlements, the International Monetary Fund, and the World Bank, these banking families gained global economic control, and, with the CIA, they would attempt to obtain political hegemony.

## AN ELITE AGENCY

In keeping with OSS protocol, Dulles recruited agents for the new intelligence agency almost exclusively from the nation's elite: millionaire businessmen, Wall Street bankers and lawyers, members of the national news media, and Ivy League scholars. The new recruits included Nelson Rockefeller, son of John D. Rockefeller Jr.; Tommy "the Cork" Corcoran, a former governor of the Federal Reserve; three Harvard-trained Wall Street lawyers; Richard Bissell, a Ford Foundation executive; William F. Buckley Jr., a Yale graduate and son of a prominent oil baron; Philip Graham, a Harvard graduate and future owner of the *Washington Post*; William Colby, a graduate of Princeton and the Columbia Law School and grandson of Gates McGarrah, one of the world's wealthiest bankers; and Richard Mellon Scaife, the principal heir to the Mellon banking, oil, and aluminum fortune. Rear Admiral Roscoe H. Hillenkoetter of the ONI became the executive director and former OSS official, and Wall Street lawyer Frank Wisner was appointed head of covert operations.[7]

## RED ALERT

The first concern of the new intelligence agency was the situation in Italy, where the Italian Communist Party (*Partito Comunista Italiano*, or PCI) was poised to take control of the government. Between late 1943 and mid-1944, the PCI had doubled, and in the German-occupied northern half of the country, an extremely radical Marxist movement was gathering strength; in the winter of 1944, over 500,000 Turin workers, waving the red flag, shut down the factories for eight days despite brutal Gestapo repression; and the Italian underground—consisting of

Communist sympathizers grew to 150,000 armed men.[8]

Postwar Italy stood poised to become the first Communist country in Western Europe. Hundreds of thousands of Northerners had either actively supported or actively fought for the partisan movement that had finally forced the German army out of Italy. It was the partisans who had captured Mussolini and who had hung him upside down with his mistress, it was the partisans who continued to assassinate fascists after the war ended, and it was the partisans who constituted the PCI. By 1946, the division in the country became acute with the people in the north wanting a Communist republic, and the people in the south wanting a Catholic monarchy.[9]

In Sicily, the rise of the PCI was even more disconcerting. Girolamo Li Causi, the island's leading Communist, stirred up the masses with his demands for the redistribution of the land's feudal holdings. His words, "we plan no Soviet rule here," cut no ice with the mob and the propertied classes but revitalized the longings of the landless poor for economic reform.[10] In 1947, the left, never previously strong in Sicily, skyrocketed out of nowhere. All of Italy was stunned by the provincial elections, which produced resounding victories for the Communists.

With national elections in Italy scheduled for 1948, US officials were faced with the specter of a coalition coming to power under Palmiro Togliatti, who had sat out the war under the hospitality of the Kremlin.[11] The first numbered document of the newly created CIA was a top-secret report entitled "The Position of the United States with Respect to Italy" (NSC 1/1). The report, which was issued on November 14, 1947, contained the following quote from a cable sent by George Kennan, director of the US State Department's Policy Planning Staff: "As far as Europe is concerned, Italy is obviously the key point. If communists were to win election there our whole position in the Mediterranean, and possibly Western Europe as well, would probably be undermined."[12]

## THE DIRTY MONEY
The heightened paranoia over the possibility of a PCI victory gave rise

to the creation of the Office of Policy Coordination within the new intelligence agency. This office was authorized to engage in "paramilitary operations as well as political and economic warfare." The authorization for such covert action, according to CIA director Frank Wisner, was included in a catch-all clause to the National Security Act of 1947, which granted the CIA the right to engage in "functions" related to "intelligence affecting the national security."[13] And nothing in 1947 seemed more of a threat to the peace and stability of America and the Western World than the threat of the Communist takeover of Italy. In the eyes of Wisner, Dulles, Donovan, and Angleton, the only individuals with the means to ward off this nightmare were Lucky Luciano and Calogero Vizzini ("Don Calo"), the *capo di tutti capi* ("boss of bosses") of the Sicilian mafia, who had been jailed by Mussolini for his support of the Christian Democrats and his opposition to fascism. The new intelligence agency, thanks to Paul E. Helliwell and the creation of the global heroin industry, now had a steady supply of cash to pay them.

Of course, the money for the muscle could not be paid to Lucky and the Don Calo clan directly. It had to be channeled through a financial firm that would not be subjected to scrutiny by US Treasury agents, Italian bank examiners, or international fiscal monitors. Only one institution possessed such immunity, and it was located in the heart of Vatican City.

## CASH AND CANDY

In the months before the 1948 national election, the CIA dumped $65 million of its black money into the Vatican Bank.[14] Much of the cash was hand delivered in large suitcases by members of Luciano's syndicate, including clerics with affiliations to the Sicilian mafia. The reception of this money by the Holy See was held in strictest confidentiality. One reason for the secrecy, as Cardinal Francis Spellman of New York later revealed, was that "subversive groups in the United States would grasp this as a very effective pretense for attacking the United States Government for having released money to the Vatican, even though indirectly conveyed."[15]

The heroin, which remained the source for the black money, continued to be supplied to the Sicilian mob by Schiaparelli, the Italian pharmaceutical giant. The dope was received by a chain of bogus businesses that had been set up in Palermo by Luciano and Don Calo.

These businesses included a candy factory, which produced chocolates that were filled with neither cherries nor cream but nuggets of 100 percent pure smack. Another company was a fruit export enterprise, which was of integral importance, since the drugs continued to be shipped to the United States, with the cooperation of the CIA, in crates of oranges, half of which were made of wax and stuffed with pure heroin.[16]

## ITALIAN ELECTION TACTICS

In the closing months of 1947, hundreds of "made men" began to arrive in Italy from New York, Chicago, and Miami to aid Luciano and Don Calo in addressing the Communist problem. Several—including Silvestro "Sam" Carolla—arrived on US military transports. The CIA's black money for mob muscle was shelled out by the Vatican bank from ecclesiastical organizations, including Catholic Action.[17] In this way, the Holy See forged an alliance with the Sicilian mafia, an alliance that would strengthen throughout the next three decades.

Murder, Inc. was now unleashed upon the Italian electorate. Don Calo and an army of thugs, including Vito Genovese's cousin Giovanni Genovese, burned down eleven Communist branch offices and made four assassination attempts on Communist leader Girolamo Li Causi. The gang, under Frank Coppola, who had been imported from Detroit by Angleton to work with Sicilian bandit Salvatore Giuliano, also opened fire on a crowd of workers celebrating May Day in Portella della Ginestra, killing eleven and wounding fifty-seven. The funds for the massacre were provided by Wild Bill Donovan through his World Commerce Corporation.[18] One of Italy's leading labor organizers, Placido Rizzotto, was found dead at the bottom of a cliff—legs and arms chained and a bullet through his brain. Throughout 1948, in Sicily alone, the CIA-backed terror attacks resulted in the killing on average of five people a week.[19]

## THE VATICAN DEATH SQUAD

In addition to the undertakings of Murder, Inc., Monsignor Don Giuseppe Bicchierai, acting upon papal authority, assembled a terror gang charged with the task of beating up Communist candidates, smashing left-wing political gatherings, and intimidating voters. The money, guns, and jeeps for the Monsignor's terror attacks were furnished by the CIA from surplus World War II stockpiles.[20]

On Election Day, Don Calo and his thugs stuffed ballot boxes and bribed voters with gifts of freshly laundered drug money, while Pope Pius remained within his chambers "hunched-up, almost physically overcome by the weight of his present burden."[21] The mob's tactics worked, and the Christian Democrats triumphantly returned to power. In his memoirs, William Colby, who would later become the CIA director, wrote that the Communists would have gained 60 percent of the vote without the Agency's sabotage.[22]

## OTHER CATHOLIC BANKS

One year after the election, renewed fears of a Communist takeover of Italy arose from Stalin's creation of the *Comecon*, the union of the Soviet Union, Bulgaria, Czechoslovakia, Hungary, Poland, and Romania, to enforce the Soviet dominion of the lesser states of central Europe.[23] In the face of this development, the CIA opted to extend support for the Christian Democratic Party in Italy and stay-behind units throughout Western Europe with billions in covert funding that could only come from the expansion of the drug trade. The CIA funds were deposited by members of Don Calo's crime family in Catholic banks throughout Italy, including *Banco Ambrosiano*. These banks, thanks to the Lateran Treaty, were safe from scrutiny by the Bank of Italy and Italy's Treasury department. A henchman for Genco Russo, Don Calo's immediate successor as *capo*, now observed: "He [Russo] is constantly in contact with priests, priests go to his place, and he goes to the bank—which is always run by priests—the bank director is a priest, the bank has always been the priests' affair."[24]

## THE VATICAN DESK

In 1949, Pope Pius XII issued a solemn decree that excommunicated not only the members of the Holy Mother Church who joined or favored the Communist party but also all Catholics who read, published, or disseminated any printed material that upheld Communist ideology.[25] In an internal memo, the CIA provided the following analysis of the pope's action:

> By this action, the two most powerful organizations for moving men to act on behalf of a doctrine are brought into open and basic conflict. The possible long-range ramifications of this conflict cannot be easily or comprehensively defined. The decree will be a very powerful factor in the East-West struggle. In Eastern Europe, it implies a struggle to the bitter end. . . . In many other areas of the world, the decree will exert a powerful and prolonged indirect pressure on both policy and action. Communist governments and Communists generally will have to accept the issue as now posed. Although the Communist governments would obviously have preferred to carry on their anti-church campaign at their own pace, the power of decision has now been taken from them. The conflict can be pressed on them with a speed and comprehensives that may well affect the satisfactory development of other Communist policies.[26]

Fearful that the decree might be insufficient to crush the "forces of godliness," Pius XII persisted to tighten his ties with the CIA into a Gordian knot that no one could unravel. The Christian Democratic Party continued to receive more than $20 million in annual aid from the Agency, and, in return, the CIA established a "Vatican desk" under Angleton.[27]

The Vatican desk reviewed all of the intelligence reports that were sent to the Holy See from papal nuncios who were stationed behind the Iron Curtain for pertinent data. During the early years of the Cold War, this became one of the only means for the Agency to penetrate the Eastern Bloc.[28] Strategies between the CIA and the Church were drafted to undermine left-wing movements throughout Europe and South America. The affairs of politically suspect members of the Curia were monitored by moles. The actions of progressive priests, particularly in Latin America, were thwarted by strong-arm techniques.[29]

# NOTES

1. "U.S. Department of State: Foreign Relations of the United States, 1945–1950, Emergence of the Intelligence Establishment." *state.gov*. Document 292, Section 5.
2. Ibid.
3. James Cameron Graham, "The Secret History of the CIA's Involvement in the Narcotics Trade," doctoral dissertation, School of Politics and International Relations, The University of Nottingham, 2009.
4. Eustace Mullins, "The CIA," from *The World Order: A Study in the Hegemony of Parasitism*, Modern History Project, 1984, http://modernhistoryproject.org/mhp?Article=WorldOrder&C=5.0.
5. David Talbot, *The Devil's Chessboard: Allen Dulles, the CIA, and the Rise of the Secret Government* (New York: Harper Collins, 2015), p. 149.
6. Ibid., p. 553.
7. Peter Dale Scott, "Operation Paper: The United States and Drugs in Thailand and Burma," *The Asia Pacific Journal*, 2008, http://japanfocus.org/-peter_dale-scott/3436, accessed May 20, 2014.
8. Alfred McCoy, *The Politics of Heroin: CIA's Complicity in the Global Drug Trade* (Chicago: Lawrence Hill Books, 2003), p. 24.
9. Philip Willan, *Puppetmasters: The Political Use of Terror in Italy* (London: Constable, 1991), p. 57.
10. Richard Cottrell, *Gladio: NATO's Dagger at the Heart of Europe* (Palm Desert, CA: 2012), p. 114.
11. Ibid.
12. National Security Council document 1/1, obtained under Freedom of Information Act. See also Philip Willan, *Puppetmasters*, p. 23.
13. Philip Willan, *Puppetmasters* p. 24.
14. Eustace Mullins, *The World Order: A Study in the Hegemony of Parasitism*, Chapter Five, *Modern History Project*, 1984, http://modernhistoryproject.org/mhp?Article=WorldOrder&C=5.0, accessed May 20, 2014. See also R. Joseph, *America Betrayed* (San Jose, California: The University Press, 2003), p. 176.
15. Cardinal Spellman's memo to General George Marshall, undated. See John Cooney, *The American Pope: The Life and Times of Francis Cardinal Spellman (New York: Times Books, 1984)*, p. 161.
16. Alexander Cockburn and Jeffrey St. Clair, *Whiteout: The CIA, Drugs, and the Press* (New York: Verso, 1998), p. 130.
17. Bradley Ayers, *The Zenith Secret: A CIA Insider Exposes the Secret War against Cuba and the Plot That Killed the Kennedy Brothers* (Brooklyn: Vox Pop, 2007), p. 82.
18. Peter Dale Scott, "Deep Events and the CIA's Global Drug Connection." ," *Global Research*, September 8, 2008, http://www.globalresearch.ca/deep-events-and-the-cia-s-global-drug-connection/10095, accessed May 20, 2014.
19. Cockburn and St. Clair, *Whiteout*, p. 137.
20. Ibid., p. 138.
21. Cockburn and St. Clair, *Whiteout*, p. 137.
22. Ibid. p. 138.

23. "The Council for Mutual Economic Assistance," Washington, D.C.: The Library of Congress; Federal Research Division, n.d., http://memory.loc.gov/frd/cs/germany_ east/gx_appnb.html.

24. Pino Arlacchi, *Mafia Business: The Mafia Ethic and the Spirit of Capitalism* (New York: Oxford University Press, 1988), p. 40.

25. Pius XII, "Excommunication of Communists," Decree of the Holy Office, July 1, 1949, http://www.geocities.ws/caleb1x/documents/communism.html.

26. CIA memo in John Cooney's *The American Pope*, pp. 167–168.

27. Ronald Kessler, "James Angleton's Dangerous CIA Legacy," *NewsMax*, March 28, 2012, http://www.newsmax.com/RonaldKessler/James-Angleton-CIA-spies/2012/03/28/id/434109/, accessed May 19, 2014.

28. Martin A. Lee, "Their Will Be Done," *Mother Jones*, July/August 1983, http://www.motherjones.com/politics/1983/07/their-will-be-done, accessed May 20, 2014.

29. Ibid.

# 28

# ONSLAUGHT OF ATROCITIES

*The Association for Responsible Dissent estimates that by 1987, 6 million people had died as a result of CIA covert operations. Former State Department official William Blum correctly calls this an "American Holocaust." The CIA justifies these actions as part of its war against communism. But most coups do not involve a communist threat. Unlucky nations are targeted for a wide variety of reasons: not only threats to American business interests abroad, but also liberal or even moderate social reforms, political instability, the unwillingness of a leader to carry out Washington's dictates, and declarations of neutrality in the Cold War. Indeed, nothing has infuriated CIA Directors quite like a nation's desire to stay out of the Cold War.*

—STEVE KANGAS, "A TIMELINE OF CIA ATROCITIES," 1994

NOT WANTING TO BE DEPENDENT ON SCHIAPARELLI, the Italian pharmaceutical giant, for the heroin to mount ongoing covert operations, the CIA worked with General Chiang Kai-shek and his Kuomintang (KMT) army to create a drug route that would lead from Southeast Asia to the United States. By 1950, thousands of General Chiang's troops had been driven into the Shan States of Burma by the Communist forces of Mao Zedong.[1] The troops were mostly members of a Muslim minority, known as the Haw, who were born and bred in southwestern Yunnan, an area dominated by the opium trade.[2] With the hope that the reconstituted KMT, now known as the 93rd Division, might still mount an invasion of China to aid in the Korean Conflict, the CIA provided for all the immediate needs of the exiled army. It was an expensive undertaking that could only be offset by cultivation of poppy fields within the mountainous regions of northern Burma and northeastern Laos.

By 1951, the CIA began supplying arms and materiel to the KMT troops, whose sole activity was opium cultivation. This venture became the second example of the CIA conducting off-the-books foreign policy with assets of which the American people and most elected officials remained completely unaware. The decisions concerning this policy were made within the Office of Policy Coordination by a very small group of elite intelligence officials whose parameters remained undefined. These officials served America's rising military-industrial complex which relied on privatized military and intelligence contractors, international bankers, and even Washington's most highly organized lobbyists.[3]

## THE WORLD COMMERCE CORPORATION

To expedite the arms-for-drugs venture in the Far East, Wild Bill Donovan resigned from the military to form the World Commerce Corporation (WCC) with a small group of very wealthy friends, including Nelson Rockefeller, Joseph C. Grew (nephew of J. P. Morgan), Alfred DuPont, and Charles Jocelyn Hambro, director of the Hambros Bank and The Bank of England with close ties to the Morgan family.

The firm, which was registered in Panama, employed mob figure Sonny Fassoulis, a notorious drug dealer, to provide "services" to General Chiang's National Army.[4] The primary function of the WCC was to buy and sell surplus US weapons and munitions to foreign underworld groups, including the KMT and the Italian mafias. In exchange for the arms, the KMT provided the opium required to create the postwar intelligence agency.[5]

The opium was flown from the mountains of Burma and Laos by Cargo Air Transport to Bangkok, where the planes were emptied and loaded with weapons for the return flight to the poppy fields. In Bangkok, General Phao Sriyanonda, director general of Thailand's national police, employed his officers to load the product on the freighters of a mysterious shipping company called Sea Supply, Inc. (SSI), a CIA front run by Paul Helliwell, who now served as the Burmese consulate in Miami.[6] In 1954, British customs in Singapore stated that Bangkok had become the major center for opium trafficking in Southeast Asia.[7] The traffic became so lucrative that Thailand abandoned its anti-opium campaign which had been launched in 1948.[8]

### INTELLIGENCE SUBCULTURE

General Phao developed a close friendship with Donovan, who became the US ambassador to Thailand. Indeed, Wild Bill became so enthralled with Phao that he nominated the Thai general for a Legion of Merit award.[9] Although he failed to capture the award, Phao, by 1953, had received $35 million in aid from the CIA, including gifts of several naval vessels and cargo planes to transport the drugs to Hong Kong, Singapore, and Marseilles.[10] The benefactions were granted with the expectation that the KMT would launch guerilla raids into China.

The WCC and Sea Supply, like Cargo Air Transport (CAT), emerged from a subculture within the intelligence community of extremely wealthy and well-connected lawyers and businessmen who, at the time, were not part of any official government agency.[11] This subculture eventually would give rise to a network of banks, including the Bank of Credit and Finance International, and proprietary businesses, including the American International Assurance Company of C. V. Starr, which were created to support and conceal the flow of money from the heroin trade.[12]

### FALSE FLAGS AND MEDIA CONTROL

As the Western World became increasingly inundated with heroin, the CIA, through spokesmen such as George White of the Federal Bureau of Narcotics (FBN), placed the blame on Chairman Mao and the People's

Republic of China, who were accused of orchestrating the movement of two hundred to four hundred tons of opium per year from Yunnan to Bangkok.[13] The Agency further presented General Phao, the linchpin in the Asian drug connection, as America's best hope in combating this drug menace. Such reports represented the first unfurling of a CIA false flag.

Knowing the importance of issuing such false reports, the CIA, under Allen Dulles, initiated Operation Mockingbird in 1953. This operation consisted of the recruitment of leading journalists and editors to fabricate stories and to create smoke screens in order to cast the Agency's agenda in a positive light. Among the news executives who took part in this undertaking were William Paley of the Columbia Broadcasting System, Henry Luce of Time Inc., Arthur Hays Sulzberger of the *New York Times*, Barry Bingham Sr. of the *Louisville CourierJournal,* and James Copley of the Copley News Service. Entire news organizations eventually became part of Mockingbird, including the American Broadcasting Company, the National Broadcasting Company, the Associated Press, United Press International, Reuters, Hearst Newspapers, ScrippsHoward, *Newsweek*, the Mutual Broadcasting System, the *Miami Herald,* the *Saturday Evening Post*, and the *New York Herald Tribune.* With over 400 journalists now on the take along with mainstream news outlets, the Agency could operate without fear of exposure.[14]

And so, the atrocities began.

## 1953

In 1953, the CIA turned its attention to Tehran, when the Iranian Prime Minister Mohammed Mosaddegh nationalized the Anglo Persian Oil Company. By purchasing the services of Iranian journalists, military officers and members of parliament, the Agency was able to spread false reports that Mosaddegh was Jewish and a Communist. These reports caused the Warriors of Islam, a group of militant extremists, to stage riots throughout Tehran. Among the rioters was the Ayatollah Khomeini, Iran's future leader.[15] After Mosaddegh was arrested and tossed out of office, the CIA replaced him with Mohammad Reza

Pahlavi, the Shah of Iran. The oil industry was denationalized and the country's national treasure was handed over to companies owned or partially owned by the House of Rockefeller.[16]

Inspired by North Korea's brainwashing program, the CIA launched its own experiments on mind control in an operation known as MK-Ultra. The project involved giving massive infusions of hallucinogens, including LSD, to American subjects without their knowledge or against their will. Others were placed into "electric dream states" through insulin overdoses, experimental drugs, and electroshock therapy. Several subjects committed suicide; others degenerated into a vegetative state.

The ultimate goal was to create human machines who would act on command of the Agency, even against their own conscience.[17] Funded by the Rockefeller and Ford Foundations, MK-Ultra also included studies in means of controlling the thoughts of the American people to by public relations, advertising, hypnosis, and other forms of suggestion.[18]

## 1954

In Guatemala, the CIA overthrew the democratically elected Jacob Arbenz in a military coup. Arbenz threatened to nationalize the Rockefeller-owned United Fruit Company, in which CIA Director Allen Dulles was a shareholder. Arbenz was replaced with a series of right-wing dictators whose bloodthirsty policies would kill over 100,000 Guatemalans in the next forty years.[19]

## 1956

Radio Free Europe, a CIA propaganda outlet, incited Hungary to revolt by broadcasting Soviet Premier Nikita Khrushchev's Secret Speech, in which he denounced his predecessor Josef Stalin. The broadcast offered assurance that the American military would support the Hungarian uprising. The support never materialized as Hungarians launched a doomed armed revolt, which precipitated a major Soviet invasion. The conflict resulted in the deaths of 7,000 Soviets and 30,000 Hungarians. The propaganda spewed from Radio Free Europe was so blatantly false that it was illegal to publish transcripts of the broadcasts in the United States.[20]

## 1959

With the assistance of the US military, "Papa Doc" Duvalier became dictator of Haiti. He created his own private police force, the "Tonton Macoutes," who terrorized the population with machetes. When Papa Doc died in 1971, his nineteen-year-old son, called Baby Doc, became "president for life." Throughout the Duvalier reign, over 100,000 Haitians were hacked to pieces. Yet the United States declined to utter a word of protest over this horrific human rights record.[21]

## 1960

In 1960, the Gladio operation turned strategic, when the Turkish stay-behind unit, known as Counter-Guerilla, joined with the military to stage a coup d'état against the government of Prime Minister Adnan Menderes. Menderes, who was planning a visit to Moscow to secure economic aid, was cast into prison, put on trial by a hastily assembled court, and executed at the gallows on the island of Imrali.[22] After civilian rule was restored by a democratic election, Col. Alparslan Turkes, one of the leaders of the uprising, formed the National Action Party and its paramilitary youth group, the Grey Wolves, with CIA funds. The new party espoused a fanatical pan-Turkish ideology that called for re-claiming large sections of the Soviet Union under the flag of a reborn Turkish empire.[23] This ideology served the interest of the money cartel, who became increasingly fixated upon seizing the vast natural resources that surrounded the Caspian Sea.

## "ESTABLISHMENT IKE"

When these atrocities took place, Dwight David Eisenhower occupied the Oval Office. Like FDR, Ike had been groomed for the presidency by the Council on Foreign Relations. He had been a four-star general who had never witnessed combat, the president of Columbia University without an academic background, and a politician who was neither a Republican nor a Democrat. He had joined the CFR before the onset of World War II, served on the editorial advisory board of *Foreign Affairs* (the CFR periodical), and chaired a CFR study group on aid to postwar Europe.[24]

As America's 34th president, Ike surrounded himself with CFR officials who took control of the government. John Foster Dulles, Allen's elder brother, became secretary of state. He was an in-law of the Rockefellers and served as chairman of the Rockefeller Foundation. He was also the chairman of the Carnegie Endowment for International Peace and a delegate to the UN's founding conference in San Francisco.[25] When Dulles died in 1959, Ike chose Christian Herter as his replacement. Herter, like Dulles, had married into the Rockefeller family and attended the Paris Peace Conference.[26] Other CFR members appointed to prominent positions by President Eisenhower include Allen Dulles as CIA director, Robert B. Anderson as secretary of the Treasury, Gordon Gray as national security advisor, Lewis Strauss as chairman of the Atomic Energy Commission; C. Douglas Dillon as undersecretary of state, and Nelson Rockefeller as undersecretary of health, education, and welfare.[27] This pattern of selecting key cabinet members, including secretaries of state, from the stable of the CFR would continue until 2017. For this reason, there was little difference which political party prevailed in national elections.

## IKE'S ATROCITIES

During his eight years in office, Ike advanced the demise of the country by halting the Reece Committee's investigation of the control tax-exempt foundations wielded over America's educational, cultural, and religious institutions, by producing national deficits that were five times greater than Harry Truman's, by promoting the growth of the military-industrial complex by unchecked defense spending, and by crushing the Bricker Amendment, which stipulated that no treaty signed by the United States could override the Constitution or infringe on the rights of

American citizens.[28] Speaking in Geneva on July 21, 1955, Eisenhower promoted the end of American sovereignty by saying:

> I have been searching my heart and mind for something I could say here that could convince everyone of the great sincerity of the US in approaching the problem of disarmament. I should address myself for a moment principally to the delegates from the Soviet Union. . . . I propose that we take a practical step, that we begin an arrangement very quickly, as between ourselves, immediately. These steps would include: to give each other a complete blueprint of our military establishments, from beginning to end, from one end of our countries to the other; lay out the establishments and provide blueprints to each other.
>
> Next, to provide within our countries facilities for aerial photography to the other country. . . .
>
> Likewise, we will make more easily attainable, a comprehensive and effective system of inspection and disarmament, because what I propose, I assure you, would be but a beginning.[29]

Eisenhower was making these concessions to a nation that was intent upon eradicating the American way of life.

Even more alarming was the Eisenhower Administration's production of a State Department document called *Freedom from War—The U.S. Program for General and Complete Disarmament*, which proposed that America should surrender all of its weapons, including its nuclear arsenals, to the United Nations. The document set forth the following objectives:

a. The disbanding of all national armed forces and the prohibition of their reestablishment in any form whatsoever other than those required to preserve internal order and for contributions to a United Nations peace force;

b. The elimination from national arsenals of all armaments, including the weapons of mass destruction and the means of their delivery, other than those required for a United Nations peace force and for maintaining general order;

c. The establishment and effective operation of an international disarmament organization within the framework of the United Nations to insure compliance at all times with all disarmament obligations.[30]

## A RAY OF HOPE

When Ike left office, Uncle Sam was in a comatose condition, but there was a flicker of hope for his survival. It came from a young senator calling for radical change and the forging of a New Frontier.

# NOTES

1.  Francis W. Belanga, *Drugs, the U.S., and Khun Sa* (Bangkok, Thailand: Editions Duang Kamal, 1989), pp. 85–87.

2.  Peter Dale Scott, *American War Machine: Deep Politics, the CIA Global Drug Connection, and the Road to Afghanistan* (Washington, D.C.: Rowman and Littlefield, 2010, p. 64.

3.  Martin McCauley, *The Cold War: 1946–2016* (New York: Routledge, 2017), p. 32.

4.  Bradley Ayers, "The War That Never Was" (New York: Bobbs Merrill, 1976), p. 78.

5.  Peter Dale Scott, "Operation Paper: The United States and Drugs in Thailand and Burma," *The Asia Pacific Journal*, 2008, http://japanfocus.org/-peter_dale-scott/3436, accessed May 20, 2014 See also Sterling and Peggy Seagrave, *Gold Warriors* (London: Bowstring, 2008), p. 324.

6.  Cockburn and St. Clair, *Whiteout*, p. 216.

7.  Alfred W. McCoy, *The Politics of Heroin*, p. 183.

8.  Ibid.

9.  Cockburn and St. Clair, *Whiteout*, p. 226.

10. Francis W. Belanga, *Drugs, the U.S., and Khun Sa*, p. 92. In his interview with David Borsamian at the University of Wisconsin – Madison, Alfred McCoy states that Marseilles became a major destination point for freighters from the Golden Triangle with shipments of heroin during the 1950s. McCoy adds that the amount of drugs that arrived in the French port from this area of Asia remains a matter of conjecture. See, http://www.lycaeum.org/drugwar/DARKALLIANCE/ciah2.html, accessed May 20, 2014.

11. Scott, *American War Machine*, p. 48.

12. Ibid., pp. 50–54.

13. Douglas Valentine, *The Strength of the Wolf: The Secret History of America's War on Drugs* (New York: Verso, 2006), p. 153.

14. Carl Bernstein, "The CIA and the Media," *Rolling Stone*, October 20, 1977.

15. Oliver Stone and Peter Kuznick, *The Concise Untold History of the United States* (New York: Gallery Books, 2014), p. 157.

16. David Talbot, *The Devil's Chessboard: Allen Dulles, the CIA, and the Rise of America's Secret Government* (New York: Harper Collins, 2015), p. 239.

17. Ibid., p. 288.

18. Steve Kangas, "A Timeline of CIA Atrocities," *Global Research*, June 9, 1997, http://www.globalresearch.ca/a-timeline-of-cia-atrocities/5348804.

19. Ibid.

20. Ibid.

21. Mark Zepezaner, "Haiti," *Third World Traveler*, 1994, http://www.thirdworldtraveler.com/CIA%20Hits/Haiti_CIAHits.html.

22. Kangas, "A Timeline of CIA Atrocities."

23. Richard Cottrell, *Gladio: NATO's Dagger at the Heart of Europe* (Palm Desert, California: Progressive Press, 2012), p. 112.

24. James Perloff, *The Shadows of Power: The Council on Foreign Relations and the American Decline* (Appleton, Wisconsin: Western Islands, 2005), p. 102.

25. Ibid., p. 104.

26. G. Vance Smith and Tom Gow, *Masters of Deception: The Rise of the Council on Foreign Relations* (Colorado Springs, CO: Freedom First Society, 2012), p. 141.

27. Ibid., pp. 141–142.

28. Perloff, *The Shadows of Power*, p. 105.

29. Dwight D. Eisenhower, quoted in G. Edward Griffin, *the Fearful Master: A Second Look at the United Nations* (Belmont, MASS: Western Islands, 1964), p. 213.

30. "Freedom from War," in Ibid., p. 217.

# PART EIGHT

# THE POINT OF NO RETURN

*At five, began studying under his cousin's tutor.*

*At nine, studied Latin, Greek, and French.*

*At fourteen, studied classical literature and additional languages.*

*At sixteen, entered the College of William and Mary.*

*At nineteen, studied law for five years starting under George Wythe.*

*At twenty-three, started his own law practice.*

*At twenty-five, was elected to the Virginia House of Burgesses.*

*At thirty-one, wrote the widely circulated "Summary View of the Rights of British America"
and retired from his law practice.*

*At thirty-two, was a Delegate to the Second Continental Congress.*

*At thirty-three, wrote the Declaration of Independence.*

*At thirty-three, took three years to revise Virginia's legal code and wrote a Public Education
bill and a statute for Religious Freedom.*

*At thirty-six, was elected the second Governor of Virginia, succeeding Patrick Henry.*

*At forty, served in Congress for two years.*

*At forty-one, was the American minister to France and negotiated commercial treaties with European nations along with Ben Franklin and John Adams. At forty-six, served as the first secretary of state under George Washington.*

*At fifty-three, served as vice-president and was elected president of the American Philosophical Society.*

*At fifty-five, drafted the Kentucky Resolutions and became the active head of Republican Party.*

*At fifty-seven, was elected the third president of the United States. At sixty, obtained the Louisiana Purchase, doubling the nation's size.*

*At sixty-one, was elected to a second term as president.*

*At sixty-five, retired to Monticello.*

*At eighty, helped President Monroe shape the Monroe Doctrine.*

*At eighty-one, almost single-handedly created the University of Virginia and served as its first president.*

*At eighty-three, died on the fiftieth anniversary of the signing of the Declaration of Independence.*

# 29

# THE NEW FRONTIER

*Kennedy's fate was sealed in June 1963 when he authorized the issuance of more than $4 billion in United States Notes by his Treasury Department in an attempt to circumvent the high interest rate usury of the private Federal Reserve international banker crowd. The wife of Lee Harvey Oswald, who was conveniently gunned down by Jack Ruby before Ruby himself was shot, told author A. J. Weberman in 1994, "The answer to the Kennedy assassination is with the Federal Reserve Bank. Don't underestimate that. It's wrong to blame it on Angleton and the CIA per se only. This is only one finger on the same hand. The people who supply the money are above the CIA."*

—JIM MARRS, *CROSSFIRE: THE PLOT THAT KILLED KENNEDY*, 1989

THE NEW FRONTIER WAS ILLUSIONARY. The promised change in the system never occurred. And, under John F. Kennedy, the key cabinet positions remained occupied by officials from the Council on Foreign Relations. Dean Rusk, the president of the Rockefeller Foundation, became Secretary of State; C. Douglas Dillon, the future CFR vice-chairman and former member of the Eisenhower cabinet, became Secretary of the Treasury. And Robert Strange McNamara, Ford Motor Company president and future president of the World Bank, became

Secretary of Defense. Other CFR appointees included McGeorge Bundy as national security advisor, Walt Rostow as deputy national security advisor, John McCone as CIA director, Roswell Gilpatric as deputy Secretary of Defense, Paul Nitze as assistant Secretary of Defense, Henry Fowler as undersecretary of the Treasury, George Ball as undersecretary of state for economic affairs; Averell Harriman as assistant Secretary of State for Far Eastern affairs, Arthur Schlesinger Jr. and Jerome Wiesner as special assistants to the president, and John J. McCloy, former president of the World Bank and chairman of the CFR, as chief of the US Disarmament Administration.[1]

## THE CUBAN FIASCOS

The Kennedy record was characterized by political embarrassment and executive indecision. He launched the Bay of Pigs invasion of Cuba under a group of 1,400 Cuban expatriates and, at the last minute, failed to provide the force with necessary air support, thereby dooming the mission to failure. Pinned on the beach, the invaders surrendered after less than a day of battle: 114 were killed, and 1,110 were placed in a prison camp.[2]

To resolve the Cuban Missile Crisis, Kennedy did not confront Nikita Khrushchev with steadfast resolve. Instead, he acquiesced to the Soviet premier's demand that the United States remove all of its intermediate range missile bases in England, Italy, and Turkey. As a further concession, Kennedy pledged that he would never again launch an invasion against Cuba and confiscated the guns and boats of all anti-Castro militants in the United States.[3]

## DAFT DECISIONS

Under Kennedy's three-year watch, the CIA launched 163 covert operations, only seven fewer than similar undertakings under the eight years of Eisenhower.[4] Several of these undertakings took place in Vietnam, including the ouster of South Vietnamese President Ngo Dinh Diem and the resettlement of thousands of villagers at gunpoint

**John F. Kennedy**
JFK was a socialist who belonged to the Fabian Society, an internationalist who sanctioned the surrender of all arms (including nukes) to the United Nations, and a supporter of the IMF/World Bank.

in barbed-wire-enclosed encampments.[5] Such actions created the instability that would lead to the Vietnam War. Other ops occurred in Latin America, including the Dominican Republic, where the CIA arranged the assassination of President Rafael Trujillo. Trujillo was replaced by the democratically elected Juan Bosch, whom the Agency ousted from office so that the country could be run by a military junta.[6]

Kennedy extended his ability to perpetuate political disasters to Central Africa. When the province of Katanga under the leadership of Moise Tshombe seceded from the Congo and declared independence, the United Nations, supported by the Kennedy Administration, launched airstrikes on Elizabethville, the capital of Katanga, followed by a full-scale invasion by UN "peace-keeping forces." The peace keepers went on a wild rampage, murdering hundreds of natives, raping women, and confiscating their belongings. But when forty-six physicians from Katanga turned to the White House for intercession, Kennedy opted to ignore their pleas.[7]

## AN UNDAUNTED SOCIALIST

JFK was a socialist who belonged to the Fabian Society, an internationalist who sanctioned the surrender of all arms (including nukes) to the United Nations, and a supporter of the IMF/World Bank.[8] On September 30, 1963, he explained the concept of global socialism and the redistribution of wealth in the following glowing terms:

> Twenty years ago, when the architects of these institutions met to design an international banking structure, the economic life of the world was polarized in overwhelming, and even alarming, measure on the United States. . . Sixty percent of the gold reserves of the world were here in the United States. . . . There was a need for redistribution of the financial resources of the world. . . . And there was an equal need to organize a flow of capital to the impoverished countries of the world. All this has come about. It did not come about by chance but by conscious and deliberate and responsible planning.[9]

But he had made enemies, including the *capos* of America's leading mafia families, who had lost their holdings in Cuba, the CIA for his failure to ensure the success of the Bay of Pigs invasion, and, last but not least, the Rockefeller family.

## ENRAGING THE ROCKEFELLERS

The Rockefeller animosity arose from Kennedy's Alliance for Progress, which he launched on March 13, 1961. This program provided massive amounts of foreign aid to Latin America. The $1.4 billion in annual aid was supposed to stimulate economic growth, redistribute wealth, and promote democratic governments.[10] The Bolivian and Chilean governments were encouraged to use their share of the aid to purchase equipment for the nationalization of mines throughout the country, including the very lucrative tin, silver, and copper mines owned by the Rockefellers. In Peru and Venezuela, the money was used to prop up state-run oil companies, much to the detriment of Standard Oil.[11] This program, which threatened the enormous interest of the House of Rockefeller south of the border, was followed by Kennedy's mishandling of the Bay of Pigs invasion, which resulted in Castro expropriating the Standard Oil refinery in Cuba and other Rockefeller holdings.

In promoting the Alliance for Progress, Kennedy said he was sick of the US government acting as the representative of private business, including the interests of the Rockefellers. He added that his administration no longer would prop up "tinhorn dictators" and "corrupt regimes" in countries like Chile, where "American copper companies [including the Rockefeller-owned Anaconda Copper] control about eight percent of all the foreign exchange. We wouldn't stand for it here. And there's no reason they should stand for it."[12]

### EXPOSING THE SNAKE PIT

Regarding JFK and the Rockefellers, David Talbot writes: "He [Kennedy] fully appreciated that the Rockefellers held a unique place in the pantheon of American power, one rooted not so much within the democratic system as within what scholars would later refer to as 'the deep state'—that subterranean network of financial, intelligence, and military interests that guided national policy no matter who occupied the White House. The Kennedys had risen from saloon keepers and ward heelers to the top of American politics. But they were still overshadowed by the imperial power of the Rockefellers."[13]

Shortly after launching his Latin American program, Kennedy appeared before the American Newspaper Publishers' Association to deliver a speech that may have sealed his fate. In a veiled reference to the House of Rockefeller and the money cartel, he spoke of a "monolithic and ruthless conspiracy" that sought to rule the world. The speech would have caused the Rockefeller brothers—David, Nelson, Laurence,

Winthrop, and John D. III—to blanch with repressed outrage, as evidenced in the following excerpts:

> The very word "secrecy" is repugnant in a free and open society; and we are as a people inherently and historically opposed to secret societies, to secret oaths and to secret proceedings. We decided long ago that the dangers of excessive and unwarranted concealment of pertinent facts far outweighed the dangers which are cited to justify it.
>
> For we are opposed around the world by a monolithic and ruthless conspiracy that relies on covert means for expanding its sphere of influence—on infiltration instead of invasion, on subversion instead of elections, on intimidation instead of free choice, on guerrillas by night instead of armies by day.
>
> It is a system which has conscripted vast human and material resources into the building of a tightly knit, highly efficient machine that combines military, diplomatic, intelligence, economic, scientific and political operations. Its preparations are concealed, not published. Its mistakes are buried not headlined. Its dissenters are silenced, not praised. No expenditure is questioned, no rumor is printed, no secret is revealed.[14]

### EXECUTIVE ORDER #11110

And, finally, there was the matter of Executive Order #11110 by which Kennedy instructed the Treasury Department rather than the Federal Reserve "to issue silver certificates against any silver bullion, silver, or silver dollars in the Treasury." This meant that for every ounce of silver in the US Treasury's vault, the government could introduce new money, with actual value, into circulation.[15] In compliance with this order, US notes in the amount of $4,292,893,815.00 were produced in two-and five-dollar denominations. This was not fiat money. It was paper currency with actual value. And, since it was issued by the government rather than the Fed, the money came interest free.

An event of alarming proportions had taken place. Kennedy, with one stroke of the pen, threatened to put the Federal Reserve out of business. The Fed no longer could manipulate the economy by producing and withholding money. It no longer could create depression or prosperity. It no longer could manufacture money from nothing. And the money cartel, including the House of Rockefeller, no longer could exact billions in interest for lending the money to pay off the national debt.[16] When Kennedy "actually minted non-debt money that does not bear the mark of the Federal Reserve; when he dared to actually exercise the leadership authority granted to him by the US Constitution," according to Colonel James Gritz, he had "prepared his own death warrant. It was time for him to go."[17]

One week after Kennedy's brains were blown away in broad daylight, Lyndon B. Johnson established a commission, under Supreme Court Justice Earl Warren, to examine the facts of the assassination and to prepare a comprehensive report. Members of the eight-man commission included Allen Dulles, the former head of the CIA who had been fired by Kennedy, and John McCloy, the former president of both the World Bank and Chase Manhattan. The 900-page investigative report ruled that Kennedy had been killed by a lone gunman, Lee Harvey Oswald. But it failed to provide anything from Oswald's past that could serve as a motive for the crime. The suspect, indeed, had publicly proclaimed his admiration of the president on numerous occasions. The report also ignored the fact that Oswald, unlike single assassins with a cause, adamantly denied his guilt and claimed that he was a patsy.[18]

The lesson was learned. In the wake of the killing, no more silver certificates were issued, and no other American president dared to defy the Fed and its secret shareholders.

# NOTES

1.  G. Vance Smith and Tom Gow, *Masters of Deception: The Rise of the Council on Foreign Relations* (Colorado Springs, CO: Freedom First Society, 2012), pp. 149–151.

2.  Staff, "Bay of Pigs Invasion," *The History Channel,* 2009, http://www.history.com/topics/cold-war/bay-of-pigs-invasion.

3.  James Perloff, *The Shadows of Power: The Council on Foreign Relations and the American Decline* (Appleton, Wisconsin: Western Islands, 2005) pp. 113–114.

4.  Oliver Stone and Peter Kuznick, *The Concise Untold History of the United States* (New York: Gallery Books, 2014), p. 178.

5.  Ibid.

6.  Steve Kangas, "A Timeline of CIA Atrocities," *Global Research,* June 9, 1997, http://www.globalresearch.ca/a-timeline-of-cia-atrocities/5348804.

7.  Smith and Gow, *Masters of Deception*, p. 294.

8.  G. Edward Griffin, *The Creature from Jekyll Island: A Second Look at the Federal Reserve,* 5th Edition (West Lake, CA: American Media, 2017), p. 109.

9.  John F. Kennedy, "Fiscal Responsibility: U.S. Must End Its Payment Deficit," a speech delivered before the International Monetary Fund in Washington, DC, September 30, 1963, http://www.copperas.com/jf k/imf.htm.

10.  Peter Smith, *Talons of the Eagle: Dynamics of US-Latin America Relations* (New York: Oxford University Press, 1999), p. 152.

11.  David Talbot, *The Devil's Chessboard: Allen Dulles, the CIA, and the Rise of America's Secret Government* (New York: Harper Collins, 2015), pp. 557–558.

12.  Kennedy, quoted in Ibid., p. 557.

13.  Ibid., p. 558.

14.  John F. Kennedy, "Address before the American Newspaper Publishers Association," April 27, 1961, https://www.jfklibrary.org/Research/Research-Aids/JFK-Speeches/American-Newspaper-Publishers-Association_19610427.aspx.

15.  John F. Kennedy, "Executive Order 11110," June 4, 1963, http://www.presidency.ucsb.edu/ws/?pid=59049.

16.  Vandita, "The Speech and the Executive Order That Got U.S. President John F. Kennedy Killed," *Anon HQ* , December 7, 2016, http://anonhq.com/the-speech-and-the-executive-order-that-got-us-president-john-f-kennedy-killed/.

17.  Colonel James Gritz, quoted in Ibid.

18.  Stone and Kuznick, *The Concise Untold History of the United States*, p. 190.

# 30

## A HELL OF A HOAX

*Having a big stake in an international foreign policy, the Rockefellers always make sure that the Secretary of State and the Director of the Central Intelligence Agency are "their boys." Marshall, Acheson, Dulles, Herter, Rusk and Kissinger have all labored to turn the backward Soviet Union into a credible power to force the Great Merger, while at the same time fighting wars to make the world safe for Standard Oil. The CIA has served as the State Department's and Standard Oil's enforcement arm, destroying genuine anti-communist movements around the world.*

—GARY ALLEN, *THE ROCKEFELLER FILE*

ON AUGUST 4, 1964, all nationally televised programs were interrupted for this urgent message from US President Lyndon B. Johnson:

> My fellow Americans: As President and Commander in Chief, it is my duty to the American people to report that renewed hostile actions against United States ships on the high seas in the Gulf of Tonkin have today required me to order the military forces of the United States to take action in reply.
>
> The initial attack on the destroyer Maddox, on August 2, was repeated today by a number of hostile vessels attacking two U.S. destroyers with torpedoes. The destroyers and supporting aircraft

acted at once on the orders I gave after the initial act of aggression. We believe at least two of the attacking boats were sunk. There were no U.S. losses.

The performance of commanders and crews in this engagement is in the highest tradition of the United States Navy. But repeated acts of violence against the Armed Forces of the United States must be met not only with alert defense, but with positive reply. That reply is being given as I speak to you tonight. Air action is now in execution against gunboats and certain supporting facilities in North Viet-Nam which have been used in these hostile operations.

In the larger sense this new act of aggression, aimed directly at our own forces, again brings home to all of us in the United States the importance of the struggle for peace and security in southeast Asia. Aggression by terror against the peaceful villagers of South Viet-Nam

**Lyndon B. Johnson**
President Johnson appointed a CFR member to virtually every strategic position in his administration.

has now been joined by open aggression on the high seas against the United States of America.

The determination of all Americans to carry out our full commitment to the people and to the government of South Viet-Nam will be redoubled by this outrage.[1]

The next morning, Johnson appeared before Congress to gain the approval for direct military involvement in the Vietnam Civil War. The resolution was passed by a vote of 416 to 0 in the House and 88 to 2 in the Senate. After the vote, Johnson said to his undersecretary of state: "Hell, those stupid sailors were just shooting at flying fish."[2]

## DEATH AND DECEPTION

The country was now involved in a war that would lead to over 50,000 deaths and millions of Vietnamese casualties. The official story of the cause remained the same throughout the course of the war. North Vietnamese torpedo boats launched an "unprovoked attack" against a US destroyer on "routine patrol" in the Tonkin Gulf on August 2—and, two days later, North Vietnamese PT boats launched a torpedo attack on two US destroyers in another act of unwarranted aggression. But there was a problem. It was all a hoax. The sailors really were shooting at flying fish. The second attack never happened. In a 2005 *New York Times* article, Scott Shane wrote: "President Lyndon B. Johnson cited the supposed attack to persuade Congress to authorize broad military action in Vietnam, but most historians have concluded in recent years that there was no second attack. The NSA historian, Robert J. Hanyok, found a pattern of translation mistakes that went uncorrected, altered intercept times, and selective citation of intelligence that persuaded him that midlevel agency officers had deliberately skewed the evidence."[3]

What's more, the first attack was not unprovoked, as the president intimated. The destroyer *Maddox* was not engaged in routine patrol. It was rather engaged in maneuvers to coordinate attacks on North Vietnam by the South Vietnamese navy and the Laotian air force.[4]

## KILLING FOR "CONTAINMENT"

By April 1965, Johnson had deployed seventy-five thousand combat troops to Vietnam—that number rose to half a million by the end of 1967. The United States dropped three times as many bombs on the tiny country of Vietnam than it did in all of World War II. The bombs included chemical weapons of mass destruction, including napalm and white phosphorus, which burned all skin from the bone.[5]

The overall policy of the Vietnam War, as developed by George

Keenan, Dean Acheson, and other CFR officials, was "containment," the attempt to confine the Communist countries to their existing borders.[6] It was the same policy that failed in Korea. Containment implied limited warfare. Victory was not an objection, but rather a liability. James E. King, in a piece published by *Foreign Affairs* in 1957, explained this new concept of limited warfare as follows:

> We must be prepared to fight limited actions ourselves. Otherwise we shall have made no advance beyond "massive retaliation," which tied our hands in conflicts involving less than our survival. And we must be prepared to lose limited actions. No limitation could survive our disposition to elevate every conflict in which our interests are affected to the level of total conflict with survival at stake. Armed conflict can be limited only if aimed at limited objectives and fought with limited means. If we or our enemy relax the limits on either objectives or means, survival will be at stake, whether the issue is worth it or not.[7]

**X-rated pornography shops**
During the Vietnam Era, America became flooded with pornography.

It was a concept that was easily sold to President Johnson, who had appointed a CFR member to virtually every strategic position in his administration.[8]

## RULES OF ENGAGEMENT

Despite the use of chemical weapons, the Vietnam War was not only to be limited but also fought with extraordinary restrictions, known as "rules of engagement." These rules prohibited American soldiers from firing at the Viet Cong unless they were being fired upon, and, even when attacked, they were forbidden to pursue the enemy forces into Laos or Cambodia. In accordance with the same restrictions, American pilots could only bomb targets that were deemed "strategic" by the Joint Chief of Staff, and they were not allowed to destroy Viet Cong missile sites that were still under construction. In 1968, Lieutenant General Ira C. Eaker observed:

> Our political leaders elected to fight a land war, where every advantage lay with the enemy, and to employ our vast sea and air superiority in very limited supporting roles only. Surprise, perhaps the greatest of the principles of war . . . was deliberately sacrificed when our leaders revealed our strategy and tactics to the enemy. . . . The enemy was told . . . that we would not bomb populated areas, heavy industry, canals, dams, and other critical targets—and thus sanctuaries were established by us along the Chinese border and around Haiphong and Hanoi. This permitted the enemy to concentrate antiaircraft defenses around the North Vietnamese targets that our Air Force was permitted to attack—greatly increasing our casualties. Missiles, oil and ammunition were permitted to enter Haiphong harbor unmolested and without protest.[9]

## THE TRADE DEAL

Of course, the US Defense Department, the Pentagon, and the Johnson Administration were well aware that over 85 percent of the war materiel for the Viet Cong came from factories within the Soviet Union. But, as

soon as Congress approved the resolution for direct American involvement in the Vietnam Civil War, David Rockefeller met with Soviet
premier Nikita Khrushchev in Moscow to draft a trade agreement that
would extend most-favored nation status within the Soviet Communist
bloc. The treaty was approved by President Johnson and went into effect
on October 13, 1966. Regarding this development, the *New York Times*
published the following report:

> The United States put into effect today one of President Johnson's
> proposals for stimulating East-West trade by removing restrictions
> on the export of more than four hundred commodities to the Soviet
> Union and Eastern Europe. . . . Among the categories from which
> items have been selected for export relaxation are vegetables, cereals,
> fodder, hides, crude and manufactured rubber, pulp and waste paper,
> textile and textile fibers, crude fertilizers, metal ores and scrap, petro-
> leum, gas and derivatives, chemical compounds and products, dyes,
> medicines, fireworks, detergents, plastic materials, metal products and
> machinery, and scientific and professional instruments.[10]

Few developments were more symptomatic of Uncle Sam's demise
than this agreement. Virtually all of the "non-strategic" items on the list
could be used as instruments of war. A machine gun, for example, was
deemed strategic and not part of the agreement, but the tools and parts
to manufacture machine guns and the chemicals necessary to propel the
machine gun bullets were considered "non-strategic."[11]

The Rockefellers became the principal benefactors of this bloody
arrangement. They set up with the House of Rothschild the International
Basic Economy Corporation to build rubber goods plants and alu-
minum-producing factories for the Vietnam People's Air Force that
was bombing American forces.[12]

### THE HIDDEN AGENDA

But more was at stake in Southeast Asia than the ideology of containment and the immediate opportunity to reap financial benefits from the

conflict. The region produced the poppy crops that were becoming one of the world's most valuable commodities. Without the flow of heroin from the Golden Triangle of Burma, Laos, and Thailand, the funding for the CIA's covert operations, which opened new markets for the money cartel, would come to an abrupt halt.

By 1958, the opium trade in Southeast Asia became so brisk that a second drug-supply line was established by the CIA. This route ran from dirt airstrips within the Annamite Mountains of Laos to Saigon's international airport for transshipment to Europe and the United States. In addition to CAT, the CIA contracted the services of small Corsican airplanes for this transport.[13] The Saigon drop would have been impossible without the cooperation of Ngo Dinh Diem, the president of South Vietnam, and Diem's brother Ngo Dinh Nhu, who served as his chief advisor. Diem, a devout Roman Catholic, had been instructed by the pope to cooperate with the strategies of the US government to thwart the gains of Ho Chi Minh and the North Vietnamese.[14] The cooperation was deemed so important by the Vatican that Cardinal Francis Spellman of New York formed a pro-Diem lobby in Washington. Through speeches and pamphlets, the people of Vietnam were presented by Spellman as a terrified throng before the cruel and blood-thirsty Viet Minh who looked upon the God-fearing Diem for salvation.[15]

The CIA now coughed up millions in covert funding for Diem and his brother to expand their scope of intelligence work and their extent of political repression.[16] The support continued even after Diem was driven from office by a CIA-supported military junta in 1963. Saigon had become a city of strategic importance.

## SAIGON SPOOKS

In 1967, Theodore Shackley and Thomas G. Clines became the CIA operatives who had been assigned to establish heroin refineries with the aid of the Corsican Mafia who permeated Saigon's underworld. In 1968, Shackley (known as the "Blond Ghost") arranged for Santo Trafficante Jr., who controlled organized crime operations in Florida, to visit

Saigon and to meet with drug lord Ving Pao in the Continental Palace Hotel.[17] The meeting concerned Pao's ability to provide the supply for the ever-increasing demand. During his stay, Trafficante also met with prominent Corsican gangsters to assure them of increased shipments to their laboratories in Marseilles.[18]

When the old Bureau of Narcotics and Drugs (BNDD) launched Operation Eagle in 1968, it found itself arresting scores of CIA employees—many of whom were working directly for Trafficante. But although it arrested several of his deputies, the BNDD could not get the Johnson or Nixon administrations to go after Trafficante directly.[19]

By 1971, Congress was getting so many complaints about GIs returning home addicted that the BNDD began to investigate. This investigation, too, went nowhere. The CIA insisted on loaning some of its select special agents to the BNDD as "investigators." The agents turned out to be the same men who had assisted in setting up the Laotians and Thais in the heroin business in the first place.[20]

## THE BODY BAGS

Business was booming. By 1971, there were more than 500,000 heroin addicts in the United States, producing a cash flow of $12 billion. Over three million Americans admitted on a government survey to using heroin at least once. Down at the morgue, where people don't lie, the numbers told a different story: 41 percent of the drug-related deaths were now linked to heroin.[21]

Southeast Asia remained the main source of opium. From Laos alone, over a ton a month arrived in Saigon on C-47 military transport planes that had been provided by the CIA to Lt. General Vang Pao of the Royal Lao Army.[22] So much opium was flowing into Saigon that 30 percent of the US servicemen in Vietnam became heroin addicts.[23] Some of this same heroin was smuggled into the United States in body bags containing dead soldiers. When DEA agent Michael Levine attempted to bust this operation, he was warned off by his superiors, since such action could result in the exposure of the supply line from Long Tieng.[24]

Cash from the network continued to be deposited by the mob in parochial banks throughout Italy. From these financial firms, the money flowed into the Vatican Bank (which continued to collect its 15 percent processing fee) before transferring the funds to privately held mob accounts in Switzerland, Liechtenstein, Luxembourg, and the Bahamas. But this system was not equipped to handle the billions generated from the heroin trade throughout the world. And so, new money laundries for the heroin trade were required, and the House of Rockefeller was more than willing to offer its service.

# NOTES

1. Lyndon B. Johnson, "Gulf of Tonkin Address," August 6, 1964, https://usa. usembassy.de/etexts/speeches/rhetoric/lbjgulf.htm.

2. Scott Shane, "Vietnam Study, Casting Doubts, Remains Secret," *New York Times*, October 31, 2005, http://www.nytimes.com/2005/10/31/politics/vietnam-study-castingdoubts-remains-secret.html?_r=0.

3. Ibid.

4. Lt. Commander Pat Peterson, "The Truth about Tonkin," *Naval History Magazine*, February 2008, https://www.usni.org/magazines/navalhistory/2008-02/truth-about-tonkin.

5. Oliver Stone and Peter Kuznick, *The Concise Untold History of the United States* (New York: Gallery Books, 2014), p. 198.

6. Michael O'Malley, "The Vietnam War and the Tragedy of Containment," History 122, George Mason University, n. d., https://chnm.gmu.edu/courses/122/vietnam/lecture.html.

7. James E, King, "Nuclear Plenty and Limited War," *Foreign Affairs*, January 1957.

8. Gary Allen, *The Rockefeller File* (Seal Beach, CA: '76 Press, 1976), p. 110.

9. Lieutenant General Ira C. Eaker, quoted in James Perloff, *The Shadows of Power: The Council on Foreign Relations and the American Decline* (Appleton, Wisconsin: Western Islands, 2005), pp. 122–123.

10. *New York Times*, quoted in Allen, *The Rockefeller File*, p. 110.

11. Ibid.

12. Ibid., p. 111.

13. Alfred W. McCoy, *The Politics of Heroin: CIA Complicity in the Global Drug Trade* (Chicago: Lawrence Hill Books, 2003), p. 153.

14. John Cooney, *The American Pope: The Life and Times of Francis Cardinal Spellman* (New York: Times Books, 1984), p. 242.

15. Ibid., p. 244.

16. McCoy, *The Politics of Heroin*, p. 160.

17. Ibid. pp. 250–251.

18. Ibid.

19. Joseph J. Trento, *Prelude to Terror: The Rogue CIA, the Legacy of America's Private Intelligence Network* (New York: Carroll and Graf, 2005), p. 44.

20. Ibid., pp. 46–47.

21. Robert Young Pelton, *The World's Most Dangerous Places* (New York: Harper Resource, 2003), p. 158.

22. Alexander Cockburn and Jeffrey St. Clair, *Whiteout: The CIA, Drugs and the Press* (New York: Verso, 1998), p. 246.

23. Ibid., p. 249.

24. Ibid.

# 31

## THE BLACK BANK

*There is at the outset a very obvious and almost facile connection between the war in Vietnam and the struggle I, and others, have been waging in America. A few years ago there was a shining moment in that struggle. It seemed as if there was a real promise of hope for the poor—both black and white—through the poverty program. There were experiments, hopes, new beginnings. Then came the buildup in Vietnam, and I watched this program broken and eviscerated, as if it were some idle political plaything of a society gone mad on war, and I knew that America would never invest the necessary funds or energies in rehabilitation of its poor so long as adventures like Vietnam continued to draw men and skills and money like some demonic destructive suction tube.*

—MARTIN LUTHER KING, JR., APRIL 4, 1967

ON JANUARY 27, 1980, two Australian policemen, driving along the Great Western Highway near the port of Sydney, came upon a 1977 Mercedes Benz parked along the side of the road. Inside the car, slumped across the front seat, was the body of a burly, middle-aged man. Searching his pockets, the policemen found the business card of William Colby, former director of the CIA. On the back of the card was Colby's itinerary for his trip to Hong Kong and Singapore. The dead man's hand was wrapped around the barrel of a new .30-calibre rifle. Next to the body was a Bible with a meat-pie wrapper as a book mark. On the wrapper were scrawled the names of Colby and California Congressman Bob Wilson, then the ranking Republican on the House Armed Services Committee.[1]

The dead man was identified as Frank Nugan, co-owner of the Nugan Hand Bank and one of the most prominent lawyers in Australia. His death was ruled a suicide despite the fact that Nugan's fingerprints were not on the rifle, and only a contortionist could have shot himself in the head from the position in which he was found in the vehicle.[2]

When Nugan's partner, Michael Hand, a former Green Beret who had served in Vietnam, learned of the death, he rushed back to Sydney from a business trip in London and began shredding enough documents in the bank to fill a small cottage. The next day, Hand held a meeting of Nugan Hand Bank directors in which he warned them that they must follow his instructions in destroying all records of transactions; otherwise they would "finish up with concrete shoes" or find their wives being delivered to them "in pieces."[3] By June 1980, Nugan Hand Ltd. was in liquidation. It owed about $50 million to creditors. Hand fled to the United States, never to be seen or heard from again.[4]

## THE NEW CENTRAL LAUNDRY
The Nugan Hand Bank had been established in 1973. Shortly after setting up headquarters in Sydney, the bank blossomed into twenty-two branches. One branch was set up in Chiang Mai, the heart of Thailand's opium industry, in the same suite as the US Drug Enforcement Administration (DEA). The DEA receptionist answered the bank's phone and took messages when the representatives were out.[5] Neal Evans, the former head of the Chiang Mai branch, told investigators that he had seen millions pass through his office, claiming that the bank operated solely "for the disbursement of funds, anywhere in the world, on behalf of the CIA, and also for the taking of money on behalf of the CIA."[6]

The money taken from the bank by the CIA was used to purchase weapons from international arms dealer Edwin Wilson for guerilla forces in Indonesia, Thailand, Malaysia, Brazil, and the white Rhodesian government of Ian Smith.[7] Wilson was a former CIA operative who was later convicted of selling arms and explosives to the Libyan government of Muammar Qaddafi.[8] Funds were also shelled out to undermine the liberal government of Prime Minister Gough Whitham, who had pulled Australian troops out of Vietnam and condemned the bombing of Hanoi. These actions were orchestrated by Theodore Shackley, the CIA's deputy director of operations. After Whitham was removed from office by John Kerr, Australia's governor-general, in 1975, the black ops money flowed to Italy and the IOR, for support of the Christian Democrats.[9]

The bank also imported heroin into Australia from the Golden Triangle. This dirty work was done by Australian police officers in service to the CIA, according to the Commonwealth–New South Wales Joint Task Force on Drug Trafficking. In 1976, one such officer, Murray Riley, organized five shipments of heroin into Australia, mostly in false bottom suitcases. For each shipment the branches of the Nugan Hand were used to transfer the purchase money from Sydney to Hong Kong. Over one hundred pounds of heroin was involved in each importation, and much of this was eventually shipped from Hong Kong to the United States. Riley was also involved in two heroin importations in July and September 1977.[10]

## THE SPOOK STAFF

The president of the Nugan Hand Bank was Admiral Earl Preston Yates, who served as the deputy chief of staff at US Pacific Command during the final stages of the US withdrawal from Vietnam. General Edwin Fahey Black, the bank's representative in Hawaii, commanded US troops in Thailand during the Vietnam War, having previously served with the National Security Council and the Office of Strategic Services. Lieutenant-General Leroy Joseph Manor, who worked for the bank in the Philippines, had been appointed chief of staff of the Pacific Command, while General Erle Cocke, a World War II veteran and former brigadier-general of the Georgia National Guard, worked as a consultant for the branch in Washington.[11]

The board of directors and administrative staff members of the Australian bank represented a "Who's Who" of prominent CIA officials. A partial list is as follows:

- Dr. Guy Parker, a financial consultant for the RAND Corporation, a CIA think tank;

- Major General Richard Secord, director of the Defense Security Assistance Agency, who worked closely with Ted Shackley in smuggling heroin money out of Vietnam in large suitcases. The money was stored in a bank account that was accessible only to Secord, Shackley, and CIA agent Thomas G. Clines;

- Walter McDonald, retired CIA deputy director and head of the Annapolis branch;

- Dale Holmgreen, former chairman CIA's Civil Air Transport and manager of the Taiwan branch;

- Theodore Shackley, former CIA deputy director for clandestine operations;

- Richard L. Armitage, special consultant to the Pentagon in Thailand who oversaw the transfer of heroin profits from Indonesia to Shackley's account in Tehran, Iran;

- Patry Loomis, former CIA advisor to the Provincial Reconnaissance Unit (PRU) in Vietnam; and

- Robert "Red" Jansen, former CIA station chief in Bangkok, who represented Nugan Hand in Thailand.[12]

## THE MAN NOBODY KNEW

William Colby served as legal consul of the Nugan Hand Bank. As the commander of the CIA station in Saigon, Colby ran intelligence operations during the Vietnam War, including Operation Phoenix, a

Stalin-like program that resulted in the assassination of an estimated forty-thousand South Vietnamese civilians. From September 1973 to January 1976, he served as the director of the CIA. He was removed from this position by President Ford after revelations of domestic spying by the Agency captured national headlines. Four years later, his business card was found in Frank Nugan's pocket.[13]

No doubt Colby, who was deeply involved with Gladio, realized the need for the establishment of a new laundry for drug money in Australia. The worldwide demand for heroin had surpassed the wildest dreams of Lucky Luciano. New heroin laboratories had sprung up in Burma, Thailand, and Laos to produce the paste that was shipped on to Hong Kong and Palermo for further refinement. The annual income from the 40 percent tax, which Shan United Army commander Khun Sa imposed on the ten to twenty laboratories along the Thai-Burma border, amounted to $200 million a year.[14]

## THE ROCKEFELLER CONNECTION

The primary shareholder of the Nugan Hand Bank was Australasian and Pacific Holding, a company that was owned and operated by the Rockefellers' Chase Manhattan Bank.[15] By 1974, the Australian bank was doing billions in business. The heroin flowing into the United States at the Andrews Air Force bank and other military installations within the body bags of dead soldiers had produced a heroin epidemic that spread from the ghettoes to the college campuses, where students mounted massive protests against the war.

The protests were funded, in part, by the House of Rockefeller, who shelled out millions to radical student organizations, including the Students for a Democratic Society. The demonstrators were paid not only to protest the war but also to call for increased government welfare, racial and gender equality, free speech, and the abolition of *in loco parentis* policies on college campuses. The executives from Exxon and other Rockefeller companies encouraged the student groups to make more and more radical demands so that agencies drafting public legislation would appear more in the center as they moved further and further to the left.[16]

## BEYOND THE LAW

The proceeds from the heroin trade, as funneled through the Nugan Hand Bank, permitted the CIA to mount hundreds of covert operations throughout the world. In Italy, the Agency initiated the "years of lead," which consisted of terror attacks that could be blamed on the Red Brigades and other Communist organizations.[17] In South America, the CIA mounted "Operation Condor" to establish military juntas and dictatorships in Brazil, Argentina, Chile, and Peru. Hugo Banzer Suarez came to power in Bolivia as the result of a three-day coup in August 1971.[18] To fund the army, Banzer ordered coca trees to be planted throughout the country's ailing cotton fields. Between 1974 and 1980, land in coca production tripled.[19] The coca was exported to Columbian cartel laboratories, including Barbie's Transmaritania. A multi-billion dollar industry was born. The tremendous upsurge in coca supply from Bolivia sharply drove down the price of cocaine, fueling a huge new market and the rise of the Colombian cartels. The street price of cocaine in 1975 was $1,500 a gram. Within a decade, the price fell to $200 per gram.[20] The CIA became an active participant in this new drug network by creating a pipeline between the Colombian cartels and the black neighborhoods of Compton and Los Angeles. The pipeline was unearthed by Gary Webb, a reporter for *San Jose Mercury News*, in 1996. Webb's findings resulted in an investigation by the US Senate, which served to confirm his claims.[21]

While the war raged, the CIA engaged in additional subversive undertakings, including the shipment of arms to the rebels in Angola and to the Kurds in northern Iraq. When news of such undertakings began to surface, the Senate established the Church Committee in 1974 to probe into the activities of the CIA. In its final report, the committee upheld the following:

The overwhelming number of excesses continuing over a prolonged period of time were due in large measure to the fact that the system of checks and balances—created in our Constitution to limit abuse of Governmental power—was seldom applied to the intelligence community. Guidance and regulation from outside the intelligence agencies—where it has been imposed at all—has been vague.

Presidents and other senior Executive officials, particularly the Attorneys General, have virtually abdicated their Constitutional responsibility to oversee and set standards for intelligence activity. Senior government officials generally gave the agencies broad, general mandates or pressed for immediate results on pressing problems. In neither case did they provide guidance to prevent excesses and their broad mandates and pressures themselves often resulted in excessive or improper intelligence activity.

Congress has often declined to exercise meaningful oversight, and on occasion has passed laws or made statements which were taken by intelligence agencies as supporting overly-broad investigations.

On the other hand, the record reveals instances when intelligence agencies have concealed improper activities from their superiors in the Executive branch and from the Congress, or have elected to disclose only the less questionable aspects of their activities.

There has been, in short, a clear and sustained failure by those responsible to control the intelligence community and to ensure its accountability. There has been an equally clear and sustained failure by intelligence agencies to fully inform the proper authorities of their activities and to comply with directives from those authorities.[22]

Ignoring the recommendations of the Church Committee, President Jimmy Carter, during the Iranian hostage crisis, encouraged the CIA not to inform Congress of its undertakings in Tehran.[23] The Agency needed no encouragement. From the time of its creation, it had opted not to inform any elected official of the full scale of its undertakings, let alone the source of its funding.

## THE BANK'S COLLAPSE

But all good things must come to an end. Within a year, the operation soon came to a screeching halt, due, in part, to the delayed repercussion from the fall of Saigon on April 30, 1975. Once the major gateway to the world market for Laotian heroin laboratories, Saigon now became a dead end to Southeast Asia's drug traffic, thanks to the anti-drug policies of the Viet Cong. Crude opium still crossed the border from Laos to service the city's declining addict population, but choice-number-four heroin was no longer available. The syndicates that had produced the high-grade product moved to markets in Europe and the United States.[24]

Other factors contributed to the bank's cash-flow problems. Between 1978 and 1980 the Golden Triangle was hit with two severe droughts. The droughts were followed by two seasons of intense monsoon rains, which reduced the region's opium production to a record low. The usual 600 ton opium harvests were cut to 160 tons in 1978 and 240 tons in 1979.[25] These natural catastrophes were accompanied by concerted efforts by the Burmese and Thai governments to eradicate poppy production. These efforts were necessitated by the fact that opium remained the main source of revenue for the Shan guerilla armies.

From 1976 to 1979, the Burmese army destroyed four major heroin laboratories near the Thai border, netting impressive quantities of precursor chemicals.[26]

## A TURNING POINT

A turning point had been reached. Southeast Asia no longer could remain the main source of heroin revenue for the CIA's covert operations. New poppy fields had to be planted within countries that possessed the proper climate and terrain—cool plateaus above 500 feet. The plants would grow rapidly and propagate easily, and the real work came with the harvesting. The poppy heads would have to be scraped as soon as the petals fell off. The scraping would cause the plants to ooze sticky sap that would have to be squeezed into banana leaves.[27] Such intensive work requires not only a slave labor force but a strong-arm government that can benefit from the production of narcotics. The Agency now set its sites on the fertile growing fields of Afghanistan.

## WAR BENEFITS

But the war was not in vain. It had produced a massive new source of cheap labor for global industrialists. The recommended minimum wage for Vietnamese workers was the lowest in the world, amounting to thirty dollars per month in 1994.[28] There was a fortune to be made by relocating American manufacturing plants to the war-ravaged country, which began to produce such American brand-name clothing and shoes as Michael Kors, Dockers, Brooks Brothers, Rockport, and Hanes underwear.[29] Companies such as Microsoft, Nike, Samsung Electronics, LG Group, Intel, Canon, Panasonic, and Toshiba have constructed multibillion dollar plants in Vietnam, thanks to funding from J. P. Morgan Chase of Ho Chi Minh City and Citibank Vietnam.[30]

# NOTES

1. Jonathan Kwitny, *The Crimes of Patriots: A True Story of Dope, Dirty Money, and the CIA* (New York: W. W. Norton and Company, 1987), pp. 19–22.
2. Penny Lernoux, *In Banks We Trust* (New York: Penguin Books, 1984), p. 69.
3. John Simkin, "Bernie Houghton," *Spartacus Educational*, June 2013, http://www.spartacus.schoolnet.co.uk/JFKhoughtonMB.htm, accessed May 21, 2014.
4. John Rainford, "How Australian Bank Financed the Heroin Trade," *Green Left* (Aus. Daily), December 7, 2013, https://www.greenleft.org.au/node/55553, accessed May 21, 2014.
5. Kwitny, *The Crimes of Patriots*, p. 207.
6. Neal Evans, quoted in Lernoux's *In Banks We Trust*, p. 71.
7. Ibid., p. 72.
8. Ibid.
9. Ibid.
10. Michael Barker, The CIA, Drugs, and an Australian Cop Killer," *Swans Commentary* (AUS), October 5, 2009, http://www.swans.com/library/art15/barker32.html, accessed May 21, 2014.
11. Rainford, "How Australian Bank Financed the Heroin Trade."
12. Lernoux, *In Banks We Trust*, pp. 69–70.
13. Jonathan Kwitny, *The Crimes of Patriots*, pp. 21–22.
14. Alfred W. McCoy, *The Politics of Heroin: CIA Complicity in the Global Drug Trade* (Chicago: Lawrence Hill Books, 2003), p. 431.
15. Kenn Thomas and David Hatcher Childress, *Inside the Gemstone File: Howard Hughes, Onassis, and JFK* (Kempton, Illinois: Adventures Unlimited Press, 1999), p. 93. See also Denise Pritchard, "Financial Takeover of Australia and New Zealand," *Opal File*, n. d., https://www.bibliotecapleyades.net/esp_sociopol_opalfile.htm.
16. James Kunen, *The Strawberry Statement: Notes of a College Revolutionary* (New York: random House, 1969), p. 112.
17. Daniele Ganser, *NATO's Secret Armies: Operation Gladio and Terrorism in Western Europe* (London: Frank Cass, s005), p. 3.
18. Robert P. Baird, "The U.S. Paid Money to Support Hugo Banzer's 1971 Coup," *Real News*, May 30, 2010, http://hcvanalysis.wordpress.com/2010/05/30/us-paid-money-to-support-hugo-banzers-1971-coup-in-bolivia/, accessed May 21, 2014.
19. Alexander Cockburn and Jeffrey St. Clair, *Whiteout: The CIA, Drugs and the Press* (New York: Verso, 1998), p. 181.
20. Ibid.
21. Gary Webb, *Dark Alliance: The CIA, the Contras, and the Crack Cocaine Explosion* (New York: Seven Stories Press, 1999), pp. 1–21.
22. U.S. Senate, "Final Report of the Select Committee to Study Government Operations with Respect to Intelligence Activities," April 26, 1976, http://www.thirdworldtraveler.com/FBI/Church_Committee_Report.html, accessed May 21, 2014.

23. L. Britt Snider, *The Agency and the Hill: CIA's Relationship with Congress, 1946-2004* (Washington, D.C.: Center for the Study of Intelligence, 2008), pp. 275–276.

24. McCoy, *The Politics of Heroin,* p. 261.

25. Alex Jones, "CIA Involvement in Drug Smuggling, Part 2," *Dark Politics*, May 2009, http://darkpolitics.wordpress.com/cia-involvement-in-drug-smuggling-part-2/.

26. McCoy, *The Politics of Heroin,* p. 429.

27. Robert Young Pelton, *The World's Most Dangerous Places*, (New York: Harper Resource, 2003), p. 158.

28. Staff, "The Future of Factory Asia: A Tightening Grip," *The Economist*, March 12, 2015, http://www.economist.com/news/briefing/21646180-rising-chinese-wages-will-only-strengthen-asias-hold-manufacturing-tightening-grip. See also Michel Chossudovsky, *The Globalization of Poverty and the New World Order* (Montreal, Quebec: Global Research, 2003), p. 171.

29. Michael Schuman, "Is China Stealing Jobs? It May Be Losing Them, Instead," *New York Times*, July 22, 2016, https://www.nytimes.com/2016/07/23/business/international/china-jobs-donald-trump.html?_r=0.

30. Dung Phan, "Vietnam: Time To Stop the Delusion of Cheap Labor," *Asean Today*, June 29, 2016, https://www.aseantoday.com/2016/06/vietnam-time-to-stop-the-delusion-of-cheap-labour/.

# PART NINE

# THE FINAL CURTAIN

*"The real rulers in Washington are invisible and exercise their power from behind the scenes."*
—JUSTICE FELIX FRANKFURTER, US SUPREME COURT.
HE SERVED FROM JANUARY 30, 1939, TO AUGUST 28, 1962.

*"I believe that banking institutions are more dangerous to our liberties than standing armies. If the American people ever allow private banks to control the issue of their currency, first by inflation, then by deflation, the banks and corporations that will grow up around the banks will deprive the people of all property—until their children wake up homeless on the continent their fathers conquered."*
—THOMAS JEFFERSON, 1802

*"I am a most unhappy man. I have unwittingly ruined my country. A great industrial nation is controlled by its system of credit. Our system of credit is concentrated. The growth of the nation, therefore, and all our activities are in the hands of a few men. We have come to be one of the worst ruled, one of the most completely controlled and dominated Governments in the civilized world, no longer a Government by free opinion, no longer a Government by conviction and the vote of the majority, but a Government by the opinion and duress of a small group of dominant men."*
—WOODROW WILSON, IN 1916, THREE YEARS AFTER SIGNING THE FEDERAL
RESERVE INTO EXISTENCE

*"The tree of liberty must be refreshed from time to time with the blood of patriots and tyrants."*
—THOMAS JEFFERSON

# 32

# TRANSFORMING THE POPULATION

*We Muslims believe that the white race, which is guilty of having oppressed and exploited and enslaved our people here in America, should and will be victims of God's wrath.*
—MALCOLM X, 1964

IN 1965, aside from the temples of the Nation of Islam (an African-American religion sect that professed doctrines and beliefs that bore no similarity to the teachings of the Prophet Mohammed), the only mosques in the United States were in Cedar Rapids, Iowa, Dearborn, Michigan, and Washington, DC (which opened in 1957)—and all three boasted fewer than 100 members. Four other cities contained miniature mosques with fewer than fifty members.[1] Small wonder, therefore, that Islam in America failed to merit the attention of religious demographers, such as Leo Rosten and Will Herberg, let alone a line of ink in the two volumes of Sydney E. Ahlstorm's *A Religious History of the American People,* which appeared in 1972.

The absence of Muslims from the millions of immigrants was due to the restrictive immigration legislation that remained in effect to safeguard the racial and religious balance of America. The Naturalization

Act of 1790 stipulated that "any alien, being a free white person, may be admitted to become a citizen of the United States."

The Chinese Exclusion Act of 1882 prohibited Chinese families from immigrating to the United States. With their strange language, customs, and dress, the Chinese were considered incapable of assimilation. The ban on the Chinese would persist until Chiang Kai-shek became a US ally during World War II.[2] The Immigration Act of 1891 reorganized the states bordering Mexico (Arizona, New Mexico, and a large part of Texas) into the Mexican Border District to stem the flow of immigrants into the United States. This act also contained a list of "undesirables" who should be prevented from entering the country.

The list included (in an apparent reference to Islam) "polygamists," along with diseased persons, convicts, paupers, idiots, and the insane. The Immigration Acts of 1903 and 1907 expanded the category of "undesirables" to include political radicals, people with physical and mental defects, and children unaccompanied by their parents.

## THE QUOTA SYSTEM

By 1924, the US Congress closed the floodgates to the country and limited the annual flow of immigrants into the country to 2 percent of each nationality who lived in the country in 1890. The reliance of this legislation on the ethnic composition of the country before the turn of the century guaranteed that the majority of new arrivals would be from Northern Europe. Since few Italians and Eastern Europeans lived in the United States in 1890, the quotas for these nationalities became fixed at marginal rates, and the number of new immigrants from "undesirable" regions was greatly reduced. The following chart shows the effects of this legislation:

## IMMIGRATION STATISTICS, 1920–1926

| YEAR | TOTAL ENTERING US | COUNTRY OF ORIGIN | | |
| --- | --- | --- | --- | --- |
| | | GREAT BRITAIN | EASTERN EUROPE* | ITALY |
| 1920 | 430,001 | 38,471 | 3,913 | 95,145 |
| 1921 | 805,228 | 51,142 | 32,793 | 222,260 |
| 1922 | 309,556 | 25,153 | 12,244 | 40,319 |
| 1923 | 522,919 | 45,759 | 16,082 | 46,674 |
| 1924 | 706,896 | 59,490 | 13,173 | 56,246 |
| 1925 | 294,314 | 27,172 | 1,566 | 6,203 |
| 1926 | 304,488 | 25,528 | 1,596 | 8,253 |

As a result of the 1924 act, immigration fell sharply. By the 1930s, it declined to 50,000 a year. During World War II, it was halted, though 400,000 displaced persons were brought to the United States following the war.[3]

## THE QUOTAS UPHELD

In 1952, the McCarran Walter Immigration Act affirmed the national-origins quota system of 1924 and limited total annual immigration to one-sixth of one percent of the population of the continental United States in 1920, or 175,455. The act exempted spouses and children of US citizens and people born in the Western Hemisphere from the quota. The new legislation angered President Harry Truman, whose veto had been overridden by both Houses of Congress: "The idea behind the discriminatory policy was, to put it boldly, that Americans with English or Irish names were better people and better citizens than Americans with Italian or Greek or Polish names. . . . Such a concept is utterly unworthy of our traditions and our ideals."⁴ Senator Pat McCarran, however, defended the legitimacy of the legislation which he had co-authored by saying:

> I believe that this nation is the last hope of Western civilization and if this oasis of the world shall be overrun, perverted, contaminated or destroyed, then the last flickering light of humanity will be extinguished. I take no issue with those who would praise the contributions which have been made to our society by people of many races, of varied creeds and colors. America is indeed a joining together of many streams which go to form a mighty river which we call the American way. However, we have in the United States today hard-core, indigestible blocs which have not become integrated into the American way of life, but which, on the contrary are its deadly enemies. Today, as never before, untold millions are storming our gates for admission and those gates are cracking under the strain. The solution of the problems of Europe and Asia will not come through a transplanting of those problems en masse to the United States. . . . I do not intend to become prophetic, but if the enemies of this legislation succeed in riddling it to pieces, or in amending it beyond recognition, they will have contributed more to promote this nation's downfall than any other group since we achieved our independence as a nation.⁵

## "SEAL OF INFERIORITY"

The push for immigration reform came from two sources. The first was a group that consisted of influential Jewish congressmen and senators, including Emanuel Celler, Jacob Javits, and Herbert H. Lehman, whose efforts to eliminate the quota system were backed by such powerful Jewish organizations as the Anti-Defamation League, the American Jewish Committee, the National Council of Jewish Women, the Hebrew Aid Society, the Synagogue Council of America, B'nai B'rith, the Jewish Labor Committee, and the Jewish War Veterans of the United States.⁶ The quota system, these legislators and activists believed, smacked of anti-Semitism and, in the words of Dr. Israel Goldstein, president of the American Jewish Committee, placed "a legislative seal of inferiority on all persons of other than Anglo-Saxon origin."[7] The Hart-Celler bill was designed to level the playing field for future generations of European Jews. It had been penned by Norbert Schlei, a prominent Jewish American lawyer in the Johnson Administration, who also had authored the Civil Rights Act of 1964.[8]

## FUNDED BY THE MONEY CARTEL

A second source of the legislation was the thought of Count Richard Nicholas von Coudenhove-Kalergi, the son of an Austrian diplomat and Japanese heiress, who has been hailed as "the father of the European Union." Upon receiving his doctorate from the University of Vienna in 1917, Coudenhove-Kalergi became an advocate for Woodrow Wilson's "Fourteen Points" and the pacific initiatives of Karl Hiller. In 1921, he joined the Masonic lodge *Humanitas*, which he used as the launching pad for his Pan Europa movement.[9] One year later, he published the *Pan Europa* manifesto, which captured the attention of Baron Louis de Rothschild and Max Warburg (father of Paul, the founder of the Federal Reserve), who opted to fund the movement to unify Europe with 60,000 gold marks.[10]

In his books *Praktischer Idealismus* and *Kampf im Paneuropa*, Coudenhove-Kalergi argued for the dissolution of national borders and the promotion of mass allogenic (genetically dissimilar) immigration.[11] The result of this immigration, Coudenhove-Kalergi wrote, would be the creation of "the men of future," whom he called *mestizos*. Such men would be of mixed Caucasian, Negro, and Asiatic blood and would appear "very similar to the ancient Egyptians."[12] The mongrelization of mankind, according to Coudenhove-Kalergi, would produce salubrious results, such as the dissolution of nationalism, the elimination of racism, and the eradication of disparities in levels of human intelligence. Since the mestizos would be of limited intelligence, Coudenhove-Kalergi maintained, they could be easily manipulated and controlled by "Jewish leaders of socialism" (*herrenmenschen*), who had been singled out by divine providence to rule the world. Although he was neither a Jew nor of Jewish descent, Coudenhove-Kalergi wrote:

> Two thousand years ago, the ancient Christians—not the Pharisees and Sadducees—were the revivers of the Mosaic tradition; today it is neither the Zionists nor the Christians, but the Jewish leaders of Socialism; because they wish, with their most exalted unselfishness, to erase the original sin of capitalism, to free people from injustice, violence, and subservience and to change the redeemed world into an earthly paradise.[13]

## PROTECTED BY THE CFR

Coudenhove-Kalergi's scheme to initiate the onset of world socialism by open borders and mass migration was derailed by the rise of fascism. His works were relegated to the bonfire by the Nazis, and he was forced to flee to France. When France fell to Hitler's forces in 1940, Coudenhove-Kalergi made his way to the United States, where he came under the care of the Council on Foreign Relations (CFR). As an advisor to the group, he helped to draft the wartime strategy of the Office of Strategic Services and the postwar plans for the revitalization of Europe. By 1949, his list of disciples included Senator William Fulbright, William J. Donovan, Allen Dulles, Thomas W. Braden, Arthur Goldberg, Jay Lovestone, and Joseph H. Retinger, who worked together to create the American Committee for a United Europe.[14] This organization gave rise to the European Coal and Steel Community, the predecessor to the European Union.

In 1950, Coudenhove-Kalergi, who had called for the elimination of the Caucasian race for the sake of a superstate, received the first annual *Karlspreis* (Charlemagne Award), for his contribution to European ideals. Throughout the next seventy-seven years, the winners of the coveted award would be ardent philo-semites and enthusiastic supporters of multiculturalism. The list of recipients included the names of British Prime Minister Winston Churchill, General George

Marshall, US Secretary of State and National Security Advisor Henry Kissinger, French President Francois Mitterrand, former Queen Beatrix of the Netherlands, British Prime Minister Tony Blair, US President Bill Clinton, German Chancellor Angela Merkel, and Pope Francis I.[15]

The ideas of the celebrated Austrian Count gave rise not only to a unified Europe but also to the belief that the white race of Americans must be eradicated for the good of humanity. Susan Sontag, one of Coudenhove-Kalergi's admirers, penned these words in 1967 for *Partisan Review*:

> If America is the culmination of Western white civilization, as everyone from the Left to the Right declares, then there must be something terribly wrong with Western white civilization. This is a painful truth; few of us want to go that far. . . .
>
> The truth is that Mozart, Pascal, Boolean algebra, Shakespeare, parliamentary government, baroque churches, Newton, the emancipation of women, Kant, Marx, Balanchine ballets, et al., don't redeem what this particular civilization has wrought upon the world. The white race is the cancer of human history; it is the white race and it alone—its ideologies and inventions—which eradicates autonomous civilizations wherever it spreads, which has upset the ecological balance of the planet, which now threatens the very existence of life itself.[16]

## A SIMPLE SYMBOLIC ACT

The Immigration and Naturalization Act of 1965 was supposed to serve as a symbolic gesture—an extension of civil rights sentiments—that would not produce a huge and sustained increase in the number of newcomers from Third World countries, let alone serve as a vehicle for globalizing immigration. Senate immigration subcommittee chairman and prominent CFR member Edward Kennedy (D–MA), who served to shepherd the bill through the Senate, offered this reassurance to his fellow legislators:

First, our cities will not be flooded with a million immigrants annually. Under the proposed bill, the present level of immigration remains substantially the same. . . . Secondly, the ethnic mix of this country will not be upset. . . . Contrary to the charges in some quarters, [the bill] will not inundate America with immigrants from any one country or area, or the most populated and deprived nations of Africa and Asia. . . . In the final analysis, the ethnic pattern of immigration under the proposed measure is not expected to change as sharply as the critics seem to think. . . . The bill will not flood our cities with immigrants. It will not upset the ethnic mix of our society. It will not relax the standards of admission. It will not cause American workers to lose their jobs.[17]

Echoing this claim, the new Attorney General Nicholas Katzenbach, a Rhodes Scholar and future CFR director, testified:

This bill is not designed to increase or accelerate the numbers of newcomers permitted to come to America. Indeed, this measure provides for an increase of only a small fraction in permissible immigration.[18]

## THE WARNINGS IGNORED

Opponents of the bill, most of them conservatives still in disarray from the rout of Barry Goldwater in the 1964 presidential campaign, argued that the Hart-Celler Bill would vastly increase the number of immigrants coming into the country and that the bulk of those immigrants would be coming from Third World nations, representing a threat to the country's existing demographic profile. Myra C. Hacker, Vice-President of the New Jersey Coalition of Patriotic Societies, warned of granting entree to "an indeterminately enormous number of aliens from underprivileged lands."[19] Whatever may be America's benevolent intent toward many people, Ms. Hacker maintained, the bill "fails to give due consideration to the economic needs, the cultural traditions, and the public sentiment of the citizens of the United States." She also said that the proposed legislation had "hidden mathematics" about which the public was not being informed.[20]

In the Senate, another opponent, Sam Ervin (D–NC), said that it was impossible not to discriminate and that it was therefore all right to favor "groups who historically had the greatest influence in building the nation."[21] To put all the earth's peoples on the same basis as prospective immigrants to the United States, Ervin argued, "was to discriminate against the people who had first settled and shaped the country." Ervin found an ally in Senator Robert Byrd (D–WV), who said the current (1965) system was "just and wise," since "additional population" from Western European countries was "more easily and readily assimilated into the American population." Byrd added: "Why should the United States be the only advanced nation in the world today to develop a guilt complex concerning its immigration policies?"[22]

The House of Representatives voted 326 to 69 (82.5 percent) in favor of the act, while the Senate passed the bill by a vote of 76 to 18. The floodgates to the New World finally had been pried open. Only Malcolm X had foreseen the enormous ramifications of this change in legislation, for he had written:

> As the Christian Crusade once went East, now the Islamic Crusade is going West. With the East—Asia—closed to Christianity, with Africa rapidly becoming converted to Islam, with Europe rapidly becoming un-Christian, generally today it is accepted that the "Christian" civilization of America—which is propping up the white race around the world—is Christianity's remaining strongest bastion.
>
> Well, if this is so—if the so called "Christianity" now being practiced in America displays the best that the world Christianity has to offer—no one in his right mind should need any much greater proof that very close at hand is the end of Christianity.
>
> Are you aware that some Protestant theologians, in their writings, are using the phrase "post-Christian" era—and they mean now?[23]

## POPULATION CONTROL

The Rockefeller family throughout the decades remained fixated on other aspects of population redistribution and control, including matters of people planning. On July 18, 1969, President Richard M. Nixon appointed John D. Rockefeller III as chairman of the newly created Commission on Population Growth and the American Future. Accepting this appointment, John D. III said: "The average citizen doesn't appreciate the social and economic implications of population growth and what it does to the quality of all our lives. Rather than think of population control as a negative thing, we should see it as enriching."[24]

One of the first reports from the Commission recommended "that present state laws restricting abortion be liberalized along the lines of New York State Statute, such abortions be performed on request by duly licensed physicians under conditions of medical safety."[25] The Commission further suggested that "federal, state, and local governments make funds available to support abortion services."[26] Thanks to this report, the New York–model abortion law, which the Commission enthusiastically endorsed, was passed in 1970 under the leadership of New York governor Nelson Rockefeller, John D. III's brother.[27] This legislation, coupled with statements from the Commission, paved the way for *Roe v. Wade.*

In the summer of 1971, Planned Parenthood of New York City, with the financial support of The Rockefeller Brothers Fund, set up the country's first large scale abortion mill. It was designed to perform 10,000 abortions a year for an average fee of eighty dollars, which was provided by Medicaid.[28] The prototype had been set. By 1976, America's second centennial, more unborn babies had been put to death in the country's abortion mills than the total number of American soldiers who had been killed in combat from the Battle of Lexington in 1776 to the last fatality in Vietnam.[29] By 2017, 59,115,995 babies had been aborted in a land once consecrated to Christian ideals.[30]

# NOTES

1. Karl Evanzz, *The Messenger: The Rise and Fall of Elijah Muhammad* (New York: Random House, 1999), p. 189.
2. Patrick J. Buchanan, *State of Emergency* (New York: St. Martin's Press, 2006), p. 229.
3. Patrick Buchanan, p. 235.
4. Harry Truman quoted in John F. Kennedy, *A Nation of Immigrants* (New York: Harper and Row, 1958), p. 236.
5. Senator Pat McCarran, *Congressional Record*, March 21, 1953, p. 1518.
6. Kevin McDonald, *The Culture of Critique: An Evolutionary Analysis of Jewish Involvement in Twentieth Century Intellectual and Political Movements* (Westport, CT: Praeger, 2002), pp. 295–355.
7. Dr. Israel Goldstein, quoted in Ibid., p. 342.
8. "Norbert Schlei, 73, Principal Authority of Civil Rights Act, Other Prominent Landmark Laws," an obituary, *Los Angeles Times*, April 21, 2003, http://articles.latimes.com/2003/apr/21/local/me-schlei21.
9. Stephen Dorill, *MI6: Inside the Covert World of Her Majesty's Secret Intelligence Service* (New York: Free Press, 2000), p. 165.
10. Dina Gusejnora, *European Elites and Ideas of Empire, 1917–1957* (Cambridge: Cambridge University Press, 2016), p. 165.
11. Richard Coudenhove-Kalergi, *Ein Leben für Paneuropa* (Wien-Leipzig, Germany: Verlag, Kremayr und Scheriau, 2016), pp. 28–32.
12. R. N. Coudenhove-Kalergi, *Praktischer Idealismus* (Wien-Leipzig, Germany: Paneuropa Verlag, 1925), p. 22.
13. Ibid., p. 27.
14. Thierry Meyssan, "The European Union's Secret History," Voltaire Network, June 28, 2004, http://www.voltairenet.org/article192787.html.
15. Der Internationale Karlspreis zu Aachen, http://www.karlspreis.de/en/.
16. Susan Sontag, "What's Happening to America?" *Partisan Review*, Volume 34, 1967, pp. 57–58.
17. U.S. Senate, Subcommittee on Immigration and Naturalization of the Committee on the Judiciary, Washington, D.C., Feb. 10, 1965. pp. 1–3.
18. Ibid., p. 8.
19. U.S. Senate, Subcommittee on Immigration and Naturalization of the Committee of the Judiciary, Washington, DC, 2/10/65.
20. Ibid.
21. U.S. Senate Report 748, 89th Congress, 1st Session, 1965.
22. Ibid.
23. *The Autobiography of Malcolm X*, (New York: Random House, 1964), pp. 376–377.
24. John D. Rockefeller III, quoted in Gary Allen, *The Rockefeller File* (Seal Beach, CA: '76 Press, 1976), p. 135.

25. Rockefeller Commission, "Human Reproduction," The Center for Research on Population and Security," 1970, http://www.population-security.org/rockefeller/011_human_reproduction.htm.

26. Ibid.

27. Allen, *The Rockefeller File*, p. 136.

28. Ibid.

29. Ibid., p. 137.

30. Guttmacher Institute, "Abortion Statistics," National Right to Life, 2016, http://www.nrlc.org/uploads/factsheets/FS01AbortionintheUS.pdf.

# 33

# ONLY THE DEAD KNOW BROOKLYN

# AND OTHER STORIES

*In the context of the modern world and considering the various crises which the Muslim world is encountered with due to highly publicized "Crusade" against Islam in the name of "War against Terrorism," it appears that America is the most suitable place where Islam can shower its infinite blessings on its people in due course; where American leadership is very much scared of Islam's inherent magnetic power that is attracting people who are in search of "Truth" and a system of life that can resolve the problems of both the worlds. The causes of this "hopeful" situation, the reasons for this upbeat approach and the possibilities of its occurrence are various and very convincing. It is in the nature of Islam that the more it is tried to be "crushed" through opposition, suppression and oppression, the more it rebounds and resurrects with great thud. The history of revival of Islam in modern Russia after the collapse of communism and that of recent Turkey are the glaring examples of this reality. Thus, America due to its predominant anti-Islam policies both at home and abroad has become the most natural place for its revival as a geopolitical entity. In fact, Allah has perhaps "selected" this land out of His infinite mercy to be the future "home" of Islam.*
—SHAMIM SIDDIQUI, *ISLAM: THE FUTURE OF AMERICA*, 2005

BY 2017, Islam had permeated nearly every aspect of American life, but the full extent of the permeation remained the X factor. But this much came to light. In 1990, fewer than 600 mosques existed in the United

States. By 2012 that number climbed to 2,106.[1] Nearly 8.5 percent of America's 330,000 houses of worship were now mosques.

A 2008 study by Cornell University projected that the number of Muslims in America had climbed from 1.6 million in 1995 to 7 million.[2] A *U.S. News and World Report* survey, which was conducted at the same time, placed the figure at 5 million.[3] The real number remained anyone's guess since the US Census Bureau neglects to collect data on religious identification.

In 2016, the Pew Research Center projected the Islamic population

**Mosques**
The Islamic boom was evidenced by reports of the new mosques and halal restaurants that had sprouted up within every major American city.

of the United States to be 3.3 million. But Pew researchers admit that their survey was not thorough since it neglected to take into account immigrant and poor black Muslims.[4] What's more, researchers only contacted Americans with telephone landlines. They failed to take into account the fact that nearly 50 percent of US residents, people ages 18–35 and nearly 100 percent of illegal immigrants communicate exclusively by cell phones.[5] Muslim organizations, such as the Council on

American-Islamic Relations (CAIR), supported the Cornell University projection of 7 million—based on mosque attendance.[6] The White House and the US State Department uphold this figure.[7]

The Islamic boom was evidenced by reports of the new mosques and halal restaurants that had sprouted up within every major American city. By 2010, according to one report, Washington, DC, boasted seven mosques and 134 halal restaurants; San Francisco, twenty-four mosques and 176 halal restaurants; Houston, fifteen and fifty, respectively; Chicago, twenty-seven and sixty-one, respectively; Cleveland,

**Empty churches**
By 2010, the average Christian church mustered a meager Sunday gathering of seventy-five.

fifteen and eleven, respectively; Boston, nineteen and sixty, respectively; Knoxville, thirty-two and six, respectively; St. Louis, twenty-one and eight, respectively; Lansing, twenty-seven and six, respectively; Toledo, seventeen and five, respectively; Buffalo, nine and eleven, respectively; Dallas, twenty-one and thirteen, respectively; Grand Rapids, nineteen and seven, respectively; New Orleans six and three, respectively; Nashville, eleven and ten, respectively; Columbia, twelve and two, respectively; Detroit, three and eighty-nine, respectively; Atlanta, nine and twenty-two, respectively; Peoria, five and one, respectively; Lincoln, twenty-five and two, respectively; and Shreveport, Louisiana, twenty-one and one, respectively. There are fourteen new mosques in Hattiesburg, Mississippi and twenty-five in Anchorage, Alaska.[8]

Many of the Islamic houses of worship were massive structures, which attracted thousands of believers to Friday afternoon prayer service (Jummah). These large mosques included the Islamic Center of America (Dearborn, Michigan), the Islamic Center of Washington, DC, the ADAMS Center in Sterling, Virginia, the al-Farooq Masjid in Atlanta, the Islamic Society of New York, Dar al-Hijrah in Falls Church, Virginia, the Tucson Islamic Center, and the King Fahd Mosque in Los Angeles.[9]

Even the smallest mosques—including the Mother Mosque of America in Cedar Falls, Iowa—could easily contain several hundred members and visitors for a single service. Much of the funding for the new mosques came from wealthy Saudi princes who sought to further the Islamic transformation of America.[10]

By 2010, the median mosque in America drew a crowd of three hundred worshippers to its Friday service,[11] while the average Christian church mustered a meager Sunday gathering of seventy-five.[12]

## THE TRANSFORMED LANDSCAPE

To come to terms with the social, political, economic, and religious impact of Islam on the US landscape, you need only pay a visit to Brooklyn—the borough of New York City once known as "the all-American neighborhood." Such a visit will make you aware not only of the Islamic transformation of US cities but also of the woeful inadequacies of religious statistics, especially those that pertain to mosques and the number of Muslims now residing within major metropolitan areas throughout the country.

Brooklyn conjures up magical images in the American imagination—Brooklyn Bridge, Coney Island, Fulton's Ferry, brownstone townhouses, and the Dodgers. It was home to William "Boss" Tweed, Currier and Ives, Margaret Sanger, Louis Tiffany, Al Capone, Gil Hodges, "Pee Wee" Reese, Leonard Bernstein, Barbra Streisand, and Ralph and Alice Kramdon of *The Honeymooners*. Brooklyn gave birth to hot dogs, roller coasters, soda pop, and more breweries than any other city in the country. One out of every seven Americans can trace their family roots to the streets of this borough.[13]

Yet Brooklyn is no longer quintessentially American. The breweries are closed, Ebbets Field remains a memory, and the hot dog stands have disappeared. Gone, too, are the Navy Yard that built such legendary warships as the *Monitor*, the *Arizona*, and the *New Mexico*, and the *Daily Eagle*, where Walt Whitman once toiled as an editor. They have vanished along with the Jewish delis, the Irish bars, and the nightclubs that had been made famous by John Travolta in *Saturday Night Fever*. Brooklyn is a city that is changing into a place that is antithetical to American sensibilities. It has become a thriving haven of Islam.

Returning to Brooklyn after a hiatus of twenty years, Sarah Honig of the *Jerusalem Post* was shocked by the changes that had occurred in her old neighborhood:

> When I climbed up the grimy station stairs and surveyed the street, I suspected that some supernatural time-and-space warp had transported me to Islamabad. This couldn't be Brooklyn. Women strode attired in hijabs and male passersby sported all manner of Muslim headgear and long flowing tunics. . . . Pakistani and Bangladeshi groceries lined the main shopping drag, and everywhere stickers boldly beckoned: "Discover Jesus in the Koran."[14]

Throughout Brooklyn, one can now hear the call of the *muezzin* five times a day from rooftop speakers: *Allahu akbar. Ashhadu an la ilaha illa-Llah*. Cab drivers pull their hacks to the side of the road and perform ritual ablutions. Shopkeepers roll out their prayer rugs toward the holy city. And life within the borough—which was once known as the "city of churches"—comes to a standstill.

The massive migration of Muslims to this borough of New York, coupled with the widespread conversion of African Americans throughout Bedford Stuyvesant and other Brooklyn neighborhoods to Islam, has been hailed as a salubrious development by many Brooklynites. The Muslim newcomers have been credited by Brooklyn mayor Marty Markowitz with closing crack houses and driving drug dealers from the crime-infested streets.

"I see more and more Muslims taking part in social life. The future is looking good," Markowitz says.[15]

Eric Bullen recalls that his store, Al's Men Shop at 1140 Fulton, was one of the few functioning businesses on what had become a block of vacant storefronts.

"It used to be so bad at times that people didn't want to even be seen out here too late. You could guarantee that, had they come through once it started to get dark, they were going to get mugged," he recalls. The Muslims, he says, were instrumental in changing things.[16]

Community Affairs Officer Steven Ruffin says that the imams of Brooklyn mosques, including Masjid al-Taqwa, have established unprecedented community cooperation with the police by creating civil patrols to police many of the borough's trouble spots.[17]

## ENEMY TERRITORY

Yet others view the Islamic transformation of the borough as something threatening and sinister. Many Jews and Christians throughout Brooklyn now display American flags and an assortment of patriotic/jingoistic banners in their front yards. These displays, for the most part, are acts of defiance.

"We're besieged," one resident told the *Jerusalem Post*. "Making a statement is all we can do. They aren't delighted to see the flag wave. This is enemy territory."[18]

Even Markowitz and others supportive of the newcomers reluctantly note that the vast majority of Muslim newcomers display an unwillingness to assimilate.[19] They continue to wear Islamic attire, maintain *halal* diets, and rigidly comply with *sharia* law. Most equate Americanism with hedonism. They shun fast-food restaurants, any food containing alcohol (including chocolate), and American cars.[20]

Few Muslim women walk the streets without a head covering; some wear full burkas that conceal their bodies and *niqabs* that conceal their faces, leaving only mesh-covered slits for their eyes. The assimilation process in Brooklyn appears to be working in reverse since the new male converts to Islam, almost all of whom are African American, now wear skull caps and long white tunics (*shalwat kameezes*), while their wives walk several feet behind them in black burkas or *abaya* gowns. They dye their beards with henna, refrain from eating pork and drinking alcoholic beverages, and greet each other in Arabic (*As-Salāmu `Alaykum*). Polygamy, among the newcomers and converts, is commonplace, and *khat*—the favorite narcotic of North African Muslims—is now cut up and sold on street corners, *halal* grocery shops, and places like the Blue Province Restaurant.[21]

In crowded flats and make-shift clinics along Atlantic Avenue, young Muslim girls—some as young as two—are subjected to the practice of female genital mutilation. Dubbed "female circumcision," this practice consists of the removal of the clitoris without the benefit of anesthesia or surgical instruments. Broken bottles or tin can lids occasionally serve as scalpels.[22] Recent statistics show that 41,000 Somali and other North African Muslims in Brooklyn and the other boroughs of New York City have been subjugated to this ordeal.[23]

While the overwhelming majority of Muslims in Brooklyn remain purportedly moderate in belief, at least 7 percent are extremely radical and support violent attacks against all nonbelievers, including the attacks of 9/11.[24] By 1989 the first North American cell of al-Khifa, an organization that would eventually morph into al-Qaeda, was implanted by Abdullah Azzam within Brooklyn's Masjid al-Farooq at 554 Atlantic Avenue, a six-story converted factory trimmed in orange and gold.

Members of this mosque came to play key roles in the assassination of Rabbi Meier Kahane, the 1993 bombing of the World Trade Center, and the planning of 9/11.[25] By 2002, they managed to raise over $20 million for bin Laden and millions more for other terrorist groups.[26] The mosque served as an arsenal, stocked with rifles, shotguns, 9 mm and .357 caliber handguns, and AK-47 assault weapons. Yet the mosque remains off-limits to law enforcement officials since it is registered as a "house of worship."[27]

Brooklyn also gave birth to Dar ul-Islam, the nation's most notorious Islamic street gang; Jamaat ul-Fuqra, a Muslim group that had been responsible for thirty terror attacks on American soil, and the Albanian mafia, which became the country's "leading crime outfit."[28]

What has taken place in Brooklyn has occurred in major cities throughout the country—most notably, Detroit, Washington, DC, Cedar Rapids, Philadelphia and Atlanta[29]—and even quaint towns and villages, such as Lodi, California; Lewiston, Maine; Hancock, New York; Commerce, Georgia; and Hamtramck, Michigan.[30]

# NOTES

1. Bob Smietana, "Muslims in USA Face Fears, Bias to Build, Expand Mosques," *USA Today*, August 3, 2010. Rachel Zoll, "U.S. Muslim Study Finds Jump in American Mosques," *Miami Herald*, February 29, 2012.

2. "Michigan Has Largest U.S. Muslim Population," *Psychiatric News*, The American Society of Psychiatrists, Vol. 40, Number 2, January 21, 2005.

3. Susan Headden, "Understanding Islam," *U.S. News and World Report*, April 7, 2008.

4. Besheer Mohamed, "A New Estimate of the U.S. Muslim Population," Pew Research Center, January 6, 2016, http://www.pewresearch.org/fact-tank/2016/01/06/a-new-estimate-of-the-u-s-muslim-population/.

5. Kathleen Parker, "Pew Study of U.S. Muslims Isn't 'Largely' Reassuring," *The Scranton Times-Tribune*, February 28, 2008.

6. http://www.cair.com/Portals/0/pdf/The_Mosque_in_America_A_National_ Portal.pdf The most rigorous estimate was from the Mosque Study Project 2000 (Bagby, Perl, and Froehle, 2001) which combined seven lists of mosques, eliminated duplicates, and attempted to verify the existence of each place. This generated a final list of 1209 mosques in 2000. The researchers then drew a sample of 631 and were successful in obtaining information about 416 of the mosques. They found that 340 adults and children regularly participated in the average mosque, and that 1629 were "associated in any way with the religious life of the mosque." This converts to a national estimate of 1,969,000 mosque-associated Muslims nationally. The study supports the projection of 6 to 7 million Muslims in the U.S. by assuming that for every Muslim associated with a mosque, three remain without association.

7. Remarks by the President on a New Beginning, Cairo University, The White House Office of the Press Secretary, June 4, 2009.

8. "America's Muslim Capitals," The Daily Beast, August 11, 2010; http://www.thedailybeast.com/articles/2010/08/11the-biggest-muslim-capitals-in-Armerica.html.

9. IPP Digital, Bureau of International Information Programs, U.S. Department of State, http://iipdigital.usembassy.gov/st/english/gallery/2011/06/20110629143232esiuol9.273708e-03.html#axzz1S81dW0y7.

10. Rachel Ehrenfeld, "Turning Off the Tap of Terrorist Funding," *Middle East Forum*, September 19, 2003; http://www.meforum.org/staff.php.

11. Ihsan Bagby, Paul Perl, and Bryan T. Froehli, "The Mosque in America: A Rational Portrait," Washington, DC: Council on American-Islamic Relations, April 26, 2001.

12. "Fast Facts," Hartford Institute for Religion Research http://hirr.hartsem.edu/research/fastfacts/fast_facts.html.

13. Ray Suarez, *The Old Neighborhood* (New York: Simon and Schuster, 1999), p. 14.

14. Sarah Honig, "A Masjid Grows in Brooklyn," *The Jerusalem Post*, July 3, 2008.

15. Sylvain Cypel, "Jews and Muslims Co-Exist Peacefully on the Streets of Brooklyn," *The Guardian*, January 18, 2011; http://www.guardian.co.uk/world/2011/jan/18/judaism-islam-new-york-cypel.

16. Jessica DuLong, "The Imam of Bedford Stuyvesant," *Saudi Aramco World,* May/June 2005; http://www.saudiaramcoworld.com/issue/200503/the.imam.of.bedford-stuyvesant.htm.

17. Ibid.

18. Ibid.

19. Sylvain Cypel, Ibid.

20. Ihsan Bagby, Paul M. Perl, and Bryan T. Foeble, "The Mosque in America: A National Portrait," Washington, DC: The Council on American-Islamic Relations, April 26, 2001; http://sun.cair.com/portals/0/pdf/the_mosque_in_america_a_ national_portrait.pdf.

21. Tom Hayes, "Khat Comes to America, Prompting a Crackdown," Associated Press, April 23, 2000.

22. Ibid.

23. Alyson Zureick, "City, State Do Little to Address Female Genital Cutting," *Gotham Gazette,* March 2009.

24. John L. Esposito and Dalia Mogahed, *Who Speaks for Islam* (New York: Gallup Press, 2007), p. 68.

25. *The 9/11 Commission Report: Final Report of the National Commission on Terror Attacks upon the United States,* Authorized Edition (New York: W. W. Norton, 2004), p. 58.

26. Steven Emerson, "Terrorism Financing and US Financial Institutions," testimony before the House Committee on Oversight and Investigations of Financial Services," March 11, 2003.

27. John Miller, "A Decade of Warning: Did Rabbi's 1990 Assassination Mark Birth of Islamic Terror in America?" *20/20,* ABC News, August 16, 2002.

28. Terry Frieden, "FBI: Albanian Mobsters 'New Mafia,'" CNN, August 19, 2004.

29. "America's Muslim Capitals," *The Daily Beast,* August 10, 210, http://www.thedailybeast.com/galleries/2010/08/10/america-s-muslim-capitals.html.

30. Sarah Pulliam Bailey, "In the First Majority-Muslim U.S. City, Residents Tense about Its Future," *Washington Post,* November 21, 2005, https://www.washingtonpost. com/national/for-the-first-majority-muslim-us-city-residents-tense-about-its-future/2015/11/21/45d0ea96-8a24-11e5-be39-0034bb576eee_story.html?utm_ term=.f99b07251993.

# 34

# THE NEW NETWORK

*What is important to the history of the world? The Taliban or the collapse of the Soviet empire? Some stirred-up Muslims or the liberation of Central Europe and the end of the cold war?*
—ZBIGNIEW BRZEZINSKI, 1998

WITH THE FALL OF SAIGON, the CIA set its sights on the Golden Crescent, where the highlands of Afghanistan, Pakistan, and Iran all converge, for a new source of drug revenue. Since the seventeenth century, opium poppies were grown in this region by local tribesmen and the market remained regional. By the 1950s, very little opium was produced in Afghanistan and Pakistan, with about 2,500 acres in both countries under cultivation.[1] At the close of the Vietnam War, the fertile growing fields of Afghanistan's Helmand Valley were covered with vineyards, wheat, and cotton.[2]

The major problem for the CIA was the Afghan government of Noor Mohammed Taraki, who sought to eradicate poppy production in the border regions of the country that remained occupied by radical Islamic fundamentalists. This attempt at eradication sprang from Taraki's desire to unite all the Pashtun tribes under Kabul rule.[3] The fundamentalists spurned such efforts not only because of their desire to keep the cash crops but also because they viewed the Taraki government as *shirk* (blasphemy). The modernist regime advocated female education and prohibited arranged marriages and the bride price. By 1975, the tension between government and the fundamentalists erupted into violence when Pashtun tribesmen mounted a revolt in the Panjshir valley north of Kabul.[4] The tribesmen were led by Gulbuddin Hekmatyar, who became the new darling of the CIA.

**Central Intelligence Agency**

The CIA got what it wanted. The holy war had begun. For the next decade, black aid—amounting to more than $3 billion—would be poured into Afghanistan to support the holy warriors, making it the most expensive covert operation in US history.

## THE MUSLIM MADMAN

Hekmatyar made his public debut in 1972 at the University of Kabul by killing a leftist student. He fled to Pakistan where he became an agent of Inter-Services Intelligence (ISI) and the leader of Hezb-e-Islami, an organization dedicated to the formation of a "pure" Islamic state ruled by the most intransigent interpretation of Sunni law.[5] Hekmatyar urged his followers to throw acid in the faces of women not wearing a veil, kidnapped rival Islamic chieftains, and, in 1977, began to build up an arsenal, courtesy of the CIA.[6] The Agency also began to funnel millions to the ISI, which became transformed into its surrogate on the Afghan border.[7]

The CIA believed that Hekmatyar, despite the fact that he was clearly unhinged, would be of inestimable value not only in undermining the Taraki government but also in gaining control of the poppy fields in the Helmand Valley. Its faith was not misplaced. Throughout 1978, a year before the Soviet invasion, Hekmatyar and his *mujahedeen* ("holy warriors") burned universities and girls' schools throughout

Afghanistan and gained feudal control over the many of the poppy farmers. The pro-Taraki militants, aware of the destabilization plot, assassinated Adolph "Spike" Dubbs, the US ambassador to Kabul, on February 14, 1979.[8]

Thanks to Hekmatyar's actions, heroin production rose from 400 tons in 1971 to 1,200 tons in 1978. After the assassination of Dubbs and the flow of millions to Hekmatyar's guerilla army, the production soared to 1,800 tons and a network of laboratories was set up by the *mujahedeen* along the Afghan-Pakistan border.[9] The morphine base was transported by caravans of trucks from the Helmand Valley through northern Iran to the Anatolian plains of Turkey.

## THE HOLY WAR

In the summer of 1979, six months before the Soviet invasion, the US State Department issued a memorandum making clear its stake in the *mujahedeen*: "The United States' larger interest . . . would be served by the demise of the Taraki regime, despite whatever setbacks this might mean for future social and economic reform in Afghanistan. . . . The overthrow of the DRA [Democratic Republic of Afghanistan] would show the rest of the world, particularly the Third World, that the Soviet's view of the socialist course of history as being inevitable is not accurate."[10]

In September 1979 Taraki was killed in a coup organized by Afghan military officers. Hafizullah Amin became installed as the country's new president. Amin had impeccable Western credentials. He had been educated at Columbia University and the University of Wisconsin. He had served as the president of the Afghan Students Association, which had been funded by the Asia Foundation, a CIA front.[11] After the coup, he met regularly with US Embassy officials, while the CIA continued to fund Hekmatyar's rebels in Pakistan. Fearing a fundamentalist, US-backed regime at its border, the Soviets invaded Afghanistan on December 27, 1979.[12]

The CIA got what it wanted. The holy war had begun. For the next decade, black aid—amounting to more than $3 billion—would be poured into Afghanistan to support the holy warriors, making it the most expensive covert operation in US history.[13] Such vast expenditures demanded an exponential increase in poppy production, which Hekmatyar and his fellow jihadists were pleased to provide.

## AFGHANISTAN DELIGHT

The war in Afghanistan delighted State Department officials, including Secretary of State Zbigniew Brzezinski. Voicing the utopian vision of what author Chalmers Johnson called the "military-industrial complex," Brzenzinski wrote of the plans to control Eurasia, including Turkey, Afghanistan, and Pakistan:

> For America, the chief geopolitical prize is Eurasia. . . . Now a non-Eurasian power is preeminent in Eurasia—and America's global primacy is directly dependent on how long and how effectively its preponderance on the Eurasian continent is sustained . . .
>
> To put it in a terminology that harkens back to the more brutal age of ancient empires, the three great imperatives of imperial geostrategy are to prevent collusion and maintain security dependence among the vassals, to keep tributaries pliant and protected, and to keep the barbarians from coming together.[14]

Brzezinski and fellow members of his "over-world" realized that the concept of democracy and freedom could never galvanize the scattered tribes and peoples of Central Asia. The people could only be unified by the cause of Allah since they were overwhelmingly Islamic. The holy war in Afghanistan, in the view of the US geostrategists, offered many benefits, including the possible downfall of the Soviet Union and the possibility of gaining access and control over the vast natural gas and oil resources of Eurasia. Months before the Soviet invasion in 1979, the CIA launched Operation Cyclone, an attempt to destabilize the Soviet Union by spreading militant Islam throughout the central Asian republics.[15] Eventually, this operation would serve to create hundreds of Islamic terror organizations, including al-Qaeda, al-Jihad, the Ulema Union of Afghanistan, the Salaafi Group for Proselytism and Combat, the Islamic Movement of Uzbekistan, al-Bada, Harakat ul-Ansar, Jamiat Ulema-e-Islam, Jamiat-ul-Ulema-e-Pakistan, Lashkar e-Toiba, and the al-Jihad Group. It would also give rise to terror attacks that would kill and maim millions of people throughout the world and the dream espoused by Fethullah Gulen and his disciples of a New Islamic World Order.

## THE BCCI

In 1972, The Bank of Credit and Commerce (BCCI) was set up in Karachi by Agha Hasan Avedi, a financier who had deep connections to Pakistan's underworld, the Turkish *babas*, and oil-rich sheikhs of Abu Dhabi. It represented the ideal spot for the CIA to set up a laundry within the Golden Crescent. Thanks to the Agency, the BCCI became registered in Luxembourg and soon mushroomed into a vast criminal enterprise with 400 branches in seventy-eight countries, including First American Bank in Washington, DC, the National Bank of Georgia, and the Independence Bank of Encino, California.[16] Virtually free from scrutiny, it engaged not only in money laundering the heroin proceeds but also arms trafficking on a grand scale, including the sale of French-made jet fighters to Chile and Chinese silkworm missiles to Saudi Arabia. By 1985, it became the seventh largest financial institution in the world, handling the money for Iraqi dictator Saddam Hussein, Panamanian strongman Manuel Noriega, Palestinian terrorist Abur Nidal, al-Qaeda chieftain Osama bin Laden, Liberian president Samuel Doe, and leading members of the Medellin Cartel.[17]

Prominent spooks, including CIA Director William Casey, made regular visits to the BCCI's headquarters in Karachi, making the Pakistani city the new haven for covert operations. The bank served the Agency in a myriad of ways by paying bribes, providing "young beauties from Lahore," and funneling cash for assassins. The enormity of the bank's operations was evidenced by its transfer of $4 billion in covert aid to Iraq from 1985 to 1989. For the Iraqi transfer, the BCCI made use of the Atlanta branch of Banca Nazionale del Lavoro (BNL), an Italian bank with ties to the IOR. Henry Kissinger sat on BNL's international advisory board, along with Brent Scowcroft, who became President George H. W. Bush's national security advisor.[18]

John R. Bath, an alleged CIA operative, became one of BCCI's directors.[19] While serving the Pakistani bank, Bath was the co-owner with future president George W. Bush of Arbusto Energy, a Texas oil company. Sheikh Abdullah Bahksh, a fellow BCCI official, served, according to the Kerry Commission, as "the principal liaison for the CIA in the entire Middle East from the mid-1960s through 1979."[20]

## PHONY AUDITS

Although a cursory investigation would have uncovered the bank's engagement in issuing phony loans, making phantom deposits, and publishing false financial reports, Price Waterhouse, the prestigious London accounting firm, published annual statements, giving BCCI its unqualified approval.[21] The Kerry Commission later concluded that the Price Waterhouse accountants "failed to protect BCCI's innocent depositors and creditors from the consequences of poor practices at the bank of which the auditors were aware for years."[22]

In 1991, the BCCI, like so many other CIA banks, went bust, leaving a financial hole of $13 billion. Creditors subsequently brought action against Price Waterhouse, claiming damages because of the firm's accounting negligence in excess of $11 billion. The matter was eventually settled out of court.[23] Ironically, in the wake of this settlement, the Vatican turned to Price Waterhouse to certify its balance sheets—a choice that journalist David Yallop characterized as "bizarre."[24]

## THE CIA'S COMPLICITY

In its opening statement regarding the CIA's relationship to BCCI, the Kerry Commission maintained:

> The relationships involving BCCI, the CIA, and members of the
> United States and foreign intelligence communities have been among

the most perplexing aspects of understanding the rise and fall of BCCI. The CIA's and BCCI's mutual environments of secrecy have been one obvious obstacle. For many months, the CIA resisted providing information to the Subcommittee about its involvement with and knowledge of BCCI. Moreover, key players who might explain these relationships are unavailable. Some, including former CIA director William Casey, and BCCI customers and Iranian arms dealers Ben Banerjee and Cyrus Hashemi, are dead. Others, including most of BCCI's key insiders, remain held incommunicado in Abu Dhabi. While promising in public hearings to provide full cooperation to the Subcommittee, to date the Abu Dhabi government has refused to make any BCCI officers available for interview by the Subcommittee. Former BCCI chairman Agha Hasan Abedi remains severely incapacitated due to a heart attack. Finally, some persons in a position to know portions of the truth have denied having any memory of events in which they participated and of documents which they reviewed.[25]

## DRUG BOOM

The Golden Triangle was now producing 80 percent of the world's opium supply. At the end of 1982, the DEA had evidence of over forty heroin syndicates and 200 heroin laboratories operating in Pakistan.[26] The CIA deposited a large share of its profits from these operations in the Shakarchi Trading Company in Lebanon, which served not only as a convenient laundry but also as a shipping firm that delivered 8.5-ton shipments of choice brown product to the Gambino crime syndicate in New York.[27]

In keeping with the policy of false flags, the sharp rise in heroin production was blamed on the Soviet generals in Kabul. "The regime maintains an absolute indifference to any measures to control poppy," Edwin Meese, President Reagan's Attorney General, said during a visit to Islamabad. "We strongly believe that there is actually encouragement, at least tacitly, over growing poppy."[28]

The increased flow of heroin affected all regions of the world, including Pakistan. Before the CIA program, there were fewer than

5,000 heroin users in Pakistan. At the end of the Soviet-Afghanistan war, there were 1.6 million heroin addicts.[29]

## ARKANSAS NARCO-BANK

But the principal laundry for the new heroin network remained the BCCI, which continued to retain its primary offices in London and Karachi. James R. Bath, a CIA associate and the business partner of George W. Bush, remained a primary director.[30] Bert Lance, an American businessman who served as the director of the office of management and budget under President Carter, emerged in 1981 as a key BCCI consultant, along with Arkansas-based power broker Jackson Stephens.[31] In accordance with the wishes of William Casey, the CIA director under President Reagan, the BCCI stood alone, financially independent, and free from congressional scrutiny.[32]

Thanks to Lance and Stephens, Western Arkansas suddenly became a hub of international drug smuggling. Cocaine was being smuggled into the small airport in Mena by CIA assets, including pilot Barry Seal. These assets also transported to Mena huge bails of cash, which was laundered by BCCI's First American Bank. First American was a Washington, DC, financial institution that had been acquired for BCCI by former Secretary of Defense W. Clark Clifford.[33] The cash came from the Gambino crime family, which was shelling out $50 million for each shipment.[34]

## BLOCKED BY NATIONAL SECURITY

The laundering at First American was conducted in conjunction with Worthern Bank (a financial institution owned by Jackson Stephens) and the Arkansas Development Finance Authority, a state agency that had been set up by Governor Bill Clinton.[35] Stephens had been a major donor to Clinton's 1982 gubernatorial campaign, and Worthern had provided the candidate with a $3.5 million line of credit.[36] The BCCI's front in the DC bank was Kamal Adham, who, according to the Kerry Committee report, operated as "the CIA's principal liaison for the entire Middle East from the mid-1960s through 1979."[37]

**Drug culture**
Cocaine and heroin were being smuggled into the United States by CIA assets.

In his attempt to probe First American, CBS correspondent Bill Plante complained there is "a trail of tens of millions of dollars in cocaine profits [from Mena, Arkansas] and we don't know where it leads. It is a trail blocked by the National Security Council."[38]

During Ronald Reagan's term in the Oval Office, the great jihad in Afghanistan grew in scope and strength, threatening to sap the USSR of its strength and resolve. The inhabitants of the five republics of the Soviet Union (Kazakhstan, Kyrgyzstan, Tajikistan, Turkmenistan, and Uzbekistan), who shared a common Turkish heritage and remained devoutly Islamic, became supportive of the *mujahedeen* in the struggle against their communist overlords. This support combined with the massive amount of Muslim recruits to the great jihad from the Arab world served to create a creeping sense of futility among the Soviet troops. To drive the "evil empire" to the point of total collapse, the CIA continued to infuse the holy war with munitions and money, until the war in Afghanistan became the Agency's most expensive covert undertaking.[39]

By 1985, the Afghan rebels were receiving $250 million a year in dirty money from the CIA to battle the 115,000 Soviet troops occupying the country. This figure was double the number of Soviet troops in 1984. The annual payments to the Muslim guerillas reached nearly $1 billion by 1988. By this time, the CIA was also shipping highly sophisticated weaponry, including Stinger missiles, to the jihadists, whom they mistakenly viewed as "freedom fighters."[40]

### MUSLIM MISSIONARIES

In an effort to supply recruits to the jihad, the CIA once again focused its attention on America's black community. This development was understandable. The Agency realized that millions of African Americans, who felt disenfranchised by the system, had converted to Islam, which they saw as "the black man's religion." This movement, prompted by such black leaders as Timothy Drew ("Noble Drew Ali"), Elijah Poole ("Elijah Muhammad") and Malcolm Little ("Malcolm X"), had given rise to hundreds of mosques within America's inner-cities."[41] By 1980, the CIA began to send hundreds of militant Muslim missionaries, all members of the radical *Tablighi Jamaat,* to the US mosques in order to call upon young black men to take up arms in the holy war to liberate their Muslim brothers.

Sheikh Mubarak Gilani, one of the first of these missionaries to arrive, convinced scores of members of the Yasin Mosque in Brooklyn to head off to guerilla training camps in Pakistan with an offer of thousands in cash and the promise of seventy *houris* in seventh heaven, if they were killed in action. The cash came from the CIA's coffers.[42]

### THE TRAINING CAMPS

Realizing that it would be financially advantageous to train the new recruits on American soil, Sheikh Gilani, with the help of the CIA, set up paramilitary training camps in rural areas throughout the country, including Hancock, New York; Red House, Virginia; Commerce, Georgia; York, South Carolina; Dover, Tennessee; Buena Vista,

Colorado; Macon, Georgia; Squaw Valley, California; Marion, Alabama; and Talihina, Oklahoma.[43]

By 1985, the international press began to report that an unspecified number of African American Muslims—all related to ul-Fuqra—had joined the ranks of the *mujahedeen* in Afghanistan and that several had been killed in action. When questioned, several of the *jihadis* imported from America would testify that they were agents of the CIA.[44]

## THE AL-QAEDA CELL

To provide more support for the *mujahedeen*, the CIA used Abdullah Azzam, Osama bin Laden's mentor, to set up a cell of al-Qaeda within *Masjid al-Farooq* on Atlantic Avenue in Brooklyn, New York. The cell, known as the al-Kifah Refugee Center, acted as a front for the transference of funds, weapons, and recruits to Afghanistan. Throughout the 1980s, this militant organization received over $2 million a year and *Masjid al-Farooq* became a very wealthy institution.[45] During this time, Azzam spent a great deal of time in Brooklyn. In a 1988 videotape, he can be seen and heard telling a large crowd of African Americans that "blood and martyrdom are the only way to create a Muslim society."[46]

By 1992, *al-Farooq* mosque had become a haven for Arabian veterans from the great jihad in Afghanistan, who were granted special passports to enter the United States by the CIA. A feud erupted between the older African American members of the mosque and the Arab newcomers, which resulted in the murder of Mustafa Shalabi, the fiery imam of the mosque, on March 1, 1991. The crime has never been solved.[47]

## NEW CIA AMIGOS

The soaring expenses for the covert war in Afghanistan coupled with the ongoing need of support for the guerilla units in Latin America and the secret armies in Western Europe caused the CIA to forge new alliances. In 1980, the Agency deployed Dewey Clarridge, its top agent in Latin America, to establish ties with Honduran drug lord Juan Matta Ballesteros, who operated SETCO, an airline that was used for smuggling drugs into the United States. In accordance with the working relationship, SETCO transported narcotics to gangs and gringos north of the border and arms to a warehouse in Honduras that was operated by CIA operatives Oliver North and Richard Secord.[48] The weapons were purchased by the Agency's cut of the deal, which in one transaction amounted to $14 million.[49] Business arrangements were made with other drug lords, including Miguel Angel Felix Gallardo, the "godfather of the Mexican drug business," whose ranch became a training ground for right-wing guerilla armies,[50] and Miguel Nazar Haro, the leader of the Guadalajara Cartel, Mexico's most powerful narcotics network.[51]

By 1990, more than 75 percent of all the cocaine entering the United States came through Mexico. Mexico also became a leading source of heroin, marijuana, and methamphetamines. The business was generating $50 billion a year, and the CIA had found a source of funding to augment its ongoing heroin trade with the *babas* and the Sicilian mafia. The new alliance meant that the Agency could launch hundreds of new operations even more ambitious than Gladio.[52]

As Americans were becoming increasingly drugged, they were becoming increasing impoverished, since the plans of the international bankers had given rise to unlimited free trade and the globalization of poverty.

# NOTES

1. Alexander Cockburn and Jeffrey St. Clair, *Whiteout: The CIA, Drugs and the Press* (New York: Verso, 1998), p. 261.
2. Ibid.
3. Alfred W. McCoy, *The Politics of Heroin: CIA Complicity in the Global Drug Trade* (Chicago: Lawrence Hill Books, 2003), p. 476.
4. Ibid.
5. Robert Pelton, *The World's Most Dangerous Places* (New York: Harper Resource, 2003), p. 342.
6. Alexander Cockburn and Jeffrey St. Clair, *Whiteout*, p. 264.
7. McCoy, *The Politics of Heroin*, p. 474.
8. Jeffrey Lord, "Jimmy Carter's Dead Ambassador," *American Spectator*, October 23, 2012, http://spectator.org/articles/34550/jimmy-carters-dead-ambassador.
9. Ibid.
10. U.S. State Department memorandum reproduced in Alexander Cockburn and Jeffrey St. Clair's *Whiteout*, pp. 262–263.
11. Ibid., p. 263.
12. Ibid.
13. Ibid., p. 259.
14. Zbigniew Brzezinski, *The Grand Chessboard: American Primacy and Its Geostrategic Imperative* (New York: Basic Books, 1997), pp. 20, 40.
15. Jagmohan Meher, *America's Afghanistan War: The Success That Failed* (New Delhi, India: Gyan Books, 2004), pp. 68–69.
16. Jonathan Beaty and S. C. Gwynne, "BCCI: The World's Dirtiest Bank," *Biblioteca Pleyades*, July 29, 1991, http://www.bibliotecapleyades.net/sociopolitica/sociopol_ globalbanking118.htm.
17. David Sirota and Jonathan Baskin, "Follow the Money: How John Kerry Busted the Terrorists' Favorite Bank," *Washington Monthly*, September 2004, http://www.washingtonmonthly.com/features/2004/0409.sirota.html, accessed May 21, 2014.
18. Lucy Komisar, "The Case That Kerry Cracked," *Alter Net*, October 21, 2004, http://www.alternet.org/story/20268/the_case_that_kerry_cracked.
19. Jonathan Beaty and S.C, Gwynne, *The Outlaw Bank: A Wild Ride into the Heart of the BCCI* (New York: Random House, 1993), p. 228.
20. Senator John Kerry and Senator Hank Brown, "The BCCI Affair: A Report to the Committee on Foreign Relations," U.S. Senate, December 1992, http://www.fas.org/irp/congress/1992_rpt/bcci/11intel.htm.
21. Steve Lohr, "Auditing the Auditors—A Special Report: How BCCI's Accounts Won Stamp of Approval," *New York Times*, September 6, 1991.
22. Kerry and Brown, "The BCCI Affair."
23. David Yallop, *The Power and the Glory: Inside the Dark Heart of John Paul II's Vatican* (New York: Carroll and Graf, 2007), p. 424.
24. Ibid.

25. Kerry and Brown, "The BCCI Affair."

26. Cockburn and St. Clair, *Whiteout*, p. 265.

27. Ibid., p. 265,

28. Edwin Meese, quoted in Ibid., p. 265.

29. Ibid., p. 269.

30. Jonathan Beaty, "A Mysterious Mover of Money and Planes," TIME Magazine, June 24, 2001, http://content.time.com/time/magazine/article/0,9171,1101911028-155760,00.html, accessed May 22, 2014.

31. John Kerry and Hank Brown, "BCCI in the United States: Initial Entry and FGB and NBG Takeovers," U.S. Senate Subcommittee Report to the Committee on Foreign Relations, 1992, http://www.fas.org/irp/congress/1992_rpt/bcci/03hist.htm.

32. David Livingston and Sahib Mustaqim Bleher, *Surrendering Islam: The Subversion of Muslim Politics throughout History until the Present Day* (Karachi, Pakistan: Mustaqim Ltd., 2010), p. 121.

33. Ibid.

34. Philip Willan, *The Vatican at War: From Blackfriars Bridge to Buenos Aires* (Bloomingon, IN: iUniverse LLC, 2003), kindle edition, 27%.

35. Cockburn and St. Clair, *Whiteout*, p. 320. See also Andrew W. Griffith, "Jackson Stephens, BCCI and Drug Laundering," Red Dirt Report, January 22, 2012,

36. Ibid.

37. John Kerry and Hank Brown, "BCCI in the United States."

38. Bill Plante, quoted in David Livingston and Sahib Mustaqim Bleher's *Surrendering Islam: The Subversion of Muslim Politics throughout History until the Present Day* (Karachi, Pakistan: Mustaqim Ltd., 2010), p. 125.

39. Alexander Cockburn and Jeffrey St. Clair, *Whiteout: The CIA, Drugs and the Press* (New York: Verso, 1998), p. 273.

40. Robert Young Pelton, *The World's Most Dangerous Places* (New York: Harper Resources, 2003), pp. 327–328.

41. Karl Evanzz, *The Messenger: The Rise and Fall of Elijah Muhammad* (New York: Vintage Books, 2001), p. 308.

42. Robert Dannin, *Black Pilgrimage to Islam* (New York: Oxford University Press), pp. 75–77.

43. Gordon Gregory and Donna Williams, "Jamaat ul-Fuqra," Special Research Report, Regional Organized Crime Information Center, 2006.

44. "Afghanistan Update," *Daily Telegraph* (UK), August 5, 1983; *Los Angeles Times*, August 5, 1983.

45. Peter Lance, *100 Years of Revenge* (New York: Regan Books, 2003), pp. 38–42.

46. Abdullah Azzam, quoted in Peter L Bergen, *Holy War, Inc.: Inside the Secret World of Osama bin Laden* (New York: Simon and Shuster, 2002), p. 136.

47. Daniel Pipes, *Militant Islam Reaches America* (New York: W. W. Norton, 2003), p. 137.

48. Alexander Cockburn and Jeffrey St. Clair, *Whiteout*, pp. 279–282.

49. Ibid.

50. Peter Dale Scott and Jonathan Marshall, *Cocaine Politics: Drugs, Armies and the CIA* (Oakland, CA: University of California Press, 1998), p. 4.

51. Peter Dale Scott, "Washington and the Politics of Drugs," *Variant*, Summer 2000, http://www.variant.org.uk/pdfs/issue11/Variant11.pdf, accessed May 24, 2014.

52. Alexander Cockburn and Jeffrey St. Clair, *Whiteout*, p. 360.

# 35

# THE GLOBALIZATION OF POVERTY

*Since the 1980s, a large share of the labor force in the United States has been driven out of high pay unionized jobs into low pay minimum wage jobs. Poverty in America's ghettoes is, in many respects, comparable to that of the Third World. While the "recorded" rate of unemployment in the US declined in the 1990s, the number of people on low wage part-time jobs has spiraled. With further declines in minimum wage employment, large sectors of the working population are pushed out of the labor force altogether. . . . In turn, economic restructuring has created profound divisions between social classes and ethnic groups. The environment of major metropolitan areas is marked by social apartheid: the urban landscape is compartmentalized along social and ethnic lines.*

—MICHEL CHOSSUDOVSKY, *THE GLOBALIZATION OF POVERTY AND THE NEW WORLD ORDER*

HENRY KISSINGER was a product of the House of Rockefeller. He graduated from Harvard in 1950 as a Rockefeller Foundation Fellow in Political science. In 1956, he was invited by the Rockefellers to join the Council on Foreign Relations, where he became a major force in shaping international policy.[1] Explaining Kissinger's rise in the CFR, J. Robert Moskin, author of *The U.S. Marine Corps Story*, writes: "It was principally because of his long association with the Rockefellers that Henry Kissinger became a force in the Council. The *New York Times* called him 'the Council's most influential member,' and a Council insider says that 'his influence is direct and enormous—much of it through the Rockefeller connection.'"[2]

During the 1960s, Kissinger served as Nelson Rockefeller's chief foreign affairs advisor and the mastermind behind Nelson's campaign for the presidency. The relationship between the two men was so close that Kissinger dedicated his memoir, *The White House Years*, to Nelson, describing him as "the single most influential person in my life."[3]

**Henry Kissinger**

Henry Kissinger was a product of the House of Rockefeller. He graduated from Harvard in 1950 as a Rockefeller Foundation Fellow in Political science. In 1956, he was invited by the Rockefellers to join the Council on Foreign Relations, where he became a major force in shaping international policy.

## WAKING "THE SLEEPING GIANT"

When Richard Nixon became president, he appointed Kissinger as Secretary of State in accordance with advice of the Rockefeller family.[4] In this position, Kissinger tirelessly advanced the agenda of the money cartel, including the promulgation of free trade between all nations. This agenda prompted him in July of 1971 to visit China, where he negotiated a trade agreement by which the Communist country would receive "most favored nation status" with the United States, a status that would permit Chinese goods to flow into America free of charge. Kissinger was accompanied by

Winston Lord, a member of the National Security Council staff, who later became president of the CFR. By the time Nixon visited China the following year, the terms of the deal had been set in stone. The treaty, which was ratified by Congress, caused David Rockefeller to gloat: "The Chinese are not only purposeful and intelligent, [but] they also have a large pool of cheap labor. So they should be able to find ways to get trading capital."[5] Of course the Chinese found ways of getting trading capital. However, the funds did not come from their own resources but rather from the IMF/World Bank, which proceeded to supply the communist country with billions of tax-free loans.[6]

## GOODBYE, MADE IN AMERICA

Manufacturing plants sprouted up throughout China. The products and goods were produced in these plants by workers making less per month than union workers in America were making per hour. Women, working in the Timberland Shoe Company in Guangdong Province, labored fourteen hours a day at twenty-two cents per hour. At a factory making Kathie Lee [Gifford] handbags for Walmart, the highest wages were seven dollars a week.[7] Compounding the problem for American manufacturers was China's manipulation of its currency. By 2010, China had devalued the yuan by 45 percent—cutting in half the cheap labor for companies moving to China and doubling the price of US goods entering the communist country. The trade deficit stood at $266 billion.[8]

Throughout America, factories began to relocate to Southeast Asia and an ever-increasing number of American workers found themselves on the unemployment line. A list of the companies that moved their manufacturing facilities to China is as follows:

AT&T

Abercrombie & Fitch

Abbott Laboratories

Acer Electronics

Ademco Security

Adidas

ADI Security

AGI—American Gem Institute

AIG Financial

Agrilink Foods, Inc. (ProFac)

Allergan Laboratories

American Eagle Outfitters

American Standard

American Tourister

Ames Tools

Amphenol Corporation

Amway Corporation

Analog Devices, Inc.

Apple Computer

Armani

Armour Meats

Ashland Chemical

Ashley Furniture

Associated Grocers

Audi Motors

AudioVox

AutoZone, Inc.

Avon

Banana Republic

Bausch & Lomb, Inc.

Baxter International

Bed, Bath & Beyond

Belkin Electronics

Best Buy

Best Foods

Big 5 Sporting Goods

Black & Decker

Body Shop

Borden Foods

Briggs & Stratton

Calrad Electric

Campbell's Soup

Canon Electronics

Carole Cable

Casio Instrument

Caterpillar, Inc.

CBC America

CCTV Outlet

Checker Auto

CitiCorp

Cisco Systems

Chiquita Brands International

Claire's Boutique

Cobra Electronics

Coby Electronics

Coca-Cola Foods

Colgate-Palmolive

Colorado Spectrum

ConAgra Foods

Cooper Tire

Corning, Inc.

Coleman Sporting Goods
Compaq
Crabtree & Evelyn
Cracker Barrel Stores
Craftsman Tools (see Sears)
Cummins, Inc.

Dannon Foods
Dell Computer
Del Monte Foods
Dewalt Tools
DHL
Dial Corporation
Diebold, Inc.
Dillard's, Inc.
Dodge-Phelps
Dole Foods
Dollar Tree Stores, Inc.
Dow-Corning

Eastman Kodak
EchoStar
Eclipse CCTV
Edge Electronics Group
Electric Vehicles USA, Inc.
Eli Lilly Company
Emerson Electric
Enfamil Estee Lauder
Eveready

Family Dollar Stores
FedEx

Fisher Scientific
Ford Motors
Fossil
Frito Lay
Furniture Brands
International

GAP Stores
Gateway Computer
GE, General Electric
General Foods
International
General Mills
General Motors
Gentek
Gerber Foods
Gillette Company
Goodrich Company
Goodyear Tire
Google
Gucci
Guess

Haagen-Dazs
Harley Davidson
Hasbro Company
Heinz Foods
Hershey Foods
Hitachi
Hoffman-LaRoche
Holt's Automotive
Products
Hormel Foods

Home Depot
Honda Motor
Hoover Vacuum
HP Computer
Honda
Honeywell
Hubbell Inc.
Huggies
Hunts-Wesson Foods

ICON Office Solutions
IBM
IKEA
Intel Corporation

J. C. Penney
J.M. Smucker Company
John Deere
Johnson Control
Johnson & Johnson
Johnstone Supply
JVC Electronics

KB Home
Keebler Foods
Kenwood Audio
KFC, Kentucky Fried Chicken
Kimberly Clark
Knorr Foods
K-Mart
Kohler

Kohl's Corporation
Kraft Foods
Kragen Auto

Land's End
Lee Kum Kee Foods
Lexmark
LG Electronics
Lipton Foods
L.L. Bean, Inc.
Logitech
Libby's Foods
Linen & Things
Lipo Chemicals, Inc.
Lowe's Hardware
Lucent Technologies
Lufkin

Mars Candy
Martha Stewart Products
Mattel McCormick Foods
McDonald's
McKesson Corporation
Megellan GPS
Memorex
Merck & Company
Michael's Stores
Mitsubishi Electronics
Mitsubishi Motors
Mobile Oil
Molex
Motorola

Motts Applesauce
Multifoods Corporation

Nabisco Foods
National Semiconductor
Nescafe
Nestles Foods
Nextar
Nike
Nikon
Nivea Cosmetics
Nokia Electronics
Northrop Grumman
Corporation
NuSkin International
Nutrilite
Nvidia Corporation
(G-Force)

Office Depot
Olin Corporation
Old Navy
Olympus Electronics
Orion-Knight Electronics

Pacific Sunwear, Inc.
Pamper's
Panasonic
Pan Pacific Electronics
Panvise
Papa Johns
Payless Shoesource
Pelco

Pentax Optics
Pep Boys
Pepsico International
PetsMart
Petco
Pfizer, Inc.
Philips Electronics
Phillip Morris Companies
Pier 1 Imports
Pierre Cardin
Pillsbury Company
Pioneer Electronics
Pitney Bowes, Inc.
Pizza Hut
Plantronics
PlaySchool Toys
Polaris Industries
Polaroid
Polo (see Ralph Lauren)
Post Cereals
Price-Pfister
Pringles
Praxair
Proctor & Gamble
PSS World Medical
Pyle Audio

Qualcomm
Quest One

Radio Shack
Ralph Lauren

RCA
Reebok International
Reynolds Aluminum
Revlon
Rohm & Hass Company

Samsonite
Samsung
Sanyo
Shell Oil
Schwinn Bike
Sears-Craftsman
Seven-Eleven (7-11)
Sharp Electronics
Sherwin-Williams
Shure Electronics
Sony
Speco Technologies/Pro Video
Shopko Stores
Skechers Footwear
SmartHome
Smucker's (see J.M. Smucker's)
Solar Power, Inc.
Spencer Gifts
Stanley Tools
Staples
Starbucks Corporation
Steelcase, Inc.
STP Oil
Sunkist Growers
SunMaid Raisins

Sunglass Hut
Sunkist
Subway Sandwiches
Switchcraft Electronics
SYSCO Foods
Sylvania Electric

3-M
Tai Pan Trading Company
Tamron Optics
Target
TDK
Tektronix, Inc
Texas Instruments
Timex
Timken Bearing
TNT
Tommy Hilfiger
Toro
Toshiba
Tower Automotive
Toyota
Toys "R" Us, Inc.
Trader Joe's
Tripp-lite
True Value Hardware
Tupperware
Tyson Foods

Uniden Electronics
UPS

Valspar Corporation

Victoria's Secret

Vizio Electronics

Volkswagen

VTech

Walgreen Company

Walt Disney Company

Walmart

WD-40 Corporation

Weller Electric Company

Western Digital

Westinghouse Electric

Weyerhaeuser Company

Whirlpool Corporation

Wilson Sporting Goods

Wrigley

WW Grainger, Inc.

Wyeth Laboratories

X-10

Xelite

Xerox

Yahoo

Yamaha

Yoplait Foods

Yum Brands

Zale Corporation[9]

## PROTECTIONISM FORSAKEN

The economic situation in America worsened as more countries, including India and Pakistan, received most-favored status. By 2010, fifty thousand manufacturing plants in America had shut down. Almost everything that Americans purchased came from overseas manufacturers: shoes, clothes, cars, furniture, TVs, appliances, bicycles, toys, cameras and computers.[10] The goods flowed into the country free of charge, violating the principles of America's Founding Fathers. Alexander Hamilton had written:

> The superiority antecedently enjoyed by nations who have preoccupied and perfected a branch of industry, constitutes a more formidable obstacle than either of those which have been mentioned, to the introduction of the same branch into a country in which it did not before exist. To maintain, between the recent establishments of one country, and the long-matured establishments of another country, a competition upon equal terms, both as to quality and price, is, in most cases,

impracticable. The disparity, in the one, or in the other, or in both, must necessarily be so considerable, as to forbid a successful rivalship, without the extraordinary aid and protection of government.[11]

Cheap foreign labor and tax-free imports also impacted the defense industry. In 2010, Senator Fritz Hollings wrote: "Today, the United States has less manufacturing jobs than in April 1941. Long before the recession, South Carolina had lost its textile industry, North Carolina its furniture industry, Michigan its automobile industry. The defense industry has been off-shored. We had to wait months to get flat panel displays from Japan before we launched Desert Storm. Boeing can't build a fighter plane except for the parts from India. Sikorsky can't build a helicopter except for the tail motor from Turkey. Under law, the Secretary of Commerce lists those items vital to our national security but Congress fails to make sure we can produce these items for our defense. Today, we can't go to war except for the favor of a foreign country."[12]

## THE WORLD TRADE ORGANIZATION

On January 1, 1995, the World Trade Organization (WTO) came into being with headquarters in Geneva, Switzerland. It was set up to integrate nations into a world order without tariffs or other economic barriers. The principal beneficiaries were the 80,000 transnational corporations with account for two-thirds of the world trade. A 2014 *New Science* study showed that 1,318 core transnational corporations, through interlocking boards of directors, owned 80 percent of global revenues, and 147 of them formed a "super entity" that controlled 40 percent of the wealth of the entire network.[13] Not surprisingly, this "super entity" was dominated by the business interests of the House of Rockefeller.

The WTO represented one of the final steps in the creation of a New World Order. It was empowered under international law to police the economic and social policies of its 164 member states, thereby derogating the sovereign rights of national governments. "Under WTO rules," noted economist Michel Chossudovsky writes, "the banks and multinational corporations (MNCs) can legitimately manipulate market forces to their advantage leading to the outright re-colonization of national economies."[14]

## THE NAFTA NIGHTMARE

Just when it seemed that the situation for American workers could not get worse, the North American Free Trade Agreement came into force on January 1, 1994. The agreement was developed by the Council on the Americas, an organization set up by David Rockefeller in 1965.[15] The Rio Grande now separated two distinct labor markets, as production facilities closed in the United States and Canada and moved to Mexico, where wages were ten times lower.[16] Thanks to this agreement, the United States suffered an additional trade deficit of $181 billion and the loss of one million more jobs. NAFTA also resulted in the displacement of more than one million Mexican *campesino*, who packed up their belongings and headed off for *el Norte* (the USA).[17]

**Abandoned factories**

By 2010, fifty thousand manufacturing plants in America had shut down. Almost everything that Americans purchased came from overseas manufacturers.

## A NATION OF TAKERS

From December 2000 through December 2010, America lost three million private-sector jobs (the worst record since 1928–1938), and 5.5 million manufacturing jobs (one out of every three Americans who worked in a plant or factory was out of work). In 1950, manufacturing constituted 27 percent of the US economy. Forty years later, that number dropped to 11 percent. By 2011, 22.5 million Americans worked for the government, while only 11.5 million worked in manufacturing. This was a reversal of the situation in 1960, when 15 million worked in manufacturing, while 7 million collected a pay check from the government. Commenting on this situation, Stephen Moore wrote the following in a piece for the *Wall Street Journal:* "More Americans work for the government than work in construction, farming, fishing, forestry, manufacturing, mining, and utilities combined. We have moved decisively from a nation of makers to a nation of takers."[18]

# NOTES

1.  G. Vance Smith and Tom Gow, *Masters of Deception: The Rise of the Council on Foreign Relations* (Colorado Springs, CO: Freedom First Society, 2012), p. 166.
2.  Robert Moskin, quoted in Ibid.
3.  James Perloff, *The Shadows of Power: The Council on Foreign Relations and the American Decline* (Appleton, WI: Western Islands, 2005), p. 145.
4.  Ibid., pp. 145–146.
5.  David Rockefeller, quoted in Gary Allen, *The Rockefeller File* (Seal Beach, CA: '76 Press, 1976), p. 121.
6.  G. Edward Griffin, *The Creature from Jekyll Island: A Second Look at the Federal Reserve* (Westlake Village, CA: American Media, 2017), p. 122.
7.  Jon E. Dougherty, "Free Trade v. Slave Trade: Brutal Chinese Working Conditions Benefit WalMart, Others," *World Net Daily,* May 24, 2000, http://www.hartford-hwp.com/archives/55/312.html.
8.  Pat Buchanan, *Suicide of a Superpower* (New York: Thomas Dunne Books, 2011), p. 13.
9.  Jie's World Staff, "American and International Companies in China."
10. Ibid., p. 12.
11. Alexander Hamilton, quoted in Ian Fletcher, "America Was Founded as a Protectionist Nation," *Huffington Post,* September 12, 2010, http://www.huffingtonpost.com/ian-fletcher/america-was-founded-as-a_b_713521.html.
12. Fritz Hollings, "Fifth Column: The Enemy within the Trade War," *Huffington Post,* March 18, 2010, http://www.huffingtonpost.com/sen-ernest-frederick-hollings/fifth-column-the-enemy-wi_b_323833.html.
13. Takis Fotopoulos, "The Transnational Elite and the New World Order," *Global Research,* October 28, 2014, http://www.globalresearch.ca/%CF%84he-transnational-elite-and-the-nwo-as-conspiracies/5410468.
14. Michel Chossudovsky, *The Globalization of Poverty and the New World Order* (Montreal, Quebec: Global Research, 2003), p. 26.
15. Fred Gardner, "The Birth of NAFTA," *Counter Punch,* February 28, 2008, https://www.counterpunch.org/2008/02/28/the-birth-of-nafta/.
16. Chossudovsky, *The Globalization of Poverty and the New World Order,* p. 76.
17. Lori Wallach, "NAFTA at 20: One Million U.S. Jobs Lost, Higher Income Equality," *Huffington Post,* n. d., http://www.huffingtonpost.com/lori-wallach/nafta-at-20-one-million-u_b_4550207.html.
18. Stephen Moore, quoted in Buchanan, *Suicide of a Superpower,* p. 16.

# PART TEN

## AMERICA, NO MORE

JEFFERSON MEMORIAL WASHINGTON, D.C. INSCRIPTION UNDER THE DOME
*". . . I have sworn upon the altar of god eternal hostility against every form of tyranny over the mind of man."*
—JEFFERSON TO DR. BENJAMIN RUSH, SEPTEMBER 23, 1800[1]

### PANEL ONE

*"We hold these truths to be self-evident: that all men are created equal, that they are endowed by their Creator with certain inalienable rights, among these are life, liberty, and the pursuit of happiness, that to secure these rights governments are instituted among men. We . . . solemnly publish and declare, that these colonies are and of right ought to be free and independent states. . . . And for the support of this declaration, with a firm reliance on the protection of divine providence, we mutually pledge our lives, our fortunes, and our sacred honor."*
—THE DECLARATION OF INDEPENDENCE[2]

### PANEL TWO

*"Almighty God hath created the mind free. All attempts to influence it by temporal punishments or burthens . . . are a departure from the plan of the Holy Author of our religion. . . . No man shall be compelled to frequent or support any religious worship or ministry or shall otherwise suffer on account of his religious opinions or belief, but all men shall be free to profess and by argument to maintain, their opinions in matters of religion. I know but one code of morality for men whether acting singly or collectively."*

## ORIGINAL PASSAGE

*"Well aware that the opinions and belief of men depend not on their own will, but follow involuntarily the evidence proposed to their minds; that Almighty God hath created the mind free, and manifested his supreme will that free it shall remain by making it altogether insusceptible of restraint; that all attempts to influence it by temporal punishments, or burthens, or by civil incapacitations, tend only to beget habits of hypocrisy and meanness, and are a departure from the plan of the holy author of our religion..."*

—"A BILL FOR ESTABLISHING RELIGIOUS FREEDOM," SECTION I[3]

# 36

# THE ROAD TO 9/11

*The excessive accumulation of money wealth from the proceeds of the drug trade has transformed the CIA into a powerful financial entity. The latter cooperates through a web of corporate shells, banks, and financial institutions wielding tremendous power and influence. These CIA-sponsored "corporations" have, over time, been meshed into the mainstay of the business and corporate establishment, not only in weapons production and the oil business, but also in banking and financial services, real estate, etc. In turn, billions of narco dollars are channeled—with the support of the CIA—into spheres of "legitimate" banking, where they are used to finance bona fide investments in a variety of economic activities.*

—MICHEL CHOSSUDOVSKY, *AMERICA'S WAR ON TERRORISM*

HEROIN BY THE TURN OF THE TWENTY-FIRST CENTURY had become one of the world's most valuable resources—a resource that could generate over $100 billion a year in revenue. Without the white powder, there would be no black ops—no means of obtaining control of Eurasia—no way of molding the global economy and political relations.

On January 27, 2000, a catastrophe occurred for covert activity when Mullah Omar and the leaders of the Taliban announced their plans to ban poppy production within the Islamic Emirate of Afghanistan.[1]

This decision sent shock waves through the US intelligence community. Afghan opium poppy harvest had grown nearly tenfold from 250 to 2,000 tons during the covert war of the 1980s, and from 2,000 to 4,600 tons during the civil war of the 1990s. The country's economy transformed from a diverse agricultural system based on herding, orchards, and sixty-two varieties of field crops into the world's first opium monocrop.[2]

**Taliban**
In June 1998, the Taliban struck a deal with Saudi officials to send bin Laden to a Saudi prison in exchange for Saudi support and US recognition of its legitimacy in ruling the country.

Thanks to the Taliban ban, the opium poppy harvest fell from 4,600 tons in 1999 to 81 tons in 2001.[3] The situation had to be addressed by the military-industrial complex in a forceful way. The ban not only brought the CIA's operations to a screeching halt but also caused a mass exodus of poppy farmers from the fertile fields of the Helmand Valley. "All the young people have gone to Pakistan," a farmer named Rashid told reporters. "Ninety percent of this area used to be cultivated with poppy. How much money can you make from wheat?"[4] Losing the crop was bad enough, but losing the farmers was devastating.

The ban also spelled disaster for the international banking and business community since heroin had become "the third biggest global commodity in cash terms after oil and the arms trade."[5] Michel Chossudovsky explains:

> Supported by powerful interests, heroin is a multibillion-dollar business which requires a steady and secure commodity flow. But the Taliban prohibition caused "the beginning of a heroin shortage in Europe by the end of 2001," as acknowledged by the United Nations Office on Drugs and Crime. . . One of the hidden objectives of the war [on terrorism] was effectively to restore the CIA sponsored drug trade to its historical level and exert direct control over the drug routes. Immediately following the October 2001 invasion, opium markets were restored. Opium prices spiraled. By 2002, the domestic price of opium in Afghanistan was almost ten times higher than in 2000.
>
> At the height of the opium trade during the Taliban regime, roughly 70 percent of the global supply of heroin originated in Afghanistan. In the wake of the US-led invasion, Afghanistan accounts for more than 85 percent of the global heroin market.[6]

## THE PLANNED PIPELINE

Heroin was one cause of the war on terrorism. Oil was another. The situation in Afghanistan had become worrisome to the House of Rockefeller, which had been instrumental in bringing the Taliban to power in 1996. Through the Union Oil Company of California (Unocal), the Rockefellers had arranged to provide the group with weapons and military instructors. This aid had enabled the Taliban to capture Kabul and to oust Afghan president Burhanuddin Rabbani from office.[7]

The Unocal gifts of arms and advisors were given with the belief that the Taliban would provide assistance in the creation of a massive oil pipeline that would run from the oil wells of Turkmenistan through the mountains of Afghanistan to the port city of Karachi, Pakistan, on the Arabian Sea. It was a project that could not take place without a dominant central regime in place to suppress the country's tribal warlords.[8]

The 1,040-mile–long pipeline would have a shipping capacity of one million barrels of oil per day and would resolve the vexing problem of seizing control of the vast wealth of oil and natural gas that surrounded the land-locked Caspian Sea.[9]

## "THE GRAND CHESSBOARD"

Unocal also planned through its subsidiary Centgas to build another pipeline—this one for natural gas that would follow the same route through Afghanistan.[10] In the great game of geo-economics, the two pipelines represented the integral parts of the plan to gain control of the "stan" countries, as Zbigniew Brzezinski had set forth as follows.

> The Grand Chessboard:
>
> The world's energy consumption is bound to vastly increase over the next two or three decades. Estimates by the U.S. Department of Energy anticipate that world demand will rise by more than 50 percent between 1993 and 2015, with the most significant increase in consumption occurring in the Far East. The momentum of Asia's economic development is already generating massive pressures for the exploration and exploitation of new sources of energy and the Central Asian region and the Caspian Sea basin are known to contain reserves of natural gas and oil that dwarf those of Kuwait, the Gulf of Mexico, or the North Sea.[11]

## RAISING THE STAKES

The Soviet Union had discovered the vast Caspian Sea oil fields in the late 1970s and attempted to take control of Afghanistan to build a massive north-south pipeline system to allow the Soviets to send their oil directly through Afghanistan and Pakistan to the Indian Ocean seaport. The result was the decades-long Soviet-Afghan war. The Russians then attempted to control the flow of oil and gas through its monopoly on the pipelines in the former Soviet republics that surrounded the Caspian Sea: Turkmenistan, Kazakhstan, and Azerbaijan. The leaders of these countries saw through this Russian monopolistic ploy and began to consult with Western oil executives, including Condoleezza Rice of Chevron (the predecessor of Rockefeller-owned Standard Oil of California).[12] Ms. Rice, a prominent CFR member, later became President George W. Bush's national security advisor.

The shadow government, under the direction of Standard Oil and the House of Rockefeller, now planned to thrust further along the 40th parallel from the Balkans through these Southern Asian Republics of the former Soviet Union. The US military has already set up a permanent operations base in Uzbekistan. This so-called "anti-terrorist strategy" was designed to consolidate control over Middle Eastern and South Asian oil and contain and neutralize the former Soviet Union.[13]

Realizing its weaker position vis-a-vis the United States, Russia joined the Shanghai Cooperation Organization (SCO), which included China, Kazakhstan, Kyrgyzstan, Tajikistan, and Uzbekistan. Its membership in the SCO represented Russia's attempt to maintain its traditional hegemony in Central Asia.[14] Thus the stakes in the chess game became sky-high since the winner gained global economic hegemony.

## THE TALIBAN IN TEXAS

Once they conquered Kabul, the leaders of the Taliban were whisked off in a US military transport to Houston, Texas, where they were wined and dined by Unocal officials, who had hired Henry Kissinger and Richard Armitage (who would become George W. Bush's deputy Secretary of State) as consultants. Concerning the gatherings, L.A. reporter Jim Crogan wrote:

> [Unocal's top executive Barry]Lane says he wasn't involved in the Texas meetings and doesn't know whether then-Governor George W. Bush, an ex-oil man, ever had any involvement. Unocal's Texas spokesperson for Central Asia operations, Teresa Covington, said the consortium delivered three basic messages to the Afghan groups. "We gave them the details on the proposed pipelines. We also talked to them about the projects' benefits, such as the transit fees that would be

paid," she says. "And we reinforced our position that the project could not move forward until they stabilized their country and obtained political recognition from the U.S. and the international community." Covington says the Taliban were not surprised by that demand.

In December 1997, Unocal arranged a high-level meeting in Washington, D.C., for the Taliban with Clinton's undersecretary of state for South Asia, Karl Inderforth. The Taliban delegation included Acting Minister for Mines and Industry Ahmad Jan, Acting Minister for Culture and Information Amir Muttaqi, Acting Minister for Planning Din Muhammad and Abdul Hakeem Mujahid, their permanent U.N. delegate.

Two months later Unocal vice president for international relations John Maresca testified before a House Committee on International Relations about the need for multiple pipeline routes in Central Asia. Maresca briefed the members about the proposed Afghan pipeline projects, praising their economic benefits and asking for U.S. support in negotiating an Afghan settlement.[15]

Despite such power players, a final agreement was not reached because the Taliban was being pursued by other oil interests, including representatives from SCO. Meanwhile, the tentative US ties to the Taliban was offset by Moscow's support for the Northern Alliance, the group of Islamic militants who ruled northern Afghanistan.[16] Pressure was applied to Mullah Omar, the leader of the Taliban, to come to a decision regarding the Unocal offer. But no commitment from the chieftain was forthcoming. And the situation was becoming increasingly untenable.

## THE EMBASSY BOMBINGS

By 1998, the American power elite realized they had to set up a more cooperative government in Kabul. Plans were made to launch a terror attack against America that could be blamed on bin Laden and the host of Islamic militants that inhabited Afghanistan, including the Taliban. On August 7, the US embassies in Kenya and Tanzania were bombed.

The attack killed 234 people, twelve of them American, and wounded 5,000 more.[17] The event sent shockwaves throughout the United States. On August 20, President Bill Clinton responded by launching a cruise missile attack on al-Qaeda's alleged residential and military complexes in Khost, Afghanistan, and the bombing of the al-Shifa Pharmaceutical Plant near Khartoum in the Sudan, where bin Laden once lived.

The CIA had informed Clinton that these attacks would catch the al-Qaeda leaders unaware, since no member of the mujahedeen would believe that the United States was capable of such decisive action. The Agency further affirmed that the al-Shifa plant was producing deadly XV nerve gas.[18]

## BILL CLINTON BILGE

Following the attack, Clinton addressed his fellow countrymen from the Oval Office by saying:

> Our mission was clear: to strike at the network of radical groups affiliated with and funded by Osama bin Laden, perhaps the pre-eminent organizer and financier of international terrorism in the world today. . . . Earlier today, the United States carried out simultaneous strikes against terrorist facilities and infrastructures in Afghanistan. It contained key elements of bin Laden's network and infrastructure and has served as the training camp for literally thousands of terrorists around the globe. We have reason to believe that a gathering of key-terrorist leaders was to take place there today, thus underscoring the urgency of our actions. Our forces also attacked a factory in Sudan associated with the bin Laden network.
>
> The factory was involved in the production of materials for chemical weapons.[19]

The Clinton announcement was of vital importance to the shadow government. It identified Osama bin Laden as mankind's greatest enemy and the Taliban as a group that served him. The announcement also informed the American public that new attacks were in the works and that weapons of mass destruction were in production to be used against them. The problem was that none of it was true. Bin Laden and his Muslim pals were not in the Khost camp. They were, as the CIA was well aware, safe and sound within a *madrassah* in Pakistan. Although the missiles struck the camps, the only casualties were local farmers and some low-level militants.[20] And the Sudan pharmaceutical plant was not involved in making nerve gas or any other chemical weapon. It produced common over-the-counter drugs, including ibuprofen.[21]

## A FALSE FLAG OPERATION

What's more, information surfaced that the attack on the embassies was not conducted by al-Qaeda, but rather a false-flag operation that could be blamed on bin Laden. A key indicator of this contention was the involvement of Ali A. Mohamed, also known as Ali "the American" in the bombing. Following the attack, he was labeled as the "point man" who had masterminded the operation. Two years after the blasts, Mohamed was arrested by the American authorities and pleaded guilty to conspiracy to murder. It then came to light that the alleged al-Qaeda bomber had an impeccable US military service record. He had been trained at Fort Bragg, North Carolina, and worked as an instructor in explosives at the John F. Kennedy Special Warfare Center and School until 1989.[22]

The official government narrative claimed that Mohamed, who was married to an American citizen and who had lived in California, was all the while working as a double agent for al-Qaeda and that he had become a blood-thirsty jihadi by the time of the embassy attacks in 1998. This narrative was circulated by the American media. One story in the *San Francisco Chronicle* in 2001 conveyed the sense of treachery as follows: "bin Laden's man in Silicon Valley—'Mohamed the American'—orchestrated terrorist acts while living a quiet suburban life in Santa Clara." In reality, throughout the 1990s, Mohamed was working for the American secret services in East Africa, including Kenya.[23]

## "VANISHED INTO THIN AIR"

"There is no way that US intelligence handlers did not know of every move made by Mohamed," Ralph Schoenman, a reporter who has spent decades investigating the 1998 bombings maintains. "This guy was recruited by the CIA in Cairo, where he was a major in the Egyptian army. He was then a handpicked graduate of Fort Bragg for American Special Forces and he went on to instruct green berets in psy-ops and explosives at the JFK School of Warfare. We are talking about the strictest security clearance in the US military. And yet the official account expects the public to believe that somehow Mohamed's connections with bin Laden's al-Qaeda slipped their attention and that he carried out the US embassy bombings in a rogue fashion for the supposed enemy."[24]

Supporting Schoenman's contention is the fact that, despite pleading guilty in a New York court in 2000 to conspiracy to murder American citizens, Mohamed has never been sentenced to confinement. There are no records of subsequent court proceedings, and his whereabouts, to this day, remain unknown. His Californian wife, Linda Sanchez, was quoted in 2006 as saying of her husband: "He can't talk to anybody. Nobody can get to him. They have Ali pretty secret. It's like he just kinda vanished into thin air."[25]

## DREAM FULFILLED

In August 1998, the dream of Cecil Rhodes came to fruition with the merger of Amoco and BP, resulting in the formation of the world's largest oil company.[26] The House of Rockefeller was now united with the House of Rothschild, and the two nations became inextricably bound both economically and politically. Billions of dollars now flowed into joint military industrial interest and such defense contractors as Lockheed Martin, Northrop Grumman, General Dynamics, Boeing, and Raytheon.[27] Britain's new Labor government under Prime Minister Tony Blair now became America's unconditional ally.[28] The two countries, in accordance with William Stead's foresight, would act in tandem during the war on terrorism, with America as the dominant partner. The movers and shakers behind the Anglo-American Establishment, in keeping with Rhodes's vision, would meet in secret at the annual meetings of the Bank on International Settlements and the Bilderberg Conference. They also would gather within the inner sanctum of the Trilateral Commission, an outgrowth of the Council on Foreign Relations that had been established by David Rockefeller in 1973. This organization, by providing loans to foreign governments, including General Augusto Pinochet in Chile, made a cadre of American and British bankers more powerful than the elected representatives of both governments.[29]

After the merger of the oil giants, the primary concern of the new power elite was the need to build the trans-Afghan pipeline and the threat to the world economy posed by the Taliban's ban on poppy production. They realized during their clandestine meetings that these problems could only be resolved by the invasion and occupation of Afghanistan and the removal of the Taliban from power.

## THREE STEPS TOWARD ENDLESS WAR

The first step toward meeting these objectives had been the bombing of the two African embassies which resulted in making the Taliban synonymous with al-Qaeda even though the two groups were sharply at odds. In 1998, Mullah Omar rejected bin Laden's repeated calls for violence against Americans and rejected the al-Qaeda chieftain's religious rulings as "null and void."[30] Moreover, the scruffy Taliban leader resented the arrogance of the Arab mujahedeen, whose aristocratic attitude toward Pashtun customs and beliefs had become intolerable. Tensions between the two Islamic militant groups became so tense that gunfire broke out between the Taliban soldiers and bin Laden's bodyguards.[31] In June 1998, the Taliban struck a deal with Saudi officials to send bin Laden to a Saudi prison in exchange for Saudi support and US recognition of its legitimacy in ruling the country.[32] Prince Turki bin Faisal, head of the Saudi General Intelligence Agency, confided to the Clinton Administration that the exchange was "a done deal."[33]

But after the missile attacks, Prince Faisal retuned to Afghanistan to find the one-eyed Taliban mullah a changed man. "Mullah Omar became very heated," the prince said. "In a loud voice he denounced all our efforts and praised bin Laden as a worthy and legitimate scholar of Islam."[34]

The second step toward legitimizing an invasion of Afghanistan was the appointment of Hamid Karzai as the head of the interim government in Kabul. Prior to this appointment, Karzai had acted as a consultant and lobbyist for Unocal in its negotiations with the Taliban and as a CIA covert operator who had funneled US aid to Mullah Omar and his band of radical Muslim students.[35]

The third and final step was the creation of an incident of enormous proportion that would warrant the planned invasion. That incident came on September 11, 2001, when Islamic terrorists hijacked four American airliners; two crashed into New York's World Trade Center, one into the Pentagon in Arlington County, Virginia, and the fourth in a field near a reclaimed coal strip mine near Shanksville, Pennsylvania. It resulted in the deaths of 2,292 Americans, public and private property destruction in excess of $21 billion, and the loss of more than 200,000 jobs.[36]

A war without end had started.

# NOTES

1. Alfred W. McCoy, *The Politics of Heroin: The CIA's Complicity in the Global Drug Trade* (Chicago: Lawrence Hill Books, 2003), p. 505.
2. Ibid.
3. Ibid, p. 518.
4. Luke Harding, "Taliban to Lift Ban on Farmers Growing Opium if US Attacks," *The Guardian*, September 24, 2001, https://www.theguardian.com/world/2001/sep/25/afghanistan.terrorism8.
5. Michel Chossudovsky, *America's "War on Terrorism"* (Montreal, Quebec: Global Research, 2005), p. 228.
6. Ibid.
7. Richard James DeSocio, *Rockefellerocracy: Assassinations, Watergate, and Monopoly of "Philanthropic" Foundations* (Bloomington, IN: Author's House, 2013), pp. 97-98. Also Richard Labeviere, *Dollars for Terror* (New York: Algora Press, 2000), p. 272.
8. Simon Reeve, *The New Jackals: Ramzi Yousez, Osama Bin Laden, and the Future of Terrorism* (Boston: Northeastern University Press, 1999), p. 190.
9. Chossudovsky, *America's "War on Terrorism*, p. 82.
10. Ibid., p. 80.
11. Zbigniew Brzezinski, *The Grand Chessboard: American Primacy and Its Geostrategic Imperatives* (New York: Basic Books, 1998), p. 125.
12. Ibid, p. 82.
13. Norman D. Livergood, "The New US-British Oil Imperialism," October 29, 2001, http://www.hermes-press.com/impintro1.htm.
14. Ibid.
15. Jim Crogan, "The Oil War: Unocal's Once Grand Plan for Afghan Pipelines," *L. A. Weekly*, November 28, 2001, http://www.laweekly.com/news/the-oil-war-2134105.
16. Staff Report, "BBC Bolsters Northern Alliance," *BBC News*, October 22, 2001, http://news.bbc.co.uk/2/hi/south_asia/1612898.stm.
17. Michael Grunwald, "CIA Helps Thwart Bomb Plot against Embassy in Uganda," *Washington Post*, September 25, 1998, https://www.washingtonpost.com/archive/politics/1998/09/25/cia-halted-plot-to-bomb-us-embassy-in-uganda/8c8fd38b-1c6f-4570-ba14-126601660bf6/?utm_term=.5af04628e933.
18. Rohan Gunaratna, *Inside Al Qaeda: Global Network of Terror* (New York: Berkeley Books, 2002), p. 63.
19. Bill Clinton, quoted in Peter L. Bergen, *Holy War, Inc.: Inside the Secret World of Osama Bin Laden* (New York: Simon and Schuster, 2002), p. 125.
20. Ibid.
21. Ibid.
22. Finian Cunningham, "Kenyan False Flag Bomb Plot Aimed at Tightening Sanctions Noose on Iran," *Global Research*, July 6, 2012, http://www.globalresearch.ca/kenyan-false-flag-bomb-plot-aimed-at-tightening-sanctions-noose-on-iran/31795.

23. Ibid.
24. Ralph Schoenman, quoted in Ibid.
25. Linda Sanchez, quoted in Ibid.
26. Chossudovsky, *America's "War on Terrorism,"* pp. 84–85.
27. Ibid., p. 15.
28. Ibid., p. 86.
29. Penny Lernoux, *In Banks We Trust* (New York: Penguin Books, 1986), pp. 241–242.
30. Bergen, *Holy War Inc: Inside the Secret World of Osama Bin Laden*, p. 166.
31. Tim Weiner, "Terror Suspect Said to Anger Taliban Hosts," *New York Times,* March 4, 1999, http://www.nytimes.com/1999/03/04/world/terror-suspect-said-to-anger-afghan-hosts.html.
32. William C Rempel, "Saudi Tells of Deal to Arrest Terror Suspect: Afghans Back-Pedaled on Hand-Over of Bin Laden after U.S. Embassy Blasts," *Los Angeles Times,* August 8, 1999, http://articles.latimes.com/1999/aug/08/news/mn-63689.
33. Ibid.
34. Prince Turki bin Faisal, quoted in Jane Corbin, *Al Qaeda: In Search of the Terrorist Network That Threatens the World* (New York: Thunder Mouth Press, 2003), pp. 69–70.
35. Chossudovsky, *America's "War on Terrorism,"* p. 88.
36. Tom Templeton and Tom Lumley, "9/11 in Numbers," *The Guardian*, August 17, 2002.

# 37

## THE MYSTERIES OF 9/11

*On September 11, 2001, the three worst structural failures in modern history took place when World Trade Center Buildings 1, 2, and 7 suffered complete and rapid destruction. In the aftermath of the tragedy, most members of the architecture and engineering community, as well as the general public assumed that the buildings' destruction had occurred as a result of the airplane impacts and fires. This view was reinforced by subsequent federal investigations, culminating in FEMA's 2002 Building Performance Study and in the 2005 and 2008 reports by the National Institute of Standards and Technology (NIST). Since 9/11, however, independent researchers around the world have assembled a large body of evidence that overwhelmingly refutes the notion that airplane impacts and fires caused the destruction of the Twin Towers and WTC 7. This body of evidence, most of which FEMA and NIST omitted from their reports, instead supports the troubling conclusion that all three skyscrapers were destroyed in a process known as "controlled demolition," where explosives and other devices are used to bring down a building.*

—ARCHITECTS AND ENGINEERS FOR 9/11 TRUTH

NO ONE CAN DOUBT that two jetliners crashed into the Twin Towers of the World Trade Center, or that another jetliner flew into the Pentagon and a fourth fell from the sky near Shanksville, Pennsylvania, on September 11, 2001. But everything else about that fateful day remains shrouded in mystery.

## MYSTERY #1 – THE PYROTECHNIC SUBSTANCE

The first mystery concerns the collapse of the twin towers which represents the worst structural failure in modern history. The official story from the National Institute of Standards and Technology (NIST), an agency of the US Department of Commerce, is that the impact of the jetliners produced fires that weakened the structure of the two skyscrapers, resulting in a gravitational collapse.[1] But the evidence supports another story—one that concerns a controlled demolition. Such evidence includes:

1. the rapid onset of destruction;

2. the constant acceleration at or near free fall of the collapsed floors through parts of the buildings that should have been paths of greatest resistance;

3. eyewitness accounts, including those of 118 members of the New York Fire Department, of explosions;

4. lateral ejections of multi-ton steel framing flying distances of 600 feet at 60 miles per hour;

5. the midair pulverization of 90,000 tons of concrete and large volumes of expanding volcanic-like dust clouds;

6. isolated explosive ejections 20 to 60 stories below the "crush zone";

7. total destruction of the buildings with 220 floors;

8. several tons of molten steel/iron among the debris; and evidence of thermite incendiaries on the steel beams.[2]

The final item is particularly telling. Neither jet fuel nor office fires can reach temperatures sufficient to melt steel (2,750 degrees Fahrenheit), much less to bring steel to a boiling point. Thermite is a mixture of iron oxide and elemental aluminum, that when ignited, reaches temperatures between 4,000 to 4,500 degrees Fahrenheit and produces aluminum oxide and molten iron in a volcanic-like display.[3] The presence of this substance among the ruins of 9/11 provided a tell-tale sign that the collapse of the Towers may have been the result of a controlled implosion.

## MYSTERY #2 – THE STAND-DOWN ORDER

The US military had spent billions developing stealth aircraft—invisible to radar—that could intercept any air attack on the homeland. But on the morning of September 11, 2001, the North American Aerospace Defense Command (NORAD) was oblivious that four jetliners were invading prohibited airspace and headed for central targets, including the Pentagon. Even after the first jetliner crashed into North Tower at 8:46 a.m., NORAD proved incapable of locating and stopping the second jetliner from crashing into the South Tower at 9:02 a.m. Yet the Northeast Air Defense Sector of NORAD was fully staffed on 9/11, and the entire staff, even when placed on high alert, remained oblivious of the third jetliner that crashed into the Pentagon at 9:37 a.m. and that the fourth jetliner, which—thanks to heroic passengers—crashed in Shanksville, was headed toward the White House. Procedures at NORAD were completely abandoned. There were fifteen to twenty minute delays in issuing warnings to air traffic controllers. Interceptor planes were not scrambled by NORAD from the bases near the targets, even when it was clear that the commandeered jets were headed toward Manhattan and Washington, DC. And fighter planes that were in the air were not redeployed by NORAD to prevent the attacks.[4]

This mystery of the prevention of interceptions is intensified by the fact that the air traffic controllers on duty that day in New York recorded a tape of all that had transpired before, during, and after the attacks. But the tape, which included vital testimony, was seized by a Federal Aviation Administration (FAA) quality assurance manager, who crushed the tape in his hand, and cut it into tiny pieces, which he proceeded to deposit in different trash containers. Kenneth Mead, the FAA inspector general, said that the destruction of the tape was merely a matter of "poor judgment."[5]

The stand-down order to NORAD had come from Vice-President Dick Cheney, who was safe and secure within a bunker beneath the White House. This fact was confirmed by Norman Mineta, the Secretary of Transportation.[6] Cheney was a director of the CFR and a former executive of Halliburton, one of America's largest defense contractors, who had given Cheney a $34 million signing bonus to serve as George W. Bush's running mate.[7]

**Dick Cheney**
The stand-down order to NORAD had come from Vice-President Dick Cheney, who was safe and secure within a bunker beneath the White House.

What accounts for such bizarre action? Why was this crucial tape seized and destroyed? Why had NORAD failed to respond to a prolonged attack in such strategic locations? The answer, in part, resides from the fact that NORAD had received a "stand down" order that its commanders were compelled to obey. The order came from Vice-President Dick Cheney, who had sought shelter from the attacks in a bunker.

## MYSTERY #3 – THE MISSING RUBBLE

Another mystery lies with the rubble (including the debris from the planes) that was removed from ground zero before it could be examined by forensic experts. The Twin Towers collapsed in a manner identical with a planned implosion. Such an implosion would have required the use of pyrotechnic substances—traces of which would have remained among the mounds of twisted steel. Yet 185,101 tons of structural steel that should have been subjected to detailed analysis were loaded on trucks and transported to salvage yards in New Jersey, where the steel was cut into fragments for recycling. A substantial amount of this recycled steel was sold at the rock bottom price of $120 per ton and shipped off to China.[8]

Given that the removal and recycling of World Trade Center steel took place over the objections of victims' families and others seeking a genuine investigation, many uttered a sigh of relief when news was announced that steel parts of the Twin Towers had been saved from the smelting furnaces. The heaviest of these steel pieces was stored in an 80,000-square-foot hangar at John F. Kennedy International Airport. These pieces included some of the base sections of the Towers' massive core columns and 13 of the 153 steel trees from the bases of the Towers' perimeter walls.[9]

Although the hangar, which reportedly held one five-hundredth of the "total debris field," remained off-limits to the public, the discovery of the existence of intact pieces of the Twin Towers' columns seemed to be good news for independent investigators who would like to test samples of steel. However, the locations of these pieces within the Towers belied reason for their preservation. The large core column sections stood on the Towers' foundations, seven stories below street level, and the perimeter column trees were from the lobby level, just above street level. Only these lower sections of the Towers were spared the blasting that shredded the steel frames down to about their fourth stories. This was evident from the facts that eighteen people survived in the lower reaches of the North Tower's core, and fragments of the perimeter walls of each Tower remained standing after the buildings collapsed.[10]

## MYSTERY #4 – THE INSIDER TRADING

Among the mysteries is the finding that an elite group of Wall Street investors purportedly possessed criminal foreknowledge of 9/11, which permitted them to make a windfall from insider trading. By 2014, one of these trades left an unclaimed gain of $2.5 million. This transaction was the result of put options that were placed on United Airlines stock. Since the planes involved in 9/11 belonged to United Airlines and American Airlines, the two companies took a major hit as a result of the attacks, with shares of United Airlines dropping from $30.82 to $17.50, and shares of American Airlines falling from $29.70 to $18.00.[11]

Put options are sold in blocks of 100 shares. They give investors the option of selling these shares at a future date at the price set when the options are issued. Thanks to these the allowance of these transactions, investors could tie up 100,000 shares of United at $30.82 and 100,000 shares of American at $29.70 which the sellers were obliged to buy. When the prices plummeted respectively to $17.50 and $18.00 per share, the holders of the options could purchase the shares of the two airlines at the rock bottom prices and immediately sell them at the price set when the options were purchased.

The firm used to purchase the unclaimed gains in put options was Bankers Trust-AB Brown, a division of Deutsche Bank, which remained under the control of the House of Rothschild.[12] Bankers Trust, a New York bank, had been established in 1903 by J. P. Morgan.[13] It merged in 1997 with Alex Brown and Sons, an investment bank founded in 1800, to become Bankers Trust – A B Brown. Alvin "Buzzy" Krongard had been the chairman of Alex Brown and Sons at the time of the merger. After the two banks combined, he became vice-chairman of the new financial conglomerate. His task was to oversee "private client relations," a position that brought him in contact with some of the world's richest people, including allegedly individuals involved in the heroin market, and the bank, according to Senator Carl Levin, became a major center for the laundering of drug money.[14] After Bankers Trust – A B Brown was sold to Deutsche Bank in 1999, Krongard joined the CIA, where he became the executive director. Few individuals had greater insider knowledge of covert operations and impending threats than Krongard, and fewer still had closer ties to the international banking community. On September 6, 2001, Bankers Trust – A B Brown, where Krongard had served as a top executive, purchased 95 percent of the puts on United Airlines and, on September 10, as part of the same investment strategy, 115,000 shares of American Airlines.[15]

## MYSTERY #5 – THE VISITOR FROM PAKISTAN

And then there is the mysterious matter of General Mahmoud Ahmad, the head of Pakistan's Inter-Services Intelligence (ISI).

Two weeks after 9/11, the FBI confirmed in an interview with ABC News that Mohammed Atta, the ringleader of terrorists who hijacked the jetliners, had been financed from unnamed sources in Pakistan. Following this announcement, several European news agencies, including Agence France Presse and the Times of India, were able to confirm that the money had been wired to Atta from Pakistan by ISI officials at the insistence of General Ahmad. Yet, on the morning of 9/11, Ahmad, the alleged "money man," was in Washington, DC, conferring with top government officials, including CIA Director George Tenet; Senator Bob Graham, chairman of the Senate Intelligence Committee; Senator John Kyl, a member of the Senate Intelligence Committee, and Representative Porter Goss, chairman of the House Intelligence Committee.[16] After the attacks, Ahmad remained in Washington to meet with Secretary of State Colin Powell, Deputy Secretary of State Richard Armitage, Under Secretary of State Marc Grossman, and Senator Joe Biden, Chairman of the Senate's Foreign Affairs Committee.[17] The fact that the man who sponsored the terror attacks was rubbing elbows with America's leading political leaders before, during, and after the attacks should cause raised eyebrows from the most ardent supporters of the war on terror.

## MYSTERY #6 – THE COLLAPSE OF BUILDING 7

A forty-seven-story skyscraper located at 7 World Trade Center I, New York City, was not struck by a jetliner. Yet it collapsed at 5:20 p.m. on 9/11 with little news coverage. The incident was not even mentioned in the official report from the 9/11 Commission.[18]

The building appeared to implode in the same manner as the

Twin Towers. Yet officials from the Federal Emergency Management Agency (FEMA) argued that the collapse had been caused by fireballs of cascading debris from the Towers. They asserted this argument even though no steel high-rise had ever before collapsed because of a fire.[19] Adding to the mystery was the fact that BBC reported the collapse of the building twenty minutes before it fell to the ground.[20]

It took eight years for the National Institute of Standards and Technology (NIST) to provide an explanation of why Building 7 was reduced to rubble. NIST insisted that the collapse was not caused by an explosion since no audible sound of a blast could be detected on existing recordings of the event. Yet eyewitnesses, including members of the New York Fire Department, reported hearing sounds of explosives immediately before Building 7 collapsed.[21]

## MYSTERY #7 – THE SEARCH FOR BIN LADEN

At eleven in the morning of 9/11, the Bush Administration announced that al-Qaeda was responsible for the attacks on the Twin Towers and the Pentagon. This announcement was made without a police investigation, a statement of guilt by the leaders of al-Qaeda, or any supporting evidence. At 9:30 p.m., the "War on Terror" was officially launched against al-Qaeda and the Taliban. The latter was singled out as being a state sponsor of the horrific events.[22]

**Osama bin Laden**
Bin Laden became the world's most wanted man on November 4, 1998, when he was indicted in US federal court on 224 counts of murder for masterminding the bombings of the US embassies in Tanzania and Kenya.

Four weeks later, on October 8, the US invasion of Afghanistan was launched. The American people were led to believe that the decision to go to war had been made on the spur of the moment without previous preparation. Since the central target was Osama bin Laden, the first casualty, as in every war, was truth. Bin Laden had been recruited by the CIA in December of 1979 to create a cadre of "holy warriors" (*mujahedeen)* to ward off the Soviet invasion of Afghanistan. The Agency provided the warriors training in guerilla warfare and indoctrination in the tenets of radical Islam so that they would view the invasion as justification for "holy war" or *jihad*.[23]

During the war in Kosovo, bin Laden and his holy warriors were used by the Clinton Administration to combat the Christian Serbs in a struggle that was designed to safeguard the Balkan route by which heroin was transported from Turkey to northern Italy and to establish the massive Camp Bondsteel military base to safeguard US economic interests.[24]

Bin Laden became the world's most wanted man on November 4, 1998, when he was indicted in a US federal court on 224 counts of murder for masterminding the bombings of the US embassies in Tanzania and Kenya. A $5 million bounty was placed on his head by the US State Department, and the leader of the *mujahadeen* became the favorite bogeyman of the press and the power elite.[25]

But the hunt was really a scam. Two months before the events of 9/11, bin Laden was a patient at an American hospital in Dubai, where he was receiving treatment for a chronic kidney infection. During his stay in the hospital, the al-Qaeda chieftain conferred with the CIA station head.[26] On September 10, 2001, the day before the attacks, bin Laden was back in the hospital—this time in Rawalpindi, Pakistan, where he received dialysis treatments. This finding was substantiated by *CBS News*.[27] The hospital in Pakistan was a military facility. It operated under the jurisdiction of the Pakistani Armed Forces, which had close links to the Pentagon.[28] If this report is accurate, then bin Laden in all likelihood was still in the Rawalpindi hospital on the morning of 9/11.[29] Despite awareness of bin Laden's whereabouts over the months before 9/11, Donald Rumsfeld, the US Secretary of Defense, announced to the press that it would be difficult to find the al-Qaeda chieftain and to extradite him. "It's like searching for a needle in a haystack," Rumsfeld said.[30]

When bin Laden was finally placed within a body bag by US Navy Seals, he had been living for five years next to an elite military academy in Abbottabad. The compound, where Osama had been living with his four wives, was not inconspicuous. It loomed over the Pakistani city like a "strange mansion," and the world's most wanted man probably could have been collared by a Boy Scout troop.[31]

# NOTES

1. Richard G. Gann et al., "Reconstruction of the Fires: Final Report in the World Trade Center Towers. Federal Investigation of the World Trade Center Disaster," National Institute of Standards and Technology, December 1, 2005, https://www.nist.gov/publications/reconstruction-fires-world-trade-center-towers-federal-building-and-fire-safety-0?pub_id=101028.

2. "Science of 9/11," Architects and Engineers for 9/11 Truth," n. d., http://www.ae911truth.org/gallery/evidence.html.

3. Ibid.

4. "NORAD Stand Down: The Prevention of Interceptions of the Commandeered Planes," *9/11Research*, n. d., 11research.wtc7.net/planes/analysis/norad/.

5. Matthew L. Wald, "Tape of Air Traffic Controllers Made on 9/11 Was Destroyed," *New York Times*, May 7, 2004, http://www.nytimes.com/2004/05/07/us/tape-of-air-traffic-controllers-made-on-9-11-was-destroyed.html?_r=0.

6. Aaron Dykes, "Secretary Mineta Confirms Dick Cheney Ordered Stand Down on 9/11," *Jones Report*, June 26, 2007, https://extremeprejudiceusa.wordpress.com/2013/08/26/secretary-mineta-confirms-dick-cheney-ordered-stand-down-on-911/.

7. Louis Jacobson, "Chris Matthews Says Cheney Got $34 Million Payday from Halliburton," *Politifact*, May 24, 2010, http://www.politifact.com/truth-o-meter/statements/2010/may/24/chris-matthews/chris-matthews-says-cheney-got-34-million-payday-h/.

8. "ETC Steel Removal," *9/11 Research*, September 9, 2015, http://911research.wtc7.net/wtc/groundzero/cleanup.html.

9. Ibid.

10. Ibid.

11. Marc Davis, "How September 11 Affected the Stock Market," *Investopedia*, May 16, 2017, http://www.investopedia.com/financial-edge/0911/how-september-11-affected-the.u.s.-stock-market.aspx.

12. Silver Report, "Rothschild Pulls His Money from Banks; Deutsche Bank Collapsing," *Main Street Bail Out*, February 23, 2017, http://mainstbailout.com/2017/02/23/silver-report-rothschild-pulls-his-money-from-banks-deutsche-bank-collapsing/.

13. Francine McKenna, "16 Years Later. Billions in Value Gets Wiped Away from Bankers Trust," *Market Watch*, October 9, 2015, http://www.marketwatch.com/story/how-bankers-trust-lost-its-value-16-years-later-2015-10-09.

14. Michael C. Ruppert, "9/11 Attacks: Criminal Foreknowledge and Insider Trading Lead Directly to the CIA's Highest Ranks," *Global Research*, April 16, 2014, http://www.globalresearch.ca/9-11-attacks-criminal-foreknowledge-and-insider-trading-lead-directly-to-the-cia-s-highest-ranks/32323.

15. *9/11 Commission Report* (New York: W. W. Norton, 2001), p. 499.

16. Michel Chossudovsky, *America's "War on Terrorism"* (Montreal, Quebec: Global Research, 2005), pp. 139–140.

17. Ibid., p. 54.

18. "7 Facts about Building 7," Remember Building 7. org., n. d., http://rememberbuilding7.org/.

19. FEMA, "World Trade Center Building Performance," The Federal Emergency Management Agency, September 1, 2002, p. 4, https://www.fema.gov/media-library/assets/documents/3544.

20. BBC TV, "September 11, 2001: 4:54 PM – 5:36 PM," September 11, 2001, https://archive.org/details/bbc200109111654-1736.

21. Staff Report, "Neue Videos vom 11. September Aufgetaucht," *Bild*, September 9, 2010, http://www.bild.de/news/2010/terror-anschlaege-world-trade-center-13892672.bild.html.

22. Chossudovsky, *America's "War on Terrorism,"* p. xi.

23. Ibid., pp. 22–25.

24. Dimiter Kenarov, "Unapproachable Light," *VQR*, Spring 2010, http://www.vqronline.org/dispatch/unapproachable-light.

25. CNN Library, "1998 U.S. Embassies in Africa Bombings: Fast Facts," *CNN*, August 3, 2016, http://www.cnn.com/2013/10/06/world/africa/africa-embassy-bombings-fast-facts/index.html.

26. Chossudovsky, *America's "War on Terrorism,"* p. 5.

27. CBS News. "Hospital Worker: I Saw Osama," *CBS Evening News*, January 28, 2002, http://www.cbsnews.com/news/hospital-worker-i-saw-osama/.

28. Chossudovsky, *America's "War on Terrorism,"* pp. 20–21.

29. Ibid., p. 21.

30. Peter Brush, "Rumsfeld: Al Qaeda Still Active," *CBS News*, June 4, 2002, http://www.cbsnews.com/news/rumsfeld-al-qacda-still-active/.

31. Natasha Bertrand, "There's an Uncomfortable Mystery behind Osama bin Laden Living in Pakistan for 5 Years," *Business Insider*. May 17, 2015.

# 38

# WAR WITHOUT END

*The period extending from the Korean war (1950–53) to the present is marked by a succession of U.S. sponsored theater wars (Korea, Vietnam, Cambodia, Afghanistan, Iraq, and Yugoslavia, various forms of military intervention, including low intensity conflicts, "civil wars" (The Congo, Angola, Somalia, Ethiopia, Rwanda, Sudan), military coups, U.S. sponsored death squadrons and massacres (Chile, Guatemala, Honduras, Argentina, Indonesia, Thailand, Philippines), covert wars in support of al-Qaeda "freedom fighters" (Soviet-Afghan war), U.S.-NATO covert wars using al-Qaeda as foot soldiers (Syria), U.S.-NATO sponsored humanitarian military interventions: Libya in 2011 (aerial bombings combined with support to al-Qaeda rebels). The objective has not been to win in these wars but in essence to destabilize these countries as nation states as well as impose a proxy government which acts on behalf of Western interests. Accounting for these various operations, the United States has attacked, directly or indirectly, some 44 countries in different regions of the developing world since 1945, a number of them many times.*
—MICHEL CHOSSUDOVSKY, *THE GLOBALIZATION OF WAR*, 2015

PROOF OF THE LIFELESS CONDITION of Uncle Sam came with the avuncular figure's failure to respond to the mysterious circumstances surrounding 9/11 and the possibility that the country had been subjected to one of the most horrendous false-flag attacks in human history.

Such attacks had become commonplace. On August 2, 1990, Saddam Hussein ordered a half million Iraqi troops to invade and occupy Kuwait. The reason for the invasion was reasonable. Kuwait, while Iraq was locked up in a deadly war with Iran, had pilfered $2.4 billion in oil from the Rumdia oil field—an Iraqi oil field—and still Kuwaiti emir Amir Jabir al-Almad refused to absolve even the interest on Iraqi's debt to his country.[1]

This development posed no threat to US national security, but it jeopardized the interests of the House of Rockefeller and the House of Rothschild, which feared that Hussein would invade Saudi Arabia and absorb the oil fields in the Persian Gulf.[2] These two banking families controlled the world's largest oil companies, including Exxon and BP. They had created Saudi Aramco in the 1930s and remained the largest purchasers of Mid-eastern oil. This position enabled them to establish oil prices—a position that became threatened when Saddam Hussein's invading army appeared at the Saudi border.[3]

The Reagan Administration, under the guidance of George Schultz and other CFR members, had sided with Iraq during the decade-long Iran-Iraq War. It had shelled out billions in agricultural credits and hundreds of millions of dollars in advanced weaponry to Saddam. The weapons were transported to Iraq by a circuitous route through Egypt and Saudi Arabia since the House of Saud was also intent upon ending the

**Saddam Hussein**

Despite the fact that Saddam Hussein was dragged from a hole, placed on trial before a kangaroo court, and lynched, no ties between the Iraqi ruler and al-Qaeda were ever substantiated.

reign of the Ayatollah Khomeini in Iran.[4] The United States, under Reagan, further equipped the Iraqi army with satellite intelligence supplemented by AWACs (Airborne Warning and Control Systems) reconnaissance that could be used to direct weapons against Iranian suicide brigades.[5]

### FALSE FLAG #1: SADDAM AS BABY KILLER

But when Saddam Hussein ventured into Kuwait, President George H. W. Bush, a prominent CFR member, became intent upon launching a war against America's old ally. Bush's ties to big-oil interests, including Standard Oil, were extensive.[6] Early in his career, he made millions with the drilling of the first off-shore oil well in Kuwait. He also became associated with the Carlyle Group, a leading defense contractor, which numbered the Saudi royal family and the government of Kuwait among its customers.[7] In this way, Bush Sr. was wired to the Rockefellers, the Saudis, and the military-industrial complex. Members of his cabinet were similarly wired. Secretary of Defense Dick Cheney, a CFR director, became the chief executive officer of Halliburton.[8] And Secretary of State James Baker, another CFR member, became senior counselor of the Carlyle Group.[9] The problem for Bush was how to justify US military involvement against Iraq. Amir Jabir al-Ahmad al-Jabir al-Sabah, the emir of Kuwait, was certainly not a sympathetic character. Stories were widely circulated about his profligate lifestyle. The emir, according to unsubstantiated accounts, was syphilitic, kept seventy wives, and married a virgin every Thursday.[10]

The answer to the problem came with the raising of a false flag. Bush and his cabinet began to circulate stories that Hussein had ordered his soldiers to enter Kuwaiti hospitals in order to remove babies from incubators and to cast them on the floor to die.[11] Repeating this concocted tale five times over the national airwaves, Bush said: "I don't think that Adolf Hitler ever participated in anything of that nature."[12]

**George H. W. Bush**
On January 14, 1991, Bush Sr. launched the Persian Gulf War, which, as it turned out, wasn't much of a war.

## THE PERSIAN GULF WAR

On January 14, 1991, Bush Sr. launched the Persian Gulf War, which, as it turned out, wasn't much of a war. But it did allow the military-industrial complex, thanks to twenty-four-hour television coverage on CNN, to showcase their latest technology in warfare: stealth bombers, cruise missiles, "smart" bombs, and laser guidance systems that pin-pointed targets and minimized civilian casualties. Within a matter of days, the Iraqi air force was obliterated, along with airfields, missile sites, and communication centers.[13] Throughout Iraq, most means of modern life were destroyed. All electrically operated installations ceased to function. Food could not be preserved. Water could not be purified. Sewage could not be pumped away. Nine thousand homes were destroyed or damaged beyond repair.[14]

Following the war, economic sanctions were placed on Iraq, which resulted in a shortage of medical supplies and food. Malnutrition and disease increased at an alarming rate. By 1998, nearly one million Iraqis, mostly young children and the elderly, had died because of the embargo.

Diseases that had been nearly eradicated reappeared, including polio, cholera, and typhoid. Cancer rates soared due to a proliferation of the uranium used in the smart bombs.[15] In 1993, physicians discovered a new disease. Iraqi mothers, too malnourished to breastfeed and unable to buy powdered milk, began feeding their babies sugared water or tea. Almost all the babies died. The doctors called them "sugar babies."[16]

Shortly after the Persian Gulf War began, Middle East Watch, a New York–based human rights organization, sent investigators to Iraq to verify the stories about Iraqi soldiers entering hospitals and removing infants from incubators. They were unable to locate any doctor, nurse, medical worker, or mother of a newly born child who could support the accounts that had caused the conflict.[17]

### FALSE FLAG #2: THE KOSOVO MASSACRES

Bush was not alone in raising a false flag to initiate a war in order to protect the interests of the CIA, the defense contractors, and the money cartel. In 1999, President Bill Clinton ordered the US Air Force, under the auspices of NATO, to conduct a bombing campaign that reduced Kosovo to a mound of rubble. Between March 24 and June 10, 37,465 missions were flown, destroying every stronghold of the Christian Serbs. The bombing was justified, Clinton and his administration argued, because the Serbs were committing genocide by murdering thousands of Muslim Albanians for the sake of ethnic cleansing. Since Kosovo was part of Yugoslavia, Clinton blamed Slobodan Milosevic for the alleged atrocities and compared the Yugoslavian president (much in the same manner that George H. W. Bush spoke of Saddam Hussein) to Adolf Hitler. "Though his ethnic cleansing is not the same as the ethnic extermination of the Holocaust, the two are related—both vicious, premeditated, systematic oppression fueled by religious and ethnic hatred," Clinton told a group of 200 Veterans of Foreign Wars members at the National Defense University at Fort McNair.[18] Stories surfaced in the *New York Times* and the *Washington Post* about a massacre in the small village of Racak, where the bodies of Muslim Albanians were left to rot

**Bill Clinton**
In 1999, President Bill Clinton ordered the US Air Force, under the auspices of NATO, to
conduct a bombing campaign that reduced Kosovo to a mound of rubble.

in the street. Investigative reporters from *Le Figaro* and *Le Monde* were
dispatched to verify these accounts. They discovered that the bodies
had been placed in unnatural positions, that the site of the "massacre"
was completely devoid of cartridges, and that the villagers were unable
to identify the victims.[19]

Another widely circulated story used to justify US intervention
concerned a mine in Trepca, where thousands of bodies of Muslim
Albanians were allegedly dumped. In the wake of the war, a French
gendarmerie spelunking team descended half a mile into the mine to
the bottom in search of bodies. They found none. Some villagers said
that the bodies were burned in a nearby furnace. A second French team
inspected the ashes. They found no teeth, no bones, and no trace of
human remains.[20]

## SIDING WITH THE ENEMY

For aid in their struggle for independence, the Muslim Albanians turned
to bin Laden and the *mujahedeen*. By 1995, more than six thousand holy

warriors from Chechnya, Egypt, and Saudi Arabia had made their way to the Balkans in preparation for the struggle against the Christian Serbs.[21]

Bin Laden visited the area three times between 1994 and 1996 to establish al-Qaeda training camps throughout the Balkans.[22] He also shelled out seven hundred million dollars to establish the Kosovo Liberation Army (KLA). The purpose of this organization was to drive the Christian Serbs from Kosovo, to topple the government of Slobodan Milosevic, and to unite the Muslims of Kosovo, Macedonia, and Albania into the Islamic Republic of Greater Albania.[23]

President Clinton, along with Secretary of State Madeleine Albright, Secretary of Defense William Cohen, and CIA director George Tenet (all CFR members), praised the KLA as "freedom fighters." In no time at all, millions of US dollars were flowing to the Muslim rebels in the form of military training and field advice.[24] The United States was now in league with the terrorist group that was purportedly intent upon its destruction. History doesn't get any crazier than this.

In the wake of the war, more than two hundred Christian churches and monasteries in Kosovo were put to the torch. Accounts surfaced of the mass execution of Serbian farmers, the murders of scores of priests, and "granny killings"—the drowning of elderly women in bathtubs.[25]

Of the two hundred thousand Serbs who lived in Kosovo before the war, only four hundred were left when the conflict came to an end.[26]

## HIDDEN REASONS FOR THE WAR

After the Christians had been purged from Kosovo, the Pentagon established Camp Bondsteel on the border of Kosovo and Macedonia. This massive military base came to house over six thousand US troops. The purpose of the camp was to protect the Balkan route whereby heroin flowed from Afghanistan via Turkey to Western Europe.[27] Another purpose of the 1,000-acre military installation was to provide protection for the trans-Balkan pipeline which was to channel Caspian Sea oil from the Bulgarian Black Sea port of Burgas to the Adriatic. The feasibility study for the pipeline had been drafted by the engineering division of Halliburton.[28]

And so the pattern persisted. False flag after false flag was unfurled to bring the United States into military conflict, while the American people, sapped of their strength and spirit, remained incapable of responding with cries of indignation, let alone outrage. America had become a corporation, and its citizens were not shareholders.

## FALSE FLAG #3 – IRAQ'S WEAPONS OF MASS DESTRUCTION

In 2003, President George W. Bush and his CFR cabinet proclaimed that Saddam Hussein was now in league with al-Qaeda and planning an attack on American soil that would eclipse the events of 9/11. Hussein, they maintained, had developed weapons of mass destruction that would soon be unleashed upon the hapless inhabitants of major US cities.

This false news was repeated over and over again on 532 separate occasions by Bush, Vice-President Cheney, National Security Advisor Condoleezza Rice, Defense Secretary Donald Rumsfeld, Secretary of

**George W. Bush**
The laboratories that Bush declared the US invading forces had found turned out to be innocuous facilities that were manufacturing hydrogen for weather balloons.

State Colin Powell, and Deputy Defense Secretary Paul Wolfowitz.[29] A sampling of their false statements is as follows:

ON AUGUST 26, 2002, in an address to the national convention of the Veterans of Foreign Wars, Vice-President Cheney said: "Simply stated, there is no doubt that Saddam Hussein now has weapons of mass destruction. There is no doubt he is amassing them to use against our friends, against our allies, and against us."[30]

ON SEPTEMBER 8, 2002, Cheney appeared on *Meet the Press* and announced: "We do know, with absolute certainty, that he [Saddam Hussein] is using his procurement system to acquire the equipment he needs in order to enrich uranium to build a nuclear weapon."[31]

ON SEPTEMBER 19, 2002, Defense Secretary Rumsfeld told Congress that Saddam "has amassed large, clandestine stockpiles of chemical weapons, including VX, sarin, and mustard gas."[32]

ON SEPTEMBER 28, 2002, President Bush in his weekly radio address to the nation said: "The Iraqi regime possesses biological and chemical weapons, is rebuilding the facilities to make more, and, according to the British government, could launch a biological or chemical attack in as little as forty-five minutes after the order is given . . . this regime is seeking a nuclear bomb, and with fissile material could build one within a year."[33]

ON MARCH 16, 2003, Vice-President Cheney appeared again on *Meet the Press.* This time he said: "We believe he [Saddam Hussein] has, in fact, reconstituted nuclear weapons."[34]

ON MAY 29, 2003, President Bush, in an interview with Polish TV, declared: "We found the weapons of mass destruction. We found biological laboratories. You remember when Colin Powell stood up in front of the world, and he said, Iraq has got laboratories, mobile labs to build biological weapons. They're illegal. They're against the United Nations resolutions, and we've so far discovered two. And we'll find more weapons as time goes on. But for those who say we haven't found the banned manufacturing devices or banned weapons, they're wrong, we found them."[35]

## BLOOD FOR OIL AND NATURAL GAS

None of it was true. No weapons of mass destruction had been found. No plans to develop nuclear bombs had been made. No biological laboratories that were fabricating sinister germ warfare. The laboratories that Bush declared the US invading forces had found turned out to be innocuous facilities that were manufacturing hydrogen for weather balloons.[36] Despite the fact that Saddam Hussein was dragged from a hole, placed on trial before a kangaroo court, and lynched, no ties between the Iraqi ruler and al-Qaeda were ever substantiated.

**Al-Qaeda**

The Libyan Islamic Fighting Group, rebels who opposed Gaddafi, was closely associated with al-Qaeda. A US intelligence report, months before the bombings, disclosed that there is a close link between al-Qaeda, jihadi organizations, and the opposition in Libya.

The war was launched to create a strategy of tension within Iraq. This allowed Anglo-American big oil companies under control of the money cartel to seize Iraqi oil fields and to further their control over the world's supply of energy.[37] Immediately after Bush announced "mission accomplished," ExxonMobil, Chevron, Shell, and BP set up shop in Iraq along with a slew of oil service companies, including Halliburton.[38]

Another purpose was to further the plans for the construction of a natural gas pipeline that would run from the North Pars, an Iranian port city on the Persian Gulf, to Damascus, Syria, via Iraq. Most European countries remained dependent upon Russia for its supply of natural gas.

Therefore, the pipeline would serve to cripple Russia economically while furthering the interests of the House of Rockefeller and the House of Rothschild.[39]

Plans for the conquest and occupation of Iraq had been in the works for several years. In *Winning Modern Wars*, General Wesley Clark writes of meeting Pentagon officials shortly after 9/11 who said the military campaign included the invasion of seven countries, "beginning with Iraq, then Syria, Libya, Iran, Somalia, and Sudan."[40]

### FALSE FLAG #4 – GADDAFI AS A MASS MURDERER

In 2011, when Islamic extremists took up arms against the government of Muammar Gaddafi in Libya, the US national news outlets, in tandem with the CFR Administration of President Barack Obama, announced that the Libyan ruler was planning the mass murder of men, women, and children in Benghazi to cower the populace into submission. Therefore, Libya had to be bombed to smithereens for the sake of humanity.[41]

Justifying the bombing, Secretary of State Hillary Clinton said: "We had a murderous dictator . . . threatening to massacre large numbers of the Libyan people. We had our closest allies in Europe burning up the phone lines begging us to help them try to prevent what they saw as a mass genocide, in their words. And we had the Arabs standing by our side saying, 'We want you to help us deal with Gaddafi.'"[42]

### UNMASKING MENDACITIES

Of course, it wasn't true. On March 17, 2011, Gaddafi announced to the rebels in Benghazi, "Throw away your weapons, exactly like your brothers in Ajdabiya and other places did. They laid down their arms and they are safe. We never pursued them at all." Subsequent investigation revealed that when Gaddafi regime forces retook Ajdabiya in February 2011, they did not attack or kill any innocent civilians. The Libyan ruler also attempted to appease protesters in Benghazi with an offer of development aid before finally deploying troops in an attempt to end the rebellion.[43]

What's more, an Amnesty International investigation in June 2011 could not corroborate any allegation of mass human rights violations by Gaddafi regime troops. It rather uncovered evidence that rebels in Benghazi made false claims and manufactured evidence. The investigation concluded: "Western media coverage has from the outset presented a very one-sided view of the logic of events, portraying the protest movement as entirely peaceful and repeatedly suggesting that the regime's security forces were unaccountably massacring unarmed demonstrators who presented no security challenge."[44]

## SIDING WITH THE ENEMY – PART II

The Libyan Islamic Fighting Group, the organization of the rebels who opposed Gaddafi, was closely associated with al-Qaeda. Secretary of State Clinton and President Obama were well aware of this fact before they deployed bombers and troops to topple the Gaddafi government. A US intelligence report issued months before the bombings contained this finding: "There is a close link between al-Qaeda, jihadi organizations, and the opposition in Libya."[45]

Oil-rich Libya was the most prosperous country in Africa. Education, medical treatment, and electricity were free, and gas sold for forty-two cents a gallon. Women who gave birth were supported with cash grants and couples, with cash gifts from the government on their wedding day. Libya's state bank provided loans without interest and provided free startup capital to farmers.[46]

## GADDAFI'S CRIME AGAINST THE MONEY CARTEL

Gaddafi's independence from big oil and the money cartel was the cause of his demise. Earlier in life Gaddafi's goal was to organize Arabs as a bloc that could withstand Western demands and depredations. He turned to Pan-Africanism and refused to join the US Africa Command. Gaddafi also attempted to introduce a gold-based African currency that would free Africans from American financial hegemony.[47]

Gaddafi used Chinese energy companies to develop Libya's energy resources, thereby passing the interests of the Anglo-American big oil and banking establishments. The power elite, already upset with Russian presence in the Mediterranean, became faced with Chinese presence as well. Gaddafi was playing ball with the wrong people and he had to go.[48]

On October 20, 2011, during the Battle of Sirte, Gaddafi was found hiding in a culvert by the rebel forces. He was beaten with rifle butts, sodomized with bayonets, and shot several times in the head.[49] Upon receiving word of Gaddafi's demise, a gleeful Hillary Clinton said: "We came. We saw. He died."[50]

## AN UNANSWERED QUESTION

Is ISIS (the Islamic State of Iraq and Syria) a creation of the Obama Administration, the CIA, and the US State Department under Hillary Clinton? This question, which was raised by Donald Trump during his campaign for the White House, was dismissed as absurd by the national media.[51] But evidence points to an affirmative answer. Gordon Duff, senior editor of *Veterans Today*, confirmed that the ISIS terrorists were trained in Jordan and Syria by US Major General (retired) Paul E. Vallely and other senior military consultants.[52] Vallely is a Fox News military analyst and the founder of the US Army Psychological Warfare School.[53] To establish his case, Duff has provided videos of Vallely and other American military officials with ISIS commandos.[54] Support for this startling assertion was provided by Aaron Klein of WorldNetDaily, who unearthed evidence that the ISIS forces were and are trained at a secret US military base in the Jordanian town of Safawi.[55] This report has been corroborated by *Der Spiegel,* Germany's leading news magazine. Additional support came from Edward Snowden, the NSA (National Security Agency) whistleblower who produced classified government documents that show that Abu Bakr al-Baghdadi, the leader of ISIS, is a CIA operative.[56]

## MUSLIM CONFIRMATION

Leaders from the Muslim world confirm these findings. Nabil Na'eem, the founder of the Islamic Democratic Party, who appeared on the pan-Arab TV station al-Maydeen to say that all current al-Qaeda affiliates, including ISIS, work for the CIA. Mr. Na'eem could be imparting false information, but his claim is upheld by Bahaa al-Araji, Iraq's deputy prime minister, and other leading Iraqi officials. Mr. Araqi is a devout Shia and Mr. Na'eem is a militant Sunni. The two men share little in common and have completely different political and religious agendas.[57]

**ISIS**

The purpose of ISIS is to create a state of "endless war" that will serve to exhaust Saudi and Iranian military resources, to bring about the dissolution of Syria and Iraq, and to collapse the Arab countries into small states that can be manipulated by the US-dominated money cartel, which seeks control of their natural resources.

## THE COVERT PURPOSE OF ISIS

According to several news analysts, the purpose of ISIS is to create a state of "endless war" that will serve to exhaust Saudi and Iranian military resources, to bring about the dissolution of Syria and Iraq, and to collapse the Arab countries into small states that can be manipulated by the US-dominated money cartel, which seeks control of their natural resources.[58] This thesis is supported by classified CIA documents that affirm that arms for ISIS came, compliments of the US, from the arsenal of Muammar Gaddafi. The shipment of these weapons to ISIS in Syria was supervised in 2012 by David Petraeus, the CIA director who would soon resign when it was alleged that he was having an affair with his biographer.[59]

## THE PATRIOT ACT

As a result of the endless wars without borders, the citizens of the United

States became stripped of the liberties, once viewed as God-given, by the Patriot Act of 2001. No longer did they possess freedom of association. The government now could monitor religious and political institutions without suspecting criminal activity to assist terror investigation. No longer were they granted freedom of information. The government closed once-public immigration hearings, secretly detained hundreds of people without charges, and encouraged bureaucrats to resist requests for the disclosure of public records. No longer did they possess freedom of speech. The government could prosecute librarians or keepers of any other records if they told anyone that the government was seeking information related to a terror investigation. No longer did they retain a right to legal representation. The government could monitor federal prison jailhouse conversations between attorneys and clients and deny lawyers to Americans accused of crimes. No longer were they free from unreasonable searches. Government could search and seize their belongings, including their personal papers, without probable cause for the sake of a terror investigation. And no longer were they granted the right to a speedy and public trial. The government now could jail anyone without a trial on charges of terrorism—including its own citizens.

**Militant feminists and gay-rights activists**
With the loss of American sovereignty, the country witnessed the rise of radical activists who professed to possess the voice of democracy.

In the past, these rights characterized the citizens of the United States, who deemed them so precious that they were willing to die to sustain and uphold them. But, at the dawn of the twenty-first century, they had surrendered them without a whimper. They were no longer Americans. They had become citizens of the world.

# NOTES

1. William L. Cleveland, *A History of the Modern Middle East,* 3rd Edition (Bolder, CO: Perseus Books, 2004), p. 479.
2. Paul Johnson, *Modern Times: The World from the Twenties to the Nineties,* Revised Edition (New York: Harper Collins, 1992), p. 769.
3. Noam Chomsky, "Gulf War Pullout," *Z Magazine,* February 1991, https://chomsky.info/199102/.
4. Mark Danner, "Taking Stock of the Forever War," *New York Times Magazine,* September 11, 2005, http://www.nytimes.com/2005/09/11/magazine/taking-stock-of-the-forever-war.html.
5. Ibid.
6. Kevin Phillips, *American Dynasty: Aristocracy, Fortune, and the Politics of Deceit in the House of Bush* (New York: Viking, 2004), p. 343.
7. Naomi Klein, "James Baker's Double Life," *Nation,* October 12, 2004, https://www.thenation.com/article/james-bakers-double-life/.
8. Jarrett Murphy, "Cheney's Halliburton Ties Remain," *CBS News, http://www.cbsnews.com/news/cheneys-halliburton-ties-remain/.*
9. Klein, "James Baker's Double Life."
10. Daniel Pipes, "Heroes and Knaves of the Kuwait Crisis," in *A Restless Mind: Essays in Honor of Amos Perlmutter,* edited by Benjamin Frankel (London: F. Cass, 1996), p. 96.
11. Craig Unger, *House of Bush, House of Saud* (New York: Scribner's, 2004), p. 137.
12. George H. W. Bush, quoted in Ibid.
13. Robert Young Pelton, *The World's Most Dangerous Places,* 4th Edition (New York: HarperCollins, 2000), p. 574.
14. Arti Ahtisaari, UN undersecretary for administration and management, *Report to the Security Council,* March 20, 1991, http://www.un.org/Depts/oip/background/reports/s22366.pdf.
15. Felicity Arbuthnot, "Cradle to Grave: The Impact of the UN Embargo," *New Internationalist Magazine,* January-February 2005, https://newint.org/features/2005/01/01/business/.
16. Ibid.
17. Unger, *House of Bush, House of Saud,* p. 137.
18. Staff Report, "Clinton: NATO Must Stop Milosevic's Atrocities against Kosovo," *CNN News,* May 13, 1999, http://www.cnn.com/ALLPOLITICS/stories/1999/05/13/clinton.kosovo/.
19. Johnson, *Modern Times,* p. 715.
20. Daniel Pearl and Robert Block, "Despite Tales, the War in Kosovo Was Savage, But Wasn't Genocide," *Wall Street Journal,* December 31, 1999, https://www.wsj.com/articles/SB946593838546941319.
21. Staff Report, "Ibrahim Rugova: Pacifist at the Crossroads," *BBC News,* May 5, 1999, http://news.bbc.co.uk/1/hi/special_report/1998/kosovo/110821.stm.
22. Marcia Christoff Kurop, "Al Qaeda's Balkan Links," *Wall Street Journal,* November 1, 2001, https://www.wsj.com/articles/SB1004563569751363760.
23. Peter Wolf, "The Assassination of Ahmad Shah Massoud," *Global Research,* September 14, 2003, http://www.globalresearch.ca/articles/WOL309A.html.
24. Tom Walker and Aiden Laverty, "CIA Aided Kosovo Guerrilla Army All Along," *Sunday Times* (London), March 12, 2000, https://www.globalpolicy.org/component/content/article/192/38782.html.

25. "Kosovo Fact-Finding Mission," A White Paper of the Religious Freedom Coalition," August 2004, http://www.documentshare.org/culture-and-the-arts/kosovo-fact-finding-mission-a%C2%80%C2%93-august-2004/.

26. Ibid.

27. Michel Chossudovsky, *The Globalization of War* (Montreal, Quebec: Global Research, 2015), p. 111.

28. Ibid., p. 118.

29. Charles Lewis, *935 Lies: The Future of Truth and the Decline of America's Moral Integrity* (New York: Public Affairs, 2014), p. 253.

30. "Vice President Speaks at VFW 103rd National Convention," Office of the Press Secretary, February 6, 2014, https://georgewbush-whitehouse.archives.gov/news/releases/2002/08/20020826.html.

31. Richard Cheney, quoted in Jonathan Stein and Tim Dickinson, "Lie by Lie: A Timeline of How we Got into Iraq," *Mother Jones*, September/October 2006, http://www.motherjones.com/politics/2011/12/leadup-iraq-war-timeline/.

32. Donald Rumsfeld, quoted in Ibid.

33. George W. Bush, "Radio Address by the President to the Nation," Office of the Press Secretary, September 28, 2002, https://georgewbush-whitehouse.archives.gov/news/releases/2002/09/text/20020928.html.

34. Richard Cheney, quoted in Stein and Dickinson, "Lie by Lie: A Timeline of How We Got into Iraq."

35. "Interview of the President by TYP, Poland," Office of the Press Secretary, May 29, 2003, https://georgewbush-whitehouse.archives.gov/g8/interview5.html.

36. Lewis, *935 Lies: The Future of Truth and the Decline of America's Moral Integrity*, p. 256.

37. F. William Engdahl, "The Secret Stupid Saudi-US Deal on Syria: Oil Pipeline War," *Global research*, October 14, 2014, http://www.globalresearch.ca/the-secret-stupid-saudi-us-deal-on-syria/5410130.

38. Antonia Juhasz, "Why the War in Iraq Was Fought for Big Oil," *CNN*, April 15, 2013, http://www.cnn.com/2013/03/19/opinion/iraq-war-oil-juhasz/index.html.

39. Ibid.

40. Wesley Clark, *Winning Modern Wars* (New York: Public Affairs, 2003), p. 130.

41. Kevin Sullivan, "A Tough Call on Libya That Still Haunts," *Washington Post,* February 3, 2016, http://www.washingtonpost.com/sf/national/2016/02/03/a-tough-call-on-libya-that-still-haunts/?utm_term=.917df391c0b8.

42. Hillary Clinton, quoted in Ibid.

43. Washington Blog Staff, "Libya War Was Based on Lies, Bogus Intelligence, NATO Supported and Armed the Rebels. British Parliamentary Report, September 23, 2016, http://www.globalresearch.ca/libya-war-was-based-on-lies-bogus-intelligence-nato-supported-and-armed-the-rebels-british-parliamentary-report/5547356.

44. Ibid.

45. Ibid.

46. Paul Craig Roberts, "Hillary's War Crime: The Murder of Muammar Gaddafi," *Global Research*, October 21, 2016, http://www.globalresearch.ca/hillarys-war-crime-the-murder-of-muammar-gaddafi-we-came-we-saw-he-died/5552094.

47. Ibid.

48. Ibid.

49. Martin Chulov, "Gaddafi's Last Moments: 'I Saw the Hand Holding the Gun, and I Saw Fire," *The Guardian*, October 20, 2012, https://www.theguardian.com/world/2012/oct/20/muammar-gaddafi-killing-witnesses.

50. Hillary Clinton, quoted in Roberts, "Hillary's War Crime: The Murder of Muammar Gaddafi."

51. Tom LoBianco and Elizabeth Landers, "Trump: Clinton, Obama 'Created Isis,'" *CNN*, January 3, 2016, http://www.cnn.com/2016/01/02/politics/donald-trump-barack-obama-hillary-clinton-created-isis/index.html.

52. Chip Tatum, "ISIS Commander Confirmed by Veterans Today," Wiki Army, 2013, http://www.wikiarmy.com/index.php/15-breaking-news/97-isis-commander-confirmed-by-veteranstoday.

53. Ibid.

54. Ibid.

55. Aaron Klein, "Blowback: U.S. Trained Islamists Who Joined ISIS," *World Net Daily,* June 17, 2014, http://www.wnd.com/2014/06/officials-u-s-trained-isis-at-secret-base-in-jordan/.

56. Staff, "ISIS Leader a Confirmed CIA Puppet," *Hang the Bankers*, July 21, 2014, http://www.hangthebankers.com/isis-leader-a-confirmed-cia-puppet/.

57. David D. Kirkpatrick, "Suspicions Run Deep in Iraq That CIA and Islamic State Are United," *New York Times*, September 20, 2014, https://www.nytimes.com/2014/09/21/world/middleeast/suspicions-run-deep-in-iraq-that-cia-and-the-islamic-state-are-united.html?_r=0.

58. Karl Nimmo, "Former Al-Qaeda Commander: 'ISIS Works for CIA," *Infowars,* July 12, 2014, https://www.infowars.com/former-al-qaeda-commander-isis-works-for-the-cia/.

59. David E. Sanger, "Rebel Arms Flow Is Said to Benefit Jihadis in Syria," *New York Times*, October 14, 2012, http://www.nytimes.com/2012/10/15/world/middleeast/jihadists-receiving-most-arms-sent-to-syrian-rebels.html.

# 39

## AFTER THE FUNERAL

*There were periods like the Gilded Age in the 1890s and the Roaring Twenties, when a situation developed similar to this, but the current period is extreme. Because if you look at wealth distribution, the inequality mostly comes from super-wealth—literally, the top one-tenth of a percent are just super-wealthy. This is the result of over thirty years of a shift in social and economic policy. If you check you find that over the course of these years the government policy has been modified against the will of the population to provide enormous benefits to the very rich. And for most of the population, the majority, real incomes have almost stagnated for over thirty years. The middle class in that sense, that unique American sense, is under severe attack.*

*A significant part of the American Dream is class mobility. You're born poor, you work hard, you get rich. The idea that it is possible for everyone to get a decent job, buy a home, get a car, have their children go to school . . .*

*It's all collapsed.*

—NOAM CHOMSKY, *REQUIEM FOR THE AMERICAN DREAM*, 2017

BY THE TIME Donald Trump ascended to the Oval Office, the brain-storm of Cecil Rhodes had transformed the world, but not quite as he intended. The New World Order did not result in the British flag flying over the earth with African aborigines, Afghan tribesmen, and Chinese clansmen communicating in English and dressed in dinner jackets. Nor was the world transformed and united by Englishmen who, aware of the "white man's burden," had set out with the missionary zeal of Jesuits to colonize and inhabit the dark regions of the planet. And the great projects that Rhodes once envisioned, including the construction of the Cairo-to-Cape Town railroad, never came to fruition.

Rhodes was neither particularly prescient nor deeply insightful. His awareness of the breaking of nations before the forces of globalization was not unique. It had been discerned by many of his nineteenth-century predecessors, including John Ruskin, John Stuart Mill, and Karl Marx. The uniqueness of Rhodes resided in his insistence that the process of globalization could be controlled by a "synarchy"—an elite group of bankers, businessmen, and industrialists, who meet in secret to chart global affairs.

Contrary to Marx, Rhodes believed that the process of history—a process that Marx called "dialectical materialism"—would result not in the formation of the "stateless state" but rather a socialist system in which the vast majority of mankind would become dependent upon big government to provide their basic needs. Outwardly, this government would be ruled by elected officials or strong-arm dictators, but, inwardly—clandestinely—it would be controlled by an elite brotherhood.

Among the original members of Rhodes's Secret Society, the most influential was Nathan Rothschild, who set up the House of Morgan to control the economic development of America. The Rothschilds would give rise to the Pilgrim Society in New York—a dining club within New York's Waldorf Astoria Hotel that was off-limits to the general public. Within this rarified setting, the wealthiest men in the country could meet to shape national policy. This group, in turn, would give rise to the American chapter of the Roundtable Movement.

The House of Morgan served as the driving force behind the creation of the Federal Reserve System, which would control the country's money supply and the prevailing interest rate. This central bank was privately owned by representatives of the world's leading banking consortia:

Morgan, Rockefeller, Rothschild, Warburg and Kuhn-Loeb. In *The Creature from Jekyll Island*, G. Edward Griffin points out: "They [the banking families] were often competitors, and there is little doubt that there was considerable distrust between them and skillful maneuvering for favored position in any agreement. But they were driven together by one overriding desire to fight their common enemy. The enemy was competition."[1]

These families represented a classic cartel. "A cartel," Griffin writes, "is a group of independent businesses which join together to coordinate the production, pricing, or marketing of their members."[2] In the case of the Federal Reserve, these elite families became joint shareholders who worked together to manipulate the US and world economy. They possessed the ability to create depression or prosperity. They could print money *ex nihilo* ("out of nothing") and lend it to the government with interest. In order for the interest to be repaid, the government was compelled to borrow more and more money from the central bank and to fall further and further into financial enslavement to the Fed's private shareholders.

The banking cartel, under the leadership of the House of Morgan, manipulated events, including the sinking of the *Lusitania*, which brought America into World War I for the purpose of creating a global government. When this failed, the cartel set up the Royal Institute for International Affairs (the Chatham House) in London and the Council on Foreign Relations, (CFR) in New York. In time, the CFR came to preside over the affairs of the US State Department.

At the onset of the Great Depression, the interlocking interests of the cartel gave rise to the establishment of the Bank of International Settlements (BIS) in Basel, Switzerland, where the banking families met in absolute secrecy. These meetings resulted in the creation of a covert economy based on real wealth, that is, gold. In keeping with this development, gold was hoarded and squirreled away in the vaults of the BIS. The gold standard was abolished, and the American government, under Franklin Delano Roosevelt, confiscated the gold of its citizens, which they relinquished without cry or whimper.

At the outbreak of World War II, the Rockefellers emerged as the dominant family within the cartel. Through the efforts of this family, the United Nations, the World Bank, the International Monetary Fund (IMF), and the World Trade Organization came into being. These organizations worked in tandem to dissolve the sovereignty of the United States. In his *Memoirs*, David Rockefeller, founder of the Trilateral Commission and chairman of the Bilderberg Group, wrote: "Some even believe we [the Rockefeller family] are part of a secret cabal working against the United States, characterizing my family and me as 'internationalists' and of conspiring with others around the world to build a more integrated global political and economic structure—one world, if you like. If that's the charge, I stand guilty, and I am proud of it."[3]

\* \* \*

Rhodes's dream of a world unencumbered by tariffs or any barriers to free trade, thanks to the cartel, had become a reality. While labor remained stationary, capital moved. America's mighty manufacturing plants were relocated in the Third World, where workers were plentiful and willing to labor long hours for a pittance. Goods were no longer made in America, but in such places as China, Japan, Indonesia, Africa, the Philippines, and Mexico. As America lost its industrial base, its citizens became more and more dependent upon the government to meet their basic needs, including health care. Democracy, in accordance with the plan of Rhodes and his Secret Society, had dissolved into socialism.

Due to the free circulation of labor and free trade between nations, labor supply far exceeded demand and employment insecurity intensified throughout the United States. This was in keeping with the designs of the Federal Reserve and the money cartel. Testifying before the US Senate Committee on Banking, Housing, and Urban Affairs on February 26, 1997, Fed Chairman Alan Greenspan said:

> An acceleration in nominal labor compensation, especially its wage component, became evident over the past year. But the rate of pay increase still was markedly less than historical relationships with labor

market conditions would have predicted. Atypical restraint on compensation increases has been evident for a few years now and appears to be mainly the consequence of greater worker insecurity. In 1991, at the bottom of the recession, a survey of workers at large firms by International Survey Research Corporation indicated that 25 percent feared being laid off. In 1996, despite the sharply lower unemployment rate and the tighter labor market, the same survey organization found that 46 percent were fearful of a job layoff.

The reluctance of workers to leave their jobs to seek other employment as the labor market tightened has provided further evidence of such concern, as has the tendency toward longer labor union contracts. For many decades, contracts rarely exceeded three years. Today, one can point to five- and six-year contracts—contracts that are commonly characterized by an emphasis on job security and that involve only modest wage increases. The low level of work stoppages of recent years also attests to concern about job security.

Thus, the willingness of workers in recent years to trade off smaller increases in wages for greater job security seems to be reasonably well documented.[4]

American workers—once the most productive and well-paid labor force in the world—became forced to submit to the increasing demands of globalization and the money cartel. Their wages dwindled; their benefits all but vanished; and their working hours became extended.[5] Two adults in a family had to work—most in the service industry—to make ends meet. The cleft between the haves and have-nots grew to such an extent that the middle class disappeared into the widening fissure.[6]

Those who sought to advance from their insecure positions were advised to seek higher education. But the cost of tuition climbed to such an astronomical level that the average student graduated from college over $100,000 in debt.[7] This debt hung over their heads like a guillotine. It was a debt that couldn't be absolved by bankruptcy. Failure to make payments resulted in garnishments, even on Social Security checks.[8]

\* \* \*

While the working class suffered and the infrastructure of America's cities fell into ruins, the money cartel continued to seize natural resources throughout the world in order to sustain their hegemony. Such seizures required conflict, and Americans, by tens of thousands, began to die in limited wars that were fought not for freedom but economic interests of the chosen few.

The same chosen few created the Central Intelligence Agency to topple governments hostile to their interest. These covert operations were funded almost solely by the sale of heroin. The heroin, cultivated and distributed under the auspices of the CIA, came from Southeast Asia, necessitating the Vietnam War, and then Afghanistan, necessitating the "war on terror." When the US military occupation of Afghanistan became precarious, the CIA worked with the Mexican drug cartels to develop poppy fields throughout the mountains of Mexico's west coast. By 2013, heroin and cocaine from Mexico—with a street value of $3 billion—flooded Chicago.[9] The heroin arrived by land, rail, and air, including 747 jetliners. When Jesus Vicente Zambada Niebla, a member of the Sinaloa cartel, was collared by Chicago police officials, he claimed to be a CIA operative under government protection. His trial was halted by federal prosecutors on the basis of the "Classified Information Procedures Act." The prosecutors claimed that Niebla's testimony would constitute a threat to national security.[10]

\* \* \*

Heroin by the turn of the twenty-first century had become one of the world's most valuable resources—a resource that could generate over $100 trillion a year in revenue. The days when heroin money could be laundered through a small circle of banks, including the Vatican Bank, were long past. By 2014, $500 billion to $1 trillion in proceeds from criminal activity and black ops were laundered through the world's leading banks—half of which were located in the United States. Narcodollars became the lifeblood of the nation's economy.[11]

The US banks developed an incredibly complex system for transferring illicit funds into the country for investments in real estate, corporations, industries, and government bonds. The financial institutions that participated in this process, according to Canadian commentator Asad Ismi, included the Bank of Boston, Republic National Bank of New York, Landmark First National Bank, the Great American Bank, People's Liberty Bank and Trust Company of Kentucky, Riggs National Bank of Washington, Citibank, and American Express International of Beverly Hills.[12] Manufacturers, Chase Manhattan, Chemical Bank and Irving Trust have admitted not reporting transfers of substantial amounts of money to the US government as required by the Bank Secrecy Act of 1970, and the Bank of America has been fined $4.75 million for refusing to provide documentation for transfers of more than $12 billion.[13]

In an attempt to address this problem, the US Congress has passed several laws, including the Money Laundering Control Act of 1986, which called for stiffer enforcement by public regulators. All of this legislation was to no avail. The banks continued their laundering, and the sum of dirty money circulated throughout the country grew exponentially. No decisive action by government officials was ever adopted since the high profits of the drug trade served as a leading buttress of the US economy. Indeed, Antonio Maria Costa, head of the UN Office on Drugs and Organized Crime, has argued that the United States was saved from total economic collapse in 2008 by the billions which flowed through American banks from the drug trade. These funds, Costa argues, represented the "only liquid investment capital" available to financial institutions.[14] And so it came to pass that the land of the free and the home of the brave became a narcocapitalistic country.

# NOTES

1.  G. Edward Griffin, *The Creature from Jekyll Island,* Fifth Edition (Westlake Village, CA: American Media, 2017), p. 12.
2.  Ibid., p. 11.
3.  David Rockefeller, *Memoirs* (New York: Random House, 2002), p. 405.
4.  Alan Greenspan, Testimony before the Committee on Banking, Housing, and Urban Affairs, U.S. Senate, February 26, 1997, https://www.federalreserve.gov/boarddocs/hh/1997/february/testimony.htm.
5.  Noam Chomsky, *Requiem for the American Dream: The 10 Principles of Concentration of Wealth and Power* (New York: Seven Stories Press, 2017), pp. 40–41.
6.  Ibid.
7.  Ibid., p. 20.
8.  Ibid.
9.  Christopher Woody, "We Have a Clearer Picture of Who's Fueling the US Heroin Epidemic—and How They're Doing It," *Business Insider,* November 15, 2015, http://www.businessinsider.com/us-heroin-coming-from-mexican-cartels.
10. James Corbett, "The CIA and the Drug Trade," *The Corbett Report,* February 7, 2017, https://www.corbettreport.com/the-cia-and-the-drug-trade/.
11. Peter Dale Scott, *America's War Machine: Deep Politics, the CIA Global Drug Connection, and the Road to Afghanistan* (Lanham, Maryland: Rowman and Littlefield, 2010), electronic edition, "Obama and Afghanistan," 51%.
12. Asad Ismi, "The Canadian Connection: Drugs, Money Laundering and Canadian Banks," *Briarpatch.* July/August 1997, http://www.asadismi.ws/cancon.html.
13. Ibid.
14. Rajeev Syal, "Drug Money Saved Banks in Global Crisis, Claims UN Advisor," *Guardian* (UK), December 12, 2009, http://www.theguardian.com/global/2009/dec/13/drug-money-banks-saved-un-cfief-claims.

# EPILOGUE

## RAISING THE DEAD

*It starts with the money. For dominant powers, it always does—from the Roman Empire to the British Empire. "Declinism" is in the air these days, but we full-time apocalyptics are already well past that stage. In the space of one generation, a nation of savers became the world's largest debtors, and a nation of makers and doers became a cheap service economy. Everything that can be outsourced has been—manufacturing to by no means friendly nations overseas, and much of what's left in agriculture and construction to the armies of the "undocumented." . . . Like Belshazzar's Babylon, when you weigh us in the balance, we're seriously wanting. Under a ruling class comprehensively inept and comfortably insulated, America has been thoroughly unbalanced: thanks largely to distortions driven by government, we have too much college, too much housing, too much financial sector, too much "professional servicing"—accounting, lawyering, and other activities necessary to keep the fine print in compliance with the regulatory state. All of these are huge obstacles to making productive use of even our non-borrowed money and to keeping America competitive with the rest of the world.*

*Even in its glory days, the Age of Abundance wasn't exactly a Balshazzaresque party for most folks: since 1973, the wages of 90 percent of Americans have grown by only 10 percent in real terms, and consumption even of cheap Chinese goods was fueled by borrowing. But eventually even that mirage fades and you see the writing on the Wal-Mart.*

—MARK STEYN, *AFTER AMERICA*, 2011

THE PLANS TO KILL UNCLE SAM were conducted during secret gatherings at the Mowbray House in London and the Waldorf Astoria in New York. The motivating factor was greed—the creation of an economic global hegemony through the formation of an Anglo-American alliance. Uncle Sam remained the chief obstacle to the scheme. He stood for isolationism, freedom from foreign entanglements, tariffs, self reliance, and democracy. The New World Order of the plotters would be based on socialism. Events would be manipulated so that the American people would become utterly reliant on the government, which the plotters would control from the shadows. The government, under their direction, would institute free trade, the offshoring of American manufacturing, and the creation of a global labor force. Wars would be conducted to break down the borders between countries and to facilitate the free flow of commerce. International agreements and agencies would be established, and Uncle Sam would be sapped of his industrial strength.

By controlling the news media and the educational system, the plotters would be able to change the way in which Americans viewed reality. The populace would be conditioned to relinquish their cherished beliefs in order to embrace the virtues of diversity and multiculturalism. In many ways, the plotters shared the views of the Marxists, who held that history consisted of a process of "dialectical materialism"—thesis and antithesis—that would culminate in universal socialism. But they differed from the Communists in their insistence that this process could be controlled for their benefit. They also held much in common with the thought of Friedrich Nietzsche, who foresaw a Godless future in which the trans-valuation of all values would take place since nothing would be held sacred. A figure like Uncle Sam who spouted a belief in moral absolutes while waving the American flag would have no place in this brave new world.

Uncle Sam's demise progressed in stages. First, they deprived him of his right to manage his own finances. His wealth in gold was stripped from his possession and shipped to a place where it could not be recovered. Swimming in debt that he could not pay, his days of manifest destiny and incredible achievements came to an abrupt halt. Next, they entangled him in foreign affairs and conflicts from which there was no escape. One war led to another with such rapidity that the old man began to lose his grip on reality. Then he was dragged with opiates and his teeth were extracted, since they were well aware that the avuncular figure could bite. His sons and daughters were taken from him, and the old man was placed in unfamiliar settings with people who were unrelated to him—people who did not know who he was, let alone what he had stood for. And they poisoned his food through bio-genetics and other means. He became filled with toxic fluids that left the old man in a comatose condition.

The only hope for even a partial recovery of Uncle Sam resided with the initiation of the following series of restorative measures.

## AUDIT THE FED

The policies of the Federal Reserve System affect average US citizens far more than legislation passed by Congress. The Fed possesses the power to increase the money supply and to keep interest rates artificially low, thereby creating a steady cycle of booms and busts in housing, stock market, and employment to serve the interests of the money cartel.

While the Fed's financial statements are audited annually, its monetary policy operations remain exempt from scrutiny by the Government Accountability Office (GAO), the investigative arm of Congress. The GAO is currently prohibited by law from examining discount windows and open-market operations, agreements with foreign governments and central banks, and Federal Open Market Committee (FOMC) directives. It is precisely this information that should be made public.

The American people must know how and why Fed officials expand the money supply, set interest rates, and conduct transactions with other central banks and foreign governments. It is not enough for the Fed to simply provide its updated balance sheet after crucial decisions and transactions have been made.[1]

## PRODUCE REAL MONEY

Following the audit, steps must be taken to convert fiat money into real money backed by precious metals. China has already taken the lead by taking measures to back the yuan with gold.[2] When this goal is accomplished, China will possess the world's most valuable currency, and the paper dollars produced out of nothing by the Fed no longer will serve the world's favored means of financial exchange. The effect of this development will be catastrophic for the US economy.

The first step toward the establishment of a commodities-based currency must be an amendment to the US Money and Finance Code of 1982 so that Americans are no longer compelled to accept Federal Reserve Notes as the only legal tender. Banks should be permitted to issue their own notes backed by real wealth, that is, precious metals. Once alternative currencies are created, the government's existing stockpiles of gold and silver should be used to back the Federal Reserve Notes that remain in circulation. The process of retiring such notes must then begin, culminating in the issuance of silver certificates from the US Department of the Treasury that are interest free.[3]

By weakening the Fed, the country's ties to the Bank of International Settlements, the International Monetary Fund, the World Bank, and the World Trade Organization will be loosened, and the money cartel will be stripped of the means of control over global events by the manipulation of the national currency. "The first panacea for a mismanaged country is inflation of the currency, the second is war," wrote Ernest Hemingway. "Both bring a temporary prosperity, both bring a permanent ruin. But both are the refuge of political and economic opportunists."[4]

## END ENDLESS WAR

By 2015, the cost of the wars in Afghanistan and Iraq exceeded $6 trillion with less than salubrious results.[5] Instead of making the world safe for democracy, the wars have served to inflame Islamic hatred against the American people. Surely this money would have been better spent rebuilding America's rotting cities, infrastructures, and transportation systems.

The end of the long war also would enable the United States to close its archipelago of 700 to 1,000 military bases in 130 countries and its vast expenditures for the military-industrial complex at home.[6] Thousands of US troops remain stationed in Europe to defend Europe against an "evil empire" that collapsed twenty-seven years ago. There are 174 base sites in Germany, 113 in Japan, and 83 in South Korea. Other bases have been set up in Aruba and Australia, Bahrain and Bulgaria, Colombia, Kenya and Qatar.[7] The cost of sustaining these overseas facilities exceeds $150 billion a year.[8] It's time to close them.

As David Vine observes, "Rarely does anyone wonder how we would feel if China, Russia, or Iran built even a single base anywhere near our borders, let alone in the United States."[9]

For the most part, the wars serve no interest of national security. Tens of thousands of American soldiers have been killed to advance the hegemony of the money cartel. To make matters worse, the United States has been dragged into these bloody conflicts by lies and acts of deception. The perpetuators of these mendacities and false-flag attacks should be subject to federal trials on charges of war crimes. The list of such culprits who merit arrest and prosecution includes several ex-presidents and the members of their cabinets.

### TERMINATE THE CIA

Since its establishment in 1947, the Central Intelligence Agency has operated at the whim of the money cartel to topple governments, institute strategies of tension, and to install strong-arm regimes in countries throughout the world. Their efforts have resulted in the creation of the *mujahedeen*, al-Qaeda, and ISIS. Its reliance on drug money to fund its black operations has resulted in the Vietnam War and the War in Afghanistan. Its covert activities undermine national security and drag the United States into costly conflicts—conflicts that only serve to sustain the economic hegemony of the money cartel.

The Senate Intelligence Committee cannot control the rogue intelligence agency. The reports of the Committee on the CIA's dirty undertakings are kept "under wraps" and free from public scrutiny on the grounds that they concern matters of national security. The CIA is compelled to report only to the president, but since Congress exercises control of the budget, it possesses the right to oversee the spy agency's undertakings.[10] It is high time for many of these undertakings to be brought to light and terminated.

Back in the 1970s, a special Senate investigative committee, headed by Senator Frank Church (D–Idaho), held a series of hearings on the crimes of the CIA, the National Security Agency, and other government intelligence arms. The public learned that the intelligence agency had plotted the assassination of foreign leaders, spied on antiwar activists, used foundations as fronts and administered LSD to hundreds of unwitting Americans as part of an experiment on mind control. In the wake of these revelations, Congress created committees in both the House and the Senate to oversee the CIA covert operations. But as events over past decades have shown, these reforms ultimately failed, and the spy agency, thanks to increased powers granted to it since 9/11, has morphed into a paramilitary organization.[11]

## ABSOLVE THE NATIONAL DEBT

Of the $19,850,000,000,000 national debt, over $5.5 trillion is owed to federal agencies. This debt has been incurred by the US Treasury Department's borrowing from the trust fund of one federal agency to give to another. For example, the Treasury routinely takes funds from Social Security to shore up other entitlement programs, including the Affordable Health Care Act. Of the remaining $14.35 trillion, the largest debt holder is the Federal Reserve, which owns over $2.25 trillion Treasury bonds, 64 percent more than China.

By absolving the debt that the federal government owes to itself and the Federal Reserve, the country will be able to expand the debt held by foreign investors and, thereby, obtain the means to address its rotting infrastructures and to forgive student loans that hang around the necks of many young Americans like albatrosses.

## STOP UNIVERSITY FUNDING

Student debt forgiveness must be accompanied by the curtailing of federal and state funding for colleges and universities that fail to provide job placement for their graduates. For the most part, these institutions of higher education fail not only to equip their graduates for employment but also to ground them in the fundamentals of academics. In 2011, a study by Richard Arun and Josipa Roska discovered that fewer than half of America's undergraduates had taken a single course in the previous semester that required twenty pages of writing. A third of the students had not taken a course that required forty pages of reading. And 45 percent displayed no improvement in critical thinking, reasoning, and writing since the time they stepped foot on college campus.[12] Even more damning is a study that shows that only 25 percent of America's college graduates scored high enough in standardized testing to be deemed proficient enough in reading and writing to function in society.[13]

Compared to forty other modernized countries, the United States currently ranks seventeenth in literacy, seventeenth in math, and twenty-first in science, according to a recent report by the Organization for Economic Co-Operation and Development.[14] This dismal performance remains unpardonable since the United States tops the world's list for spending on education, with the federal government shelling out a whopping $68 billion annually as the country grows progressively dumber.[15]

The cutoff of government funding is justified not only on the basis of the pitiable results of higher education but also by the fact that many colleges and universities really don't need the money. Harvard University has an endowment of $37.6 billion, Texas A&M (College Station) of $9.75 billion, Yale University of $25.5 billion, Stanford University of $22.2 billion, the Massachusetts Institute of Technology of $13.5 billion, and the University of Michigan (Ann Arbor) of $9.8 billion.[16] All of these schools receive substantial federal and state funding, and of the sixty-four institutions with endowments in excess of $1 billion, sixteen are state-operated universities.[17]

## INVESTIGATE THE FOUNDATIONS

Upon matriculation, the college students are subjected to such courses as "Women's Studies," "Pretty, Witty, and Gay," and "Queer New Media." These "academic" offerings comply with the demands of the Rockefeller, Carnegie, and Ford Foundations for "curriculum transformation"—an insistence that race, gender, and sexual consciousness be injected into every department and every discipline.[18]

Throughout the twentieth century, the foundations increased their influence over America's educational system until they became the source of 20 percent of the total income of America's private and public colleges and universities.[19] By shelling out hundreds of millions of dollars to boost the administration and instructional staff of these institutions, they could dictate what courses should be offered and (by providing the funding to develop the textbooks) how such courses should be taught.

In this way, they managed to control the thought of America's college students, so they would embrace the tenets of globalism, including the acceptance of diversity as a national virtue.

The influence of the tax-exempt foundations exceeded past the realm of education to include the once celestial fields of American Christianity. The Rockefeller Foundation gave rise to the National Council of Churches and the World Council of Churches, organizations which campaigned for abortion-on-demand, same-sex marriage, and liberation theology. In Africa, they provided funding to armed Communist guerillas who mounted bloody revolutions in Angola, Mozambique, and Namibia. In Zimbabwe (formerly Rhodesia), they armed the Patriotic Front, a group of Communist guerrillas whose campaign of indiscriminate terror claimed the lives of 207 white civilians, 1,721 blacks, and 9 missionaries as well as their children.[20]

During the 1950s, Congressmen Eugene E. Cox (D–GA) and Carroll Reece (R–TN) launched an investigation to determine which "foundations and organizations are using their resources for purposes other than the purposes for which they were established, and especially to determine which such foundations and organizations are using their resources for un-American and subversive activities or purposes not in the interest or tradition of the United States."[21] This investigation was brought to a halt by President Dwight D. Eisenhower, whose ascent to the Oval Office had been funded by the House of Rockefeller.[22] It is high time for this investigation to begin anew.

## DOWNSIZE THE GOVERNMENT

Absolving the federal debt owed to the Federal Reserve and the federal government must be accompanied by downsizing the federal government, which spends five dollars for every three that it collects in taxes. The problem is untenable. Were tax increases used to balance the federal budget, the tax load on individuals and corporations would have to rise by 67 percent.[23] For this reason, partial debt forgiveness must be accompanied by the following measures:

1.  A two-year freeze on all federal salaries.

2.  A two-year suspension of cost-of-living adjustments to all entitlement programs.

3.  An investigation of individuals who are receiving welfare and disability benefits for which they are not entitled.

4.  A hiring freeze in the federal work force.

5.  An elimination of bailouts to state governments, which should be compelled to handle their own financial affairs.

6.  A halt on foreign aid unrelated to national security.[24]

## IMPOSE TARIFFS

To reduce its dependency on foreign goods, the United States must impose tariffs on all imports, and it must use the revenue amassed in this manner to reduce the taxes on goods produced in the United States. Free trade, the religion of Cecil Rhodes, has resulted in the loss of manufacturing plants, which once represented a central source of employment for the American people. Tariffs would achieve the following results:

1. A reduction of imports, since the cost of foreign goods would rise, creating a concomitant increase in made-in-America goods.

2. A rise in employment with full-time benefits since new workers would be needed to meet the demand for labor. The income and payroll taxes of these workers would replace the sinking tariff revenue from falling imports.

3. An increase in capital investment since foreign companies would shift production to the United States in order to retain their share of the American market.[25]

## DRAIN THE SWAMP

Members of Congress have been corrupted by their dependence on money from lobbyists—and from the special interests hiring those lobbyists—to fund their reelection campaigns. By 2016, the amount spent on campaigns by all candidates for Congress soared beyond $4 billion, with incumbents spending between 30 to 70 percent of their time fundraising rather than legislating.[26] This was all well and good, since the time that they spent legislating was, for the most part, advancing the policies of their benefactors.

The problem was typified by Senator Max Baucus (D–Montana), chairman of the Senate Committee on Finance, whose position gave him a critical role in the debate over President Obama's healthcare proposal. Baucus received $5 million in campaign contributions from the financial, insurance, and health industries. The money helped to guarantee that single-payer health insurance was not on the table when the legislation was written.[27]

The corruption is *systemic* and *systematic*: Every year, lobbyists spend $3.5 billion, or about $6.5 million per each elected member in Congress to advance the interests of their big business and banking sponsors. Convicted lobbyist Jack Abramoff, as part of a series hosted by the Center for Ethics, described how offering a Senator or Congressperson a high-paying job on K Street (home of the leading lobbying firms in

Washington, DC) is, in effect, a way of hiring them on the spot. They may be two years from the end of their terms, Abramoff said, but from that moment—with no money down—the members of both Houses of Congress are, in the back of their minds, serving their future employers.[28] Abramoff's testimony is supported by facts. Fifty percent of the US Senators and 42 percent of the Representatives become lobbyists with seven-figure salaries upon leaving public office.[29]

Thanks to legislators serving the interests of lobbyists of the global agribusiness, the federal government shelled out more than $70 billion subsidizing corn production between 1995 and 2009. As a result, every $1 of profits earned by food conglomerate Archer Daniels Midland's corn-sweetener operation costs American consumers $10. The subsidies made high-fructose corn syrup cheap and raw corn so inexpensive that some farmers feed it to their cattle. Corn sweeteners—now present in 40 percent of the food on grocery shelves—have been implicated in the obesity and diabetes epidemics. And the cattle—which can't digest corn properly—developed gastrointestinal bacteria that had to be treated with antibiotics, in turn facilitating the evolution of drug-resistant "super bugs" that can infect humans.[30] "You begin to poison people through the food-production system," Lawrence Lessig, the director of the Safra Center for Ethics at Harvard University, says. "There's *nobody* on the right who can say this is a good thing. And people on the left who might have supported this system originally, because it was going to support family farms—they don't like this either. Yet think about the political will that would be necessary to turn this spigot off! I don't think we have that political capacity."[31]

The problem runs deep and can only be rectified by a cutoff of all funding from lobbyists to people serving or seeking public office and the institution of term limits for everyone elected to federal office.

## OVERTHROW JUDICIAL TYRANNY

Due to the tyranny of the US Supreme Court, secularism has become the official state religion. Prayers, the Bible, and the Ten Commandments have been expelled from the country's schools. Nativity scenes have been banished from public squares. Abortion, homosexuality, and same-sex marriage have been declared constitutional rights. And children have been bused far from their friends and families to achieve a fanciful sense of racial balance.

The decisions made by the country's highest court that stand in conflict with the will of the people must be overturned. The judges must be subjected to ten-year term limits, and their reign of tyranny must be brought to an end. Congress must attach a rider to every law dealing with social policy that it is not subject to judicial review. And should the Supreme Court continue to act in a dictatorial manner, their rulings should be ignored. This is in keeping with American tradition. Abraham Lincoln in his first inaugural address said: "If the policy of the government upon vital questions affecting the whole people is to be irrevocably fixed by decisions of the Supreme Court . . . the people will have ceased to be their own rulers, having to that extent practically resigned their government into the hands of that eminent tribunal."[32]

## UPHOLD STATES RIGHTS

By 2017, the country had become so fractionated by political and cultural dissent that a movement for secession took root in California, where Democrats held every state office, both Senate seats, two-thirds of both houses of the state legislature, and three out of every four congressional seats. In no way could California be reconciled with the red (Republican) states that favored the construction of a wall along the southern border, the elimination of sanctuary cities, the right to bear arms, the sanctity of marriage, and the revitalization of industries that threatened the environment. California favored unencumbered federalism—big government that regulated the lives of its citizens and corporations and provided an array of social benefits, including universal health care and free college tuition, while the red states favored a government that would confine its activities to securing the border, fighting defensive wars, and creating inter-state means of transportation.

The situation had become so polarized that the only solution resided in the devolution of power and resources away from the federal government and back to states, cities, and towns, so that the citizens of various regions of the country could resolve their own problems in their own way and in accordance with their own principles.[33] This development would be in accordance with the long-forgotten Tenth Amendment of the Constitution, which stipulated: "The powers not delegated to the United States by the Constitution, nor prohibited by it to the States, are reserved to the States, respectively, or to the people."

### RESTRICT IMMIGRATION

To prevent the ongoing mongrelization of the American people, a moratorium must be placed on immigration. Such a measure is not incongruous with US history as witnessed by the restrictive immigration measures of the 1920s and the imposition of a quota system. Such a moratorium should be designed to achieve the following results:

1. A rise in employment for US citizens since existing jobs no longer would be gobbled up by foreign workers, many of whom work "under the table" while tapping into entitlement programs.

2. The erection of a wall along the southern border to prevent the ongoing invasion of illegal aliens.

3. The deportation of all those who have entered the country illegally.

4. The imposition of stiff fines on businesses and corporations that employ undocumented workers.[34]

These measures must be accompanied by a correct interpretation or a repeal of the Fourteenth Amendment, which permits any child born to an illegal alien or foreign visitor on American soil to become automatically a US citizen.

## THE TIE THAT BINDS

America was once a nation where the people shared a country and a culture. They spoke the same language, shared the same literature, learned the same history lessons, celebrated the same heroes, attended the same sporting events, observed the same holidays, went to the same movies, watched the same television programs on the same three networks, read the same newspapers, danced to the same music, ate the same foods, and believed in the same future.

That America is gone and will never return.

Yet there remains hope that the United States, once again, can be united into a cultural and racial melting pot as envisioned by our forefathers. Americans no longer share the same history and heritage. Not even the same European roots or common language. But, for the most part, they share the same religion. In 2017, over seventy percent of the inhabitants of the United States identified themselves as Christians.[35] The vast majority, even those who rarely, if ever, darkened the doorway to a church, continued to share the same faith and to worship the same God as the American forefathers. This faith can be rekindled by the winds of revival. Such a monumental spiritual event has happened twice before on American soil.

## THE FIRST GREAT AWAKENING

By the start of the eighteenth century, New England had lost its original Puritan fervor. Men became totally absorbed in worldly pursuits, conversions became fewer in number, the churches were occupied by people who had never experienced the reality of God, and the vast majority remained unsaved and un-churched. Morality reached low ebb. From this environment rose the First Great Awakening. It was initiated by a series of sermons that Jonathan Edwards preached in Northampton, Massachusetts, in December 1734. Men and women were stirred into profound manifestations of repentance, hundreds were filled with the Holy Ghost, and thousands gave testimonies of their conversions. The movement spread from New England to New Jersey, New York, Pennsylvania, and the other colonies.[36]

These separate outbreaks of revival became bound together by George Whitefield, a Methodist preacher, who arrived in 1739. From New York City he traveled to Charleston, South Carolina, making the longest journey ever made by a white man. Everywhere he went, he preached. His sermons always ended with the same altar call: "Come poor, lost, undone sinner, come just as you are to Christ."[37] By the time, Whitefield returned to England one year later, millions of American colonists had been touched. Denominational lines had been superseded. Colleges and Indian missions were established. And the anti-slavery campaign began.[38]

## THE SECOND GREAT AWAKENING

The Second Great Awakening originated shortly after the Revolutionary War. It brought a revival throughout the thirteen colonies and the Appalachian frontier. Religious and moral conditions on the frontier were abominable. The great mass of settlers and frontiersmen remained un-churched and heedless of the tenets of scripture. The educated class, who resided in New England, embraced Deism, which held that God is an indifferent Being, who does not intervene in the affairs of human history.[39] In 1793, the Kentucky legislature felt that prayer was so useless that it voted to get rid of its chaplain.[40]

It was in Kentucky that the second outburst of revival began. In the East, Deism was abandoned and colleges, including Harvard, Yale, and Princeton, became populated with spirit-filled Christians. Itinerant preachers transformed the frontier. One crossed the mountains into Kentucky only ten years after Daniel Boone, and he gained thousands of miles on Boone's successors. He reached Oregon and California ahead of the first arrivals of immigrant settlers from the east coast.[41] By 1820, the lights from camp meetings flowed throughout the country.

The Second Great Awakening transformed American Protestantism. The leaders of the revival, including Lyman Beecher, Peter Cartwright, and Charles Finney, shared an impatience with institutional religion, including liturgies, creeds, and theologies, and placed the emphasis of their preaching on the personal. The deep stirrings of a person's spiritual emotions became understood as the most authentic workings of faith.

In this way, the revival encapsulated the spirit of the frontier with an emphasis on individualism, emotionalism, and a lack of intellectual restraint.[42]

The revival resulted in the establishment of mission societies which overran denominational lines, including societies that cared for widows and orphans, prison reform, temperance movements, the Abolition movement, the Underground Railroad, and the American Bible Society to promote Christian education.[43] The effects of this Awakening still reverberate throughout the country's homeland, where people continue to attend church, to adhere to the teachings of scripture, and to pray for a new movement of God.

## PARTING WORDS

It can happen again.

The principalities, powers, and rulers of the darkness who have taken control of the government to accomplish their own financial ends may be driven from the land by the mighty wind of a Pentecost.

A new generation of spirit-filled men and women can be educated for higher office at Christian schools, such as the River School of Government, to enact the required restorative measures.

The globalization of war and poverty can be halted.

Righteousness can prevail over a country that has fallen into decay and decadence.

Eternal values can be recaptured.

Uncle Sam can be revived and restored to health—But only by one person.

His name is Jesus.

# NOTES

1.  "About Audit the Fed," Campaign for Liberty, n. d., http://www.campaignforliberty. org/audit-fed/.
2.  Nathan Lewis, "China Is Laying the Foundation for the Next Gold Standard," *Forbes,* May 5, 2016, https://www.forbes.com/sites/nathanlewis/2016/05/05/china-is-laying-the-foundation-for-the-next-world-gold-standard-system/#35a4c104689e.
3.  G. Edward Griffin, *The Creature from Jekyll Island,* Fifth Edition (Westlake Village, CA: American Media, 2017), p. 576.
4.  Ernest Hemingway, quoted in Scott Horton, "Hemingway on the Politics of War," *Harper's Magazine*, September 17, 2007, https://harpers.org/blog/2007/09/hemingway-on-the-politics-of-war/.
5.  Paul Bedard, "Report: Price of Iraq, Afghan War Hits a Staggering $6 Trillion," *Washington Examiner*, March 7, 2015, http://www.washingtonexaminer.com/report-price-of-iraq-afghan-wars-hits-a-staggering-6-trillion/article/2560928.
6.  Patrick Buchanan, *Suicide of a Superpower* (New York: Thomas Dunne Books, 2011), p. 410.
7.  David Vine, "The United States Probably Has More Foreign Military Bases Than Any Other People, Nation, or Empire in History," *The Nation*, September 14, 2015, https://www.thenation. com/article/the-united-states-probably-has-more-foreign-military-bases-than-any-other-people-nation-or-empire-in-history/.
8.  "US Spending Over $150 Billion Annually on Overseas Military Bases," *Mint Press News*, March 7, 2016, http://www.mintpressnews.com/214492-2/214492/.
9.  David Vine, quoted in Ibid.
10.  David Wise, "Can Congress Control the CIA?" *Reuters*, March 13, 2014.
11.  Ibid.
12.  Mark Steyn, *After America: Get Ready for Armageddon* (Washington, DC: Regnerey, 2011), p. 340.
13.  Doug Lederman, "Graduated But Not Literate," *Inside Higher Education*, December 16, 2005.
14.  Jamie Lee, "The Untold History of Modern U.S. Education: The Founding Fathers," *Waking Times*, January 28, 2014, http://www.wakingtimes.com/2014/01/28/untold-history-modern-u-s-education-founding-fathers/.
15.  Lauren Camera, "Federal Education Funding: Where Does the Money Go?" *US News and World Report*, January 14, 2016, https://www.usnews.com/news/blogs/data-mine/2016/01/14/federal-education-funding-where-does-the-money-go.
16.  Ilana Kowarski, "10 Universities with the Biggest Endowments," *US News and World Report*, October 4, https://www.insidehighered.com/news/2005/12/16/literacy 2016, https://www.usnews. com/education/best-colleges/the-short-list-college/articles/2016-10-04/10-universities-with-the-biggest-endowments.
17.  "Understanding College and University Endowments," *American Council on Education*, 2014, http://www.acenet.edu/news-room/Documents/Understanding-Endowments-White-Paper.pdf.
18.  Jamie Lee, "The Untold History of Modern U.S. Education: The Founding Fathers."
19.  Gary Allen, *The Rockefeller File* (Seal Beach, CA: '76 Press, 1976), p. 45.

20. Jacob Laskin, "National Council of Churches: Worldviews, Activities, and Agendas," *Discover the Networks*, 2005, http://www.discoverthenetworks.org/Articles/nccexpandedagenasactivities.html.

21. Statement of Cox Committee, quoted in Allen, *The Rockefeller File*, p. 42.

22. Ibid., p. 43.

23. Patrick J. Buchanan, *Suicide of a Superpower* (New York: Thomas Dunne Books, 2011), p. 415.

24. Ibid., pp. 415–416.

25. Ibid., p. 419.

26. "Cost of Election," Center for Responsive Politics, 2017, https://www.opensecrets.org/overview/cost.php.

27. Jonathan Shaw, "A Radical Fix for the Republic," *Harvard Magazine*, July-August 2012, http://harvardmagazine.com/2012/07/a-radical-fix-for-the-republic.

28. Ibid.

29. "Term Limits for Congress," *Term Limits for Congress PAC*, August 6, 2017, http://www.termlimitsforuscongress.com/why-term-limits.html.

30. Shaw, "A Radical Fix for the Republic."

31. Lawrence Lessig, quoted in Ibid.

32. Abraham Lincoln, quoted in Buchanan, *Suicide of a Superpower*, p. 426.

33. Patrick J. Buchanan, "Is Succession a Solution to Cultural War?" Patrick J. Buchanan—Official Website, February 24, 2017, http://buchanan.org/blog/secession-solution-cultural-war-126571.

34. Buchanan, *Suicide of a Superpower*, pp. 421–422.

35. "Religious Landscape Study," Pew Research Center, 2017, http://www.pewforum.org/religious-landscape-study/.

36. Will Herberg, *Protestant, Catholic, Jew* (Garden City, New York: Anchor Books, 1960), p. 101.

37. George Whitefield, quoted in Ernest G. Borman, *Force of Fantasy: Restoring the American Dream* (Carbondale, Illinois: South Illinois Press, 1985), p. 74.

38. Herberg, *Protestant, Catholic, Jew*, p. 102.

39. James Sire, *The Universe Next Door: A Basic Worldview Catalog* (Downers Grove, Illinois: InterVarsity Press, 2009), pp. 59–64.

40. Herberg, *Protestant, Catholic, Jew*, p. 103.

41. Ibid.

42. Ibid., p. 106.

43. Stephen Combs, *A Tribute to Our Christian Heritage* (Raleigh, NC: Lulu, 2012), pp. 56–57.

# AMERICA IN THE TWENTY-FIRST CENTURY

## BY DR. RODNEY HOWARD-BROWNE

To the land of stars and stripes we go

Our land of our adoption

We were invited by the lady with the lamp come and rest yourself.
The land of freedom, the land of dreams becoming reality. The land
of the eagle, buffalo, and bear

From marsh and swamps to rolling hills with blue grass to mountains
that tower like huge breasts

Concrete jungles with crowded buildings as many flock to seek their
place in the sun. Amusement centers from a wheel to a mouse try to
attract many to fill the void, as unhappiness sweeps the masses for
what they don't have.

Beautiful rivers now polluted by toxic waste as pollutants pour into
once pure fish-laden streams.

Now containing disease from sewage and chemicals,

The natural giving way to the fake,

The imitation,

From implants to veneer,

It's not real, it's not what it seems, all's not gold that glitters,

Anything for the dollar, it's worshipped, and families are sold for a few.

Intoxicants and enhancements now needed,

As many retreat into a cyber existence of someone else's life lived through a big screen.

As Hollywood has set the norm and lowered the bar, morality has been taken away.

Anything goes,

As long as it feels good no matter whom it hurts.

What happens here stays here,

They hide behind the mask,

An ash on the forehead makes it right. Live like there is no tomorrow, no afterlife.

Decisions made based on what's good for the moment,

Instant gratification if it's longer than four hours then see a doctor; he will make it right,

Medication that masks giving temporary relief with side effects bringing on death.

However, that's collateral damage that must be accepted en route to create that next income.

People want it and it's expected, so the end justifies the means.

The food that's not food but imitation. Looks like the real but cannot be digested by the body, as the racks in the super markets contain hybrid genetically altered chemical edibles that have a shelf-life longer than a human. Kids growing up thinking of self-parents that have shown them the wrong way even though their words sounded right, the actions spoke louder—what the parents did in moderation, the children did in excess.

The result is a culture that has no anchor,

Nothing to cling to,

Superman, Spiderman, and everybody's a hero,

Even a leader who promised the sun; however, he can't change a light bulb. False weights and balances,

The promise of happiness.

The emotion and the high at the end of the day leaves one empty and thirsty and dry. Schools that dumb down and narrow the view, universities that lengthen and educate the few,

While ignorance reigns supreme. As some think San Francisco is the home of the Queen.

A skewed worldview where some don't know that Mexico borders Texas and the World Series is played among us with no one from the world; communication is filtered with its political correctness.

No offense, I won't tell it like it is.

My yes is not yes, and my no is not no, go means stop, and stop means go.

White is black and black is white.

Good means bad, and bad means good;

All are sad and don't know why a third are under treatment for depression for unreasonable expectations.

It's someone else's fault. My family's dysfunctional; can't you see a new trailer, pickup, and dog for me?

A wife, oh I have had one, two, or three. Fly now, pay later; I will live beyond my means.

Everybody give me a hand out; you owe it to me: welfare,

Clothing, food, and a car.

I will strike it rich, I'll spin the wheel.

I will pull the arm of a god; as I worship, I will put a coin in, hoping he will have mercy on me and spit a jackpot on me;

Rags to riches as millions I'll find, now problems start, lawyers, CPAs and financial advisors all want their dime. A litigious society we now have, your word is not your bond as covenants are broken.

Promises made that are not kept, vows broken.

It will be all right; my intention was better than the way it turned out! While the talk is about a better future, a dream, the future looks bleak, and the dream becomes a nightmare as everything spirals out of control.

The politicians that are more interested in their pensions, the bailout of AIG shows, paper money printed,

As more and more banks close,

Shrinking the credit of those whose bills are paid up to date not because they can't afford it or their payment is late.

They have no money, and everything is faked.

Wall Street's just numbers.

They play,

Inflated wealth on paper,

As junk bonds and debts are bought in a batch and sold for a song, collateral means nothing even land that's paid off.

You can't leverage, they won't give you money based on your worth because they don't have it.

They are bankrupt.

The Feds losing 10 billion dollars, they don't know what happened, they can't explain;

Bonnie and Clyde are saints,

Al Capone and organized crime eradicated,

I think not.

They hide behind their interpretation of the law,

And laws can be changed as liberal judges seek to move the boundaries and ancient marks that have held a society for centuries.

Checks and balances are now being lost.

Modern-day slavery as millions now form the mundane nine-to-five workplace for minimum wage,

Because of no education, illiteracy abounds;

Someone's eaten my cheese,

And there's a Heffalump and Woozle. Image is everything, or so it seems, even though everything is coming apart at the seams.

We will hold it together with duct tape, I bought it from the mart.

The odometer rolled back, it's a deal it's a deal.

Spring sale, Labor Day, and Thanksgiving too,

Christmas in July, and this is only a few.

March madness, Valentine's, Mother's Day too,

Fathers and secretaries, they are gonna get you.

Drinking hot coffee from a Styrofoam benzene cup, no wonder I can't remember, Alzheimer's and the shakes.

Imitation sweeteners,

I can't concentrate,

I took a pill, it came from Mexico,

Canada made the way,

A baby was aborted right in the birth canal, it wasn't out yet, it did not even breathe air.

Its voice will not be heard nor will its little fingers play,

The right of a woman and man to walk their promiscuous way.

AIDS/HIV, homosexual same-sex marriage, all is the norm.

No one will be ready, there's coming a perfect storm;

However, I will save the planet,

The earth's getting warmer,

I will hug a tree, did you see that spotted owl? No hunting, take away their guns,

Give them medication, let them smoke medicinal weed.

They will kill themselves, their elderly they will put to sleep,

The money stealers, five life sentences they will have, but murderers and rapists are up for parole.

Millions of laws on the statute books, but it's left to interpretation as attorneys take retainers but won't produce,

It's better to keep this going for as long as they can.

It's a cash cow; I tell you whether guilty or not,

Who cares? It's about job security.

Don't feel like working, never put off today what you can put off tomorrow,

I take what's not mine,

Others' reputation, money, and time and expect to be paid, this right is mine,

Someone owes me.

Have you not seen my résumé? Just give me the dollars,

Give it to me now, salary advance.

Hey, you can get your tax back, before the date,

Take the cruise, tomorrow is another day,

Holiday, vacation, I don't want to work hard.

I have many gifts and talents; however, that's not in my job description.

If they want me to do that, they will have to pay me more;

That's why I work three jobs.

I have to have more,

Jack of all trades and master of none.

I just want my money, and blondes just want to have fun. Hot dogs and hamburgers and pizza too, cotton candy, that carousel;

That looks pretty on you.

I am covered, so sue me; see if I care, I know it was in the contract, but I am no longer there,

Someone else bought your loan, it's changed hands a few times.

The piece of the equipment, it's out of date and what do I care your payment is late, the lifetime guarantee,

Whose life, that of a flea,

Misrepresent yourself,

Promise the moon, make up stories, something will take soon, someone will be duped,

Someone will be conned, and when they find out, too late, I will be gone.

The suit doesn't fit the tickets, nonrefundable, that is not covered in your policy,

You were told that.

Oh well, it's take it or leave it, or you can go to, there's a hurricane coming, go get some water and we better batten down the hatches because this house is made out of wood,

Built in thirty days, something for humanity.

The mayor's toupee is now in another county.

Body bags are piling up, but only a few deaths, the media will squash it, we can't have fear.

Tell them all is safe and all is well.

Buy something, eat something; if you don't, you can all go to the ball game,

Best out of seven;

Why if it's just one then maybe it was not a win; rigged fights,

staged matches, future payouts, money for promotions,

give the people want they want; they will pay,

it's on demand, it's pay per view, pornography, Internet access,

we are surfing in cyberspace, online relationships,

we've been talking, looking for a mate, cybersex,

A camera, I can view,

Wonder why I am so empty, how about you? No feeling, no touch, no breath.

Hollywood beautiful airbrushed complexions, no blemishes or wrinkles, live out their last years lonely and spinsters.

MTV generation pimping their rides, makeovers,

This Old House, Extreme Makeover, Clean Sweep,

Wife Swap, The Nanny,

Dr. Phil, Oprah Winfrey,

Judge Judy, and CSI, Whodunnit?, Agatha Christies and Hitchcocks on steroids—

We TV'ed it.

We will use it to retreat to,

Lost in a fantasy world, forget about your problem, get your mind off it, it will all go away;

I just received another credit card, whose line is it, anyway? YouTube and Google and Facebook too, you tweet you twit it's all up to you

The remote, the channels, too many to choose; when you look again, all time is gone.

Creativity lost as you are living a fantasy.

You will never know what could have come out of you,

Your life's faded away, always hoping for tomorrow, waiting for a better day. It's Thanksgiving, but no one's thankful; it's Christmas and Hanukkah, and what meaning is this?

Time to make some more money; they are looking for happiness, the most wonderful time.

Lonely,

Broken homes, separation, single parent homes,

I should have given you up for adoption, you should have never been born;

In primary school and on Discovery, I see that we all came from monkeys and should still be swinging in trees,

The world the minds say just evolved.

Wow, it takes more faith to believe that than stories of old. Everyone's looking for happiness and the American way.

They all looking for a brighter day.

The hustle and bustle and traffic jams too,

Waiting with your buzzer at a restaurant, it's just a table for two, the GPS is not working, I could not find the place,

My cell has no coverage, and my check is in the mail, an apple's not an apple, in looks only you will see, there's a worm in the apple,

I just bit one, you see. It's America, it's progress, it's the twenty-first century, and we are free!

# AMERICA—
# OUR CONTINUED FIGHT FOR FREEDOM

America is today 241 years old—born July 4, 1776—birthed out of pain and a hunger to worship freely, wise men with their dreams came from the East; the first winter survived, through the red man they were blessed. Thanksgiving, a yearly reminder, we were blessed out of their provision. The new land yielding of her bounty, the fight for a new world is made, from east to west, new frontiers, covenants made, trail of tears, the red man would also give his blood as covenants were broken.

Over the decades, and down through the years, through all the pain, sorrow, and many tears, many a man would lay down his life for freedom's dream, and so while the sword and cannon spoke, the pen being mightier than them all, produced a Bill of Rights; wise fathers penned the Constitution. From this Constitution we cannot sway, not one jot or tittle can be allowed to be taken away—not even by the highest courts of the land—for if it is altered, America no more shall stand.

One nation under God, united, defeated the enemy's might. Our flag was still flying by the dawn's early light, propped up by our flesh, as men would resist to lower the flag, the broad stripes and bright stars that would signal a nation had been born—tyranny swept aside—the flag was still waving over the land of the free and the home of the brave.

Many wars were fought on every front, even among us brother to brother—the blue and the gray as the red blood flowed—giving way to the red, white, and blue. Slavery, the curse of every family, the cry of every mother—brought to a halt—the desire of all to be free. We hold these truths to be self-evident—all men are created equal, and from this Declaration of Independence we cannot sway.

Ellis Island would be the place where the stranger would come seeking freedom—the Lady with the Lamp the way beaming—give me your huddled and tired masses, they will find rest on my shores. Thirteen states that became one nation under God would grow to become a jubilee of fifty nations within our borders. Many times, over the years, the balance of power would sway. Thankfully, three divisions of government would equally tip the scales—the checks and balances by our Founding Fathers laid—the dream that all would be equal from a mountain the Promised Land was seen that we would not be judged by the color of our skin. America would become the Land of Jubilee, the place of the dream.

This nation has walked away from its plumb line, three million-plus laws on the statute books you'll find, replacing the Ten Commandments. Prayer taken out of schools, our people oppressed by drugs and alcohol, slaves to pornography and STDs, HIV, millions of unborn babies aborted. While many are trying not to retain God in their knowledge, they are given over to a reprobate mind, professing themselves to be wise, they become fools, something has to be done and must be done soon. This cannot be done without Divine Intervention.

This is the day, this is the hour—we must hear from Heaven and so now we pray.

You have guided us these many years, now hear from Heaven, forgive our sin, and heal our land—for You were seen in the watch-fires of a hundred circling camps, altars were built in the evening dews and damps. As You died to make men holy, so we will live to make them free, Your truth is marching on.

O Sovereign Heavenly Father, in Jesus's mighty name, we pray, grant mercy on us one more time—as You have each century—a generation now lost their way, may we still say "in God we trust" and be "one nation" under Thee. Heavenly Father, we as a generation refuse to give up—we will stand as one—and humble ourselves and pray, and seek Your face and turn from our wicked ways. You have promised to come and heal our land—a new generation is rising up with faith, and the anointing to set the captives free, and marching through the land to see another Great Awakening. This is our purpose, this is our goal—*igniting a generation*—for a nation to fulfill its call!

—POEM BY DR. RODNEY M. HOWARD-BROWNE

# LOOKING FOR SOMEONE TO BLAME? CONGRESS IS GOOD PLACE TO START

BY CHARLEY REESE OF THE SENTINEL STAFF

Politicians, as I have often said, are the only people in the world who create problems and then campaign against them.

Everything on the Republican contract is a problem created by Congress. Too much bureaucracy? Blame Congress. Too many rules? Blame Congress. Unjust tax laws? Congress wrote them. Out-of-control bureaucracy? Congress authorizes everything bureaucracies do. Americans dying in Third World rat holes on stupid U.N. missions? Congress allows it. The annual deficits? Congress votes for them. The $4 trillion plus debt? Congress created it.

To put it into perspective just remember that 100 percent of the power of the federal government comes from the U.S. Constitution. If it's not in the Constitution, it's not authorized.

Then read your Constitution. All 100 percent of the power of the federal government is invested solely in 545 individual human beings. That's all. Of 260 million Americans, only 545 of them wield 100 percent of the power of the federal government.

That's 435 members of the U.S. House, 100 senators, one president and nine Supreme Court justices. Anything involving government that is wrong is 100 percent their fault.

I exclude the vice president because constitutionally he has no power except to preside over the Senate and to vote only in the case of a tie.

I exclude the Federal Reserve because Congress created it and all its power is power Congress delegated to it and could withdraw anytime it chooses to do so. In fact, all the power exercised by the 3 million or so other federal employees is power delegated from the 545.

All bureaucracies are created by Congress or by executive order of the president. All are financed and staffed by Congress. All enforce laws passed by Congress. All operate under procedures authorized by Congress. That's why all complaints and protests should be properly directed at Congress, not at the individual agencies.

You don't like the IRS? Go see Congress. You think the Alcohol Tobacco and Firearms agency is running amok? Go see Congress. Congress is the originator of all government problems and is also the only remedy available. That's why, of course, politicians go to such extraordinary lengths and employ world-class sophistry to make you think they are not responsible. Anytime a congressman pretends to be outraged by something a federal bureaucrat does, he is in fact engaging in one big massive con job. No federal employee can act at all except to enforce laws passed by Congress and to employ procedures authorized by Congress either explicitly or implicitly.

Partisans on both sides like to blame presidents for deficits, but all deficits are congressional deficits. The president may, by custom, recommend a budget, but it carries no legal weight. Only Congress is authorized by the Constitution to authorize and appropriate and to levy taxes. That's what the federal budget consists of: expenditures authorized, funds appropriated and taxes levied.

Both Democrats and Republicans mislead the public. For 40 years Democrats had majorities and could have at any time balanced the budget if they had chosen to do so. Republicans now have majorities and could, if they choose, pass a balanced budget this year. Every president, Democrat or Republican, could have vetoed appropriations bills that did not make up a balanced budget. Every president could have recommended a balanced budget. None has done either.

We have annual deficits and a huge federal debt because that's what majorities in Congress and presidents in the White House wanted. We have troops in various Third World rat holes because Congress and the president want them there.

Don't be conned. Don't let them escape responsibility. We simply have to sort through 260 million people until we find 545 who will act responsibly.

# THE TAX POEM

## AUTHOR UNKNOWN

Tax his land,
Tax his bed,
Tax the table,
At which he's fed.
Tax his tractor,
Tax his mule,
Teach him taxes
Are the rule.
Tax his work,
Tax his pay,
He works for
peanuts anyway!
Tax his cow,
Tax his goat,
Tax his pants,
Tax his coat.
Tax his ties,
Tax his shirt,
Tax his work,
Tax his dirt.
Tax his tobacco,
Tax his drink,
Tax him if he
Tries to think.

Tax his cigars,
Tax his beers,
If he cries,
Tax his tears.
Tax his car,
Tax his gas,
Find other ways
To tax his ass.
Tax all he has,
Then let him know
That you won't be done
Till he has no dough.
When he screams and hollers,
Then tax him some more;
Tax him till
He's good and sore.
Then tax his coffin,
Tax his grave,
Tax the sod in
Which he's laid…
Put these words
Upon his tomb:
"Taxes drove me to my doom…"

When he's gone,
Do not relax.
It's time to apply
The inheritance tax.
Accounts Receivable Tax
Building Permit Tax
CDL license Tax
Cigarette Tax
Corporate Income Tax
Dog License Tax
Excise Taxes
Federal Income Tax
Federal Unemployment Tax
    (FUTA)
Fishing License Tax
Food License Tax
Fuel Permit Tax
Gasoline Tax
Gross Receipts Tax
Hunting License Tax
Inheritance Tax
Inventory Tax
IRS Interest Charges
IRS Penalties (tax on top of tax)
Liquor Tax
Luxury Taxes
Marriage License Tax
Medicare Tax
Personal Property Tax
Property Tax
Real Estate Tax
Service Charge Tax
Social Security Tax
Road Usage Tax
Recreational Vehicle Tax
Sales Tax

School Tax
State Income Tax
State Unemployment Tax (SUTA)
Telephone Federal Excise Tax
Telephone Federal Universal Service
    Fee Tax
Telephone Federal, State and Local
    Surcharge Taxes
Telephone Minimum Usage
    Surcharge Tax
Telephone Recurring and
    Nonrecurring Charges Tax
Telephone State and Local Tax
Telephone Usage Charge Tax
Utility Taxes
Vehicle License Registration Tax
Vehicle Sales Tax
Watercraft Registration Tax
Well Permit Tax
Workers Compensation Tax

STILL THINK THIS IS FUNNY?
Not one of these taxes existed 100
    years ago, and our nation was
the most prosperous in the world.
We had absolutely no national debt,
    had the largest middle class
in the world, and Mom, if agreed,
    stayed home to raise the kids.
What in the heck happened? Can
    you spell "politicians?"
I hope this goes around THE USA
    at least 545 times!!! YOU can
help it get there!!!

# ANNEX

The "Mother box" contained 12 "Baby" boxes that each contained $250 billion, for a total of $3 trillion in the "Mother box."

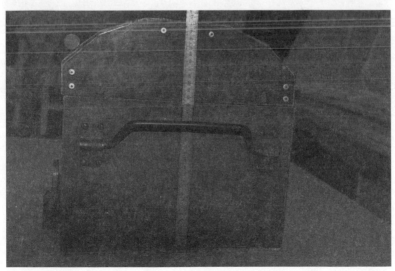

These sealed bronze and copper containers containing 12 "Baby" boxes, 6 on the left, 6 on the right, and 1 smaller box called the "Mother Control Box" in the center with a scroll.

The Treaty of Versailles "Mother box" and the scroll. These boxes were placed in each central bank allowing each bank to print their money backed by the dollar. This is the reason that the dollar was the currency of the world. This is also the reason why Switzerland was neutral during the war, because the Bank of International Settlements housed the "Mother boxes" for all of Europe.

The "Baby" boxes contained $250 billion each.

The contents of the "Baby" boxes and "Mother Control Box."

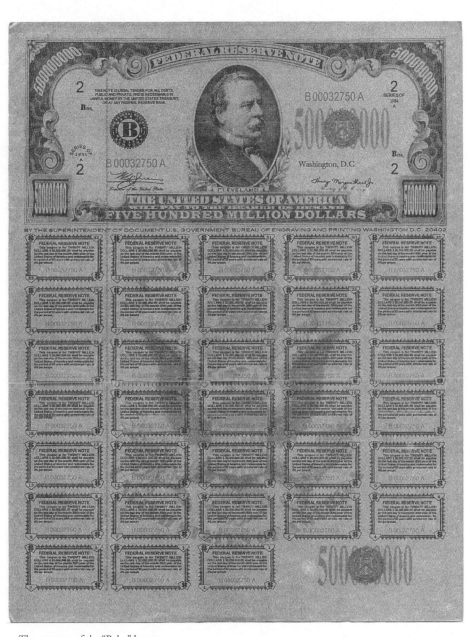

The contents of the "Baby" boxes.

Back of $500 Million Dollar bond issued by the Federal Reserve.

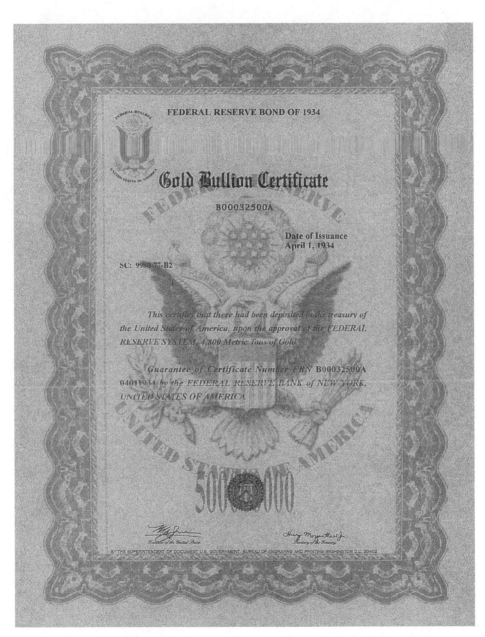

Gold Bullion Certificate.

Inventory list found in the "Mother Control Box."

# APPENDIX

MEMBERS OF THE COUNCIL ON FOREIGN RELATIONS WHO

WERE CABINET MEMBERS UNDER US PRESIDENTS

MEMBERS OF THE COUNCIL ON FOREIGN RELATIONS WHO WERE
CABINET MEMBERS UNDER PRESIDENT HARRY S. TRUMAN:

Edward R. Stettinius Jr., Secretary of State
Dean G. Acheson, Secretary of State
Henry Morgenthau Jr., Secretary of the Treasury
James Forrestal, Secretary of Defense
Robert A. Lovett, Secretary of Defense
Henry L. Stimson, Secretary of War
Robert P. Patterson, Secretary of War

MEMBERS OF THE COUNCIL ON FOREIGN RELATIONS WHO WERE
CABINET MEMBERS UNDER PRESIDENT DWIGHT D. EISENHOWER:

John Foster Dulles, Secretary of State
Christian A Herter, Secretary of State
Robert B. Anderson, Secretary of the Treasury
Neil H. McElroy, Secretary of Defense
Thomas S. Gates Jr., Secretary of Defense
William P. Rogers, Attorney General
Lewis L. Strauss, Secretary of Commerce

CABINET MEMBERS UNDER PRESIDENT JOHN F. KENNEDY:

Dean Rusk, Secretary of State
C. Douglas Dillon, Secretary of the Treasury
Robert S. McNamara, Secretary of Defense
Robert F. Kennedy, Attorney General

MEMBERS OF THE COUNCIL ON FOREIGN RELATIONS WHO WERE CABINET MEMBERS UNDER PRESIDENT LYNDON B. JOHNSON:

Dean Rusk, Secretary of State
C. Douglas Dillon, Secretary of the Treasury
Henry H. Fowler, Secretary of the Treasury
Robert S. McNamara, Secretary of Defense
A. B. Trowbridge, Secretary of Commerce

MEMBERS OF THE COUNCIL ON FOREIGN RELATIONS WHO WERE CABINET MEMBERS UNDER PRESIDENT RICHARD M. NIXON:

Henry A. Kissinger, Secretary of State
Elliot L. Richardson, Secretary of State
David M. Kennedy, Secretary of the Treasury
George P. Shultz, Secretary of the Treasury
William E. Simon, Secretary of the Treasury
Melvin R. Laird, Secretary of Defense
Elliot L. Richardson, Secretary of Defense
Elliot L. Richardson, Attorney General
Peter G. Peterson, Secretary of Commerce
Elliot L. Richardson, Secretary of Health, Education, and Welfare

MEMBERS OF THE COUNCIL ON FOREIGN RELATIONS WHO WERE CABINET MEMBERS UNDER PRESIDENT GERALD R. FORD:

Henry A. Kissinger, Secretary of State
William E. Simon, Secretary of the Treasury
James R. Schlesinger, Secretary of Defense

MEMBERS OF THE COUNCIL ON FOREIGN RELATIONS WHO WERE
CABINET MEMBERS UNDER PRESIDENT JAMES E. CARTER:

Cyrus R. Vance, Secretary of State
Edmund S. Muskie, Secretary of State
W. Michael Blumenthal, Secretary of the Treasury
G. William Miller, Secretary of the Treasury
Harold Brown, Secretary of Defense

MEMBERS OF THE COUNCIL ON FORFIGN RELATIONS WHO WERE
CABINET MEMBERS UNDER PRESIDENT RONALD REAGAN:

Alexander M. Haig Jr., Secretary of State
George P. Shultz, Secretary of State
Donald T. Regan, Secretary of the Treasury
Nicholas F. Brady, Secretary of the Treasury
Caspar W. Weinberger, Secretary of Defense
Frank C. Carlucci, Secretary of Defense
Malcolm Baldrige, Secretary of Commerce

MEMBERS OF THE COUNCIL ON FOREIGN RELATIONS WHO WERE
CABINET MEMBERS UNDER PRESIDENT GEORGE H. W. BUSH:

Lawrence S. Eagleburger, Secretary of State
Nicholas F. Brady, Secretary of the Treasury
Richard Cheney, Secretary of Defense

MEMBERS OF THE COUNCIL ON FOREIGN RELATIONS WHO WERE
CABINET MEMBERS UNDER PRESIDENT BILL CLINTON, BORN
WILLIAM JEFFERSON BLYTHE IV:

Warren M. Christopher, Secretary of State
Madeleine Albright, Secretary of State
Lloyd Bentsen, Secretary of the Treasury
Robert E. Rubin, Secretary of the Treasury
Lawrence H. Summers, Secretary of the Treasury
Les Aspin, Secretary of Defense
William J. Perry, Secretary of Defense
William S. Cohen, Secretary of Defense

Bruce Babbitt, Secretary of Interior
Ronald H. Brown, Secretary of Commerce
Donna E. Shalala, Secretary of Health and Human Services
Henry G. Cisneros, Secretary of Housing and Urban Development

CABINET MEMBERS UNDER PRESIDENT GEORGE W. BUSH:
Retired General Colin Powell, Secretary of State
Condoleezza Rice, Secretary of State
Donald H. Rumsfeld, Secretary of Defense
Robert Gates, Secretary of Defense
Elaine Chao, Secretary of Labor

MEMBERS OF THE COUNCIL ON FOREIGN RELATIONS WHO WERE
CABINET MEMBERS UNDER PRESIDENT BARACK OBAMA:

Tim Geithner, Secretary of the Treasury
Jacob Lew, Secretary of the Treasury
Robert Gates, Secretary of Defense
Chuck Hagel, Secretary of Defense
Ashton B. Carter, Secretary of Defense
Tom J. Vilsack, Secretary of Agriculture
John Bryson, Secretary of Commerce
Penny Pritzker, Secretary of Commerce
Sylvia M. Burwell, Secretary of Health and Human Services
Ernest Moniz, Secretary of Energy
Eric Shinseki, Secretary of Veterans Affairs
Janet Napolitano, Secretary of Homeland Security
Jeh Charles Johnson, Secretary of Homeland Security

# BIBLIOGRAPHY

Ahamed, Liaquat, *Lords of Finance: The Bankers Who Broke the World*, New York: Penguin Books, 2009.

Allen, Gary with Larry Abraham, *None Dare Call It Conspiracy*, San Diego, California: Dauphin Publications, 2013.

Arlacchi, Pino, *Mafia Business: The Mafia Ethic and the Spirit of Capitalism*, New York: Oxford University Press, 1988.

Ayers, Bradley, *The War That Never Was*, New York: Bobbs Merrill, 1976.

Ayers, Bradley, *The Zenith Secret: A CIA Insider Exposes the Secret War against Cuba and the Plot That Killed the Kennedy Brothers*, Brooklyn: Vox Pop, 2007.

Allen, Gary, *The Rockefeller File*, Seal Beach, California: '76 Press, 1976.

Aston, P. E., *The Raid on the Transvaal by Dr. Jameson*, London: Dean and Sons, 1897.

Bailey, Alice A., *Ponder on This: A Compilation*, Washington, DC: Lucis Publishing, 2003.

Baratta, Joseph Preston, *The Politics of World Federation: United Nations, UN Reform, Atomic Control*, New York: Praeger, 2004.

Beaty, Jonathan and S. C. Gwynne, *The Outlaw Bank: A Wild Ride into the Heart of the BCCI*, New York: Random House, 1993.

Belanga, Francis W., *Drugs, the U.S., and Khun Sa*, Nangkok, Thailand: Editions Duang Kamal, 1989.

Bergen, Peter L., *Holy War, Inc.: Inside the Secret World of Osama Bin Laden*, New York: Simon and Shuster, 2002.

Best, Gary Dean, *Pride, Prejudice, and Politics: Roosevelt Versus Recovery, 1933-1938*, New York: Praeger, 1991.

Blavatsky, H. P., *The Secret Doctrine*, Madras, India: Theosophical Publishing House, 1938.

Blair, Clay, *Hitler's U Boat Wars: The Hunters, 1939-1942*, New York: Random House, 1998.

Blake, Robert, *A History of Rhodesia*, London: Eyre Methuen, 1977.

Bodley, John H., *Cultural Anthropology: Tribes, States, and the Global System*, New York: Rowman and Littlefield, 2016.

Bontekoe, *The Nature of Dignity*, New York: Rowman and Littlefield, 2008.

Borman, Ernest G., *Force of Fantasy: Restoring the American Dream,* Carbondale, Illinois: South Illinois Press, 1985.

Bostaph, Samuel, *Andrew Carnegie: An Economic Biography*, New York: Rowman and Littlefield, 2015.

Brzezinski, Zbigniew, *The Grand Chessboard: American Primacy and Its Geostrategic Imperative*, New York: Basic Books, 1997.

Brown, Robin, *The Secret Society: Cecil John Rhodes's Plan for a New World Order,* New York: Penguin Books, 2015.

Buchanan, Patrick J., *Churchill, Hitler, and the Unnecessary War*, New York: Crown Publishing, 2008.

Buchanan, Patrick J., *State of Emergency: The Third World Invasion and Conquest of America,* New York: St. Martin's Press, 2006.

Buchanan, Patrick J., *The Suicide of a Superpower,* New York: St. Martin's Press, 2011.

Carnegie, Andrew *The Autobiography of Andrew Carnegie and His Gospel of Wealth*, New York: Signet Classics, 2006.

Carnegie, Andrew *Triumphant Democracy: Sixty Years' March of the Republic*, New York: Charles Scribner's Sons, 1886.

Cassell, Gustav, *The Downfall of the Gold Standard*, New York: Augustus Kelly, 1966.

Chambers, John Whiteclay, *The Oxford Companion to American Military History*, New York: Oxford University Press, 2000.

Chernow, Ron, *The House of Morgan: An American Banking Dynasty and the Rise of Modern Finance*, New York: Grove Press, 2001.

Chernow, Ron, *Titan: The Life of John D. Rockefeller, Sr.,* New York: Vintage Books, 2004.

Chomsky, Noam, *Requiem for the American Dream: The 10 Principles of Concentration of Wealth and Power*, New York: Seven Stories Press, 2017.

Chossudovsky, Michel, *The Globalization of Poverty and the New World Order*, Montreal: Global Research Publishers, 2003.

Chossudovsky, Michel, *The Globalization of War: America's "Long War" against Humanity*, Montreal: Global Research Publishers, 2015.

Clark, Wesley, *Winning Modern Wars* (New York: Public Affairs, 2014.

Cleveland, William L., *A History of the Modern Middle East*, Boulder, Colorado: Perseus Books, 2004.

Cockburn, Alexander and Jeffrey St. Clair, *Whiteout: The CIA, Drugs, and the Press*, New YORK: Verso, 1998.

Coetzer, Owen, *Fire in the Sky: The Destruction of the Orange Free State*, Johannesburg: Covos Day, 2000.

Combs, Stephen, *A Tribute to Our Christian Heritage*, Raleigh, North Carolina: Lulu, 2012.

Cooney, John, *The American Pope: The Life and Times of Francis Cardinal Spellman*, New York: Times Books, 1984.

Cooper, John, *The Unexpected Story of Nathaniel Rothschild*, New York: Bloomsbury Publishing, 2015.

Corbin, Jane, *Al Qaeda: In Search of the Terror Network That Threatens the World*, New York: Thunder Mouth Press, 2003.

Corrodus, Geraldine, et alia, *Oxford Big Idea - - Geography, History* (South Melbourne, Australia: Oxford University Press, 2013.

Cottrell, Richard, *Gladio: NATO's Dagger at the Heart of Europe*, Palm Desert, California, Progressive Press, 2012.

Coundenhove-Kalergi, Richard, *Ein Leben fur Paneuropa*, Wien-Leipzig, Germany: Verlag, Kremayr and Scherian, 2016.

Coundenhove-Kalergi, Richard, *Prakitscher Idealismus*, Wien-Leipzig, Germany, Paneuropa Verlag, 2016.

Cross, F. L., editor, *The Oxford Dictionary of the Catholic Church*, London: Oxford University Press, 1957.

Curtis, Lionel, *The Commonwealth of Nations: An Inquiry into the Nature of Citizenship in the British Empire and into the Mutual Relations of the Several Communities*, London: Macmillan and Company, 1916.

Dall, Charles B., *FDR: My Exploited Father-in-Law*, Washington, DC: Action Associates, 1970.

Dannin, Robert, *Black Pilgrimage to Islam*, New York: Oxford University Press, 2002.

DeLaura, David L., *Hebrew and Hellene in Victorian England*, Austin: The University of Texas Press, 1969.

DeSocio, Richard James, *Rockefellerocracy: Assassinations, Watergate, and the Monopoly of "Philanthropic" Foundations*, Bloomington, Indiana: Author's House, 2013.

Doril, Stephen, *Inside the Secret World of Her Majesty's Secret Intelligence Service*, New York: Torchstone, 2000.

Dowd, Kevin and Richard Henry Timberlake, *Money and the Nation State: The Financial Revolution and the World Monetary Systems*, Oakland, California: Independent Institute, 1998.

Durant, Will, *The Reformation*, Volume VI, *The Story of Civilization* (New York: Simon and Schuster, 1957.

Eichengreen, Barry J., *Gold Fetters: The Gold Standard and the Great Depression*, New York: Oxford University Press, 1992.

Emerson, Edwin and Marion Mills, editors, *The Nineteenth Century and After*, New York: Leonard Scott, 1902.

Engdahl, F. Williams, *Gods of Money: Wall Street and the Death of the American Century*, San Diego, California: Progressive Press, 2011.

Esposito, John L. and Dalia Mogahed, *Who Speaks for Islam?* New York: Gallup Press, 2007.

Estulin, Daniel, *The True Story of the Bilderberg Group*, Waterville, Oregon: Trineday, 2009.

Evanzz, Karl, *The Messenger: The Rise and Fall of Elijah Muhammad*, New York: Random House, 1999.

Felix, David, *Biography of an Idea: John Maynard Keyes and the General Theory of Employment, Interest, and Money*, Piscataway, New Jersey: Transaction Publishers, 1955.

Ferguson, Neil, *Empire: The Rise and Demise of the British World Order and the Lessons for Global Power*, New York: Basic Books, 2002.

Flynn, John Thomas, *The Roosevelt Myth*, Auburn, Alabama: Ludwig von Mises Institute, 2008.

Folsom, Burtom, *The Myth of the Robber Barons: A New Look at the Rise of Big Business in America*, Herndon, Virginia: Young America's Foundation, 1991.

Fosdick, Raymond E., *John D. Rockefeller, Jr.: A Portrait*, New York: Harper and Brothers, 1958

Frend, W. H. C., *The Early Church*, Philadelphia: J. P. Lippincott Company, 1966.

Ganzer, Daniele, *NATO's Secret Armies: Operation Gladio and Terrorism in Western Europe*, London: Frank Cass, 2005.

Gardner, Laurence, *The Shadow of Solomon: The Last Secret of Freemasons Revealed*, London: HarperCollins, 2009.

George, Susan, *A Fate Worse Than Debt: The World Financial Crisis and the Poor*, New York: Grove Press, 1990.

Goodson, Stephen Mitford, *A History of Central Banking and the Enslavement of Mankind*, London: Black House, 2014.

Gosch, Martin A. and Richard Hammer, *The Last Testament of Lucky Luciano,* Boston: Little, Brown, and Company, 1974.

Griffin, G. Edward, *The Creature from Jekyll Island: A Second Look at the Federal Reserve,* Westlake Village, California: American Media, 2008.

Griffin, G. Edward, *The Fearful Master: A Second Look at the United Nations,* Belmont, Massachusetts: Western Islands, 1964.

Green, Jack and Alessandro Massignani, *The Black Prince and the Sea Devils: The Story of Valerio Borghese and the Elite Units of Decoma MAS,* Cambridge, Massachusetts: DeCapo Press, 2004.

Green, Roger J., *The Life and Ministry of General William Booth: Founder of the Salvation Army,* Nashville: Abingdon Press, 2006.

Grose, Peter, *Continuing the Inquiry: The Council on Foreign Relations from 1921 to 1996,* Washington, DC: Council on Foreign Relations Press, 2006.

Gunarana, Rohan, *Inside Al Qaeda: Global Network of Terror,* New York: Berkeley Books, 2002.

Gusejnora, Dina, *European Elites and Ideas of Empire,* Cambridge: Cambridge University Press, 2016.

Haberstam, David, *The Best and the Brightest,* New York: Random House, 1972.

Hall, Manly P., *The Lost Keys of Freemasonry,* Richmond, Virginia: Macoy Publishing, 1923.

Hallett, Robin, *Africa Since 1875: A Modern History,* Ann Arbor, The University of Michigan, 1974.

Hamilton, Alexander, James Madison, John Jay, *The Federalist,* Franklin Center, Pennsylvania: Franklin Library, 1977.

Hammond, John Hays, *The Truth about the Jameson Raid,* Boston: Marshall Jones, 1918.

Herberg, Will, *Protestant, Catholic, Jew,* Garden City, New York: Anchor Books, 1960.

Higham, Charles, *American Swastika,* New York: Doubleday, 1985.

Hillgruber, Andreas, *Germany and the Two World Wars,* Cambridge, Massachusetts: Harvard University Press. 1981.

Hohne, Heinz and Herman Zolling, *The General Was a Spy: The Truth about General Gehlen and His Spy Ring,* New York: Coward, McCann, and Geoghegan, 1972.

Hoover, Herbert, *Memoirs of Herbert Hoover, 1929-1941, The Great Depression,* New York: Macmillan, 1952.

Hoover, Herbert and Hugh Gibson, *Prefaces to Peace: A Symposium,* New York: Simon and Schuster, et alia, 1948.

Iden, V. Gilmore, *The Federal Reserve Act of 1913: History and Digest*, Philadelphia: The National Bank News, 1914.

Iseliyt, Charlotte Thomson, *The Dumbing Down of America*, Ravenna, Ohio: Conscience Press, 1999.

Johnson, Paul. *Modern Times: The World from the Twenties to the Nineties*, New York: HarperCollins, 1992.

Kah, Gary, *En Route to Global Occupation: A High-Ranking Government Liaison Exposes the Secret Agenda for World Unification*, Lafayette, Louisiana: Huntington House, 1991.

Kennedy, John F., *A Nation of Immigrants*, New York: Harper and Row, a958.

Kinzer, Stephen, *The Brothers: John Foster Dulles, Allen Dulles, and Their Secret War*, New York: Times Books, 2013.

Klos, Felix, *Churchill on Europe: The Untold Story of Churchill's European Project*, London: I. B. Tauris, 2016.

Koss, Peter, *Carnegie*, New York: John Wiley and Sons, 2002.

Kruger, Henry, *The Great Heroin Coup: Drugs, Intelligence and International Finance*, Boston: South End Press, 1980.

Kunen, James, *The Strawberry Statement: Notes of a College Revolutionary*, New York: Random House, 1969.

Kwitny, Jonathan, *Crime of Patriots: A True Story of Dope, Dirty Money, and the CIA*, New York: W. W. Norton and Company, 1987.

Labeviere, Richard, *Dollars for Terror*, New York: Algora Press, 2000.

Lance, Peter, *100 Years of Revenge*, New York: Regan Books, 2003.

Larson, Erik, *Dead Wake: The Last Crossing of the Lusitania*, New York: Crown, 2015.

Lebor, Adam, *Tower of Basil: The Shadowy History of the Secret Bank That Runs the World*, New York: Public Affairs, 2013.

Lernoux, Penny, *In Banks We Trust*, New York: Penguin Books, 1986.

Le Sueur, Gordon, *Cecil Rhodes: The Man and His Work*, London: john Murray, 1913.

Lewis, Charles, *935 Lies: The Future of Truth and the Decline of America's Moral Integrity*, New York: Public Affairs, 2014.

Link, Arthur, *Wilson and the Progressive Era*, New York: Harper and Brothers, 1954.

Livingston, David and Sahib Mustaqim Bleher, *Surrendering Islam: The Subversion of Muslim Politics throughout History until the Present Day*, Karachi, Pakistan: Mustaqim Ltd., 2010.

Lundberg, Ferdinand, *America's 60 Families*, New York: Vanguard Press, 1937.

Mackey, Albert, *Encyclopedia of Freemasonry*, Chicago: Masonic History Company, 1924.

McCauley, Martin, *The Cold War, 1946-2016*, New York: Routledge, 2017.

McCoy, Alfred W., *The Politics of Heroin in Southeast Asia*, New York: Harper and Row, 1972.

McCoy, Alfred W., *The Politics of Heroin: CIA Complicity in the Drug Trade*, Chicago: Lawrence Jill Books, 2003.

McDonald, Kevin, *The Culture of Critique: An Evolutionary Analysis of Jewish Involvement in Twentieth Century Intellectual and Political Movements*, Westport, Connecticut: Praeger, 2000.

McIlhany, William H., *The Tax-Exempt Foundations*, Westport, Connecticut: Arlington House, 1980.

Malcolm X, *The Autobiography of Malcolm X*, New York: Random House, 1964.

Manchester, William, *The Last Lion: Winston Spencer Churchill: Visions of Glory, 1874-1932*, New York: Random House, 1991.

Marsh, David, *The Brundesbank: The Bank That Rules Europe*, London: William Heinemann, Ltd., 1992.

Meher, Jagmohan, *America's Afghanistan War: The Success That Failed*, New Dehli, India, Gyan Books, 2004.

Meredith, Martin, *Diamonds, Gold and War: The British, the Boers, and the Making of South Africa*, New York: Public Affairs, 2008.

Miller, Robert Moats, *Henry Emerson Fosdick: Preacher, Pastor, Prophet*, New York: Oxford University Press, 1985.

Milner, Alfred, *The Milner Papers, 1897-1905*, London: Cassell, 1933.

Mitchell, Sir. Lewis, *The Life of Right Honorable C. J. Rhodes*, London: Edward Arnold, 1910.

Monteith, Stanley, *Brotherhood of Darkness*, Oklahoma City: Bible Belt Publishing, 2000.

Mullins, Eustace, *Secrets of the Federal Reserve*, New York: Kasper and Horton, 1982.

Mullins, Eustace, *The World Order: A Study in the Hegemony of Parasitism*, Staunton, Virginia: Ezra Pound Institute for Civilization, 1985.

Nasaw, David, *Andrew Carnegie*, New York: Penguin Press, 2006.

Newman, Simon, *March, 1939: The British Government in Poland*, Oxford: Clarendon Press, 1976.

O'Sullivan, Christopher D., *Harry Hopkins: FDR's Envoy to Churchill and Stalin*, New York: Roman and Littlefield, 2014.

Pakenham, Thomas, *The Boer War*, New York: Random House, 1979.

Pelton, Robert Young, *The World's Most Dangerous Places*, New York: Harper Resource, 2003.

Perloff, James, *The Shadows of Power: The Council on Foreign Relations and the American Decline*, Appleton, Wisconsin: Western Islands, 2005.

Peterson, E. N., *Hjalmar Schact: For or Against Hitler: A Political Economic Study of Germany, 1923-1945*, Boston: Christopher Publishing House, 1954.

Phillips, Kevin, *American Dynasty: Aristocracy, Fortune, and the Politics of Deceit in the House of Bush,* New York: Viking, 2004.

Pike, Albert, *Morals and Dogma*, Charleston: South Carolina: Supreme Council of the Thirty-Third Degree of the Scottish Rite, 1871.

Pipes, Daniel, *Militant Islam Reaches America*, New York: W. W. Norton, 2003.

Quigley, Carroll, *Tragedy and Hope: A History of the World in Our Time*, New York: Macmillan, 1966.

Rauschenbusch, Walter *A Theology of he Social Gospel*, New York: Abington Press, 1918.

Reeve, Simon, *The New Jackals: Ramzi Yousez, Osama Bin Laden, and the Future of Terrorism,* Boston: Northeastern University Press, 1999.

Rich, Mark, *The Hidden Evil: The Financial Elite's Covert War against the Civilian Population*, Raleigh, North Carolina: Lulu Press, 2009.

Rockefeller, David, *Memoirs*, New York: random House, 2002.

Roosevelt, Franklin D., *The Public Papers and Addresses of Franklin Roosevelt*, New York: Random House, 1938.

Rotberg, Robert I., *The Founder: Cecil Rhodes and the Pursuit of Power*, New York: Oxford University Press, 1988.

Rothbard, Murray N., *The Case against the Fed*, Auburn, Alabama: Ludwig von Mises Institute, 2007.

Ruskin, John, *Selected Writings of John Ruskin,* New York: Oxford University Press, 2009.

Seagrave, Sterling and Peggy, *Gold Warriors: America's Secret Recovery of Yamashita's Gold,* London: Bowstring, 2008.

Schlafly, Phyllis and Chester Ward, *Kissinger on the Couch* (New Rochelle, New York: Arlington House, 1975.

Schlesinger, Arthur, Jr., *A Thousand Days: John F. Kennedy in the White House*, Boston: Houghton Musslin, 1965.

Scott, Peter Dale, *America's War Machine: Deep Politics, the CIA Drug Connection, and the Road to Afghanistan*, Washington, DC: Rowman and Littlefield, 2010.

Scott, Peter Dale and Jonathan Marshall, *Cocaine Politics; Drugs, Armies, and the CIA*, Oakland, California: University of California Press, 1998.

Seagrove, Sterling, *The Marcos Dynasty*, New York: Harper and Row, 1988.

Shillington, Kevin, *Encyclopedia of African History*, New York: Routledge, 2004.

Sire, James, *The Universe Next Door: A Basic Worldwide Catalog*, Downers Grove, Illinois" Inter-Varsity Press, 2009.

Smith, G. Vance and Tom Gow, *Masters of Deception: The Rise of the Council on Foreign Relations*, Colorado Springs, Colorado: Freedom First Society, 2012.

Smith, Peter, *Talons of the Eagle: Dynamics of US-Latin America Relations*, New York: Oxford University Press, 1999.

Stead, William T., *The Last Will and Testament of Cecil John Rhodes*, London: Review of Review Books, 2009.

Snider, L. Britt, *The Agency and the Hill: CIA's Relationship with Congress*, Washington, DC: Center for the Study of Intelligence, 2008.

Sterling, Claire, *Octopus: How the Long Reach of the Sicilian Mafia Controls the Global Narcotics Trade*, New York: Simona and Schuster, 1990

Steyn, Mark, *After America: Get Ready for Armageddon*, Washington, DC: Regnery, 2011.

Stone, Oliver and Peter Kuznick, *The Concise Untold History of the United States*, New York: Gallery Books, 2014.

Talbot, David, *The Devil's Chessboard: Allen Dulles, the CIA, and the Rise of the Secret Government*, New York: HarperCollins, 2015.

Taylor, A. J. P., *The Origins of the Second World War*, London: Hamish Hamilton, 1961.

Thomas, Evan, *The Very Best Men: Four Men Who Dared*, New York: Touchstone, 1985.

Thomas, Ken and David Hatcher Childress, *Inside the Gemstone File: Howard Hughes, Onassis, and JFK* Kempton, Illinois: Adventures Unlimited Press, 1999.

Toland, John, *Adolf Hitler*, New York: Doubleday, 1976.

Toland, John, *Infamy, Pearl Harbor and Its Aftermath*, New York: Doubleday, 1982.

Trento, Joseph, *Prelude to Terror: The Rogue CIA, the Legacy of America's Private Intelligence Network*, New York: Carroll and Graf, 2005.

Trollope, Anthony, *South Africa*, Cape Town: A. A. Balkema, 1973.

Unger, Craig, *House of Bush, House of Saud*, New York: Scribner's, 2004.

Van der Poel, Jean, *The Jameson Raid*, Cape Town: Oxford University Press, 1951.

Vierick, George Sylvester, *The Strangest Friendship in History: Woodrow Wilson and Colonel House*, New York: Praeger, 1976.

Valentine, Douglas, *The Strength of the Wolf: The Secret History of America's War on Drugs*, New York: Verso, 2006.

Wall, Joseph Frazier, *Andrew Carnegie*, Pittsburgh: The University of Pittsburgh Press, 1989.

Webb, Gary, *Dark Alliance: The CUA, the Contras, and the Crack Cocaine Explosion*, New York: Seven Stories Press, 1999.

Weiner, Tim, *Legacy of Ashes: The History of the CIA*, New York: Doubleday, 2207.

Wesseling, H. I., *Divide and Rule: the Partition of Africa, 1880-1914*, Westport, Connecticut: Praeger, 1996.

Whyte, Frederick, *Life of W. T. Stead*, New York: Houghton Muffin, 1925.

Willan, Philip, *Puppetmasters: The Political Use of Terror in Italy*, London: Constable, 1991.

Willan, Philip, *The Vatican at War: From Blackfriars Bridge to Buenos Aires*, Bloomington, Indiana: iUniverse LLC, 2003.

Williams, Mira, *The History of Foreign Investments in the United States, 1914 to 1945*, Cambridge, Massachusetts: Harvard University Press, 2004.

Wise, Jennings, *Woodrow Wilson: Disciple of Revolution*, New York: Paisley Press, 1938.

Wormser, Rene, *Foundations: Their Power and Influence*, New York: Covenant House Books, 1993.

Wrigley, E. A., editor, *Nineteenth Century Society: Essays in the Use of Quantitative Methods for the Study of Social Data*, Cambridge: Cambridge University Press, 2008.

Yallop, David, *The Power and the Glory: Inside the Dark Heart of John Paul II's Vatican*, New York: Carroll and Graf, 2007.

Yergin, David, *The Prize: The Epic Quest for Oil, Money, and Power*, New York: The Free Press, 2008.

Ziegler, Phillip, *Cecil Rhodes: The Rhodes Trust and Rhodes Scholarship*, New Haven, Connecticut: Yale University Press, 2008.

# INDEX